C0-AWW-804

GLOBAL READINGS

GLOBAL READINGS

A Sri Lankan Commentary on Paul's Letter to the Galatians

David A. deSilva

CASCADE *Books* · Eugene, Oregon

GLOBAL READINGS
A Sri Lankan Commentary on Paul's Letter to the Galatians

Copyright © 2011 David A. deSilva. All rights reserved. Except for brief quotations in critical publications or reviews, no part of this book may be reproduced in any manner without prior written permission from the publisher. Write: Permissions, Wipf and Stock Publishers, 199 W. 8th Ave., Suite 3, Eugene, OR 97401.

Cascade Books
An Imprint of Wipf and Stock Publishers
199 W. 8th Ave., Suite 3
Eugene, OR 97401
www.wipfandstock.com

ISBN 13: 978-1-61097-707-4

Cataloging-in-Publication data:

DeSilva, David Arthur

Global readings : a Sri Lankan commentary on Paul's letter to the Galatians / David A. deSilva.

xii + 336 p. ; 23 cm. — Includes bibliographical references and index(es).

ISBN 13: 978-1-61097-707-4

1. Bible. N.T. Galatians—Commentaries. I. Title.

BS2685.53 D25 2011

Manufactured in the U.S.A.

In loving memory of my grandparents,
Stephen Frederick de Silva
and
Mary Kathleen Crofton de Silva

7/30/2012 Yankee 969740

Contents

Preface

THIS COMMENTARY IS THE fruit both of the study of Galatians as a communication composed by Paul under the constraints of a particular, historical situation, crafted by him to achieve specific ends within that situation, and of collaborative reading of Galatians as a word to Christians living within the particular situation, and facing the particular challenges, of Sri Lanka.[1] Naturally, this dialogue also included what I have heard from my own students and from reading the works of other North American scholars interested in discerning a contemporary word to the churches in my Western context.

We have learned much in recent decades about the importance of listening to sisters and brothers reading the biblical texts in contexts other than our own. My particular social location shapes my ability to "see" what is in a text and to "hear" what that text is challenging my community and me to desire, to do, and to become. Any reading from a single social location runs the very real risk of being inadequate, since the lenses cast over our eyes by our social location, its ideologies, and its interests threaten to overwhelm the voice of the text (or, I might say, the voice of God in the text), at least at those points where Scripture would most challenge the ideologies and interests that drive the society in which we have been nurtured. But a reading informed by readings from multiple social locations allows us to triangulate beyond the blinders of our own social location, to see much more of the vision for discipleship

---

1. The idea was inspired by the method of "reading with" people from a different social location that lies at the heart of such groundbreaking works as Daniel Patte, ed., *The Global Bible Commentary*.

and life together in the text, to hear much more clearly its challenge to us within our social location (hence, its fuller relevance to us).

I have approached the writing of this commentary from a model of interpretation that actively seeks to employ such triangulation so as to develop a reading and interpretation that is as fully informed by multiple social locations, and thus as little hampered by the lenses of a single social location as possible. The first reading location is, of course, my own and that of my Protestant, broadly evangelical, North American reading community. I have been reading Galatians from this location off and on for about thirty years. The second location is that of my Protestant, evangelical, Sri Lankan students and newfound colleagues at Colombo Theological Seminary. The third location is that of Paul and his Galatian Christian converts.

Solid historical exegesis is an exercise in cross-cultural hermeneutics. We are trying to hear a text within a profoundly different culture (first-century Mediterranean, generally Northeastern Mediterranean) with a political system, political ideology, economics, social institutions, and religious culture profoundly different from our own. I strenuously reject the easy identification of historical exegesis as "Eurocentric": it is, rather, cross-cultural. And most of these early Christian texts are addressing places that are clearly not European (Syria, various provinces in what is now Turkey), and certainly not dominant-cultural European even when the audience is in Macedonia, Greece, or Rome. Reading from three locations, each reading from one's own location is challenged, refined, expanded. We realize, both from listening to one another across the room and listening to Paul across the millennia, that the text is addressing questions that we did not ask, and challenging ideological assumptions that we did not question.

The setting for the principal collaboration was a master's level seminar on Galatians at Colombo Theological Seminary. The students, who came from a diversity of denominational settings and among whom were both Sinhalese and Tamil individuals, were asked to give substantial time to the following questions in preparation for the seminar: (1) How would you describe your social context as a starting point for reading and interpreting Galatians? (2) As you read through Galatians, what information, images, or points strike you as particularly important for you or others in your setting? (3) Where does Galatians connect for you with your life context and the challenges you face as a Sri Lankan and as a Christian disciple? (4) How does the text help you to think about your life context? (5) What kind of response to these challenges and this context does your reading of Galatians nurture? What would it look like to live out more fully the vision, the ideals, and/or the challenges that emerge from this text in your shared life context? The goal was to encourage each student to come with an initial reading of Galatians "from *this* place."

At the conclusion of the seminar, the participants were asked to return to these questions in regard to one chapter of Galatians, engaging the questions again in dialogue with their understanding of the principal questions raised and addressed in that chapter in its presenting situation. Each participant presented his or her reading, received comments from his or her peers, and revised accordingly. Their final papers provided a wealth of insights upon which to draw in the composition of this commentary, in which I am now able not only to speak myself, but to facilitate their speaking about Galatians to their fellow leaders in the churches of Sri Lanka. It was my hope that this collaborative approach would better honor the life setting of Sri Lankan Christianity by inviting the participation of brothers and sisters who were themselves involved in ministry in the Sri Lankan context.

This volume and its author, therefore, are deeply indebted to Christy Balandran, Dharshan Fernando, Naresh Sathiyaseelan, Sashicala Sriskandarajah, and Kumar Subramaniam, for their participation in this intensive seminar and its lively dialogue, and for their thoughtful contributions to Sri Lankan reflection on Galatians. Two colleagues on the faculty of Colombo Theological Seminary, Dr. Vinodh Gunasekera and Rev. Prabo Mihindukulasuriya, attended all or part of the class sessions and contributed meaningfully to the discussions of how Galatians intersects with the challenges facing Sri Lankan Christians. Dr. and Mrs. Vinoth Ramachandra gave several afternoons to conversation with me, and each made substantive contributions to my thinking about the church and Christian mission in Sri Lanka. The entire project, however, would have come to nothing were it not for the faith and gracious hospitality of the Principal and the Academic Dean of the seminary, Rev. Ivor

Poobalan and Mrs. Mano Emanuel, who warmly welcomed me into their visiting faculty and entrusted their students to me. All of these sisters and brothers have enriched this book through their collaboration and made it thereby a more authentic word to the churches in Sri Lanka. For their partnership I am truly grateful.

I wish to thank the Lilly Foundation for its generous award of a Faculty Fellowship, administered by the Association of Theological Schools, which made it possible for me to enjoy a full six months' leave from my regular duties at Ashland Theological Seminary to pursue this project and which provided the means for a two-month stay in Sri Lanka. I am also grateful to the President and Dean of Ashland Theological Seminary, and to the Board of Trustees of Ashland University, for allowing me to take advantage of this fellowship and for supporting me in this, as in all my research and writing. The introduction to this commentary incorporates portions of chapter 12 from an earlier book, *An Introduction to the New Testament: Contexts, Methods & Ministry Formation* (Downers Grove: InterVarsity Press, 2004), and I am grateful to InterVarsity Press for allowing me to incorporate much of that material here. All translations of New Testament texts are my own unless otherwise indicated.

Introduction

AUTHORSHIP

WHILE SCHOLARS OFTEN DEBATE the authorship of several letters attributed to Paul (notably Ephesians, Colossians, and the Pastoral Epistles), no one seriously disputes the fact that Paul authored this letter to the Galatian Christians.[1] It has all the hallmarks of being shaped by a specific and unrepeatable situation in the ministry of Paul and in the life of his congregations, and it offers a response thoroughly conditioned by that situation. It does not, thus, have the appearance of trying to reclaim an apostle's voice and authority to address some later problems in the church or to provide generally useful theological or practical guidance. The personality and passion of the author shine through this letter to a degree that is unmatched among Paul's letters save, perhaps, for 2 Corinthians, but not in a way that could ever be the result of a pious fiction. Galatians shows us "Paul under fire," long before he became so widely revered a figure that any early Christian would find it useful or advantageous to write fictitiously under Paul's name.

This widespread tendency to affirm Pauline authorship of Galatians makes this letter an especially important source both for the biographical study of Paul and his ministry and, to a slightly lesser extent, for the study of the history of the early church, particularly as this history took shape around the question of how to incorporate Gentile believers into the predominantly Jewish Jesus Movement. Because Galatians is written firsthand by one of the major players in that history, it tends to be privi-

1. Betz, *Galatians*, 1. A brief review of the few attempts to challenge Pauline authorship can be found in Burton, *A Critical and Exegetical Commentary on the Epistle to the Galatians*, lxix–lxxi.

leged as an historical source over Acts of the Apostles when it comes to reconstructing the complexities of that history. Nevertheless, as the commentary proper will emphasize, we cannot lose sight of the fact that what Paul shares of his own story and the church's story is shared with a view to achieving certain goals in the Galatian situation. That is to say, the purpose behind every autobiographical statement in Galatians, or every narrative of an earlier event in Galatians, is not to provide material for later historians and biographers of Paul, but to win the debate in Galatia and bring these congregations back around to looking to Paul for the "truth of the Gospel" (2:5, 14).

Richard Longenecker has asserted that most commentators, in their analysis of Galatians, have not adequately dealt with "the probable presence of an amanuensis"—a secretary or scribe—"in the composition of the letter."[2] According to him, Paul's command to the readers, "See with what large-sized letters I wrote to you" (6:11), is a signal of a change in handwriting at that point, with the implication being that Gal 1:1—6:10 was dictated by Paul to a co-worker or even to a hired scribe functioning as a secretary.[3] It was indeed typical for people to use a professional scribe or secretary when writing letters or business documents like bills of sale. There is clear evidence in several of Paul's letters that Paul himself involved someone else—most likely a fellow Christian on his mission team—in the writing of those letters. In many cases, he names members of his team as co-authors or co-senders (see 1 Cor 1:1; 2 Cor 1:1; Phil 1:1; Col 1:1; 1 Thess 1:1; 2 Thess 1:1; Phlm 1), though the precise manner of their contribution to the letters remains unknown. In some cases, Paul explicitly draws attention to a change of handwriting near the end of a letter as a way of providing the more "personal" touch and authenticating the letter as genuinely his own. In 1 Corinthians, there is a clear transition to a new hand and an explicit reference to the same: "This greeting is in my own hand, that of Paul" (*ho aspasmos tē emē cheiri Paulou*, 1 Cor 16:21). This personally written postscript presumably extends to 16:24. *Exactly* the same six Greek words appear at the close of Colossians (4:18) and 2 Thessalonians (3:17), introducing shorter postscripts. Tertius, a fellow disciple, provided secretarial

2. Longenecker, *Galatians*, lix.

3. Ibid., lxi; so also Betz, *Galatians*, 1.

support for Paul in the composition of Romans, even adding greetings of his own (Rom 16:22), though with no corresponding greeting from Paul explicitly in Paul's own hand.

In these four instances, Paul's use of a secretary (amanuensis) is certain. However, 2 Corinthians, Ephesians, Philippians, and 1 Thessalonians give no indication of a closing change of handwriting as a means of authentication (unless in 2 Corinthians this happens as early as 10:1), nor do any of the Pastoral Epistles. We could assume either that they were written entirely in Paul's own hand, or (I think less likely) entirely in the hand of a secretary or co-author without Paul caring to add a closing greeting in his own handwriting. It is against this range of Pauline practice (and not simply the practice of 1 Cor 16:21; Col 4:18; 2 Thess 3:17) that I would consider the evidence of both Philemon 19 and Gal 6:11, the two other places where Paul refers to his own handwriting.

In Philemon 19, Paul emphasizes the fact that he is writing in his own hand in order to give weight to the "I.O.U." ("I owe you") he is rhetorically providing Philemon on behalf of Onesimus: "I, Paul, wrote with my own hand: I will pay you back." Paul's reference to employing his own handwriting here has nothing to do with the convention of closing a scribed letter with one's own handwriting, but with the practice of giving writs of debt, which have force only when written or somehow identified with the handwriting or seal of the debtor. Galatians 6:11 is also quite different from the formula of writing a closing greeting in one's own handwriting: "Look at the large letters I used as I wrote with my own hand." Paul is calling attention to the *size* of the letters, perhaps as a way of highlighting Paul's agitation as he writes. The amplitude of the letters signals the urgency of the matters he raises and his own investment in the outcome. There is also no clear indication that Paul is referring only to 6:11–18. Indeed, it makes far better sense to read 6:11 as an invitation to the Galatians to look back at the handwriting of the preceding chapters that Paul wrote in his agitation.[4] I also find that the

---

4. I would not, therefore, read *egrapsa* as a so-called "epistolary aorist," where the author chooses to use a past-tense verb to capture his or her action of writing (in his or her present moment) from the time perspective of the readers, who will read these words some time after they were actually written down. I would, instead, read it as

awkward start-and-stop style of passages like 2:3–5 (in the Greek, at least) suggests the lack of mediation between Paul, his thoughts, and the parchment or papyrus before him.

PAUL'S MINISTRY IN GALATIA

The Roman province of Galatia covered a vast territory during Paul's active ministry. It included the central portion of what is now Turkey, the principal cities being Ancyra, Pessinus, and Tavium. It stretched up to the northeast to include the cities of Side and Trapezus on the coast of the Black Sea. It extended down to include the regions often referred to as Lycaonia, Pisidia, and part of Phrygia, and thus the cities of Pisidian Antioch, Iconium, Lystra, and Derbe. The northern region of Roman provincial Galatia was the "historic" home of the original Celtic people who migrated to this area, while the southern region was joined to the northern region under the Roman Republic to form a single administrative unit. Which of these regions housed the congregations to which Paul sent his letter to the "Galatians" remains a much-debated issue among scholars, to which we will return later.

Paul himself gives us no details about the precise geographic location of the addressees. It is only when Galatians is read within the framework of Paul's mission work in Acts that this question can even be raised, let alone answered. What Paul *does* tell us about his founding visit to the congregations addressed by Galatians is quite different from anything we read in Acts.

> You know that I first proclaimed the message of good news to you on account of bodily illness, and you neither scorned nor rejected the trial you endured in my flesh, but rather you received me as God's messenger (or, "angel"), even as Christ Jesus. (Gal 4:13–14)

According to his own account, Paul appears to have evangelized in the city or cities to which he now writes because an illness prevented him from moving ahead to the destination he himself had in mind. Paul

a straightforward aorist: Paul is, in the moment, referring to the paragraphs he has already written.

offers an example here of a truly positive and Spirit-led response to the frustrations of being hindered in one's plans by sickness, seeking out God's provision of otherwise unexpected opportunities. The fact that he himself was afflicted by illness could have been expected to arouse scorn for his message. After all, how could a person who clearly was not experiencing divine favor proclaim the ready availability of divine favor in Christ? Those brought up in Greek culture, moreover, came to expect a good show from public speakers. Manner of presentation, physical grace and poise, and vocal beauty were all as important as what was said. Those who lacked these qualities in their speaking could arouse ridicule and public scorn rather than an attentive hearing. Against all such expectations, however, the Galatians received him warmly and embraced both Paul and his message. Paul also recalls for them how they experienced the reality of God's presence and power through the manifestations of God's Holy Spirit in their midst in conjunction with Paul's preaching, and experienced this newfound power invading their own lives and selves as well (Gal 3:1–5).

What was Paul's message in Galatia? Paul identifies the central feature of his Gospel here, as in Corinth, as "Christ crucified" (Gal 3:1; 1 Cor 2:2). This would have required some unpacking especially for the Gentiles in Galatia. Jesus as the "Christ," or "Messiah," was a foreign concept, and crucifixion was a sign of utter degradation. Greek culture, however, could envision a divine being suffering excruciating torments, and this specifically on behalf of humanity. The myth of Prometheus, for example, typifies this pattern. Zeus, the king of the gods, was angry with humankind and planned to destroy them. Prometheus, a Titan, sought to save humankind by equipping them with the starting point of all technology—fire, stolen from the gods. His reward was to be chained to a rocky peak and to be visited every day by an eagle, which tore into his abdomen to eat his liver (being immortal, Prometheus's liver grew back every night). Jews among Paul's audience were also familiar with pious Jewish men and women who allowed themselves to be tortured to death rather than prove disobedient to God's covenant, and how the obedient death of the righteous could restore God's favor toward the larger, disobedient people (see 2 Macc 6:16—8:5; 4 Macc 6:27–29; 17:17–22).

The Gospel of "Christ crucified" is the good news about the rescue that Jesus' offering of himself brought to human beings and about the change it produced in their relationship with God. Throughout Galatians, Paul refers to Jesus as one who, in death, "gave himself on behalf of our sins" (Gal 1:4), who "loved me and gave himself up for me" (Gal 2:20), who "rescues" believers "from the present, evil age" (Gal 1:4). The condensed formulas that Paul uses here suggest that Paul had spoken of these topics at much greater length before and could assume the Galatians' familiarity with these concepts from his earlier visit. Paul presented Christ's crucifixion in terms of a benefactor who poured himself out completely in order to bring benefit to his clients. This terminology of "giving oneself," or "pouring oneself out," is frequent in Greek and Latin inscriptions honoring benefactors. The shameful death of the cross was thus transformed into a noble act of supreme generosity and benefit. Giving himself "for our sins" (Gal 1:4), Jesus presented his extreme and complete obedience to God as a representative act on behalf of the many who were disobedient and unmindful of God. In this way, his death—the outcome of his perfect obedience—removed the obstacles, the sins against and affronts to God, that stood in the way of humanity experiencing God's favor rather than God's sentence.

Paul's claim that Jesus died in order to "rescue us from this present evil age" (1:4) recalls the apocalyptic framework of his earlier preaching in Galatia. According to this framework, this world and its history are a temporary phenomenon, one in which the justice of God and the rewards of God for the righteous cannot fully be manifested. The death and resurrection of the Messiah signaled, for Paul, the beginning of the end of this current age and the imminence of the "coming age," a better, eternal age in which God's purposes are completely fulfilled and God's people enjoy their full reward. The good news, then, was that Christ's death brought rescue *from* this world and its fate at God's judgment so that those who were rescued could enjoy the benefits of living with God in the age to come.

The way to share in the benefits of the Messiah's self-giving death and resurrected life was by "faith," trusting in the effectiveness of his death on behalf of others and in his ability to connect people with God. Those who are "of faith" trust that Jesus is a competent patron, able to procure the favor of the ultimate Patron, God. They trust that the provisions they receive by virtue of their association with Christ—most notably, the Holy Spirit—are sufficient to bring them where God wants them to be. Included within this "faith" is uncompromising loyalty to Jesus and obedience to him ("faithfulness"). The response of loyalty and gratitude toward Christ and the God he makes known would require a complementary turning away from every idol and all involvement in the worship of the no-gods that they represent. This was fundamental to the Gentile's response to the Gospel (as in 1 Thess 1:9–10), and Paul would have had a wealth of anti-idolatry polemic at his fingertips from the writings of Hellenistic era Jews (for example, the *Letter of Jeremiah*, the *Wisdom of Solomon*, and the like). Moreover, Greek and Roman philosophers had long emphasized the essential oneness of God, who was worshiped imperfectly in the many partial guises and inadequate representations of traditional Greco-Roman religion. Paul could connect this with his own understanding that the One God of the Jews was also the One God of the Gentiles. His cosmopolitan approach would certainly have been more appealing than the traditional Jewish appeal that stressed the ethnic particularity of the One God and the way of life by which one could please him.

The indisputable sign for Paul that Jesus' work was sufficient and effective on the Galatians' behalf is the Galatians' reception of the Holy Spirit. When these Jews and Gentiles responded with trust to the message Paul brought about Christ crucified, God "showed up," pouring out God's Holy Spirit upon them (Gal 3:1–5). This experience of the Holy Spirit is a common feature of the Pauline mission (see also 1 Cor 2:1–5 and Heb 2:1–4).[5] As an experience of divine power in their midst, the Galatians would have been quite aware that a decisive change had occurred in them and in their relationship with God, and that they had in fact received the Spirit of God. Paul reminds his converts of this experience, since he believes that this should have been enough to show that God had made them part of God's family. The Gentile converts among them were no longer unclean, no longer outside the people of promise,

---

5. I include Hebrews 2:1–4 as a witness from another member of Paul's team to the clear divine authentication that accompanied Paul's preaching and the birth of the congregations that were a part of his mission.

since God himself had acted to show God's own acceptance of them into that household.

THE PASTORAL CHALLENGE IN GALATIA

Paul's clear shock at what he has learned about his converts in Galatia since leaving them (1:6) suggests that he parted from them under the conviction that his work there rested on a firm foundation. What happened to shake that foundation in the months that followed his visit? We have only Paul's passionate response to the situation in Galatia as a witness to the situation itself, and must exercise some caution as we attempt to see the situation through the mirror Paul holds up to the same.[6]

New teachers have appeared on the scene, saying some new things about the "Good News" of Christ, and the Galatian Christians appear to be listening to them, even to be close to being persuaded by them (1:6–9). The fact that Paul first speaks of their message as "another Gospel" before correcting himself to say that it is "no Gospel at all" suggests that he knows them to be Christians themselves. Paul does not say much about the specific message of these rival teachers. He does indicate that persuading the Gentile converts to receive circumcision was a notable feature of their message (explicitly in 5:2; 6:12–13; indirectly in 5:11–12), as well as the adoption of some of the practices commanded in the Torah (4:10), and suggests that this was tied somehow with a concern to be "justified" before God on the basis of doing at least part of what the Torah commanded (5:4).[7]

Paul never names these rival teachers or suggests where they came from.[8] He refers to them only as "agitators" or "troublemakers" (1:7; 5:10b), clearly not welcoming their intrusion or their interpretation

6. A very helpful theoretical discussion of this process of careful historical reconstruction of a situation from one party's response to the situation is Barclay, "Mirror-Reading a Polemical Letter," 73–93.

7. So also Betz, *Galatians*, 6–7.

8. This does not mean, however, that Paul does not have a good deal of firsthand information about them and that he does not know who they are (against the inference of Witherington, *Grace in Galatia*, 23). Making vague and uncertain references to one's opponents was a standard rhetorical strategy, almost as if naming them spe-

of the Gospel. He likens their influence to the "evil eye," the magical calling down of a curse upon someone out of envy (often translated, therefore, as "bewitching" the Galatians; 3:1). He speaks of them as ill-mannered athletes who have "cut in" on the lane of the Galatian Christians, tripping them up as they run (5:7). Paul suggests that the motives of these new teachers are far from pure. They are pretending to have the Galatian Christians' best interests at heart, but are really trying to deprive the Galatians of their place in Christ so that they will, instead, become dependent upon the teachers (4:17). They are too cowardly to endure the opposition that preaching the truth of the Gospel arouses. Instead, they are trying to escape persecution themselves (from their fellow Jews) by making the Galatian Christians adopt Jewish practices, hence making the Christian movement and its message more acceptable to non-Christian Jews (6:12). They aren't even fully committed to all the practices of the Torah, the Jewish law, themselves, but are trying to use the Galatian Christians as an opportunity to enhance their own reputation (6:13).

What Paul wants to see happen within this situation is clear: his converts should reject outright the course of action that those teachers have proposed (5:1), show the new teachers the door, and slam it behind them (4:30).

Despite Paul's hostile presentation of these teachers, the fact that Paul needs to write Galatians at all suggests that these rival teachers had a persuasive message that many among Paul's converts were giving a ready hearing. Paul did not leave before answering all the questions that would arise for the Galatians about their new life in Christ and their relationship to prominent aspects of God's former dealings with

---

cifically or suggesting too great an interest in them would be to show them more respect than they merit.

Much depends on how Paul was informed about the emerging situation in Galatia. J. Louis Martyn (*Galatians*, 14) highlights the importance of an often overlooked group within the Galatians churches, namely the "catechetical instructors" (6:6). Martyn suggests that these instructors were local leaders appointed by Paul to continue the nurture of the congregations in the Pauline Gospel, the Pauline interpretation of the Jewish Scriptures, and so forth. These leaders would have been the likeliest candidates for traveling to Paul with news of developments in Galatia as well as returning from Paul to the congregations to read Paul's response in the assemblies.

the people of God. We can only speculate about what some of these questions were, but speculation here is rooted in the probabilities borne out by most if not all Gentiles who have come to faith in this Jewish Messiah. (1) If Torah is a God-given law for God's historic people, are we obliged to follow it or any part of it? It seems to dominate all of God's dealings with God's people from Moses to Malachi. Should we give it more attention, if we really want to be sure that we're right with God? (2) If we really have God's Spirit, why do we still struggle so much with temptation and fall so often into sin? How do we even know what is sin versus what is legitimate pleasure or a just course of action? Not everyone following the Spirit agrees on the answer to this question, so perhaps it's not enough just to have the Spirit, if we want to really know what God expects of us.[9] These were precisely the sorts of questions that the rival teachers were poised to answer, and answer persuasively. If the Galatian converts weren't already asking these questions, the rival teachers could certainly have introduced them and impressed upon the Galatian Christians the importance of finding reliable answers to them.

Who, then, are these rival teachers? Scholars are almost unanimous in affirming that they are representatives of another Christian mission, led by Jewish Christians, presenting Torah observance as a necessary part of responding to God's favor offered in Jesus Christ.[10]

9. Betz (*Galatians*, 8) also focuses on the dissonance in the converts' experience of being "in the Spirit" while also still liable to their lower drives as a problem for which Paul had not adequately prepared them, but for which "Paul's opposition had concrete help to offer," thus as a pressing problem precipitating the crisis.

10. Some scholars have occasionally suggested that the rival teachers are Gentile Christians who have adopted the Jewish way of life, or that they are non-Christian Jews who are reaching out to Gentile Christians. In favor of the first of these positions, Munck (*Paul and the Salvation of Mankind*, 87–89) argues that the "Judaizers" were actually Gentile Christians from within Paul's churches, but Paul consistently speaks of these rival teachers as people who have come into the congregations from the outside, not as insiders who have gone wrong (Bruce, *Galatians*, 25; see also Dunn, *The Theology of Paul's Letter to the Galatians*, 8). More recently, Mark Nanos tries to revive the second of these positions (*The Irony of Galatians*, 193). According to him, both Jewish and Gentile Christians in Galatia are still attending worship in the local synagogue, with the non-Christian Jews urging their Gentile [Christian] "guests" and "visitors," whom they commend for their desire to be "righteous," to take the necessary step of circumcision so as to separate themselves from the pagan world to which they still belong (*Irony*, 317–18). Nanos believes that these Gentile Christians would

These missionaries sought to keep the new Christian movement firmly anchored within the historic covenant between God and Israel. The activity of this kind of mission is reflected in Acts 15:1–4, which tells of Jewish Christians from Judea coming to Antioch, the home base of Paul and Barnabas's mission, seeking to impose circumcision and Torah-observance on the converts there.[11] Galatians suggests that such missionaries were active beyond Antioch as well. Paul refers briefly to this rival mission again in Phil 3:2–21, presenting them as a foil for Paul's own model of discipleship.[12]

---

still regard circumcision and full inclusion into the Jewish people as complementary to their faith in Jesus (*Irony*, 227). The principal objection to this view is Paul's own presentation of the situation as one in which a rival "Gospel" is being proclaimed, not a term he would have used if the source of the troublesome teaching was the synagogue, as well as the otherwise well-attested phenomenon of early (Jewish) Christians wrestling with the implications of the Christ-event for the ongoing observance of Torah and for Jewish-Gentile relations within the Christian churches.

11. F. F. Bruce (*Commentary on Galatians*, 55) regards the situation in Galatia to have been very close in time and kind to the situation described in Acts 15:1–2.

12. More complicated theories about Paul having to fight on two separate fronts in Galatia enjoyed some popularity in an earlier period of scholarship. Lütgert (*Gesetz und Geist*) and Ropes (*The Singular Problem of the Epistle to the Galatians*) thought that the congregations were afflicted both by Judaizers who had come from outside and by "libertines" who believed that Christian freedom meant freedom from all (or many) traditional moral restraints. Paul wrote Galatians to urge the former to embrace Christian freedom and to warn the latter not to misuse or abuse it. Richard Longenecker (*Galatians*, xcix) also thinks that Gal 5:21 signals a problem of libertinism: "I warn you, *as I did before*, that those who live like this will not inherit the kingdom of God" (5:21; emphasis and translation his). In either form, this theory would represent an excess of mirror-reading. Paul's instructions about Christian ethics need not imply a wanton neglect of morality among the Galatian Christians. It is better to regard 5:13—6:10 as an alternative solution to the problem of finding an adequate moral compass in the midst of "Christian freedom" (whether raised by the Judaizers or by the Galatians themselves out of their desire to live righteously before God), which the Judaizers solved through recourse to Torah.

The theory of Walter Schmithals ("Die Häretiker in Galatien," 25–67; *Paul and the Gnostics*, 13–64) that Paul is combating the influence of Jewish Christian Gnostics also relies on excessive mirror-reading of Paul's rather casual use of terminology in Galatians that might also have meaning within (later) Gnosticism, such as the concept of "perfection" in 3:3. F. F. Bruce (*Galatians*, 25) rightly counters, "Gnosticism has really to be read into the teaching of these people as reflected in Paul's attack on them before it can be read out of it."

Despite Paul's allegations, the primary motivation of the rival teachers was probably theologically grounded. They preserve the integrity of the Covenant, and set the work of Jesus the Messiah within the context of this Covenant (Torah). Jesus was still the one who brought light to the Gentiles, bringing about the gathering in of the nations at the end of this age, but he would accomplish this by bringing the Gentiles fully into the Jewish people through circumcising them and getting them to take upon themselves the "yoke of Torah," at least to a certain extent. These rival teachers were also concerned about the unity of the church. Like Paul, they sought to enable Jew and Gentile to come together in Christ in one worshiping body, the one Body of the redeemed. Unlike Paul, they believed it was essential that the Gentiles, and not the Jews, alter their behavior to make that fellowship possible. (This particular issue appears to stand at the heart of the dispute in Antioch related by Paul in Gal 2:11–14.)

The rival teachers acted out of their own zeal for the Torah and their commitment to keep God's people distinct from all the other peoples of the earth as required by the holiness code of Leviticus. Luke relates a particular rumor about Paul that was, he claims, running rampant in Jerusalem, to the effect that Paul was leading Jews to abandon the Torah and forsake the covenant (Acts 21:20–21). Such a rumor was not entirely inaccurate. Paul claims to have become a Jew to Jews and Gentile to Gentiles (1 Cor 9:19–23). He violated Torah's standards of purity (at least, as the Pharisees interpreted these standards) by eating with his Gentile converts, perhaps even eating food improper for Jews (1 Cor 10:25–30). He encouraged his Jewish coworkers to do the same for the sake of the mission and the Gospel, setting aside those restrictions within Torah designed to keep Jews from freely associating with Gentiles, and hence being polluted by those contacts. Moreover, he encouraged his Jewish converts to do the same with regard to his Gentile converts, to "welcome one another as Christ welcomed you" (Rom 15:7), and to regard the keeping of kosher laws or special observances of Sabbaths and other days as matters of personal choice (Rom 14:1–6). Paul might well have been seen to promote willful neglect of, if not apostasy from, the covenant.

For Jewish Christians convinced of the eternal validity of the Torah and the covenant it sustained, Paul's teaching and practice on this point would be unacceptable. Indeed, Paul was endangering the Jewish people as a whole by loosening Jewish Christians' commitment to observe the boundary-maintaining laws of Torah faithfully and rigorously. After all, the God who enforced the covenant threatens all the curses of Deuteronomy 27–28 upon the nation of Israel if they neglect and transgress the covenant, walking in the ways of the non-Jewish nations.

For Jewish Christians who might themselves be disposed to agree with Paul in principle, there was also the very real danger posed by more zealous, non-Christian Jews, who might react vigorously and violently when their fellow Jews turned away from Torah for the sake of mingling more easily with the Gentiles. Zeal for the Torah had led Paul himself to persecute Jewish Christians prior to his own conversion (Gal 1:13–14, 23; Phil 3:6), and led other non-Christian Jews to continue to apply significant pressure on Christian Jews (see, for example, 1 Thess 2:14–16). Such expressions of zeal for the Torah and the covenant were firmly rooted in the tradition of Phinehas, who struck down an Israelite man and his Moabite concubine and so won for himself the promise of perpetual priesthood and saved Israel from being destroyed by a plague for its apostasy (Num 25:1–13). It was rooted in the tradition of Mattathias and his sons at the outset of the Maccabean Revolt, as they purged Israel of the apostate and lapsed Jews in its midst and thus "turned away [God's] wrath from Israel" (1 Macc 2:15–28, 42–48; 3:6, 8).[13]

A significant movement within Jewish Christianity, therefore, wanted to make it clear to both non-Christian and Christian Jews that the Jesus movement was in no way a movement that promoted apostasy from the ancestral law. By reinforcing Jewish (Christian) adherence to the Torah, and all the more by bringing Gentiles to the light of the Law,

13. Robert Jewett ("The Agitators and the Galatians Congregation," 198–212) suggests that the rival teachers undertook their Judaizing mission specifically as a means of appeasing the growing Zealot party at home, for whom Jewish association with Gentiles was highly suspect and might provoke reprisals. While he is right to take seriously the indications in Galatians that non-Christian Jews are putting significant pressure on Jewish Christians (and perhaps Gentile Christians as well), "pressure from the Zealots in Judea" represents "only one possible background" (so, rightly, Borgen, "Paul Preaches Circumcision and Pleases Men," 37–46, especially p. 42).

the rival teachers could save themselves, the church in Judea, and the churches in the Diaspora where non-Christian Jewish communities were strong, from the intramural persecution that perceived apostasy could invite. Judaism could tolerate Messianic sects, but not the negation of its most central identity markers (like circumcision, Sabbath obedience, and care regarding foods).

It is impossible to say, however, that the particular rival teachers Paul confronts in Galatia were primarily motivated by a desire to avoid persecution. It is equally likely that they chose their path based on their convictions concerning the eternal validity of the Torah as the way to live pleasingly before God, to have a part among God's covenant people, and thus to enter into the community of the promise. If encouraging Gentile obedience to the Torah provoked strong opposition from the Roman or local Gentile authorities, they might well have embraced persecution for their devotion to the Torah, in the tradition of the martyrs of the Maccabean period whose devotion to the Torah was tested and proven through their endurance of torture to the point of death, a devotion that Jews would prove again in many different contexts (e.g., in the pogroms in Alexandria, Egypt, during the reign of Caligula, in persecutions under Hadrian in the wake of the second Jewish Revolt, and in persecutions by Christians after the church merged with imperial power).

THE "GOOD NEWS" ACCORDING TO THE RIVAL TEACHERS

What, then, was the "other Gospel" proclaimed by the rival teachers? They have left no testimony of their own, but we can reconstruct probable elements of their message from two sources. First, Paul's response to their message surely highlights the topics and the specific positions that his rivals used when they presented their case. In order for Paul's rebuttal to be a rebuttal at all, their message would have had to include points like (1) circumcision is the manner by which one joins the family of Abraham and becomes an heir of the promises given to Abraham; (2) Christ's death allows both Jews and Gentiles to enter together anew into the historic covenant God has made with God's people, the Torah, which is God's gift to all who would "choose life" (Deut 30:15–20); and (3) the Torah is God's provision for us to make progress in our life in Christ and in our struggle to master the passions of the flesh and experience freedom from their power over us.

Second, this information can be supplement by investigating primary texts that display Jewish reflection about these topics or that advance positions similar to those Paul feels compelled to address in Galatians. Hellenistic Jews energetically sought to build bridges with Greek culture, and many of their writings, in which they explain the benefits and wisdom of keeping Torah and of circumcision, survive. It is likely that the rival teachers would have drawn on such well-articulated and widely-attested arguments as resources for their own attempts to bring Gentiles over to the Jewish way of life.

The Case for Circumcision

In the opinion of Gentiles, the Jewish rite of circumcision was not one of the more admirable features of that way of life, though it was certainly the best known (alongside avoidance of pork and avoidance of all work on the Sabbath). It amounted to a mutilation of the human form, and was often disparaged as barbaric (see Philo, *De Specialibus Legibus* 1.1.1–2.).[14] What would make circumcision suddenly so appealing, so pressing an option, for the Gentile Christians in Galatia?

The Jewish Scriptures promoted circumcision as a positive and powerful ritual. Paul himself had affirmed the value of the Jewish Scriptures in his preaching, looking to these texts as essential resources for knowing the One God and for understanding the believers' place in God's family. The rival teachers were able to ground their message fully in the sacred Scriptures themselves. After all, Scripture says that the promises were given to Abraham and his children. And how does one become a part of the family of Abraham? How does one become an heir of the promises given to Abraham? The Scriptures are unambiguous on this point—through circumcision.

---

14. On Gentile criticism of Judaism and Jewish apologetics, see deSilva, *An Introduction to the New Testament*, 100–105, and the literature therein cited.

When God made the covenant with Abraham, promising him that he would be the "ancestor of a multitude of nations," God gave Abraham circumcision as the absolute, unavoidable, and essential sign of that covenant:

> "This is my covenant, which you shall keep, between me and you and your offspring after you: Every male among you shall be circumcised. . . . Any uncircumcised male who is not circumcised in the flesh of his foreskin shall be cut off from his people; he has broken my covenant." (Gen 17:10, 14 [NRSV])

Gentiles wishing to join God's people must likewise circumcise themselves, following both the command of God and the example of Abraham, the first Gentile proselyte![15] As in ancient Israel the Gentile sojourner was made fit to participate in the life and worship of the community of Israel (Exod 12:48–49), so now this continues to be the case. Moreover, only the circumcised have any part in the heavenly Zion, the life of the age to come, for it is written: "Awake, awake, put on your strength, O Zion! Put on your beautiful garments, O Jerusalem, the holy city; for the uncircumcised and the unclean shall enter you no more" (Isa 52:1 [NRSV]). Likewise Ezekiel, speaking of the heavenly temple, says: "Thus says the Lord GOD: No foreigner, uncircumcised in heart and flesh, of all the foreigners who are among the people of Israel, shall enter my sanctuary" (44:9 [NRSV]). The sacred oracles of God demonstrate, therefore, that circumcision is the means by which to join the family of Abraham and the people of God. Indeed, it is key to participation in the age to come.

Circumcision, moreover, has great moral significance, as do all of the Jewish laws and customs when viewed symbolically and observed in both mind and body (see Philo, *Migr.* 89). Circumcision "is a symbol for the cutting away of pleasures and the passions" of the flesh that lead the reason astray from its proper course, as well as an acknowledgment that the human male is not capable of producing offspring without the help of God, and therefore also a remedy for pride (Philo, *Migr.* 92; *Spec.*

---

15. Barclay, *Obeying the Truth*, 54. For early Jewish texts describing Abraham as a Gentile convert to the worship of the One God, see *Apocalypse of Abraham* 1–8; *Jubilees* 11:15–17; Philo, *Virtues*, 212–16.

1.2.9–11; *Quaest. Gen.* 3.48). The rite may also be seen as a symbolic initiation into a way of life that will facilitate mastery of the passions —those desires, sensations, and emotions that belong to our human nature and so often hinder us from following the dictates of virtue and righteousness.

Torah as the Way to Perfection

Circumcision is a good beginning, but it is only an initiation. God's covenant was made with Israel in the Torah, and all who hope to share in the blessings of Israel, and avoid the curses upon the disobedient, must submit to the yoke of Torah, as it stands written, "Cursed be everyone who does not uphold the words of this law by observing them" (Deut 27:26 [NRSV]). The person who keeps the commands of Torah shall live to God by means of Torah (Lev 18:5).[16]

The way of life prescribed by Torah is far from a collection of barbaric, ethnocentric rules, as some Gentile critics claimed. For the person who is confused about how to make progress in living a God-pleasing life of virtue, as the newly converted might certainly be, Torah provides the God-given guide for the perplexed. Jewish defenses of the enlightened quality of the Torah focused on the virtues that a Torah-observant way of life nurtured. Philo, as we have already seen in regard to circumcision, draws out the hidden moral meaning behind those particular commands that most clearly distinguish Jews from Gentiles. The author of the *Letter of Aristeas* takes a similar approach. For example, he explains that the dietary laws are to be understood in terms of the characteristics of the particular animals that are classified as either clean or unclean, commending the former and warning against imitation of the latter (*Let. Aris.* 128–169). Vultures and eagles, for example, are unclean because they live by feeding on the dead bodies of other creatures or preying violently upon weaker animals, teaching Jews never to prey upon the weak or the vulnerable. Weasels are unclean because they conceive through their ears and give birth through their

---

16. Paul recites these two verses from the Torah in Gal 3:10, 12, but it appears he is pushed to take account of them because they are significant pieces of the rival teachers' argument.

mouths (apparently ancient zoology had a few holes in its research), teaching Jews not to participate in internalizing or passing along gossip. Animals that have split hooves and chew their cud are designated as "clean," commending to Jews the virtue of distinguishing carefully between virtue and vice and only setting their foot upon the virtuous path (the split hoof) and always meditating on virtue and righteousness ("ruminating").

One particular Hellenistic Jewish defense of the value of Torah, *4 Maccabees*, provides an exceptionally informative background. *4 Maccabees* offers itself as a philosophical "demonstration" of the thesis that the mind that has been trained by following Torah is able to master the passions of the flesh (*4 Macc.* 1:1, 13–17). Rising above these passions was a central topic of Greco-Roman philosophical ethics, since the passions—whether emotions like fear or anger, sensations like pleasure or pain, or desires like greed or lust—were deemed the most potent obstacles to living a virtuous life. Unchecked, the passions of the flesh would clamor louder than one's reasoning faculty, derailing a person's commitment to virtue and ability to walk in line with virtue.[17] The battle against these forces became the true battle for honor, the most noble athletic competition. The Jewish Law provides a complete exercise regimen for the strengthening of the rational faculty and the subduing of the passions. The dietary laws and prohibitions against coveting exercise one in self-control (*4 Macc.* 1:31–2:6a); the regulations concerning debt-release and leaving the gleanings of the harvest subdue greed (*4 Macc.* 2:7–9a); limits on vengeance and actions against enemies subdue the passion of enmity or hate (*4 Macc.* 2:14). Torah is lauded as that which "teaches us self-control, so that we master all pleasures and desires, . . . courage, so that we endure any suffering willingly; . . . justice, so that in all our dealings we act impartially, and . . . piety, so that with proper reverence we worship the only living God" (*4 Macc.* 5:23–24).

This is precisely the kind of argumentation that the rival teachers would have had ready at hand to use as they encountered the Galatian converts, still painfully aware of being at the mercy of their own fleshly impulses and desires. The final chapters of Paul's letter (5:12—6:10) have often been viewed as nothing more than an afterthought, a bit of moral

17. See deSilva, *4 Maccabees*, 52–58.

19

exhortation added to the letter once his real argument was completed. However, these chapters were an integral, essential part of his counter-argument against the position of the rival teachers, who presented, in Torah, the reliable guide to virtue and the discipline that would develop virtue and inhibit vice that the Galatians sorely knew they needed. These converts "needed concrete help, and the opponents of Paul could provide it."[18] The rival teachers presented the Torah as the best trainer in virtue, the way to perfection in terms of ethical progress, a proven discipline for mastering the "passions of the flesh." Paul, then, would have to demonstrate that the Galatians had already received all that they needed to rise above the passions and embody the virtues that God sought for in God's people—in the Spirit, in which they were to learn to walk.

Whom Should the Galatians Trust?

Both Paul's defensiveness in Galatians and the well-established practice of attacking a rival's credibility in order to make room for one's own position make it highly likely that the Jewish Christian missionaries had called Paul's reliability into question in the course of seeking to win the Galatian Christians to their position. At the very least, these rival teachers would have needed to be able to answer the question posed by the Galatian believers: "Why didn't Paul tell us any of this, and why should we trust *you* on these matters when our beloved Paul said nothing about circumcision or taking on the yoke of Torah?"[19]

Judging from Paul's response, their attack on his credibility plausibly included the following elements. First, the rival teachers claimed to represent the Jerusalem apostles, who supposedly supported a much stricter observance of Torah than Paul. James was well known for his piety, even among non-Christian Jews. Peter had wavered on this is-

18. Betz, *Galatians*, 72.

19. Witherington (*Grace in Galatia*, 25) suggests that the rival teachers did not come overtly attacking Paul's apostleship, although the very fact of questioning the adequacy of Paul's message seems to include questioning his reliability or credibility as a representative of the Gospel. It appears that they did make some remarks about Paul that he found particularly objectionable, as reflected in Paul's rebuttal in Gal 5:11 (and this personal attack on Paul may have been a primary motivator for his personal, and rather uncouth, rejoinder in Gal 5:12).

sue, but the rival teachers themselves might have been the first to bring up the Antioch incident (Gal 2:11–14) to prove that Peter had come to his senses and remained true to the original, Torah-observant Gospel. Paul preached circumcision in other instances, but probably thought that would make his message less welcome or successful here, so he left it out (Gal 5:11; 6:17).[20] Whatever his reasons for not preaching "the whole truth of the Gospel," they were not ultimately in the Galatians' best interests. Second, Paul's authority and knowledge of the Gospel—like those of the rival teachers themselves—are dependent upon the Jerusalem "pillars," as Paul's travels to Jerusalem demonstrate. If Paul's message differs from the rival teachers' message, then, the rival teachers would have to assert, it is Paul who has been an unreliable and unfaithful messenger (Galatians 1–2).

Unlike Paul, the rival teachers assured the Galatians that they would teach them the whole truth about the Gospel.[21] Even though it involved difficulties, like the rite of circumcision, they would not keep anything back from the Galatian Christians just to win their assent or avoid difficult arguments. The plain sense of Scripture supported their position. The Galatians could trust them to bring them the next step in their journey toward righteousness.

OVERVIEW OF PAUL'S RESPONSE

Such a reconstruction of the rival teachers' position would well account for each of the three major parts of Paul's response to the situation in

20. This was observed as early as the fifth century by John Chrysostom: "They accused [Paul] too of acting a part, saying: 'this very man who forbids circumcision observes the rite elsewhere, and preaches one way to you and another way to others'" (*Commentary on Galatians* 1:1–3; cited by Longenecker, *Galatians*, l).

21. George Howard (*Crisis in Galatia*, 9) suggests that the rival teachers might well have understood themselves to be "completing" Paul's Gospel and mission work by introducing Torah, even to be amicably disposed to Paul, considering him their ally in a mission equally dependent upon the Jerusalem apostles as they themselves were in theirs. The attention Paul gives to defending his credibility, and especially the fact that he raises topics about his consistency in a manner suggesting that specific charges have been made to the contrary (notably, 5:11), indicates to me that the rival teachers were not wholly amicably disposed toward Paul.

Galatia: the opening portion focused on issues of Paul's call, confirmation of the same, and steadfastness therein (1:10—2:21), the middle portion that constitutes a series of arguments against making a place now for reliance on the Torah in one's walk with God (3:1—4:21), and the closing portion that turns to focus on ethical guidance. In effect, Paul appears to be addressing three primary questions:

1. Why should the Galatians trust Paul, rather than the rival teachers whom Paul, in effect, curses in 1:8–9?[22]

2. What does Paul have to say about the role of Torah and circumcision in God's economy, and thus the Christian relationship to the Law given by God, in response to the "other Gospel" that is no Gospel?

3. If we aren't going to rely on Torah to help us progress toward righteousness before God, what do we have to guide us?

Each of these questions, and therefore every part of Galatians, can thus be read as integrally related to the challenge posed by the situation in Galatia.

22. I would disagree with Witherington (*Grace in Galatia*, 29) here on the fundamental purpose of Gal 1:10—2:14. He suggests that "the *function* of the narrative material we find in Gal 1–2 is to provide examples to the audience of what sort of behavior to adopt or shun (shun—Paul's pre-Christian behavior, the behavior of Peter and Barnabas at Antioch, and the behavior of the false brothers; adopt—Paul's post-conversion life style and behavior and the behavior of the pillars when Paul met with them in Jerusalem and did not compel Titus' circumcision and endorsed Paul's mission to the uncircumcised Gentiles) . . . He intends to show his audience what sort of behavior to emulate and what sort to avoid."

Aside from the fact that Paul at no point draws explicit attention to the exemplary purpose of these episodes ("Don't be like Peter or Barnabas"; "Take the pillars for your example"), the specific points Paul establishes in regard to this string of episodes all answer—and answer very well—questions other than "Whom should we imitate?" These would include: (1) "What is the source of Paul's commissioning and message, and therefore his authority to speak on behalf of God?" (2) "What is the nature of Paul's relationship with the Jerusalem pillars?" (3) "Who has shown the greatest consistency in regard to the 'truth of the Gospel' and what is required of Gentiles to become part of God's people in Christ?" The purpose of Paul's narrative is not to provide examples of behavior, but to affirm the ultimate reliability of Paul's Gospel vis-à-vis the "other Gospel."

WHO WERE THE GALATIAN CHRISTIANS?

The Christians Paul addresses were Paul's own converts, with whom he felt he had established a deeply personal connection (Gal 4:12–15). He calls them his "children," in line with his tendency to use the language of parenting or nursing when referring to his relationship to people whom he has personally brought to faith in Christ (Gal 4:19; see also, for example, 1 Cor 4:14–15; 1 Thess 2:7–8, 11–12). These might be rather recent converts, if Paul's remark of astonishment is to be read as indicating the small amount of time that has passed since their first "call" into God's favor (1:6), though other readings of the verse are certainly possible.

Scholars tend to assume that these congregations are composed mostly, if not entirely, of Gentiles. J. Louis Martyn, for example, remarks that Paul makes no distinction in his letter between Gentile Christians, who would be contemplating circumcision, and Jewish Christians, for whom the question of whether or not to receive circumcision was rendered moot by their parents on their eighth day of life. He finds nothing said about the harmlessness of the circumcision received by Jewish males prior to their coming to faith in Jesus. Paul explicitly speaks of the idolatrous past of his addressees (4:8–9), differentiating no one in the audience who had previously worshiped the God of Israel.[23]

Martyn's observations do not, in my opinion, adequately take into account the nature of the focal problem. His conclusion is just slightly less erroneous than the suggestion that there are no women among the congregations addressed by Galatians, since Paul says nothing explicitly to women comparable to the attention he gives to circumcision and the Gentile Christian *men* contemplating it. The question directly on the table in Galatia concerns only the Gentile converts, for whom circumcision is not yet a fait accompli, and whose motivations for undertaking the rite show a misalignment of their theologies and trust. Paul is most concerned about what the *Gentile* Christians among his audience are contemplating doing. Naturally, they and their imminent choices are the focus of his attention and his arguments.

23. Martyn (*Galatians*, 16) uses these observations to support a North Galatian destination, on the supposition that the cities there housed no Jewish population in the mid-first century CE as far as we know. Longenecker (*Galatians*, lxix), however, considers this assumption to be "patently false."

Despite this focus, much of what Paul says in Galatians would speak to any Jewish Christians "bystanders" in the audience, giving them adequate guidance concerning how to process the fact of their own circumcision (2:15–16; 3:23–26; 4:4–7; 5:5–6; 6:15–16). A Jewish Christian would not be threatened by Paul's dire words concerning the consequences of circumcisions performed *now* (Gal 5:2–4); rather, Paul's words about the harmlessness of circumcisions already performed upon the bodies of Jewish males who have since come to trust in Christ would speak directly to their state: "Neither circumcision nor uncircumcision matters, but only faith working through love" or "a new creation" (5:6; 6:15).

While the presence of Jewish Christians among the Galatian congregations cannot be positively proven, any more than their presence can be ruled out, several factors weigh in favor of the former position. First, Paul is particularly interested in creating *one* people of God out of the two peoples formerly alienated from one another by virtue of the boundary-maintaining power of the Torah. Ephesians 2:11–22 celebrates this as, in effect, the heartbeat of Paul's mission. The Antioch incident that Paul recounts represented a dangerous threat to this unity, and Paul's (over)reaction to the behavior of Peter, Barnabas, and the other Jewish Christians in that church is a measure of his passion for this unity. By withdrawing to separate tables, Peter, Barnabas, and the other Jewish Christians were only reaffirming Jewish commitment to live by Torah. It is only because Paul could not conceive of a divided church—a church of Jewish Christians and a church of Gentile Christians—that he interpreted this as an act that would "compel the Gentiles to take up the Jewish way of life" (Gal 2:14b). Second, the pattern of Paul's preaching in Acts, if it is to be valued as a historical source for the Pauline mission, consistently presents Paul beginning his mission work in a local synagogue, gathering a core of Jewish and "God-fearing" adherents (see, in regard to cities in provincial Galatia, Acts 13:43; 14:1), before moving out from there into the home of one of these early adherents to continue his outreach and his nurturing of a congregation, or simply moving on to a new location. Mixed congregations of Jewish and Gentile Christians, then, would seem to be the norm both in terms of Paul's ecclesiology and reputed practice.

WHERE WERE THE GALATIAN CHRISTIANS?

Were the addressees of Galatians, then, residents of the cities of southern Galatia like Pisidian Antioch, Iconium, Lystra, and Derbe, which Paul and Barnabas evangelized in the mission work narrated in Acts 13:14–14:23, or does Paul write to churches in the major cities of northern Galatia like Ancyra, Pessinus, and Tavium, which he ostensibly evangelized on the journey narrated in Acts 16:6; 18:23? Scholars of considerable ability and repute have weighed in favor of both the "South Galatian" and the "North Galatian" hypothesis,[24] so that one must admit that the evidence is far from conclusive on either side.[25] Nevertheless, I will attempt to lay out here why I would favor the former view, reading Galatians as perhaps Paul's earliest letter, written in the thick of the unresolved issues swirling around the question of how Gentiles can become full participants alongside Jewish Christians in the assemblies of God in Christ.

Acts and Galatians

One of the decisions that every historian of early Christianity must make concerns the historical reliability of the Acts of the Apostles, and

24. On locating these churches in the northern territory of Galatia, see Lightfoot, *St. Paul's Epistle to the Galatians*; Moffatt, *An Introduction to the Literature of the New Testament*, 83–107. The "North Galatian Hypothesis" reaches back into the patristic period. This is fully understandable, however, given that the Roman province of Galatia had been, by the mid-second century CE, reduced once again to its northern territories. Between 74 and 137 CE, the territories of Lycaonia and Pisidia/Phyrgia were detached from the province of Galatia and joined to other provinces, with the result that Antioch, Iconium, Lystra, and Derbe were no longer known as "Galatian" cities (Longenecker, *Galatians*, lxiii). The patristic commentators on Galatians were simply reading the address in terms of their own contemporary geography (Bruce, *Galatians*, 6).

W. M. Ramsey made the "classic" case for locating these churches in the southern cities of Galatia in his *Historical Commentary on St. Paul's Epistle to the Galatians*; see also Hemer and Gempf, *The Book of Acts in the Setting of Hellenistic History*, 277–307. Longenecker (*Galatians*, lxiii–lxxii) provides an exceptional summary of the issues involved and of the positions taken.

25. So rightly Bruce, *Galatians*, 18; Dunn, *The Epistle to the Galatians*, 7.

thus the role that Luke's historical framework should play in discussions concerning the historical setting of other books of the New Testament that fall within the scope of Luke's narrative. This is an especially important decision in the case of Galatians since Paul actually relates a fair amount of early Christian history therein (at least in regard to seventeen years of his own activity, including some important interactions with other principal figures in the early church). Scholars tend to approach this question from one of three basic positions:

1. Acts and Galatians are both completely historically reliable; they can and must be harmonized (i.e., Galatians must be read within the framework of Acts).

2. Acts and Galatians are both generally reliable, but must be read and evaluated in terms of the authors' different perspectives, knowledge of events, principles of selection, and goals for shaping the story in the way that each author does. Together, each can *contribute* to a reliable picture of the history of the early church. Privilege tends to be given to Galatians as a firsthand testimony to events.

3. Acts and Galatians are documents written to tell "history" in such a way as supports the authors' agenda (usually this is applied far more forcefully to Acts than to Galatians). The framework of Acts is especially open to revision, as it reflects Luke's idealized portrait far more than it reflects than the "facts." Privilege is always given to Galatians.

This discussion of Galatians proceeds mainly from the second theoretical position. I find that Luke's account is reliable to a considerable extent. For example, the details of the movements of Paul and his team from Thessalonica to Athens and Corinth in Acts 17:1–18:5 closely follow the same movements about which Paul himself speaks in 1 Thess 1:7–8; 2:17—3:6. Such correspondences increase my confidence in Luke's care investigating such details. However, we must also take seriously the discrepancies between Luke's account of Paul's conversion and early mission and Paul's own account of the same in Galatians:

1. Paul insists that, immediately following his conversion, he "did not confer with flesh and blood" (Gal 1:17), but rather went immediately into Arabia, then returned to Damascus, and only then went to Jerusalem (Gal 1:17–18). According to Luke, Paul confers immediately with Ananias and remains with the disciples in Damascus for "some days" or "many days" and next goes to Jerusalem (Acts 9:10–26).

2. According to Luke, Paul is introduced to all the apostles by Barnabas and even preaches openly in Jerusalem until being forced to flee (Acts 9:26–30); according to Paul, he only met Peter and James the Just on a visit to Jerusalem a full three years after his conversion, and remained "unknown by face to the churches in Judea" (1:16–22).

3. Luke makes no mention of a visit undertaken by Paul and Barnabas to Jerusalem for a private meeting with Peter, James the Just, and John, specifically involving Titus and the question of whether or not Titus needed to be circumcised in order for his conversion to the One God through Christ to be valid, as well as the Jerusalem pillars' confirmation of the validity of Paul's apostolic work thus far (Gal 2:1–3). Instead, Luke tells of Paul and Barnabas going to Jerusalem to deliver funds for famine relief (Acts 11:27–30), and then going yet another time for the "Jerusalem Conference" in response to the activity of Judaizers in Antioch (Acts 15:1–29). (None of Luke's accounts of Paul's visits to Jerusalem in the first part of his ministry square absolutely with Paul's firsthand accounts of the same.)

4. Luke also makes no mention in Acts of the "Antioch incident" and the falling out between Paul and Peter (and Barnabas!) that looms so large in Paul's memory as he writes Galatians (Gal 2:11–14).

5. Luke makes no mention of Paul's illness in the Acts account of the first evangelizing visit to the cities either in the southern part of the Roman province of Galatian (i.e., Pisidian Antioch, Lystra, Iconium, Derbe) or the northern part of the same

(Ancyra, Pessinus, and Tavium), although this is prominently featured in Paul's account of this visit (Gal 4:13–14).[26] (If the visits to the Galatian territory in Acts 16 represent a new evangelization effort in the cities of Northern Galatia, Acts gives us no details about these whatsoever, even omitting the mention of any cities Paul visited.)

These are important discrepancies and, while in my opinion they do not diminish the value of the historical framework of Acts as a resource for understanding the history leading up to the crisis in Galatia, they do suggest that we keep several principles in mind as we read Galatians alongside Acts in an attempt to locate Galatians in the life and ministry of Paul and of the early church.

First, Luke is clearly selective in what he chooses to report. Even a report that is highly accurate in what it includes can create bias by virtue of what it excludes. Luke has chosen to minimize division and uncertainty within the inner circle of apostles where the inclusion of the Gentile Christians and related issues are concerned. Luke was deeply concerned with giving his Gentile Christian readers "certainty" and "security" (Luke 1:4) about their place in the people of God. It did not suit his purposes to speak of the sharp division between Peter and Paul at Antioch over the matter, nor about James's apparent difficulties with Jewish Christians playing loose with Torah to eat with uncircumcised Gentiles (Gal 2:11). Nor would it help to recall the ways in which key figures like Peter and Barnabas may have vacillated on this issue.

Second, while Luke did accompany Paul and continued to be a part of the Pauline mission for some time (Col 4:4; Phlm 24; 2 Tim 4:11), he was not a "player" in its early stages. He may not have been privy to information about the private meeting between Paul, Barnabas, Peter,

---

26. James Moffatt (*Introduction*, 99) puts this forward as an argument against identifying the churches addressed by Galatians with those churches in southern Galatia evangelized by Paul and Barnabas, but this objection holds only to the extent that we expect Luke to tell his story entirely in line with Paul's memory (and much more *recent* memory) of the same, and to the extent that we are willing, in effect, to accept an argument from silence in regard to Paul's evangelization of North Galatia. That is to say, it is not so much that Luke says nothing contradictory to Paul in regard to evangelizing particular churches because he fell ill, as the fact that Luke says *nothing* about founding other churches in Galatia at all.

James, and John. Paul only speaks of this once, and that only when absolutely pressed. Luke writes Acts after the end of the Jewish Revolt in 70 CE, and thus well after James the Just, Paul, and Peter have been killed.[27] As Luke composed Acts, none of these major players were available to him for further investigation of these events that took place well before Luke himself appeared on the stage of this story. From another angle, James, Paul, and Peter were also therefore unavailable to correct Luke's story, reminding Luke or his readers that it was really a lot rougher sorting out the question of Gentile inclusion than Acts suggests.

Paul's Visits to Jerusalem in Galatians and Acts

We come, then, to the question of Paul's visits to Jerusalem. Luke tells of five visits that Paul made to Jerusalem over the course of his Christian career. The first occurs shortly after Paul's conversion (Acts 9:26–30), in which Paul is introduced to the apostles by Barnabas and spends some time coming and going in their midst and preaching in Jerusalem.[28] The second occurs in connection with relief funds taken up in Antioch for those affected by the famine in Judea (Acts 11:27–30), which Paul and Barnabas deliver to the elders of the church there. The third occurs in response to the appearance of Jewish Christian missionaries in Antioch claiming that Gentile converts must also be circumcised and observe

27. It is commonplace to read that Mark, Matthew, and Luke were all written after the destruction of Jerusalem in 70 CE that effectively brought the first Jewish Revolt to an end. This is only certain, however, in the case of Luke, who alters predictions of Jesus about the "end" (see Mark 13:14–19; Matt 24:15–21), replacing the allusive language Jesus used, referring to the "abomination of desolation" and the like, with clear descriptions of the siege of Jerusalem of 70 CE (Luke 21:20–24), which Luke understood to be the fulfillment of Jesus' predictions. Since Luke presents Acts unambiguously as the sequel to his Gospel, it follows that Acts, too, was composed after 70 CE. James the Just was lynched in 62 CE; Paul and Peter are both believed to have been executed in Rome under Nero, hence before 68 CE, and most likely before or in connection with the fire of 64 CE.

28. Since Paul regards himself as "still unknown by face" to the churches in Judea after this point (Gal 1:22), one must wonder if Luke has colored his depiction of this visit (Acts 9:26–30) with stories of Paul openly preaching and debating in Jerusalem as a means of making his transformation—now becoming what once, in Stephen, he persecuted—more dramatic and vivid.

the Torah, resulting in the Jerusalem Conference at which the issue was decided: Gentiles do not need to be circumcised, nor observe Torah. They would only need to avoid foods sacrificed to idol, fornication (of course), eating meat from animals that had been strangled (hence with the blood still in the tissues), and from all ingestion of blood (Acts 15:20, 29). A fourth visit is probably to be inferred in Acts 18:22, where, upon Paul's return to Caesarea after his missionary work in Achaia, he "went up and greeted the church." Within Palestine, one "went up" to Jerusalem and "went down" again to wherever one's home was. The fifth visit results in Paul's imprisonment of several years and voyage to Rome to stand trial (Acts 21:17).

In Galatians, Paul speaks only of two visits to Jerusalem. The first occurs three years after his conversion (Gal 1:18–20). Paul's purpose for this visit was to make Peter's acquaintance, and to this end he stayed with Peter for two weeks. He declares on oath that he saw none of the other apostles "except James, the Lord's brother." The second visit occurs fourteen years later, counting either from Paul's conversion or, as would be more natural and therefore likely, from the first visit (Gal 2:1–2). The central feature of this visit, according to Paul, was a private meeting involving himself, Barnabas, Peter, James the Just, and John (Gal 2:2b) for the purpose of seeking their confirmation of how God was at work both through Peter, taking the Gospel to the Jewish people, and through Paul, taking the Gospel to the non-Jewish nations (Gal 2:7–9). At stake for Paul was the pillars' acknowledgment of the fundamental unity of their missions, though it was being carried out with a focus on different spheres. Paul finds it relevant that these three pillars did not see fit at that time to demand that Titus, Paul and Barnabas's Gentile companion and co-worker, be circumcised: as far as Paul is concerned, this should serve as precedent enough to settle the issue now facing the Galatian Gentile converts (Gal 2:3–5). According to Paul, the pillars did not seek to correct Paul's Gospel or his manner of incorporating Gentiles into the Church at all, only urging him to "*continue* to remember the poor," which was already fixed in Paul's own heart (Gal 2:10).

The activities that Paul mentions in Galatians are the following, in narrative order:

1. Out of zeal for the Torah and his ancestral tradition, Paul was formerly hostile toward the Jesus movement in Palestine and beyond, "persecuting and seeking to destroy it" (Gal 1:13; cf. Acts 8:3; 9:1–2).

2. Paul encountered the Glorified Christ and was turned instantly from persecutor to proclaimer of the faith (Gal 1:15–16; cf. Acts 9:3–6, 19b–22).[29]

3. Paul visits Jerusalem for the first time after his conversion/commission in the third year after that event (Gal 1:18–20; Acts 9:26–30?).

4. After this first visit, Paul returned to work in the regions of Syria (the home of Antioch) and Cilicia (the home of Tarsus; Gal 1:21; Acts 9:30; 11:25–26).

5. Paul visits Jerusalem a second time, taking Barnabas and Titus, for a private meeting with the pillars (Gal 2:1–10; Acts 11:28–30? 15:2–21?).

6. Peter visits Paul and Barnabas and the church in Antioch. Later, some "men from James" arrive and Peter feels pressured into eating with them at a separate table from the Gentile believers, reinstating the social boundaries that Jewish observance of Torah's dietary laws create between Jew and non-Jew (Gal 2:11–14; not in Acts).

7. Paul preaches the Gospel in the cities of Galatia (Gal 4:11–16), possibly with Barnabas (Acts 13:13–14:28? 16:6?).

8. After Paul's departure, rival teachers come to Galatia urging the Gentile converts to accept circumcision and some facets of

29. At this point, Paul may be exercising the greater selectivity in his version. He denies conferring with "flesh and blood" (Gal 1:16), by which he means to emphasize the independence of his Gospel and apostolic commission from the Jerusalem apostles and utter dependence upon God for both. His omission of any mention of Ananias and the disciples in Damascus (see Acts 9:10–19) is therefore understandable as being beside the point and potentially damaging to his claims. Both accounts agree that Paul continued on in Damascus for a time, though Luke gives the impression of a much shorter stay there (Gal 1:17; Acts 9:20–25).

Torah observance as a means to making their place in God's family secure and making progress in the life of discipleship (Gal 1:8–9; 5:7–12; 6:11–14; not in Acts, though see Acts 15:1, 5).

How does all this match up with the narrative of Acts, and how can this help us locate Galatians in Paul's ministry, and the Galatian churches on the map? Both Paul himself and Luke speak consistently regarding Paul's former zeal for Torah, expressed in the suppression of deviant Jewish groups, and his stunning transformation from persecutor to apostle. Both Paul and Luke agree that Paul visited Jerusalem not too long after his conversion in order to become acquainted with the leaders of the Christian movement (Gal 1:18–20; Acts 9:26–30), though they differ significantly in the details. These differences, however, are readily attributable to Paul's interests for recounting his early relationship with Jerusalem and Luke's greater distance from the events (and possibly the unavailability of any firsthand witnesses to Paul's first visit). Both also speak of Paul's carrying out of his apostolic commission in the provinces of Syria and Cilicia after this initial visit.

It is at this point that greater disagreement arises among scholars, who are fairly evenly divided on the question of whether to identify the second visit recounted by Paul in Gal 2:1–10 with the second visit mentioned by Luke (Acts 11:28–30) or the third visit, undertaken in conjunction with the Jerusalem Conference (Acts 15:1–30).[30] Reading Acts alongside Galatians, Acts 11:28–30 occupies the same spot in the narrative flow that one would assign to the conversations about which Paul writes in Gal 2:1–10.[31] Paul's narrative suggests that prior to the

30. These are by no means the *only* options, though they are the preferred ones. John Knox (*Chapters in a Life of Paul,* 64–73) and Kirsopp Lake (*The Beginnings of Christianity,* 5.195–212) have both suggested that Luke has heard two different accounts of what was actually a single visit, but treated them as if they were accounts of separate visits. Lake thus identifies Gal 2:1–10 with both Acts 11:28–30 and 15:6–21, while Knox identifies Gal 2:1–10 with both Acts 15:6–21 and 18:22. Lake's position has been adopted and advanced by Haenchen, "The Book of Acts as Source Material for the History of Early Christianity," 271; Haenchen, *Acts of the Apostles,* 400–404, 438–39.

31. Burkitt, *Christian Beginnings,* 116. In favor of this identification, see Ramsay, *The Teaching of Paul in Terms of the Present Day,* 372–92; Bruce, *Galatians,* 43–56.

visit of 2:1–10 he worked only in Syria and Cilicia. If his missionary travels were more extensive in this interim, it would have been easy for him simply to add the names of a few more provinces, or to omit specific reference to two provinces when he was referring to a period that included mission beyond those two. In other words, the most natural reading of Galatians 1–2 suggests that the meeting of Gal 2:1–10 happened exactly where Luke places the visit of Acts 11:28–30—between Paul's work in Tarsus and Antioch (11:19–26) and Paul and Barnabas's mission to the cities of southern Galatia (Acts 13–14).[32]

Luke's account of this visit is so different from Paul's, however, that many scholars have looked instead to Acts 15, where at least the basic subject matter (circumcising a Gentile, whether Titus as test case or all Gentile converts) seems closer to the conversation that Paul relates in Gal 2:1–10. The differences between Acts 11:28–30 and Gal 2:1–10 may be accounted for by the fact that Luke—and perhaps any of Luke's informants—looked upon this meeting from the outside, underscoring the visit as part of a famine relief program (Acts 11:27–30). The phrasing of Gal 2:10, in which the Jerusalem apostles urge Paul and Barnabas to "continue to remember the poor" while Paul asserts that he had already been eager to do this very thing, would complement the "relief fund" aspect of this visit. Paul, however, looks at the visit as an insider, being privy to the private meeting with James, Peter, and John. While Paul is intent on demonstrating his essential independence from these Jerusalem pillars, this also affords him an opportunity to affirm their validation of his calling at the same time.

James Dunn objects to identifying Gal 2:1–10 with the visit of Acts 11:28–30, since, "if . . . the issue of circumcision was resolved as decisively as Gal. ii.1–10 indicates, with the full and formal approval of the Jerusalem leadership (ii.3, 6–9) in the face of strong internal pressure to the contrary (ii.4–5), it is difficult to see how it could have become an

---

32. The objection that this does not give Paul sufficient missionary experience and achievement to claim that he has been entrusted with "apostleship for the Gentiles" (see Stein, "Relationship of Galatians 2:1–10 and Acts 15:1–35," 239–42) does not take sufficient account of Paul's understanding of his calling. For him, "apostleship to the Gentiles" was a part of his understanding of his call from his experience of God's revelation of Jesus. It would also have been sufficiently enacted by this point in his activity in "Arabia," Syria, and Cilicia (Longenecker, *Galatians*, lxxxi).

issue once again in Acts xv."[33] Dunn, however, may be assuming—like Paul himself!—that the meeting of Gal 2:1–10 resolved more than it actually did. From the perspective of the pillars, it may have only resolved questions of two separate but equal missions, one to Jews and one to Gentiles. The Antioch Incident (Gal 2:11–14) appears to have raised new issues that some people at the table in the conversations of Gal 2:1–10, most notably Peter, but perhaps also James, did not regard as having been settled at that time. The agreement of Gal 2:1–10 does not appear to have envisioned a congregation of Jewish Christians alongside Gentile Christians, and the pressure applied to Jewish Christians in Antioch to eat at a separate table where greater attention was paid to purity regulations need not be seen as in any way a breach of the earlier agreement.

Identifying Gal 2:1–10 with the visit of Acts 11:28–30 raises some challenges for chronology as this pertains to the reconciliation of Galatians with the framework of Acts.[34] According to Paul, three years pass between his calling and his first visit to Jerusalem, and then fourteen years pass between visits. The Jerusalem Conference, however, cannot be dated past 49 CE, to give Paul time to make it Corinth by the time of Gallio's tenure there as proconsul (Acts 18:12), which can be firmly dated to 50/51 CE (perhaps the one firm date in early Christian chronology). There is, however, still sufficient time between Jesus' crucifixion and the Jerusalem Conference for these time intervals if we are willing to grant at least two of the following three presuppositions:

1. Paul is counting partial years as whole years;

2. the three years and the fourteen years are concurrent, both beginning with Paul's life-changing encounter with the glorified Christ;[35]

---

33. Dunn, *Galatians*, 38.

34. Hemer, "Acts and Galatians Reconsidered," 81–88, especially p. 87.

35. Robinson, *Redating the New Testament*, 37; Martyn, *Galatians*, 180–82. Of the three, this is the one that I would least favor granting. It is far more natural to read these as subsequent rather than concurrent time periods.

3. the crucifixion occurred in 29 or 30 CE, and not later, with Paul's conversion occurring by 32 or 33 CE.[36]

I find these assumptions generally easier to grant than those required by dating Galatians after the Jerusalem Conference (thus identifying the visit of Gal 2:1–10 with Acts 15:6–21).

Scholars who identify the visit of Gal 2:1–10 with the meeting of Acts 15:6–21 generally do so because, in their opinion, "the central issue, key participants and principal arguments are so close that the two accounts must be variant versions of the same episode."[37] It is true that Barnabas, Paul, Peter, and James are all present at both meetings, and that the subject of whether or not Gentile converts need to accept circumcision as part of their initiation into Christ arises in regard to both. Beyond this, however, the "variants" are extensive. Paul speaks of a private meeting with the apostles (he is, indeed, emphatic on this point, Gal 2:2b), a meeting that was chiefly focused on confirming Paul's calling as apostle to the Gentiles. The particular "test case" of Titus was a secondary matter. Luke speaks of the convening of a more general assembly (Acts 15:5–7, 12–13, 22), focused mainly on the question of what Gentile converts were required to do to be part of the new people of God formed from both Jews and Gentiles. In Paul's account of his second visit, he and Barnabas go away with only one stipulation placed on his work, namely that they continue to remember the poor (Gal 2:10). In Acts, four stipulations are laid upon all Gentile believers, including the avoidance of the ingestion of blood (e.g., left in the tissues of strangled animals) and the avoidance of meat from animals that had been sacrificed to idols, as a kind of "bare minimum" in the way of purity requirements for being part of the new people of God.

Aside from these discrepancies, two significant problems arise if we identify the visit of Gal 2:1–10 with the Jerusalem Conference. First, Paul recounts his own story under a self-imposed oath in Galatians 1–2, which suggests that he is attempting to lay out his visits to Jerusalem

36. Longenecker, *Galatians*, lxxxiii. Colin J. Hemer ("Observations on Pauline Chronology," 3–18, especially 13) adds that the events of Acts 1–8, to the extent that they are historical, need not have occupied more than a few months—such was the vigor of the early Christian movement at its inception.

37. Dunn, *Galatians*, 88; so also Schlier, *Der Brief an die Galater*, 115–16.

and other events in his life with careful attention to chronology and completeness, at least where his dealings with Jerusalem and the Jerusalem church powers are concerned, to establish certain points about his relationship to those powers. Omission of an entire visit, especially when he has invoked an oath about the truthfulness of his report at an earlier juncture (Gal 1:20), would seriously undermine the credibility of the remainder of his report. The argument that Paul simply considered the famine relief visit irrelevant is beside the point: he would need to have mentioned it and declared its irrelevance so as not to leave himself vulnerable to disconfirmation. Second, the "Apostolic Decree" (Acts 15:22–29) would have direct bearing both on the question of circumcision raised in Galatia and the question of table fellowship with the Gentile Christians raised in Antioch (Gal 2:11–14). If it had been published in connection with Paul's second visit, it is difficult to understand why Paul remains silent about the council's ruling on the question of the necessity of circumcising Gentiles, when that ruling would have been the perfect trump card to play against the rival teachers' position. However, Paul could also not speak of that ruling as "adding nothing" to his own message and the practice of his churches (Gal 2:10), since it did involve specifically calling for observance of four prohibitions on the part of Gentile converts.

In my estimation, then, it makes better sense to view the conversation related in Gal 2:1–10 as a preliminary conversation about two missions and mutual affirmation of the practice of these missions without yet considering the implications for, for example, table fellowship between the circumcised and uncircumcised, between the kosher and the non-kosher, in a single congregation. Paul reads more into the non-compelling of Titus to be circumcised than Peter did, to judge from the confrontation in Antioch. This meeting took place in conjunction with Paul and Barnabas's delivery of relief funds for Judean Christians, and thus in 47 or 48 CE.[38] The situation in the South Galatian churches contributes to bringing this issue to a head, and thus to resolution at the Jerusalem Conference. Paul's mission work in Galatia follows after this second visit, but predates the Jerusalem Conference, aligning

---

38. So Becker, *Paul: Apostle to the Gentiles*, 31; Witherington, *The Paul Quest*, 314–18; Alexander, "Chronology of Paul," 115–23, especially 122–23.

thus with Luke's report on Paul and Barnabas's mission to the cities of Lycaonia and western Phrygia (i.e., South Galatia; Acts 13:1—14:28).[39] Paul would, then, be writing to the congregations in these cities in 49 CE, shortly before the Jerusalem Conference.

Considerations of Paul's co-workers—both those who are named and *not* named in Galatians—tends to confirm this dating and destination. The prominence with which Barnabas is mentioned (2:1, 9, 13) more naturally presumes acquaintance with Barnabas on the part of the addressees. This would point to the churches founded by both Paul and Barnabas in southern Galatia (Acts 13:1—14:28), but not to churches in northern Galatia, if we are to read Acts 16:6; 18:23 as referring to a mission in northern Galatia, since Barnabas does not travel with Paul for long after the Jerusalem Conference (Acts 15:22, 35–41). While it is always *possible* that the addressees of Galatians could have learned of Barnabas indirectly,[40] the emphatic character of Paul's remark that "*even* Barnabas was caught up in this play-acting" (2:13) suggests rather that Barnabas's "defection" should be more surprising to the audience than Peter's, thus presuming personal acquaintance with Barnabas and his previous, more inclusive vision.[41] The absence of any mention of Timothy also weighs in favor of an earlier date as well as a South Galatian destination. Timothy is Paul's constant missionary companion from

39. The fact that Luke does not refer to this region as "Galatia" himself in Acts 13–14 is not significant (against Moffatt, *Introduction*, 93). The important point is that these cities were, in fact, part of the province of Galatia and could be referred to as cities of Galatia. Whether or not Luke chooses to do so is by no means decisive for the question of whether or not Paul would do so.

40. Martyn (*Galatians*, 17–18) asserts, on the contrary, that "it seems probable that that knowledge came from the Teachers," that is, from the rival mission. He does not, however, offer any argumentation in support of his claim that this is actually "probable."

41. Dunn, *Galatians*, 17; Bauckham, "Barnabas in Galatians," 61–71. The fact that Paul writes Galatians without naming Barnabas as a co-sender may point to the fact that they had not yet reconciled since their falling out in Antioch. If we rely on the record of Acts, Paul and Barnabas are reconciled with one another at the Jerusalem Conference and work together for a brief span afterwards (Acts 15:22–35). Witherington (*Grace in Galatia*, 11) takes this as further evidence that Galatians was written within this window prior to the Conference while Paul and Barnabas were still at odds.

Acts 16:1–4 (starting from Lystra) through the journey to Jerusalem (Acts 20:4), and named as a co-sender in 2 Corinthians, Philippians, Colossians, 1 and 2 Thessalonians, and Philemon. If the letter is addressed to churches that both evangelized together, or if it was written after Paul had been working together with Timothy, it is strange that Paul never mentions Timothy.[42]

The objection has been made that Paul would not have addressed the Christians in Pisidian Antioch, Iconium, Derbe, Lystra (and perhaps other towns as well) as "Galatians," since the term originally referred to people of a particular ethnic background (i.e., the Celts who migrated to and settled in central Anatolia, hence the northern region of provincial Galatia). While most among Paul's congregations in Southern Galatia would not have shared that particular ethnic background, it would still have been perfectly appropriate for Paul to address the people in the southern part of the province as "Galatians" as well.[43] William Ramsay documents the fact that as early as the second century BCE, "the Phrygian origin of the larger half of the Galatian population was forgotten by ordinary people of the surrounding countries, and the whole state was thought of as Galatia and its people Galatians."[44] When Galatia was expanded to include Lycaonia in 25 BCE, the same would hold true. The status of each person was that of a "provincial" as the Roman Empire designated provinces. Orators would therefore address populations by their provincial identity, not their original ethnicity. Hence, Paul would be following standard procedure by addressing *any* congregations within Galatia as "*Galatae*, i.e., members of the Roman empire as being members of the Province Galatia."[45] More to the point, no other single term besides "Galatians" would have been sufficiently

---

42. Longenecker, *Galatians*, lxx–lxxi.

43. Whether or not he ought to have called them "*foolish* Galatians" (Gal 3:1) is another matter.

44. Ramsay, *A Historical Commentary on St. Paul's Epistle to the Galatians*, 84.

45. Ramsay, *Galatians*, 120. Witherington (*Grace in Galatia*, 4) cites several first-century inscriptions as evidence that the entire region was commonly called "Galatia" during Paul's lifetime, not just the historic northern part where the Celts had originally settled.

inclusive to use to address people from Antioch, Iconium, Lystra, and Derbe (i.e., people from the sub-regions of Phrygia and Lycaonia).[46]

Fundamentally, however, the question needs to be asked afresh whether there even was a *Pauline* mission to North Galatia. The theory that Galatians addresses Christians in the cities of northern Galatia rests on the slender evidence of the two references in Acts to "the Phyrgian and Galatian region" (16:6) and "the Galatian region and Phrygia" (18:23). These passages are often taken as Luke's *extremely* brief mention of a Pauline mission to North Galatia, on the strength of reading "the Phrygian and Galatian region" as a specific way of indicating two originally independent territories by their older, ethnic designations. But it is far from clear that Luke intended such an inference to be made (or that his use of ethnic versus provincial designations is indeed all that precise). Tracing out the movements of Paul and his team as related in Acts 16:6–9 on a map of ancient Asia Minor might more readily suggest the following picture.

After the Jerusalem Conference, Paul and Barnabas returned to the cities of South Galatia (specifically Derbe and Lystra) to deliver the decision of the Jerusalem leadership (Acts 16:1, 4) and pass on from there to the remaining cities of "the Phrygian and Galatian region" (Acts 16:6), namely the portion of the Roman province of Galatia associated with Pisidia and Phrygia (hence, southern Galatia), with the intention of planting churches in the major cities of the Roman province of Asia (on the West coast of Asia Minor). If Paul's team's goal was to preach in Ephesus, there is a fairly direct route through Pisidian Antioch and thence through Phrygia (a region that sits half in the province of Galatia and half in province of Asia) to the eastern parts of Roman Asia with their bustling cities. The Spirit prevents them from preaching in Asia, so Paul and his team head north through Phrygia (quite possible through that part that lies within Roman Asia) until they reach the edge of Mysia. At this point they contemplate heading northeast into Bithynia, but, under the Spirit's guidance, head directly west through Mysia to the port city of Troas instead and embark upon the Macedonian mission.

A tour through Ancyra and Pessinus and, even more so, Tavium, at this point in Luke's narrative (i.e., Acts 16:6) would represent an exten-

---

46. Burton, *Galatians*, xxix; Bruce, *Galatians*, 16.

sive detour (more than two hundred kilometers!) for a missionary who left Lystra intending to head for Ephesus.[47] It would be even stranger for Luke to pass over entirely any description of mission work in this new region. If this reconstruction of the itinerary of Acts 16:1–9 is accepted, then Paul once again returns to the churches of south Galatia and Phrygia in Acts 18:23 shoring up his congregations there before finally pursuing his mission in the Roman province of Asia (Acts 19).[48]

47. Witherington, *Grace in Galatia*, 5–6.

48. So also Hemer, *The Book of Acts*, 120; Witherington, *Grace in Galatia*, 6. There is some disagreement concerning whether "the Phrygian and Galatic region" (Acts 16:6; compare "the Galatic region and Phrygia" in 18:23) refers to one region or two. Burton (*Galatians*, xxxii) argues that this phrase designates a single region, with the noun *chōra* ("region") being described by two proper adjectives joined by a single article in both references. Even if Luke intends to name two geographic areas, he may be joining a provincial with an older regional term, aware that they are somewhat overlapping, because he finds this to give a more precise indication of the apostle's trajectory from Derbe toward Ephesus.

Several approaches to the question of dating Galatians relative to Paul's other letters are fundamentally flawed. One approach treats the content or theological perspective of each letter as a reliable indicator of date. Thus the strong eschatological orientation of 1 Thessalonians, contrasted with the relative lack of interest in eschatology in Galatians, suggests to some that Paul could not have written the two letters within a short span of each other. This argument ignores the more fundamental issue governing the content of Paul's letters, namely the situations of, and issues faced or raised by, the addressees of each particular letter (rightly Fung, *Galatians*, 23). Similarly, the absence of the "faith-works" antithesis in the Corinthian and Thessalonian letters is not due to Paul's not having yet formulated it, such that Galatians and Romans should both be dated among the later of Paul's letters, but to its irrelevance to the challenges in the situations being addressed in those letters (Bruce, *Galatians*, 49).

Arguments based on content also produce strikingly different results. Galatians and Romans clearly treat many of the same topics and are profitably read in connection with one another, but this observation does not help us determine *when* Galatians was written. J. B. Lightfoot argues that the similarities in content between Galatians and Romans presuppose that Galatians was written shortly before Romans. John Drane, however, focuses more on the theological distance between Galatians and Romans (as well as the Corinthian Letters). Galatians is much more negative in terms of the role of Torah in the life of the believer, and much more confident in the sufficiency of the Spirit, than he is in Romans and the Corinthian letters, suggesting to him that some significant time had to elapse between the writing of Galatians and Romans (Drane, *Paul, Libertine or Legalist?*, 140–43; also Betz, *Galatians*, 12). Whether one focuses on the similarities or the differences between Galatians and Romans leads to opposite conclusions regarding their proximity in time.

PAUL, LETTER-WRITING, AND THE ART OF PERSUASION

Two important contexts for thinking about Galatians in terms both of Paul's objectives and the text's impact upon the Christians he addresses are the contexts of ancient letter-writing (epistolography) and rhetoric. Scholars often ignore one context favoring the other, or argue that only one is truly applicable. Such approaches are needlessly one-sided. Each background needs to be considered for what it can contribute to the illumination of Galatians.

Handbooks on letter-writing and on the art of persuasion written during or near to the period of the composition of the New Testament texts have survived from antiquity, giving us firsthand information about how people native to that time and culture thought about both arts.[49] The reader of these handbooks will notice at once that the handbooks on letter-writing are extremely brief, while handbooks on rhetoric tend to cover a far greater amount of ground in far greater detail. Since the arts of argumentation and persuasion were absolutely foundational to Greek and Roman education in any formal setting, it is likely that writers of handbooks on letter-writing felt that they could assume a lot in terms of their readers' ability to compose appropriate arguments and address necessary topics. In other words, writers on the art of letter-writing appear to have been *supplementing* a foundation in logic and

Arguments based on "tone" are even less helpful. Readers of Paul cannot help but notice that Galatians and 2 Corinthians contain some of Paul's most virulent attacks regarding rival teachers and his own converts' stupidity for listening to them, while Paul also defends his own apostolic legitimacy. The shared tone, however, does not provide any solid evidence that the two letters were written in close proximity, only that Paul responded with a similar degree of intensity when he felt his own apostleship to be called into question and saw his converts shifting their loyalty to his critics. The fact that Paul's rivals in both Galatians and 2 Corinthians are Jewish Christian teachers also tells us nothing about the dating of the letters since most early Christian leaders and teachers were, in fact, Jewish Christians. Moreover, Paul's rivals in Corinth do not appear to have been Judaizers, *per se*.

49. The two most important handbooks on letter-writing are those by Pseudo-Demetrius and Pseudo-Libanius, the original texts and translations of which can be found in Malherbe, *Ancient Epistolary Theorists*. Handbooks on classical rhetoric are in greater abundance, the most important including the following: Aristotle, *Art of Rhetoric*; Anaximenes, *Rhetorica ad Alexandrum*; Pseudo-Cicero, *Rhetorica ad Herrennium*; Cicero, *De inventione* and *De oratore*; and Quintilian, *Institutio Oratoria*.

rhetoric rather than trying to provide everything a letter-writer needed to know in their brief treatments.

Galatians as Ancient Letter

Galatians clearly presents itself as a letter from the outset, using an expanded form of the typical letter opening wherein a sender names himself or herself, then the recipient, and opens with words like "greetings," or "peace," or "greetings and good health." Paul would have far preferred to have been present with the Galatians to address his speech to them personally, in his own voice and embodied presence (4:20), but he is unable or unwilling to leave his present location at that precise moment, and so he sends this letter, probably in the hands of the Galatian Christian or Christians who came to him to seek his help, to achieve the same goal.

Richard Longenecker compiled a list of typical expressions from surviving, authentic letters from the period as a means of identifying transitions within, and indications of Paul's shifting goals for, Galatians.[50] These formulas include:

Opening Formula ("A to B, greetings [*chairein*]")

Thanksgiving ("I give thanks for . . . ")

Prayer ("above all else, I pray for your . . . ")

Expression of Joy ("I rejoiced exceedingly when . . . ")

Astonishment/Rebuke ("I am amazed how . . . ")

Expression of Grief or Distress ("I am anxious because . . . ")

Reminder of Past Instructions ("as I have asked you before . . . ")

Disclosure of Information ("I want you to know . . . "
    or "I would not have you unaware . . . ")

Request ("I beg you to . . . ", "I entreat you to . . . ")

Use of Verbs of Hearing or Learning ("I was grieved to hear
    that . . . ")

Introduction of Topics with *Peri* ("Now about . . . ")

Notification of Upcoming Visit ("I hope to come to you . . . ")

50. Longenecker, *Galatians*, cv.

References to Writing ("You wrote that . . . " or "I have written that . . . ")

Use of Verbs of Speaking or Informing ("Alexander will tell you how it is with us . . . .")

Use of the Vocative to Indicate Transition ("Brother," or "Friend, I urge you to . . . ")

Closing Formula ("I wish you good health [*errōsthai se boulomai*]" or the like)

When he applied the full inventory to Galatians, he discovered clusters of these formulas in a number of passages, suggesting that these passages indicated important transitions within the letter.[51]

1:1–3 (salutation and greeting)

1:6–13 (astonishment-rebuke formula; disclosure statements)

3:1–7 (vocative; verb of hearing/learning; disclosure statement)

4:11–20 (expression of distress; request formula; disclosure statements; travelogue and a visit wish)

4:28—5:13 (vocatives; appeal; disclosure formula; expression of confidence)

6:11–18 (subscription, benediction, grace wish, vocative)

This suggests, in turn, the following epistolary structure, with the particular prominence of topics and formulas of "rebuke" and "request" providing the clues to the primary letter types that Paul has combined in Galatians:

1:1–5: Salutation

1:6—4:11: Rebuke Section

4:12–6:10: Request Section

6:11–18: Subscription

---

51. Here Longenecker (*Galatians*, cvii-cviii) followed the insight of Mullins ("Formulas in New Testament Epistles," 380–90, especially 387) to the effect that the use of one formula tends to precipitate the use of one or more others, making these clusters especially helpful markers of transition in the writer's thought.

Galatians would likely have been heard by its audience, then, as a letter of a "mixed type," primarily combining the "rebuke letter" and "request letter" types.[52] This goes a long way toward giving us a reliable, preliminary orientation to Galatians, but we need also to draw on the insights of classical rhetoric to discern more precisely how Paul positions the Galatian Christians both to receive his rebuke and respond to his request, as well as the specific nature of that request.

Galatians as Ancient Rhetoric

In the centuries leading up to Paul's time, writers on the art of public speaking distinguished between three basic types—or "genres"—of rhetoric. Each of these types aligned with one of the three principal goals for a speech in one of the three principal settings for oratory in civic life. Oratory was born out of the practical needs of the Greek city and the institutions required for the regulation of civic life. A city's enrolled citizens met to determine what course of action they should take on behalf of the city to meet some particular need. This was the home of "deliberative rhetoric," the object of which was to discover the most advantageous course of action for the (usually immediate) future. Speakers promoting a particular course of action would try to establish that it was the *right* thing to do (that it, it was in keeping with the culture's core values, like courage, prudence, justice, or generosity), the *expedient* course to pursue (tending to preserve existing goods, gain other advantages, or ward off ills), a *feasible* course (the resources to un-

52. Longenecker, *Galatians*, cix. Hansen (*Abraham in Galatians: Epistolary and Rhetorical Contexts*, 34–43) has collected several examples of mixed "rebuke-request" letters from among actual papyrus letters from the late Roman period. Pure types can be found in postcard-length letters from antiquity, but are rare in actual correspondence of any length.

Hans Dieter Betz (*Galatians*, 15) had asserted that Galatians be read as an example of the "apologetic letter," in keeping with his view of Galatians primarily as a specimen of judicial rhetoric, the goal of which was to persuade the Galatian Christians about the authenticity of Paul's apostleship and the reliability of his presentation of the Gospel. Betz listed several texts as examples supporting the existence of such a genre (Plato, *Epistle* 7; Demosthenes, *De corona*; Isocrates, *Peri Antidoseōs*), but further inspection of these examples revealed that none presents a genuine "letter." See Hanson, *Abraham in Galatians*, 25–27; Witherington, *Grace in Galatia*, 39.

dertake the course being available), an *honorable* response (embodying virtues, tending toward the praiseworthy), and the like.[53] Speakers trying to dissuade the assembly from pursuing a particular course would use the opposite topics.

A second principal setting for the development of a distinctive kind of rhetoric was the law court, where enrolled citizens would be called upon to assess the innocence or guilt of a particular person in regard to some past action identified as a wrongdoing. This was another area of competition between speakers (a prosecutor and an advocate), with each seeking a particular judgment from the audience (the jury) in regard to whether or not a particular person committed a particular wrong. "Judicial" or "forensic" rhetoric typically relied on the testimony of witnesses, oaths, material evidence, and logical probabilities for reconstructing the past event and assigning guilt.

A third genre of rhetoric, "epideictic" or "demonstrative" oratory, was much broader in scope. This category included speeches given on civic occasions to remember and to praise the honored dead or to acknowledge exceptional benefactors, in which the goal was to lay out the virtues and achievements of the subject and win, essentially, "assent" from the audience concerning the virtue of the subject and the value of the qualities he, she, or they embodied (and thus the audience's ongoing commitment to those qualities as well).[54] This category also included speeches aimed at the demonstration of a particular thesis or proposition where, again, the goal of the speech was assent to the thesis or proposition.

The strategies employed in these three genres of rhetoric were by no means limited to the particular settings in which they originated. Wherever some group needed to make a decision about a future course of action, deliberative strategies would be employed by those involved. Questions of wrongdoing were not only raised formally in law courts, such that forensic strategies would be employed in many informal settings where one person accused another of wrongdoing, putting him or

---

53. For a fuller discussion, see *Rhet. Alex.* 1421b21—1423a12; *Rhet. Her.* 3.2.2—3.4.9.

54. This last point was often explicit in commemorative speeches. See Thucydides, *History*, 2.44; 4 *Maccabees* 18:1–2; Dio Chrysostom, *Or.* 29.21.

her on the defensive in the eyes of some group (whether it be a family, a circle of friends, or a voluntary association). Paul uses forensic strategies throughout 2 Corinthians 1 and 2, where Paul must acquit himself of "charges" about his truthfulness and sincerity, and prove that he did not injure the believers by sending his painful letter rather than making a promised visit. Only after this could Paul and the church move forward in their relationship together.

Real speeches were also rarely "pure" in regard to a single genre of rhetoric. This was already true in Aristotle's time.[55] Epideictic rhetoric could be incorporated into a defense speech to remind the jury of the proven virtue and merit of the defendant. Epideictic rhetoric could be incorporated into a deliberative speech to hold up the praiseworthy memory of people who, in the past, had followed a course of action similar to the one being proposed, or to remind the audience of the dishonor that befell people who failed, in similar circumstances, to act as the speaker now urges. Forensic strategies could be employed within a deliberative speech to tear down the credibility of a rival speaker, or to set aside prejudice that had been aroused against oneself by "setting the record straight" (as Paul does in the opening of 2 Corinthians). A nuanced rhetorical analysis does not merely try to decide that a speech is deliberative, but to discern the ways in which epideictic and forensic topics, if present, support the overarching deliberative goal.

What kind of rhetoric does Paul exhibit in Galatians? In a groundbreaking study that sought to read Galatians in light of the rhetorical practice of Paul's day, Hans Dieter Betz proposed that Galatians was essentially an example of forensic or judicial rhetoric, written as Paul's "self-apology" or defense against claims that had been made against his reliability as an apostle and his character: "the addressees are identical with the jury, with Paul being the defendant, and his opponents the accusers."[56] Betz identifies the letter as a whole as an "apologetic letter," a defense speech sent in the form of a letter.

---

55. See Aristotle, *Rh.* 1.3.5; also *Rhet. Alex.* 1427b31–35; *Rhet. Her.* 3.8.15. A similar phenomenon appears in the discussions of types or categories of letters in the ancient theorists of epistolography, where the "mixed" type is an expected category (see Pseudo-Libanius, *Epistolary Styles*, 46, 92).

56. Betz, *Galatians*, 24. Hester ("The Rhetorical Structure of Galatians 1:11–14,"

While Betz will always enjoy the honor of having been a pioneer in restoring rhetorical criticism's place in the study of the New Testament, he essentially misdiagnosed Paul's principal goals in Galatians and, therefore, the kind of rhetoric Paul is employing on the whole. The best way to determine what genre of rhetoric a text is likely to represent is to study it first with a view to answering one fundamental question: what does the author most want from the readers or hearers as a result of their receiving this communication? Does the author want to promote a decision about whether or not someone's past action was right or wrong? The communication is seeking, then, a judicial end. Does the author want to promote a decision about what course of action the recipients will take in the (possibly very near) future? The communication is seeking a deliberative end. Does the author want to promote adherence to certain basic values, virtues, or principles? The communication is operating in primarily epideictic modes.

In regard to Galatians, Paul's overarching goal for the speech is not the rendering of a verdict on the part of the audience (i.e., on his innocence as a sincere missionary or on the rivals' guilt as deceivers with ulterior motives), but the selection of a particular course of action to pursue (i.e., deciding against the course of allowing themselves to be circumcised in response to the rival teachers' urging). It is essentially a piece of *deliberative* rhetoric, all aimed at forestalling one imminent course of action (5:1–4) in favor of another (5:16).[57] All the material

---

223–33) also treats Galatians as a specimen of judicial rhetoric.

57. Kennedy, *New Testament Interpretation through Rhetorical Criticism*, 144–52; Joop Smit, "The Letter of Paul to the Galatians: A Deliberative Speech," *New Testament Studies* 35 (1989): 1–26; Witherington, *Grace in Galatia*, 27–28. Martyn (*Galatians*, 21) upholds the usefulness of rhetorical criticism, as long as this does not become a straitjacket either for the text or its analysis. I would take issue, however, with his dismissal of "deliberative *rhetoric*" as a description of Galatians. Rejecting "deliberative *speech*" as a label, however, would have been justified as a criticism of attempting to fit Galatians strictly into a formal category. On the other hand, to call Galatians "a reproclamation of the gospel in the form of an evangelistic argument," as Martyn (*Galatians*, 22) does, or to call "the body of the letter" a "sermon centered on factual and thus indicative answers to two questions, 'What time is it?' and 'In what cosmos do we live?'" is to relinquish the close connection between the situation that occasioned Galatians and Galatians as a situation-specific address, losing sight of Paul's rhetorical purpose in developing answers to these questions at all, namely

in Galatians regarding Paul's sincerity and reliability (i.e., the opening chapters that appear very much to present a "self-defense") and the questionable reliability of the rival teachers (found mostly at the opening and closing of the letter) serves the purposes that appeals to ethos would in any kind of speech (see below), and is not itself an indication of the rhetorical genre. The principal topics of Gal 3:1—5:12, moreover, appeal to categories that are typical in deliberative rhetoric—the honor and advantages that have been gained in Christ, and that would be lost by turning now to Torah's regulation of the human relationship with God (3:2b–5, 13–14, 23–29; 4:8–11; 5:1–4); the injustice that would be done by looking to Torah on this side of Christ's self-giving death (2:21); the lack of feasibility inherent in the rivals' course (3:11–12, 21b). Such topics are typically used to move an audience to choose one course (the course that preserves advantages and honor) over another course.

A prominent topic in classical rhetorical handbooks alongside genres of rhetoric is the typical *form* that an oration would tend to follow. Judicial and deliberative speeches tended to consist of four (following Aristotle) or five (following Roman theory) sections, each section having particular functions.[58] The opening of a speech was called the "exordium," and it generally sought to give a foretaste of the subject matter, put the hearers in a receptive and attentive frame of mind (*Rhet. Her.* 1.4.7), and deal with issues related to the speaker's credibility and, if applicable, the lack of credibility of opposing speakers (Aristotle, *Rh.* 3.14). This would be followed, particularly in judicial speeches, by a narration of the events under dispute. This narration would present a strategically shaped and colored rehearsal of events, putting certain parties in the best light possible, and certain parties in the worst light possible, depending on the specific goal of the speech. Generally the narration led up to the proposition, the main point to be demonstrated, followed by the fourth section, the proofs (*probation*), the core of the speech establishing the speaker's position as the better-founded one. The speech generally closed with a "peroration," a conclusion that brought together

---

to dissuade the hearers from entering the Sinaitic covenant and adopting a Torah-observant lifestyle.

58. Epideictic speeches generally followed different sorts of outlines, and displayed the greatest freedom in this regard.

the main points, offered a concluding exhortation, left the audience in a strategically selected emotional state, and took parting shots at the opposing speakers and their cases (Aristotle, *Rh.* 3.19).

New Testament interpreters using rhetorical criticism have often come under fire—and often justifiably—for trying to fit a particular New Testament text into this mould. While it can readily be demonstrated that early Christian authors, like others in less formal settings where persuasion is a necessary skill, used many of the argumentative strategies known from the more formal settings, most attempts at outlining a Pauline or other epistle against the framework of the four- or five-part oration are forced, at least at some points, thereby bringing the whole enterprise of rhetorical criticism into disrepute.

That being said, Galatians comes *closer* to fitting this overall outline than any other New Testament text.[59] Its opening (1:1–10) and closing (6:11–18) accomplish many of the functions traditionally assigned to the exordium and peroration. The opening *is* followed by a lengthy narrative (1:11–2:14) that clearly has an argumentative edge to it, relevant to the situation at hand. This narrative culminates in a series of propositions that, again, seem to be germane to the overarching goal of the communication (persuading the Galatian Christians *not* to turn now to Torah observance as a means of making progress in their new relationship with God). The middle portion of Galatians is a clearly defined sequence of argumentative proofs (3:1—4:31) in support of Paul's position that righteousness, or being made right with God, does not come through Torah-observance and that Christ's death was not in vain (2:16, 21). The third major section (5:1—6:10) contains a lot in the way of exhortation, all of which is grounded in the preceding arguments. There is need for some fluidity in the application of the classical outline, to be sure, and nothing to be gained by forcing the text into the outline at any point. However, in regard to Galatians knowledge of the basic functions of each part of the classical outline can help us discern the function of many of the parts of Galatians.

Using classical rhetorical theory as a tool for investigating New Testament writings does not presuppose that a particular New Testament

59. In part, this may be due to the nature of the situation and Paul's very clear and singular goal for his letter.

author received formal training in rhetoric, and certainly does not presuppose that the author in question had a copy of Aristotle's *Art of Rhetoric* or some such textbook at his side as he thought about how to address a particular pastoral challenge. It does presuppose, however, that discussions from within the ancient, Greco-Roman world about how arguments are constructed, what kinds of responses particular topics typically evoked, and what contributes to successful persuasion are useful for thinking about the construction and impact of early Christian texts written within and for that world.

These handbooks provide snapshots of a wide range of rhetorical techniques, approaches, and topics to which New Testament authors and audiences would both potentially have been exposed, and thus open a window into an important facet of the cultural environment within which early Christian authors and teachers lived and moved and upon which they could potentially have drawn.[60] While these handbooks came to be used "prescriptively" as textbooks for aspiring orators, they are rooted in the "descriptive" work of observing the oratorical practice of their authors' times and the analytical work of simply laying out the strategies these authors observed at work in real oratory.[61] The fact that these handbooks come from the world of the early Christian movement, in my mind, greatly enhances their value for New Testament interpretation. Far from being a foreign imposition upon New Testament texts, classical rhetorical theory is native to the same world as those New Testament texts.

60. My working premise is that early Christian authors, to the extent that they learned the "art of persuasion," learned it inductively through observing and hearing public speakers, itinerant philosophers, and even synagogue preachers in the cities in which they dwelt (whether in the cities of Judea and Galilee or the cities of Syria and Asia Minor), although a few (like the authors of Hebrews and Luke-Acts) possess such a facility in the art of argumentation, reproduce known patterns from the *Progymnasmata*, and attend to matters of style to such a degree as suggests some formal training. "We should be cautious in assuming too much formal rhetorical knowledge . . . but we should not sell them too short as uncultured and uneducated" (Royalty, "The Rhetoric of Revelation," 600).

61. Martyn (*Galatians*, 23), for example, objects that Paul "shows relatively little concern with observing certain rules set out in the standard teaching of rhetoric," but the rhetorical handbooks are not about following prescriptive rules, but descriptive analyses of "what works" in the various kinds of speeches given in various settings.

In Paul's particular case, however, it is worth contemplating the extent to which he might, indeed, have enjoyed some formal training in the art of argumentation and persuasion. According to Luke, Paul was a native of Tarsus (Acts 9:11; 21:39; 22:3). When Luke's Paul claims to be "a citizen of no unimportant city" (Acts 21:39), he is engaging in considerable understatement. Tarsus was a cultural center of the Roman province of Cilicia, concerning which the Greek geographer Strabo writes:

> The people at Tarsus have devoted themselves so eagerly, not only to philosophy, but also to the whole round of education in general, that they have surpassed Athens, Alexandria, or any other place that can be named where there have been schools and lectures of philosophers . . . Further, the city of Tarsus has all kinds of schools of rhetoric; and in general it not only has a flourishing population but also is most powerful, thus keeping up the reputation of the mother-city. (Strabo, *Geography* 14.5.13; trans. Reasoner)

Strabo's comments date from roughly the time of Paul's boyhood. If the historical Paul enjoyed any formal education in this city, it likely would have included those subjects for which the city was renowned, notably including the art of argumentation and public speaking.

Nevertheless, again according to Luke, Paul actually received at least the more formative part of his education in Jerusalem, "at the feet of Gamaliel, educated strictly in line with the ancestral law" (Acts 22:3). Gamaliel was a respected teacher whose name is well attested, and much revered, in later rabbinic literature. Such an education would be in keeping with Paul's parents' dedication to piety, as well as to Paul's own witness to his training as a Pharisee and his intense zeal for the traditions of the elders (Phil 3:6; Gal 1:14). It does not by any stretch mean, however, that his education was entirely parochial and that he was thereby insulated from Greek influence and learning.

Jerusalem itself was a cosmopolitan city connected with the Greco-Roman world, not isolated from it.[62] The city had been the focal center

62. See Hengel, *The Pre-Christian Paul*, 57–61. Jewish education in Greek, including the art of argumentation, was pursued in Jerusalem at least from the time of Herod.

for Hellenization—the introduction of Greek language, culture, and political organization—in Judea several centuries before (2 Macc 4:7–17). While certain elements of Hellenization were staunchly resisted (particularly where this encroached upon Jewish monotheism, dedication to the way of life and values promoted by Torah, and the preservation of the temple cult) during the Maccabean Revolt, the Hellenization of Palestine nevertheless made substantial progress during the Hellenistic period, and was given renewed attention during the period of Roman domination.[63]

Many of Rabbi Gamaliel's own students were said to have been "trained in the wisdom of the Greeks."[64] In Gamaliel's school, perhaps similar to what one would have found in the Jerusalem-based school of Yeshua Ben Sira two centuries before,[65] Paul would have learned not only of Torah and its rules of application, but the art of argumentation,[66] the Jewish wisdom tradition (which energetically combined Greek, Egyptian, and Jewish wisdom), and quite probably continued his study of Greek as well. Fluency in Greek would have been of great importance as the means by which to communicate with and instruct Greek-speaking Jews from the Diaspora residing in Palestine, visiting during pilgrimages, or encountered in a teacher's travels away from Palestine. It was also essential to political and economic success in Greek-dominated, then Roman-dominated, Judea.[67] Conversations

63. See the landmark studies by Martin Hengel: *Judaism and Hellenism*; *Jews, Greeks, Barbarians*; *The Hellenization of Judaea in the First Century After Christ*.

64. Daube, "Rabbinic Methods of Interpretation and Hellenistic Rhetoric," 239–64.

65. A sizable sample of Ben Sira's curriculum, as it were, can be found in the Apocryphal book known alternatively as Ecclesiasticus, Sirach, or the Wisdom of Ben Sira.

66. Even if this did not include specific training in the Greek art of rhetoric, Jewish traditions of argumentation, especially as seen in the more fully developed forms of wisdom literature (see deSilva, *Introducing the Apocrypha*, 169–75), would have given Paul an ample foundation upon which to keep building as he encountered and absorbed Greco-Roman rhetorical strategies in his missionary work.

67. An important archaeological datum in this regard concerns the language of inscriptions found in Jerusalem, dating from the early Roman period. A full third of these are written in Greek, while an additional 7 percent are carved in both Greek and a Semitic language (Hebrew or Aramaic). See Hengel, *Pre-Christian Paul*, 55, 136 n. 258.

with Jews from the Diaspora would have afforded ample opportunity for Paul to learn more of Greco-Roman philosophy and ethical traditions, as would have debates with Gentile philosophers resident in Palestine. The essential skill of letter-writing would not have been neglected, as Hellenistic letter-forms had been practiced in Jerusalem at least since the rise of the Hasmoneans.

This comprehensive curriculum would have remained thoroughly "Jewish" insofar as it was rooted in the sacred history and literature of Israel (as opposed to being based on the sacred literature of the Greeks, notably the writings of Homer and Hesiod), conducted within the framework of a Torah-observant lifestyle (as opposed to the Greek lifestyle nurtured by the educational institution of the "gymnasium" and "lyceum"), and geared toward participation in the distinctive in-stitutions of Judea and Jewish culture generally. [68] The compatibility of strict alignment with the "ancestral (Jewish) law" with competence in Greek language, rhetoric, and philosophical ethics is widely demon-strated throughout the Hellenistic Jewish world (for example, by Philo of Alexandria and the authors of 4 Maccabees and *Letter of Aristeas*), and the same would have held true for the *Hellenized* Jerusalem of Paul's youth.

Even while we stress ways in which Paul exhibits facets of the clas-sical arts of argumentation and persuasion, there are significant ways in which Paul expressed reservations about rhetoric and relying too much on performance-based persuasion. While this topic does not emerge in Galatians, Paul is rather explicit about it in 1 Corinthians. Ancient orators gave significant attention not only to developing strong appeals, but to decorating their speeches to delight the ears of the hearers with many kinds of verbal ornamentation (like alliteration and word play, such as one often hears in sermons today) and to developing the use of their voice and gesture to give their speech greater impact. Paul refused, in particular, to play to these cultural norms, because he wanted the

---

68. Hengel (*Pre-Christian Paul*, 38) speaks of Paul receiving a *Jewish* education in *Greek*, and considers both aspects to be important. While Paul was thoroughly acquainted with Greek language, argumentation, and the like, his education would have been based on the Septuagint and other Jewish writings in Greek, rather than on Hesiod and Homer, the standard fare of Greek education among Gentiles.

power of his own proclamation and the response of his hearers to be focused more fully on the life-transforming message of the cross and on the encounter with God that the proclaimed Word facilitated (1 Cor 1:17; 2:1–5).

This observation cannot be turned into a warrant for saying that Paul did not give a thought to rhetoric, since even the claim to avoid using the flashiness of presentation to awe an audience so as to focus them on the content of the message was a rhetorical device.[69] On the contrary, Paul's critical reflection upon those aspects of rhetorical practice that he would *not* weave into his proclamation of the Gospel (and, by extension, into his letters) confirms his acquaintance with the larger "art of persuasion" and helps direct us more precisely where to look for his employment of the same.

Throughout this commentary, we will aim to strike a balance in the use of ancient rhetorical theory as a window into how Paul strategically framed his address to his Galatian converts in order to move them to adopt a particular course of action while rejecting another course of action being urged upon them by rival speakers. In particular, we will consider throughout how Paul may be attending to each of the three basic kinds of "appeal" that orators and others in the business of persuading typically incorporated. These are appeals to questions of character ("ethos"), appeals to the emotions of the hearers ("pathos"), and appeals to rational argumentation ("logos").[70]

The appeal to *ethos* is foundational to all the others (Aristotle, *Rh.* 1.2.4). People are more likely to accept the arguments of, and be persuaded by, the speaker whom they trust more. "Credibility" was generally created as a speaker impressed upon the hearers that he or she was

69. This particular device was used also by the great orator Dio Chrysostom: "My purpose is . . . neither to elate you nor to range myself beside those who habitually sing such strains, whether orators or poets. For they are clever persons, mighty sophists, wonder-workers; but I am quite ordinary and prosaic in my utterance, though not ordinary in my theme. For though the words I speak are not great in themselves, they treat of topics of the greatest possible importance" (*Or.* 32.39; LCL).

70. See Aristotle, *Rh.* 1.2.3: "Now the proofs furnished by the speech are of three kinds. The first depends upon the moral character of the speaker, the second upon putting the hearer into a certain frame of mind, the third upon the speech itself, in so far as it proves or seems to prove."

morally upright, expert in the matters on which he or she spoke, and well-disposed to the hearers, such that all that he or she would urge would be in their best interest (Aristotle, *Rh.* 2.1.3; *Rh.* 2.1.5; Quintilian, *Inst.* 3.8.13). Any prejudice that might exist against the speaker must be eliminated before he or she could effectively address the subject matter of his or her speech.[71] By extension, speakers often found it necessary, or at least advantageous, to cast doubt on the sincerity, reliability, and good will of opposing speakers.

The wise speaker also paid attention to the emotional state of the audience, seeking to arouse those emotions that would dispose an audience more readily to move in the direction that speaker wished. People make different decisions depending on whether they are calm or angry, confident or afraid, compassionate or indignant (Aristotle, *Rh.* 1.2.5; 2.1.2, 4, 8). An orator seeking a verdict of not guilty would seek to rouse pity toward a defendant; an orator wishing to dissuade an audience from taking a certain course of action might seek to arouse feelings of fear or shame in regard to the consequences of that action, and so forth. Aristotle provides an especially helpful list of topics and situations that tend to arouse eleven particular emotions, helping attune us to this aspect of the potential impact of an address on an audience (*Rh.* 2.2—2.11).

Of course, a speaker also has to have something to say to make his or her case and, if applicable, refute the case being made by opposing speakers. This is the province of *logos*, the crafting of rational argumentation. Speakers would tend to use a variety of types of argument, some involving deductive logic, others involving a more inductive approach—appealing to historic examples, looking at analogous situations to build a case, calling on popular wisdom or appealing to authoritative texts (like Homer and Hesiod for a non-Christian, or the Septuagint for Christians and Diaspora Jews). In Galatians, for example, Paul uses the historical example of Abraham (3:6–9), analogies drawn from the raising of children in an affluent household (3:23–25; 4:1–7) and from the legal practice of making a will (3:15–18), popular wisdom (for example, proverbial sayings about yeast and reaping what one sows in 5:9; 6:7), as

---

71. See especially *Rhet. Her.* 1.9 on eliminating prejudice through the "subtle approach."

well as arguments based on more formal, deductive reasoning that we will need to unpack carefully. The use of words like "for" (*gar*, thirty-five times in Galatians) and "because" (*hoti*, nine times) often signal the presence of more formal, deductive argumentation.[72]

While Paul does not by any means confine his rhetorical strategies, topics, and arrangement to the strategies laid out in surviving rhetorical handbooks from his period, the descriptions of the various kinds of appeal (ethos, pathos, and logos) in those handbooks often illumine Paul's argumentation and help the modern reader discern the rhetorical force of his writings paragraph by paragraph as well as they would illumine an address by Cicero or Dio Chrysostom.

WAS GALATIANS EFFECTIVE?

Did the churches in Galatia uniformly reject the proposals of the rival teachers and send them on their way after hearing Paul's letter? Were the rival teachers, in the end, able to rebut Paul's arguments and insinuations, retaining and solidifying their hold on the congregations? James Dunn finds the very survival of the letter and its eventual incorporation into the collection of Pauline writings to be a sign "that Paul won a significant victory in Galatia."[73] He also points to the fact that, when Paul writes to the Corinthian churches about the collection project for the poor in Judea, he tells them to do exactly as he "instructed the churches in Galatia" (1 Cor 16:1). Assuming that Galatians was, in fact, written prior to 1 Corinthians, this would probably imply that Paul had ongoing interaction with the Galatian Christians after sending his letter to them, no doubt a good sign that he had some positive response from them.

Unfortunately, the preservation of Galatians need not imply Paul's *victory* in Galatia. If even a small number of disciples in those congregations remained loyal to him, they would have preserved the letter themselves, forming new congregations loyal to Paul's Gospel in that region.[74] Galatians would have still come to be treasured by Pauline

72. Longenecker, *Galatians*, cxvi.

73. Dunn, *Galatians*, 19.

74. Martyn (*Galatians*, 14), for example, points to an often overlooked group within the Galatians churches, namely the "catechetical instructors" (6:6), local lead-

Christians throughout the Mediterranean (notably the provinces of Asia, Macedonia, and Achaia), therefore enjoying a broader circulation and being positioned to become part of the Pauline "canon." While Paul apparently gave the Galatians instructions about participating in the collection project (1 Cor 16:1), it is striking that, when he writes to the Roman Christians about the collection, he says only that "Macedonia and Achaia were pleased to make a certain contribution for the poor among the saints in Jerusalem" (Rom 15:26). Did the Galatian churches, in the end, elect not to participate? Would this be a signal of their having broken with Paul, or at least having taken a significant step back from partnership with Paul?

Participation or non-participation in the collection notwithstanding, Luke portrays Paul enjoying ongoing relations with the churches in Galatia. After the Jerusalem Conference, and thus, by our accounting, well after Paul sent his letter to the Galatians, Paul and Barnabas return to the cities of South Galatia (specifically Derbe and Lystra) to deliver the decision of the Jerusalem leadership (Acts 16:1, 4). They may indeed return to these cities once again when Paul goes through "the Galatian region and Phrygia, strengthening all the disciples" (Acts 18:23). This would suggest that Paul continued to have generally strong relations with at least a good portion of the congregations in Galatia, leaving open, though, the question of Paul's silence in regard to their participation in the collection. The failure of Torah-observant Christianity to flourish outside of Palestine and Syria (where the Ebionites and Nazarenes, for example, took deep root) testifies, in its own way, to Paul's ultimate victory in Galatia and throughout the Diaspora Christian mission generally.

---

ers appointed by Paul to continue the nurture of the congregations in the Pauline gospel, the Pauline interpretation of the Jewish Scriptures, and so forth. These leaders would have been the likeliest candidates for traveling to Paul with news of developments in Galatia as well as returning from Paul to the congregations to read Paul's response in the assemblies.

Commentary

1:1-5: PAUL'S OPENING GREETING

Paul, an apostle not sent out from human beings nor through a human being's agency, but through Jesus Christ and the Father God who raised him from among the dead, [2]and all the brothers who are with me, to the churches of Galatia: [3]May generous kindness and peace be yours from our Father God and the Lord Jesus Christ, [4]who gave himself for our sins to rescue us out from the present, evil age according to the will of our God and Father, [5]whose is the glory into the ages of ages, Amen!

Just as we have adopted standardized ways of opening and closing letters, so letters in the ancient world tended to use a standard formula identifying the sender and the intended recipient or recipients, and adding a word of "greeting"—literally *a* word (in letters written in Greek, *chairein*, "rejoice," "greetings"; in Hebrew letters, *shalom*, "peace"). We find a good example of this formula in Acts 23:26: "Claudius Lysias to his Excellency the governor Felix, greetings (*chairein*)." The basic framework of this formula remains intact in Paul's letter openings, though he feels free to expand and modify it in several ways, sometimes expanding his own self-identification,[1] sometimes expanding upon the identification of the recipients, and always replacing the standard word of "greeting" (*chairein*) with a wish that the recipients will be experiencing "grace" (*charis*) and "peace" (*eirēnē*, the Greek representation of the

---

1. See Rom 1:1-7, in which 1:1-6 represents Paul's expansion of his self-designation.

Hebrew *shalom*) from God. Sometimes the nature of Paul's expansions gives us some clues concerning what's on his mind and how he begins to fulfill the typical goals for the opening of an address as early as the letter-opening itself.

One of the goals a speaker would seek to achieve from the outset of a speech is to establish his or her credibility—his or her "authority" to address a particular issue and his or her investment in the well-being of the audience whom the speaker is trying to lead along toward making a particular decision. Paul addresses the issue of his authority head-on as he expands his self-designation as the sender of the letter. He emphasizes his direct authorization by God to act as an apostle of the Gospel, denying that he relies on any human authorization. Paul claims that he has neither been sent out as an apostle as a representative "from human beings" nor received his commission as an apostle "through a human being."[2] James might have commissioned other Jewish Christian teachers who went out from Jerusalem to check on daughter churches in the nearby provinces (Gal 2:11); other people might be commissioned as messengers or apostles on behalf of particular churches (see 2 Cor 8:23); James and his fellow apostles might select and commission people like Judas and Silas to represent them, distributing and explaining the Apostolic Decree among the churches (Acts 15:22–27). Paul, however, claims that his own commission to represent God and God's Messiah in the proclamation of the Gospel came directly "through Jesus Christ and the father God" (Gal 1:1). Ultimately, Paul is answerable to God, not to the Jerusalem apostles and, if not them, *certainly* not to the rival teachers who have come to Galatia claiming, perhaps, the authority of the Jerusalem church for their own message and mission. It is highly likely, given Paul's extended treatment of his own commission and his careful delineation of his relationship with the Jerusalem apostles in Gal 1:11—2:10, that Paul is already working from the first lines of this letter to "destroy prejudice" aroused against him by the rival teachers.

2. Following the practice of the New American Standard Version (NASV) and New Revised Standard Version (NRSV), I have introduced the phrase "not sent out" in my translation of Gal 1:1 in order to capture the verbal facet of *apostolos* ("sent one," "envoy") in relation to the adverbial prepositional phrases that follow ("from human beings," "through a human being's agency").

Paul often names a co-worker as a co-sender of an epistle (1 Corinthians: Sosthenes; 2 Corinthians, Philippians, Colossians, Philemon: Timothy; 1 and 2 Thessalonians: Silvanus and Timothy; Romans, Ephesians, 1 and 2 Timothy, Titus: none). Here, however, and uniquely here, he creates a picture not just of a single teammate, but of "all the brothers and sisters who are with me" standing beside Paul in solidarity with him, addressing their fellow Christians in Galatia. In part, this could be explained by the likelihood that Paul does not have a teammate at present, since Galatians may well have been written in that narrow window between his falling out with Barnabas in Antioch and their reconciliation before testifying together at the Jerusalem Conference. Nevertheless, rather than simply address the Galatians on his own, he includes the Christians present with him in the city from which he writes Galatians to emphasize the fact that his message is not his own idiosyncratic invention, but the shared testimony of Christian community.[3]

At this point, we should also observe Paul's use of kinship language already at the outset of this letter—a theme that will dominate Galatians as well as the ethos of the early Christian Church as a whole. God is "father" (1:1, 3); the believers in Christ are "sisters and brothers" (1:2) to one another, even across great distances. Paul, like other early Christian leaders, uses the language of family to speak of the relationships between Christians throughout the evangelized world, inviting believers not only to accept a new relationship in regard to the One God (sons and daughters), but a new relationship with one another (brothers and sisters). Those who are by birth "outsiders" to one another in terms of blood relations are called upon to accept one another, and look out for one another, as "insiders." They are called upon to give one another the gifts that accompany being siblings—cooperation, sharing of material resources and other advantages, truth-telling and faithfulness, the nurturing of harmony and unity, investing in advancing one another's interests—and to approach one another from this vantage point. As people who have been brought together into a single family, they are called upon to banish all those things that would be unseemly within a natural family—competition, looking out for one's own interests at

---

3. Bruce, *Galatians*, 74; Fung, *Galatians*, 38.

another's expense, manipulation and withholding truth and true intentions, and the like. So much of the ethical vision for Christian relationships and community in the New Testament can be traced directly back to the understanding that God was fashioning a new *family* out of the many, unrelated people redeemed by Christ's blood—and therefore related *by blood*.[4]

Three other goals usually attended to in the openings of speeches involved (1) announcing the principal themes that would be taken up in the speech, (2) capturing the hearers' attention, showing that the question at hand is one of importance, and (3) arousing prejudice against speakers who were trying to lead the same audience in a different direction (see Aristotle, *Rhet.* 3.14.6–7; *Rhet. Alex.* 1436a33–37). Galatians 1:3–4 certainly begins to contribute to the first of these as he describes the character of the "Lord Jesus Christ" whose favor ("grace," *charis*) and peace he wishes upon the audience.

Paul first recalls the fact that Jesus "gave himself for our sins," announcing the theme of Jesus' sacrificial generosity toward Paul and his audience. Both Paul and his hearers would have been familiar with the virtuous hero who brought benefit to the people by his or her death "for them." This was a topic commonly used to praise military leaders and common soldiers, who gave up their own lives in order to bring safety or other advantage to their people. Greek tragedies frequently celebrated the person who was willing to sacrifice himself or herself for the greater good of another or of the city or people as a whole. In Jewish tradition, those martyrs who had accepted death by torture rather than release from torment at the cost of breaking God's covenant were remembered as heroes who gave themselves up for their nation, since their obedience to God was accepted by God as a representative offering of obedience to the covenant on behalf of the whole people, toward whom God turned again in mercy.[5]

Jesus, then, lavished his generosity upon Paul and his audience to the utmost, namely to the point of death, so committed was he to

---

4. See, further, deSilva, *Honor, Patronage, Kinship & Purity*, 157–240.

5. See 2 Macc 7:1—8:5; 4 Macc 6:28–30; 17:21–22. The ultimate root of this theology of martyrdom and representative offering of oneself in obedience to God is probably Isaiah 52:13—53:12.

bringing benefit to them (and to all people) in line with God's plan for extending blessing to all the nations. This is the manifestation of "grace," of "generous kindness," that Paul will himself be so careful not to "set aside" by turning to other, older supports like Torah (see 2:19–21), that Paul will return to in describing how people were able at last to exchange, as it were, Torah's curse for Abraham's promised blessing (3:10–14), and that Paul fears the Galatian converts are devaluing and, therefore, cutting themselves off from as they contemplate trusting circumcision and Torah observance to do what they doubt Christ and the Spirit can do (5:2–4).

Jesus' death is further described as deliverance from "the present, evil age," which introduces the apocalyptic framework within which Paul understands God to be working. According to this view, time and space are divided into two ages—the present age, and the "age to come." Although God created the heavens and the earth "good," this present cosmos was corrupted by the disobedience of both angels and human beings.[6] Humanity—from the individual person to the political, economic, and religious systems maintained by the participation of countless human beings—has fallen under the powers of Sin, Death, Flesh, and the Devil and the demonic. Creation itself has departed from the good and natural order instituted by God. The present age has been so corrupted that it cannot be redeemed. The "age to come," however, is God's new creation: it is a renewal of all things, or a replacement for all things, in which God's vision for humanity, community, nature, and relationship with the Divine all comes to pass in perfected reality. It is the world in which righteousness will be at home and have its reward, the time when all of God's promises will be fulfilled, the time when the suffering of this present age will be swallowed up in the goodness and righteous shepherding of God's people by God's own self.

---

6. Jewish apocalypses do not look so much, or exclusively, to the story of the fall in Genesis 3 for an explanation of evil or understanding of the fallenness of this age, but to the story of the angels who were aroused by the beauty of human females, left their proper station to have sexual relations with them, lived among humankind and taught them all manner of forbidden skills and arts, and fathered a race of giants who wrought havoc upon the earth. This story had its roots in Genesis 6:1–4, but was greatly expanded in the centuries before Paul's birth. The most important and influential representation of this story is found in *1 Enoch* 6–36.

A major feature of the age to come, at least in the strand of apocalypticism represented by Jewish Christians like Paul and John and by non-Christian Jews like the authors of 4 Ezra or Daniel, is that the righteous who have died are not excluded from its rewards and blessings. Rather, God will raise to life again those who have died in faithfulness to God, so that they, too, can share in the age of come. This, in turn, leads to the expectation that *all* who enter into the age to come will share in the life of the resurrected body, over which Death itself no longer has any power. For Paul, the resurrection of the *one* righteous person, Jesus, was the signal that the present, evil age was nearing its close and that the age to come was, in fact, finally at the threshold. His letters dramatically reflect his awareness of living at the seam of these two ages, or at the place where the two ages were "grating together," as it were, as the one receded into oblivion and the other began to emerge.

By his death, and by the consequent giving of the Holy Spirit to all who turned to God trusting Jesus, Jesus rescued people from passing away along with the present, evil age and from the grip of all the powers that therein corrupt human beings and turn them aside individually and communally from God's good vision for human existence. Paul will return to this theme again when he speaks of Jesus' coming "in the fullness of time" (Gal 4:1–7) and when he stresses the *sufficiency* of the deliverance Jesus provides, giving us all that we need to deal with the power of the "flesh" as it manifests itself within and among us, so that, by the empowering and guidance of the Spirit, we are moving toward embodying the righteousness that God seeks in us and has always sought in his people (5:5–6, 13–25).

1:6-10: PAUL ANNOUNCES THE PRESENTING PROBLEM

⁶I am astounded that you all are so quickly turning aside from the one who called you in [Christ's] generous kindness and toward another message of good news. ⁷It's not really another message of good news, but there are some people troubling you, desiring to pervert the good news about Christ. ⁸But even if we ourselves or an angel from heaven should proclaim as a message of "good news" something other than what we

formerly proclaimed to you as good news, may that person be accursed! [9]As we have said before, now I say again: If anyone proclaims to you as "good news" a message besides that which you received, may that person be accursed. [10]Am I now, then, campaigning for human support, or God's? Or am I trying to please people? If I were still trying to please people, I would not be Christ's slave.

Paul continues to attend to the goals normally associated with the openings of speeches in this next paragraph, namely (1) announcing the principal themes that would be taken up in the speech; (2) capturing the hearers' attention, showing that the question at hand is one of importance; (3) arousing prejudice against speakers who were trying to lead the same audience in a different direction; and (4) returning to the topic of his own reliability, destroying prejudice that has been previously aroused against him by the rival teachers.

After an expanded greeting formula, Paul usually opens a letter with a paragraph expressing thanksgiving (see Rom 1:8–12; 1 Cor 1:4–9; Phil 1:3–11; Col 1:3–14; 1 Thess 1:2–10; 2 Thess 1:3–12; 2 Tim 1:3–7; Phlm 4–7) or benediction (2 Cor 1:3–7; Eph 1:3–14), often including some report of the prayers Paul offers on behalf of the addressees. Here, however, he opens with an expression of shock and amazement (Gal 1:6–7) followed by the pronouncement of a curse rather than a prayer (1:8–9). The Galatians, of course, would not know that this was uncommon, but they would immediately recognize that Paul was about to take them to task for what they've done in his absence.

The verb Paul uses (*thaumazō*, "I am astonished") is a typical feature of rebuke letters in the Hellenistic world, introducing the behavior that prompts the writer's rebuke and attempt to correct the addressee.[7] Paul has learned, perhaps from people he has left in some leadership capacity there (the instructors whom he commends in 6:6?), that his converts have been listening to other teachers who have brought a message different from Paul's, and that they are close to being persuaded by them to adopt a Torah-observant lifestyle as a means of cementing their place in the people of God and advancing in God-pleasing righteousness.

7. Longenecker, *Galatians*, cv, 14.

The rival teachers promoted circumcision and some degree of Torah observance as elements that would be complementary with the Galatian converts' trust in Jesus. Indeed, they could well have presented this as the next step forward in their spiritual journey to becoming full-fledged children of Abraham and their ethical journey to a transformed life of virtue. What the rival teachers would join together, Paul radically rends asunder as he opens his letter. For him, the course of action they are contemplating is not a complement to their faith in Jesus, but an act of desertion and repudiation of their divine Benefactor, a "turning aside from the one who called you in [Christ's] generous kindness and toward another message of good news" (1:6).[8]

Paul's opening is well calculated to arouse feelings of shame among the hearers. That Paul is "shocked" at their behavior indicates that they have fallen far short of his expectations of them. He accuses them of having proven unfaithful ("turning away from," even "deserting") to the God who invited them into a relationship of "grace" or "favor," an especially shameful response given the emphasis throughout the letter on the immenseness of the generosity God has shown in Christ, which should arouse only the deepest loyalty and commitment on the part of the beneficiaries. Paul adds that they have done this "with such speed," perhaps indicating the short amount of time that has elapsed since he left them, thinking them to have been well grounded at the time, but perhaps saying this simply to add to the shame of their desertion. That it happened "so quickly" amplifies Paul's own sense of disapproving surprise and calls their reliability into question even more, since their loyalty was so easy to subvert. As it happens, it potentially calls their intelligence into question as well—given the nature of the "gospel" to which they are turning "so quickly." Paul will explicitly question their intelligence in a second section calculated to arouse feelings of shame

---

8. In regard to Gal 1:6, there is strong and widespread support for the longer reading ("in *Christ's* grace"), though an early papyrus manuscript from the third century CE (P[46]) and several early church fathers who are quoting this verse read simply "in grace." A very few manuscripts read "in Jesus Christ's grace" and one "in God's grace." This may be best explained by adopting the shortest (and oldest attested) reading as the original, understanding the desire of scribes to provide helpful glosses to specify this "grace" as "Christ's grace." There would be no explanation for the earliest scribes omitting "Christ's" if it were already present in the manuscript they were copying.

for not having seen through the rival teachers' arguments and held their ground better (Gal 3:1–5, especially 3:1, 3).

The message of the rival teachers is not a "second installment" of the Gospel, but a "different gospel." Paul immediately corrects himself by calling this "different" gospel "no 'gospel' at all," but a perversion of the true Gospel (Gal 1:7). This is the point he will need to prove in order to bring the Galatian Christians back to his own understanding of the Gospel and the response to the Gospel that God is seeking. Galatians 2:14—5:12 can largely be read as a demonstration of the inadequacy of the rival teachers' "gospel," while Gal 5:13—6:10 could be read as Paul's further demonstration of how the Gospel that he preached included within it all the resources the Galatians would need to see God's righteousness manifested within them and in their midst as a community.

Paul begins to create prejudice against the rival teachers by referring to them as "agitators" or "troublemakers" in the Galatians' midst and as people whose goal is to "pervert" the Good News about Christ (see also Gal 5:7, 10). Paul speaks of the rival teachers as disturbers of the peace, as it were, within the Galatian congregations, the equivalent of rabble who stir up trouble amongst an otherwise harmonious and prospering community. Creating distance between the hearers and these rival speakers will continue to be a major goal throughout Galatians.

With two solemn curse formulas (Gal 1:8–9), Paul underscores the complete incompatibility of the message they are hearing with the Gospel they had received. The word *anathema* ("cursed," "handed over to God") is routinely used in the Septuagint (the Greek translation of the Old Testament) to translate *herem*, the "ban" according to which spoils, a city, or a people were "devoted" to God—a transaction carried out by their utter destruction (see, for example, Josh 6:17–18). The stakes of receiving the Gospel—and receiving it rightly—are so high that Paul thinks that anyone who would interfere with this preaching and hearing of the genuine Gospel of Jesus Christ (for example, by changing the message so that people are thrown off course) merits such a sentence.[9]

9. When Paul says in 1:9, "As we said before, so now I am saying again," it is not clear what he is referring to as the first time he uttered this warning. Some commentators take it to refer to the immediately preceding verse (1:8; so Schlier, *Galater*, 40; Bruce, *Galatians*, 84). Others suggest that Paul is referring to a warning that he had

What is of special interest in these curses is that Paul does not claim himself to be the final authority: the message that he had brought to the Galatians when he evangelized them, the message that the holy God confirmed by working wonders and sharing his Spirit with those who listened with trust, is the final authority. The Galatians should hold on to what they received as people who have been well grounded in the experience of Christ's love and God's acceptance. If a new group of teachers, or Paul himself, or a shining angel from heaven comes along now to tell them differently, they should not be swayed from the course on which they began, on which God himself had set them (3:1–5).

Paul returns to the topic of his credibility as he rounds out the opening of his letter with two rhetorical questions: "Am I now, then, campaigning for human support, or God's? Or am I trying to please people? If I were still trying to please people, I would not be Christ's slave." The translation of the Greek verb *peithō* in the first half of the verse is a bit difficult and significantly affects interpretation. It essentially means "persuade" or "win over by argument," but often carries negative connotations of "speaking in order to please" or even "to placate."[10] We also have to decide if Paul expects different answers to the different halves of this first question ("No, I'm not trying to persuade/placate people, but I am trying to persuade/satisfy God"), or the same answer to both halves ("No, I'm not trying to persuade either people *or* God").

The second half of the verse, however, is quite clear. Paul denies that he preaches the Gospel with a view to trying to please human be-

---

given during one of his two visits to these churches (either the evangelistic visit or the second visit on his return trip, when he confirmed them in their new Christ-centered way of life; so Longenecker, *Galatians*, 17; Fung, *Galatians*, 47). The second position is probably correct. Paul elsewhere refers to instruction previously given, but clearly *not* in the letter, and therefore on a previous visit (5:21). He also uses a plural verb to refer to the previous warning ("as *we* said before"), which is distinct from his use of a singular verb referring to his current, repeated warning in 1:9 ("so now *I* am saying"), suggesting a memory of a warning given while Paul was visiting them with at least one co-worker (Barnabas?).

10. See Fee, *Galatians*, 33; Longenecker, *Galatians*, 18. Martyn (*Galatians*, 138) looks closely at the use of the verb in the context of speaking about the activity of popular speakers, who play to the crowds with a view to winning them over, who are more interested in gaining quick assent than in the more painstaking and disciplined tasks of discovering and teaching the truth.

ings, because he knows that he cannot be a slave to human opinion and approval and a reliable slave of Christ at the same time (1:10b). This suggests that we read the first half of the verse as a similar denial of seeking to "persuade" people in the sense of "speaking so as to gain their support." Since Paul clearly implies that he does want Christ's approval as Christ's faithful servant, we might be right to read the second half of the opening question in this direction as well: Paul does speak with a view to enjoying God's support, as perhaps even the invocation of a divine curse in the preceding two verses demonstrates. Martyn helpfully points to a similar statement in 1 Thess 2:4–5, where Paul reflects on his preaching thus: "just as God tested and approved us to be entrusted with the Gospel, so we speak not as those pleasing human beings, but as those pleasing God who continues to test our hearts." This, too, would point to Paul's awareness of seeking God's approval (seeking to proclaim the Gospel faithfully so as to acquit oneself well before God) far and above seeking his audience's approval and assent.

The abrupt introduction of the idea that Paul is a people-pleaser, which hits the reader in 1:10 without any warning or preparation, suggests that his rivals brought it up first.[11] This need not imply undue malice on their part, but only a defense of their own position. When they arrived in Galatia urging Gentiles already converted to trust in Jesus also to accept circumcision and the basic contours of a Torah-driven life, the converts would reasonably have asked, "Why didn't Paul mention any of this? Why should we now listen to you when the person through whom we came to experience God in our midst never said a word about circumcision?" The rival teachers could readily have responded that Paul wanted to make it easier for them to come to faith, and so adapted the message to make it more pleasing to the Galatians. Perhaps Paul's strategy had merit, given its results; perhaps it was a sign of an underlying weakness on his part. Either way, you converts ought to be ready now, and sufficiently grounded in God, to hear the whole truth.

Paul takes the suggestion that he is a "people-pleaser" very seriously, and responds energetically to prove otherwise. His makes his opening statement in Gal 1:6–9 as provocative as he does precisely to show the Galatians that he is not timid about causing offense for the sake of

11. Fee, *Galatians*, 33.

preserving the truth of the Gospel and making sure his converts walk in line with that truth. His story of his second visit to Jerusalem and of the incident at Antioch (2:1–14) also address this topic very directly: Paul does not alter his message in order to please others, and is more than willing to confront Christian teachers who do put people-pleasing ahead of walking in line with the Gospel (as did Peter in Antioch). Unlike his opponents (as he will assert in 6:12–13), he will not be swayed from holding to the true gospel, nor blunt its force because that gospel might make him unpopular or even bring him hardship. He understands that being a people-pleaser is incompatible with being a reliable servant of Christ.

This opening is rhetorically effective indeed. Paul captures the hearers' attention (the main goal of the *exordium*, or opening of a speech) by presenting their situation as one of the gravest peril, since they find themselves in danger of proving disloyal to their great Benefactor, Jesus, forcing them to be open to reconsidering the relationship between faith in Jesus and circumcision. Paul makes great strides toward re-establishing his credibility as a reliable messenger of God, and a strong beginning toward calling the rival teachers' credibility into question. Perhaps most importantly, he reminds the hearers of the tremendous benefits Jesus has won for them at tremendous cost to himself, making them sensitive from the outset to Paul's proposals concerning how best to honor, and show gratitude for, Jesus' generous kindness—namely, moving forward with confidence in the sufficiency of the gifts he has brought to them.

1:11–17: THE DIVINE SOURCE OF PAUL'S DRAMATIC TRANSFORMATION AND GOSPEL

[11]I want you to know, brothers and sisters, that the message of good news that I proclaimed is not one devised by a human being. [12]I didn't receive it from a human being, nor was I taught it, but I received it by means of a revelation of Jesus Christ. [13]You have heard, no doubt, of my conduct when formerly in Judaism, that I used to persecute God's assembly beyond all bounds, seeking to destroy it. [14]I was making greater progress in Judaism than many of my peers among my race,

being abundantly zealous for the traditions of my forebears. [15]But when it pleased the one [or, the God] who set me apart from the time I was in my mother's womb and who called me through his generous kindness [16]to make his son known through me, in order that I should proclaim the good news about him among the nations, it wasn't with flesh-and-blood humans that I went to confer immediately, [17]nor did I go up to Jerusalem to those who were apostles prior to me, but I went, rather, into Arabia and I returned again to Damascus.

Paul signals the beginning of a new segment of his letter with the phrase "I want you to know" (*gnōrizō gar hymin*), a typical transition formula in Hellenistic letters.[12] This segment extends at least through 2:14, and, since it is impossible to determine within 2:14–21 where Paul's report of his response to Peter ends and his fresh statement of his position for the benefit of the Galatian converts begins, effectively through 2:21. The narrative that Paul crafts in Gal 1:11—2:14 is not an attempt at autobiography. Rather, it is an attempt to restore credibility in the eyes of his converts. He carefully selects episodes from his past and, especially, his interactions with the Jerusalem apostles, and constructs a narrative that communicates the following major points:

1. Paul's commissioning and message come directly from God, and so his presentation of the Gospel must be deemed more authentic and authoritative than that now preached by the rival teachers.

2. His authority is not dependent upon, or derivative from, the Jerusalem apostles, and therefore he is not ultimately answerable to them or to their position.

3. Despite this, Paul has worked collegially with them and his apostleship has been recognized as valid by them.[13]

---

12. Longenecker, *Galatians*, cv, 22.

13. As Bengt Holmberg (*Paul and Power*, 15) rightly observes, "the dialectic between being independent of and acknowledged by Jerusalem is the keynote of this important text."

4. Paul is the one who has all along, in the face of any and all pressures, walked "straightforwardly in line with the truth of the gospel" (Gal 2:14), the truth God revealed to him and seeks to reveal through him, and so is most plausibly the one doing that now in regard to the embodiment of the Gospel in Galatia.

The first major point that Paul stresses is the divine origin of the Gospel he originally brought to the Galatians (Gal 1:11–12). The first and best reason they should resist the leading of the rival teachers is that Paul brought them exactly and fully the message God had for them: "the message of good news that I proclaimed is not one devised by a human being. I didn't receive it from a human being, nor was I taught it, but I received it by means of a revelation of Jesus Christ." The prepositional phrase *kata anthropon* in 1:11 is a bit difficult to capture. This kind of construction is prevalent in Paul, who uses it with a variety of nouns like "flesh" or "spirit" (*kata sarka, kata pneuma,* and the like), apparently to communicate a sphere of influence. Thus he claims that his message does not derive from, nor fall in line with, the human sphere, which is precisely how the following verse explains the phrase, adding a positive statement about its source: "a revelation of Jesus Christ."

"Jesus Christ" appears in Greek in the genitive case, the case used when a speaker or writer wishes to use one noun (here, "Jesus Christ") to describe or qualify another noun (here, "revelation") in some way. The genitive case can indicate a wide range of such descriptive relationships indeed, a fact that is the source of some lively exegetical and theological debate in Galatians (see below on "the faith *of Jesus Christ*"). In this instance, the most probable senses are either "source" or "object": Paul's Gospel either came "through a revelation that Jesus Christ gave" him or "through an unveiling of who Jesus Christ really was." If one is inclined to read this in light of the much more detailed story of Paul's conversion in Acts 9, then the second option seems the obvious choice.[14] The main point of 1:12, however, is to stress the divine source of Paul's Gospel, such that Paul might intend us to hear, in effect: "I did not receive the Gospel that I preached from a human being, but from Jesus Christ him-

---

14. So Betz, *Galatians*, 63; Bruce, *Galatians*, 89; Fung, *Galatians*, 53.

self (through a revelation)."[15] I prefer to allow the ambiguity to remain rather than force a decision, all the more as Paul's main point is not jeopardized on either reading. If Paul is referring to his vision of Christ on the Damascus road, naming Christ as the "content" revealed, it is still clear that Paul's commission and message come from a divine rather than a human source.

As proof of this bold claim, Paul reminds the Galatians of the encounter that had turned his own life around, and of the "before" (1:13–14) and "after" (1:21–23) of his activities that prove, in effect, that something miraculous had to have happened to bring about such a change. In what Paul calls his "former life," he had been more on fire for the Torah and the covenant relationship with God that the Torah sustained than his rivals could ever be. He devoted himself to the Pharisaic way of life, being fully dedicated to Torah as interpreted and extended through the "ancestral traditions" that eventually multiplied and became associated with rabbinic Judaism.[16] It is striking that Paul actually refers to "Judaism" (*Ioudaismos*, 1:13, 14) here. This was a relatively rare way of speaking about the Jewish way of life, unique here within the New Testament. The term appears to have been coined by Jews in opposition to Hellenism.[17] The first literary occurrence of the term is 2 Macc 4:13, where the word represents the Jewish way of life specifically as something set apart from and distinct from the way of life of the Greeks (which was being foisted and even forced upon Jerusalem and Judea by its Hellenizing Jewish elites).[18] Paul's use of the term here to describe the way of life he embraced and zealously defended may signal his aware-

---

15. So Longenecker, *Galatians*, 23–24. Although a different author's usage is hardly determinative for how Paul should be read, it is interesting that this same phrase appears at the outset of Revelation (Rev 1:1), where Jesus is clearly intended to be understood as the source of the revelation, as part of the "chain" of revelation that begins with God and passes through John to the rest of the believers addressed.

16. It is striking that Paul refers to his devotion to "the traditions of my forebears" rather than "the Law of God." This may be an early sign in this letter that Paul has moved far from regarding his former life as service to God and God's Law, which he now understands quite differently as the law of love (5:14; 6:2), toward regarding it as slavish devotion to what is ultimately a human tradition.

17. Dunn, *The Theology of Paul the Apostle*, 347.

18. See deSilva, *Introducing the Apocrypha*, 276–78.

ness of the importance of maintaining its distinctiveness, maintaining the boundaries that marked Israel off as "holy," as well as his awareness of the importance that such "boundary issues" would have throughout his career (as in Antioch, Galatians, the Jerusalem Conference, and Romans).

At no point does Paul seem to have become disillusioned with the Torah-driven life—despite persistent attempts to read Rom 7:14–25 as Paul's confession of his personal inadequacy to keep the Torah. Paul himself claims to have lived in perfect conformity with the demands of Torah: "as regards righteousness under the law," Paul was "blameless" (Phil 3:6).[19] Torah would certainly not have represented a lifeless religion for Paul. Rather, Torah was the gift of God to Israel, sanctifying Israel and inviting Israel into a covenant relationship with God. The doing of Torah was a response to God's choice of Israel to be God's own, the path to security and peace for the nation and the path to life for the individual. As a Pharisee, Paul would have shared in the hope for the resurrection and the life of the world to come as the reward for fidelity to the covenant. This apocalyptic framework would provide an important means by which to make sense of his encounter with Jesus, the resurrected One.

So great was Paul's zeal—his passionate and even fanatical devotion to the covenant—that he took it upon himself to act as the defender of the covenant to the point of devoting himself to the punishment and even elimination of deviant Jews like the early Christian movement taking root in the Jewish communities of Jerusalem and Damascus (see also Phil 3:6, where Paul similarly connects "zeal" with persecution of deviants). Paul had several important models that guided him in the way he directed his "zeal." In Moses' generation, Phinehas manifested "zeal" for God specifically by killing an Israelite male and his Midianite

19. Martin Hengel (*The Pre-Christian Paul*, 79) rightly opposes looking for psychological explanations for Paul's conversion, for example in a supposed discontentment with Torah, in alleged inner struggles, and the like. Phil 3:6 betrays no such struggles. Not the deficiencies of his religion, but an unexpected encounter with the divine, best explains the radical change. Paul's claim to be "blameless" would not imply that Paul thought he never sinned: there was a detailed, Torah-prescribed system of sacrifices that would keep a rightly-intentioned Jew "blameless" in regard to accidental sins and slips, at least.

concubine, defending the boundaries of the people of God (Num 25:1–13). According to the Scriptures, Phinehas's zeal atoned for Israel's transgression and turned away God's wrath (Num 25:11). In more recent history, Mattathias and his son Judas Maccabaeus, heroes of the Maccabean Revolt, expressed their "zeal" in a similar way. Mattathias rushed forward to kill a Jew and a Syrian official as the former stepped forward to break faith with the covenant by offering a pagan sacrifice at the latter's invitation. Mattathias and his family then gathered together a guerilla force, inviting "everyone who is zealous for the law and supports the covenant" to join them (1 Macc 2:27). This "zeal" was directed especially against Jews who were deserting the covenant, enforcing obedience to the Torah or depriving the renegades of life (1 Macc 2:44–47). Thus they, too, "turned away wrath from Israel" (1 Macc 3:8).[20]

Paul thus acted in line with a well-formed role as a watchdog for the ancestral ways.[21] He clearly saw the Jesus movement, particularly as it came to expression among repatriated Diaspora Jews like Stephen, as a threat to the nation's fidelity to the covenant, as at least the beginnings of the same sort of departure from Torah that had provoked God's anger in the past and had led to God's punishing the nation through some foreign power. Rome's presence in Judea made it an ever-present candidate for such use.[22] Paul was thus seeking to protect Israel's covenant loyalty and Israel's place in God's favor through punishing those who threatened to violate that covenant bond and incur God's wrath against the

---

20. See, further, deSilva, *Introducing the Apocrypha*, 257–58, 265; Dunn, *Theology*, 351–52.

21. Paul clearly disagreed with his teacher Gamaliel's policy of "live, let live, and leave it to God" (Acts 5:38–39). This may indicate that Paul himself was more in line with Pharisaism as taught in the school of Shammai (which would have indeed aligned him with the "strictest sect" of his religion, as in Acts 26:5), even though Gamaliel, a disciple of the school of Hillel, was his teacher. The school of Shammai was indeed stricter in its application of the Torah than the school of Hillel, and the fact that Paul studied under Gamaliel (a Hillelite) would not preclude his moving away from his teacher's opinions to follow the stricter application of the Shammaite Pharisees. See, further, Wright, *What Saint Paul Really Said*, 26–29.

22. The author of the *Psalms of Solomon*, in fact, understood the Roman Pompey's invasion of Jerusalem in 63 BCE, and the havoc he wrought there, as divine chastening for the transgressions and injustice of the later Hasmonean kings and the aristocracy.

whole people.[23] Paul emphasizes his former life "in Judaism" to make two points: first, no one, including the rival teachers, can pretend to know more about the Torah-observant way of life than Paul; second, only God indeed could have turned such a person into what he is now, a preacher of a Torah-free Gospel.

It was when his zeal for Torah was at its most fevered pitch, and his opposition to the Jewish Christian movement in its full strength, that the inexplicable happened: "when it pleased the one [or, the God] who set me apart from the time I was in my mother's womb and who called me through his generous kindness to make his son known through me, in order that I should proclaim the good news about him among the nations, it wasn't with flesh-and-blood humans that I went to confer immediately" (Gal 1:15–16). The first thing to notice about this verse is that those subjects that are probably most interesting to us—God's revelation of Christ, Paul's commission to proclaim Christ to the non-Jewish nations—are not Paul's focal concern. Paul's chief point is that, after this life-changing experience, he didn't present himself to the Jerusalem apostles as a pupil or ministry candidate, nor present himself thus to any other "flesh and blood" body of Christians that could then claim ownership of and authority over him. What he understood to be the significance of the Christ-event and the nature of the message he was to proclaim (and that specifically to the Gentile nations) took shape independently of the Jerusalem-based Jesus movement.

Scholars have debated whether God's dramatic intervention in Paul's life should be considered a conversion or a prophetic call,[24] but

---

23. Nor was Paul alone in this commitment. Even as he writes Galatians, there are non-Christian Jews expressing their zeal for the Torah by putting various kinds of pressures upon Christian Jews. The rival teachers, Paul will claim, are themselves promoting circumcision and Torah observance among the Christian movement precisely to appease more zealous (non-Christian) Jews (Gal 5:11; 6:12–13). The motivation of these non-Christian Jews was quite sincere, as they also no doubt saw themselves as defenders of the covenant between God and the Jewish people.

24. Krister Stendahl (*Paul among Jews and Gentiles*, 7), for example, is reluctant to speak about Paul's conversion at all since Paul was still responding to the same God (the God of Judaism and the God of the Church). Paul did not leave behind the faith of Abraham in order to embrace the faith of Christ, and saw himself rather as embracing the fulfillment of what God had promised and been driving toward all along (so, correctly, Hagner, "Paul and Judaism," 75–105, especially 93.). Nevertheless, if we

the debate misses the point. It was both at the same time.[25] Paul immediately left off those pursuits that were incompatible with the revelation of Jesus as the Messiah (notably, the persecution of his followers), came to a new understanding of who Jesus was in God's plan for God's people, and radically shifted his allegiance from Torah to Jesus as Messiah. From that standpoint, it was a conversion. Paul also understood this revelation as a commission to proclaim the good news about Jesus to the Gentiles, and from that standpoint, it was a call. It would be a mistake, however, to think of the "conversion" facet of this encounter in terms of Paul's "personal decision for Christ." It was more an encounter with divine destiny and an acceptance of that destiny. In other words, God had made a "personal decision" for Paul, revealed to him the errors in his understanding and direction (hence, converted him), and personally revealed what Paul's task was now to be (hence, commissioned him).

When Paul speaks about God's intervention, he weaves in language reminiscent of God's commissioning of earlier prophets and messengers:

"Before I formed you in the womb, I knew you,

And before you were born I consecrated you;

I appointed you a prophet to the nations." (Jer 1:5 NRSV)

The Lord called me before I was born;

While I was in my mother's womb he named me . . .

---

allow that "conversion" can happen as one moves between groups that have different expressions and understandings of a single religion, then Paul was certainly "converted." If joining the Essene community would have constituted "conversion" for a Pharisee, joining the Christian community would have done so all the more since Saul the Pharisee came to embrace the beliefs and practices of a distinct group that he had formerly opposed, and even persecuted.

25. Scholars have indulged in debates over the question of "which came first," conversion or commission (see Kim, *Paul and the New Perspective*, 4–13, 36), but the essential point is rather that the encounter with the Risen Jesus, the Glorified Christ, changed both Paul's understanding of what God was doing in his generation and of what Paul's role as a servant of God would be.

> And now the LORD says, who formed me in the womb to be
> his servant, . . .
>
> "I will give you as a light to the nations." (Isa 49:1, 6 NRSV)

Aside from the subtle support Paul gives to his own claim to be called by God through his use of language from biblical call narratives, Paul also shows here how integral the mission to the Gentile nations is to his own sense of God's call on his life. Paul brings this out explicitly in 1:16: God's called Paul "in order that I should proclaim the good news about him among the nations."

The intervening phrase calls for closer investigation. It is often translated "when it pleased [God] . . . to reveal his Son *to me*," but the Greek underlying "to me" in this translation is *en emoi*, woodenly, "in me." Because of the overshadowing force of Luke's description of Paul's conversion in Acts 9, there is a strong tendency to read this phrase as a reference to that event, hence God's showing God's Son *to* Paul, to correct Paul's perceptions of who Jesus is.[26] It is also possible, however, that Paul is moving past this encounter itself (the event in which God "called me through his generous kindness," 1:15) to a statement about God's purposes in turning Paul's life around. Paul would be seen, in this reading, to understand that God's transformation of Paul from persecutor to preacher itself was a revelation of the power and reality of God's Son to all who saw the change and heard Paul's Gospel.[27] The next purpose clause ("that I should proclaim the good news about him among the nations") would offer a more human angle on the opening clause of 1:16, which presents the God's-eye view on the same activity: God was revealing God's Son "in" Paul as Paul went about fulfilling his divine commission to "proclaim Christ among the Gentiles." This is another point of genuine ambiguity in the text.

Paul becomes a living paradigm of God's gracious action.[28] He was "called by God's grace" (1:15) just as the Galatians were (1:6).[29] He was

---

26. So Martyn, *Galatians*, 158.

27. See Gaventa, "Galatians 1 and 2," 309–26.

28. Lyons, *Pauline Autobiography*, 171; Fee, *Galatians*, 46.

29. Early manuscript evidence is fairly well divided over the inclusion of "God" in Gal 1:15. P[46] and Codex Vaticanus do not explicitly specify "God" as the subject of the verb (though they and their readers would still have understood God to

himself quite overtly an enemy of God's Messiah on account of his own devotion to Torah and the preservation of Israel's exclusive covenant, but God turned him into an emissary of that Messiah to proclaim God's acceptance of *all* people on the basis of trust in God's provision in Christ. Paul was in need of such an act of gracious intervention precisely when he was *most* committed to "works of Torah," persecuting the Jewish Christians who, in his eyes, were violating God's covenant and thus jeopardizing the Jewish nation. The idea that assuming Jewish identity would be required in order to be accepted by God was something Paul's own experience belied: he had been the Jew par excellence, but still found himself opposing God outright.

Since Paul claims that his commission and Gospel come essentially from this encounter with the living, glorified Christ (1:11–12), we would do well to explore what Paul brought to this encounter and, thus, how this encounter changed Paul's mind about his most fundamental convictions.[30] Paul knew enough about the "Way" to know that it presented a threat to what he held most dear, namely Torah and Israel's covenant with God, and to devote himself to silencing its preachers and pressuring their followers to renounce their deviant way of life. Jesus had been recently crucified as a blasphemer, who had himself profaned the Sabbath, violated purity regulations, and had claimed far too much authority for himself (for example, the authority to forgive sins), perhaps even claiming to be the Messiah. He had violated Torah (at least, as Paul and the Pharisaic party interpreted it), stood condemned under Torah, and had been justly executed under its curse.[31] To proclaim such

be the one setting Paul apart from the womb and being pleased to reveal his Son); Codex Alexandrinus and Codex Sinaiticus do include "God" explicitly as the subject. I would understand the shorter reading here to be closer to Paul's original, since it was the habit of scribes (as it is the natural habit of translators) to clarify the identity of the pronouns in the Greek text for their readers' sake.

30. See the thoroughgoing attempt to demonstrate this in Kim, *The Origins of Paul's Gospel*; and Kim, *Paul and the New Perspective*.

31. This "curse" pertains not only to the curse pronounced upon "anyone hung on a tree" (Deut 21:22–23), a text applied to victims of crucifixion during the Roman period (see 1QT 64:7–12; Hengel, *Pre-Christian Paul*, 83), but more broadly to the curse pronounced upon "anyone who does not uphold the words of this law by observing them" (Deut 27:26; Hengel, *Pre-Christian Paul*, 84). Jesus' frequent conflicts with the Pharisees over matters of *halakha*—over how to walk in the way of the Law—showed

a one now as the "Righteous One" was clearly an affront to Torah's definition of "righteousness." Paul saw in the Jesus movement a tendency
toward the relaxation of Torah's commands in the name of this crucified
one, with the probable result that God would again punish Israel for
tolerating such flagrant violations of the covenant in its midst.

When Paul was confronted, then, with the *resurrected* Jesus, his
former interpretation of the world and God's action in that world, which
had seemed so secure and certain, was violently and irreparable shaken.
For Jesus to be alive—and glorified, no less—meant that God himself
had vindicated Jesus against the claims of Jesus' enemies (including the
authorities whom Paul revered and followed). God had approved Jesus
and shown that Jesus was righteous in God's eyes. It is, as it were, that
God said afresh to Paul: "*This* is my beloved Son. Listen to Him!"

Well before Paul was born, Jews had connected resurrection with
God's vindication of the righteous person who had been unjustly killed.
Premature death and the loss of covenant blessings could not be the
last word in the life of a person who had shown God due obedience:
such punishment was fitting for the ungodly, not for those who loved
and honored the covenant. Thus pious Jews clung to the hope of resurrection as a consequence of their belief that God was just—so just, that
if justice was not done for the righteous in this life, it certainly would
be done for them in the life beyond death.[32] If Jesus was condemned to
death under Torah as a transgressor and blasphemer, but was actually
so righteous in God's sight that God had *already* raised him from the
dead (Jesus would be the first to enter into the *resurrected* life!), then
the Torah itself was no longer a reliable guide to what God counted as
righteous, nor could it be embraced as something that would reliably
make its devotees righteous before God. The problem for Paul was not
that Torah *could* not be obeyed, but that Torah was not the final and
ultimate revelation of God's righteousness. Jesus was that revelation. A

him to be at odds with walking according to Torah as Paul the Pharisee understood
it, and thus at odds with Torah itself from his point of view.

32. See especially 2 Maccabees 6–7, a text known, if not written, in Palestine in
the late second century/early first century BCE, and Wisdom of Solomon 3:1–9, a
Diaspora Jewish text written in Greek from the turn of the era. These texts are further
discussed in deSilva, *Introducing the Apocrypha*, 142–44, 277.

critical change in Paul's mind, then, is that the center of authority and revelation shifts from the Torah to Jesus.[33]

If Jesus was righteous in God's sight, then his followers must be correct in their acclamation of him as Messiah and in their commitment to take their bearings from his teachings above (or as the interpretive key to) Torah. Encountering Jesus as a *resurrected* One, furthermore, signaled to Paul that the "last days" had begun. The general resurrection of the dead was an event expected at the end of this age, such that Jesus' resurrection from the dead is interpreted as the firstfruits of this end-time harvest. It is at this point that the connection between Paul's encounter with the *resurrected* Jesus and his commitment to proclaim Jesus as the Messiah to the Gentiles is forged. Part of the Jewish hope for the messianic age was that the Gentiles would come to worship the One God of Israel, bringing their glory to Jerusalem. Paul himself cites some of the oracles of God that fed this hope in Romans 15:9–12:

> As it is written,
>
> "Therefore I will confess you among the Gentiles,
>
> and sing praises to your name";
>
> and again he says,
>
> "Rejoice, O Gentiles, with his people";
>
> and again,
>
> "Praise the Lord, all you Gentiles,
>
> and let all the peoples praise him";
>
> and again Isaiah says,
>
> "The root of Jesse shall come,
>
> the one who rises to rule the Gentiles;
>
> in him the Gentiles shall hope."

Paul's own nurture in the Old Testament Scriptures would naturally lead him to connect the coming of the Messiah with the arrival of the time for the ingathering of the Gentiles.[34] What was special to his

33. See Beker, *Paul the Apostle*, 182–89. God's resurrection of this crucified Christ signaled that Torah's jurisdiction had come to an end and that God's saving acts were now moving into a new stage.

34. See Wright, *What Saint Paul Really Said*, 36–37.

own calling was that he should take part in this mission to the Gentiles as an ambassador of the Messiah. The author of Luke-Acts effectively captures the connection of Old Testament hope and the Pauline mission by using Isa 49:6 to illumine both the significance of Jesus and the mission of Paul: "I have set you to be a light to the Gentiles, to bring salvation to the uttermost parts of the earth" (Luke 2:32; Acts 13:47; see also Acts 26:18), a text to which Paul himself may already have alluded in Gal 1:15.

Paul's commission to proclaim good news to the Gentiles connects also with Paul's realization that the final authority of the Torah had come to an end with the resurrection of the One whom Torah had pronounced "cursed." The Torah essentially kept Jew and Gentile separate, maintaining the "dividing wall of hostility" between Jew and Gentile (Eph 2:14–15). A fully Torah-observant person could find himself, as did Paul, as starkly opposed to God as any "Gentile sinner," and thus as one who stood in equal need of God's gracious intervention. In Christ's death and the outpouring of God's Holy Spirit, God has intervened on behalf of both Jew and Gentile—and so both Jew and Gentile find themselves reconciled to God and brought back in line with God's standards of righteousness in precisely the same way. In such a situation, it no longer made sense to Paul to try to make Jews out of Gentiles—all that was important now was to be newly created in the Messiah by the power of God's Spirit.

This ingathering of the Gentiles was ultimately grounded, for Paul, in the *Shema* itself, the foundational creed of Israel: "Hear, O Israel: the LORD your God, the LORD is One" (Deut 6:4). The dividing wall of Torah, erected between Jew and Gentile, seemed to belie this essential truth. As Paul would later remark in Romans, "Is God the God of the Jews only? Is God not also God of the Gentiles? Yes, of the Gentiles also, since 'God is One'" (Rom 3:27–31)." The Oneness of God was to be reflected in the oneness of God's people (Gal 3:19–28).[35] Paul became convinced through his encounter with the risen Lord that he was the

35. Another important stream of tradition that would feed this expectation concerns the universal dominion of the Messiah, reflected in Pss 2:7–8; 72:8; 89:27 (Wright, *What Saint Paul Really Said*, 55). From this angle, again, Paul would be led to expect One Lord for Jews and Gentiles.

one to bring the promises of God to the Gentiles—the promises given long ago to the Gentile Abraham—by announcing this new act of God's favor, the arrival of the Messiah and the possibility of salvation through trust in this Mediator of God's favor.

Much of Paul's theological orientation can be traced back, therefore, to his encounter with the risen Jesus. Of course, it would remain for him to wrestle with the implications of this revelation for the remainder of his life in the variety of situations he encounters, but the fundamental lines are drawn in this encounter—hence he can truly claim that his gospel came through "a revelation of Jesus Christ" (Gal 1:11–12) rather than through human agency or consulting "flesh and blood" (1:16).

Paul gives us no specifics regarding his travels or destinations within "Arabia," nor does he report on his activity there. Neither does he report on his activities in Damascus following his return, nor his activities in Syria and Cilicia (1:21). What he *does* say is that, following all this activity, the churches in Judea were hearing reports that their former persecutor was now proclaiming the faith he once sought to stamp out (1:23). This would imply at the very least that Paul was actively preaching the Good News about Jesus Christ in Syria and Cilicia; it might also suggest that Paul immediately went about his task of proclaiming Jesus to the Gentiles in the cities of Arabia (for example, the Nabatean capital of Petra) and in Damascus following his return.[36] It is popular to regard Paul's journey into Arabia as a time of solitude and reflection, picturing the wastelands of Arabia as the location. Paul says nothing, however, that would suggest this, either here or elsewhere (nor, for that matter, does Luke in his picture of Paul's early post-conversion experience).

Paul's whole purpose here, though, is not to arouse his readers' curiosity about what he *did* do in Arabia and Damascus, but on what he did *not* do by remaining in those regions after his conversion. Paul did *not* present himself to the authorities in the Jerusalem church for their "orders," nor did he present himself to them as their student and disciple. Paul's goal is thus simply to stress his independence from the Jerusalem apostles in regard both to his commission and his understanding of God's revelation in Jesus Christ. While Paul doubtless would continue

36. This understanding would be supported by Schlier, *Galater*, 58; Betz, *Galatians*, 74; Bruce, *Galatians*, 94; Fung, *Galatians*, 69.

to work out the implications of that communication for decades, he insists that the whole Gospel was given to him there in seed form.

1:18–24: PAUL'S FIRST VISIT TO JERUSALEM AND WORK IN SYRIA AND CILICIA

[18]Then after three years I went up to Jerusalem to visit with Cephas, and I stayed with him for fifteen days. [19]I didn't see any of the other apostles except for James, the Lord's brother. [20]In regard to the things I am writing to you, look—before God, I swear I am not lying. [21]Then I went into the regions of Syria and Cilicia, [22]and I was unknown by face among the Judean assemblies that are in Christ. [23]They were just hearing reports that "the one who used to persecute us is now proclaiming as good news the faith that he was formerly trying to destroy," [24]and they were giving God honor *for what God was doing* in me.

Paul was active as an ambassador of the risen Christ for roughly three years before he made contact with the Jerusalem apostles. Even then, Paul insists, he met only with "Cephas" (the Aramaic form of Peter's name),[37] and that for only fifteen days, though he admits that he did also see James, Jesus' half-brother (see Mark 6:3; Matt 13:55), during that brief visit. Paul's purpose for this visit was "to make Peter's acquaintance" (Greek, *historēsai*).[38] Paul went not as a schoolboy, but as a fellow apostle and preacher of the Gospel. No doubt Paul learned a great deal from Peter, notably about the earthly life and the teachings of Jesus, whom Paul had not known "in the flesh." But Paul wants it clear that his visit was a meeting of equals, perhaps also a sign of Paul's desire to

37. In several places (here in 1:18; later in 2:11 and 2:14) the earliest manuscripts refer to Peter by his Aramaic name, "Cephas." Since "Cephas" was better known as "Peter" throughout the church, it is not surprising to find scribes beginning to replace "Cephas" with "Peter" in these three passages. This explains the difference between the KJV and most modern translations, which have the benefit of the knowledge of these earlier manuscripts (only brought to public light centuries after the KJV was undertaken), at these points.

38. Longenecker, *Galatians*, 37–38; Fung, *Galatians*, 73–74.

begin to establish collegial relationships between two major branches of the Christian mission.

At this point, Paul invokes a solemn oath, calling God as a witness to the truth of Paul's narrative up to this point (Gal 1:20). This alerts us again to the fact that he is making a quasi-formal case, and not merely sharing his "faith journey" or reminiscing for the sake of reminiscing.[39] He is especially interested, it would appear, in affirming the truthfulness surrounding his claims about his interaction with the Jerusalem apostles—or, better, the strict limitations on that interaction. There was no room for the suggestion that Paul was a convert of those apostles, that he was originally taught about the Gospel and about what would be required of converts from the apostles, or that he was commissioned by the apostles to preach Christ. Paul got all of that from God himself.[40] While this oath could be read as narrowly applying to the details of this first visit,[41] I think it more likely that Paul would want to affirm the utter truthfulness—at least from his perspective—of *all* the details in this entire narrative (such that he would not leave out all mention of an intervening visit between 1:18–20 and 2:1–10, if such a visit had happened).[42]

After this brief encounter, Paul focuses on the provinces of Syria and Cilicia for his early evangelistic efforts. Luke tells us very little of Paul's work during this time, save for the fact that he goes to Tarsus (in Cilicia) after his visit to Jerusalem (Acts 9:30) and that Barnabas is able to find him there when he wants help for the work in Antioch (in Syria, Acts 11:11–26).[43] By Paul's account, however, he was a more active mis-

39. Paul Sampley sees Paul's interjection of such a voluntary oath as "a forceful and even dramatic means to emphasize both the seriousness of the issue and his own truthfulness" ("'Before God, I do not lie' [Gal. i. 20]," 477–82, especially 481–82).

40. It is possible—but just possible—that he is also trying to affirm that he did not carry out his own mission in the mission fields of the predominantly "circumcised," being sent by God to deliver the Gospel to the Gentiles (and on *God's* terms, not the circumcised Christians' terms). This question may at least have bearing on the agreement with Peter in 2:1–10 about their respective mission fields.

41. So Schlier, *Galater*, 62.

42. So Burton, *Galatians*, 61; Longenecker, *Galatians*, 39–40, at least in regard to 1:13–19; Fung, *Galatians*, 79.

43. On the differences between Paul's and Luke's accounts of Paul's first post-con-

sionary in both provinces than Luke cares to report at this point in his version of the story, since news of his work on behalf of the Gospel travels back to the churches in Judea (1:23–24).

Paul claims that he remained "personally unknown" to the Christian assemblies in Judea, a claim that confirms both that he did not spend any significant time in Judea, let alone Jerusalem, during the time since his encounter with the glorified Christ and that he understood his commission specifically as "apostle to the nations" from the very beginning, leaving the evangelism of Judea to others. Nevertheless, these Judean Christians hear reports of Paul's missionary activity in Syria and Cilicia (and perhaps Arabia) and bear witness to the activity of God in having turned their former persecutor into a promoter of "the faith" (*tēn pistin*, 1:24).[44] Paul makes the Judean Christians into witnesses, therefore, to the divine power at work in his call and apostleship since, observing the transformation in Paul's activity, they attribute the change to God's intervention: "they were giving God honor *for what God was doing* in me."[45]

---

version visit to Jerusalem (Gal 1:18–19, 22–23; Acts 9:26–30), see the Introduction.

44. Paul does not normally use the noun "the faith" to indicate the basic content of the Gospel and the way of life it promotes, preferring to use this term more for the dynamic relationship of trust and faithfulness that exists between Christians and Jesus and God. This use here may indeed stem from the way Judean Christians were talking about Paul's transformation and "the faith" (= the message, the content of the Gospel) he now proclaimed, or it may just be Paul's own choice. This becomes important when assessing the date and provenance of other texts like Jude, which use "faith" in terms of "the message and teachings about Christ handed done to us" (as in Jude 4). Often it is argued that such a petrified use of "faith" is a sign of a later date, when Paul's dynamic "faith" as "trust in Jesus" has been replaced by "faith" as a body of doctrines to be preserved. The usage of "faith" in Gal 1:24—even if it is Paul's usage, but all the more if it reflects the usage of earliest Judean Christianity—renders such an argument against an early date for Jude's Letter invalid.

45. This phrase, translated more woodenly, might read "they were giving God glory in me (*en emoi*)," but the preposition *en* ("in") is being used more in the sense of the ground or basis for an action (*why* the Judean Christians were praising God) than the location of an action (*where* the Judea Christians were praising God, or where God was when the Judean Christians were praising him). See Longenecker, *Galatians*, 42; Fung, *Galatians*, 84.

READING GALATIANS 1 WITH SRI LANKAN CHRISTIANS

The Gospel and the Majority Religions in Sri Lanka

As Paul opens his letter, he announces several important, even central features of the "Good News" of Jesus. Jesus gave himself over on account of our sins. God raised this Jesus from among the realm of the dead. Jesus rescues us from the present, evil age in line with God's good will for us. This God can be known, in some sense, as "Father" (1:3–4). The Gospel message both speaks to, and stands aloof as alien within, the context of Sri Lanka's majority religions.

Both Buddhists and Hindus would resonate with the description of the realm of human experience as a realm of suffering (Buddhism), or as a realm in which people are subject to the malice of evil spirits, against which they must take precautions (Hinduism). Both would resonate with the hope of deliverance from this realm, though framed very differently as deliverance from the cycle of rebirth and death. Classical Buddhism does not make room for divine intervention in human problems. The gods are caught also in the wheel of rebirth, not agents of deliverance therefrom. There is certainly no room for the expectation that a god would take active interest in one's deliverance as a father caring for a child in distress. It also places a high value on self-effort in overcoming the triple traps of delusion, desire, and anger. Hinduism would question whether or not it is possible for one person to take upon himself (i.e., Jesus) the suffering that others have earned through their evil deeds.

Despite these differences, the Gospel says some powerful things within a Buddhist and Hindu context, speaking to some root perceptions about existence shared by Christians, Buddhists, and Hindus. People are trapped by their own hatred, cravings, and ignorance, and suffer the consequences of the same. These are indeed cankers that gnaw at the heart of human existence and human community, condemning us to suffering. There is something fundamentally diseased about the entire social and spiritual system within which we live, and we need to find a cure. Humanity and the Divine are not right with each other, and we are at pains to discover how we can appease the Divine.

Within such shared perceptions, the Gospel affirms that there is an escape from the cycle of karma-samsara, but it takes the form of a person entering our existence from the divine realm, dying on our behalf, and rising again from the dead to a life that is no longer subject to death (including no longer being subject to rebirth). There is a God who has taken such an interest in the human predicament of suffering and of slavery to sin (including anger, delusion or ignorance, and misdirected cravings) that he has acted decisively to break the cycle by sending his Son in the flesh to take upon himself the due consequences of our evil, freeing us for a new experience of God's favor and for a new life lived beyond the power of ignorance, desires, and hatred.

The differences in worldview may nevertheless seem insurmountable, but we need to remember that when Paul preached the Gospel in Galatia or Thessalonica or Corinth he was proclaiming a message that was no more at home in the context of the worldview of Greeks and Romans. We also need to remember that Paul did not rely on the strength of his own arguments or persuasive power to bridge the gaps. He relied, rather, on the overwhelming presence of God showing up where the Gospel was proclaimed (Gal 3:1–5; 1 Cor 2:1–5; compare also Heb 2:3–4). An encounter with God can dispel agnosticism. An experience of God's love and acceptance mediated through the Holy Spirit tends to confirm that one man (Jesus) can indeed free others from the consequences of their sins and allow them to experience divine favor without the need for Kavadi. And an experience of the indwelling presence and power of the Holy Spirit successfully fighting the battle against hatred, the desires of the flesh, and delusion can make one reconsider the importance of self-reliance along the path.

Are We Preaching Another Gospel?

Gordon Fee suggests that, rather than read 1:6–9 as though we stand alongside Paul against others who have "gotten it wrong," it might be more profitable for us—and certainly more in keeping with the virtue of humility—to read 1:6–9 as an invitation to examine ourselves, to discover the extent to which we might be proclaiming and living "another

Gospel, which is no Gospel."[46] If we do this, what would we see? In the Galatians' situation, this "other Gospel" focuses on conforming Gentile Christians to the traditional practices of Jews—the practices that Paul sees more now as cultural "baggage" from his own Jewish upbringing, the residue from his pre-Christian existence. In our churches, it manifests itself perhaps most obviously as insisting upon certain behaviors or practices that one Christian group has adopted as a meaningful manner of expressing commitment to God as the *only* meaningful manner of expressing commitment to God.

The "other Gospel, which is no Gospel" is preached when one group insists that all true Christians will worship God on Saturday, the original Sabbath, and that worshiping God on Sunday is a mark of the Beast, a doing away with a commandment of God (Exod 20:8–11; Deut 5:12–15). Paul will insist in Romans, however, that, in the freedom of the Spirit, some Christians "judge one day to be better than another, while others judge all days to be alike. Let all be fully convinced in their own minds. Those who observe the day, observe it in honor of the Lord," and, since Paul's treatment of eating or abstaining from certain foods is a fully parallel case, those who observe all days as the same do so honoring God and giving thanks to God for each day (Rom 14:5–6). The "other Gospel" is preached when we insist that people who were baptized as infants and have grown up in the love of God and come to a place of faith in and commitment to Jesus be baptized again as professing believers—and often baptized in a particular way, as if only immersion counted, or only immersion following a certain formula (naming or not naming the three persons of the Trinity). Rather than rejoicing in the work of the Holy Spirit, we impose new regulations and claim that people are not part of the Body of Christ apart from submitting to certain rituals in certain ways. The "other Gospel" is preached when we insist that disciples must tithe (and, specifically, tithe to *our church*) in order to be genuine Christians. Rather than encourage generosity toward the church as a whole and all who are in need, to the fullest extent that the Spirit would enable, we return to the Torah to legislate giving for the sake of our own financial security. The "other Gospel" is preached when we insist that Christians must speak in tongues as the

46. Fee, *Galatians*, 27.

necessary evidence that they have received the anointing of the Holy Spirit and, in some extreme case, as a necessary sign that they have been saved. Rather than rejoice in *any* manifestation of the Spirit's gifts and fruit in the lives of each disciple, we establish a test that people must either pass or fail (and one on which it is, moreover, rather easy to cheat!).

Decisions we've made for ourselves about what kinds of beverages are suitable for us as Christian disciples, what manner of dress, what forms of entertainment and social engagements become decisions that we then make for everyone, denying them the same freedom in the Spirit that we exercise when we choose to abstain. For, according to Paul, both the decision to abstain *and* the decision to receive with thanksgiving are decisions we are free to make in the Spirit, and commanded to honor in the other person. Yes, we can engage in conversations with one another about these decisions. Yes, we can hold up what we think to be the merits of our particular decision. Yes, we can challenge one another to make sure that we are listening to God and not to our own "flesh." And yes, we should always bear in mind our freedom to curtail our freedom where it would give offense to another or lead another disciple to act against his or her conscience (Rom 14:13–23). But no, we cannot legislate for others the decisions we have made about whether we will abstain or receive with thanksgiving—at least, we cannot do this and expect to remain friends with Paul, and perhaps not even exempt from his anathema.

Before we jump to defend our favorite "works" of our new Torahs by pointing out the scriptural "proofs" for our positions that we find so convincing and unassailable, we need to remember that it was, in fact, the Judaizers and not Paul who had Scripture more clearly on their side in the dispute over circumcision and Torah observance.

Are They Preaching "Another Gospel"?

A striking feature of Sri Lankan Christianity is that, despite being a small minority on the island, it still has room for all the diversity and divisions that one finds in countries where Christianity (especially Protestant Christianity, with its tendency toward fragmentation) has been the majority religion for centuries. The fragmentation of the church has been a source of criticism and a stumbling block to evangelism in the West; this same fragmentation gives the non-Christian majority in Sri Lanka the opportunity to shame Christians for their lack of cohesiveness and their lack of clarity and agreement concerning the faith and religious practice for which they are leaving behind their ancestral religions and breaking with their neighbors. Alongside the Roman Catholic Church, still the largest single entity within Sri Lankan Christianity, sit an Anglican, Methodist, Reformed, Baptist, and Pentecostal presence. Alongside these sit yet other and more diverse Christian groups, many of which are simply independent congregations representing "denominations unto themselves." Across this landscape, churches also have to contend with new teachings (some of which, like the "prosperity gospel," are undesirable Western imports) blowing through like ill winds, trying to change the Christian Gospel of transformation toward the likeness of the self-giving and obedient Jesus and rescue from this present, evil age into a way to manipulate God into giving us more to enjoy in this present, evil age.

In such an environment, we need to observe two realities that are in constant tension. First, no one church, denomination, or Christian group has a perfect and complete grasp of the Good News, God's vision for God's people, or the challenge the Gospel poses to the lives, practices, and attitudes of disciples and communities of disciples. Second, Paul reminds us that there are "boundaries" on the Good News and there are ways in which Christian teachers, well-intentioned or otherwise, can cross those boundaries such that they are presenting a perversion of the Good News that is, therefore, no longer the life-giving, life-changing message that we received from the apostles.

The first of these two realities calls us to discern when the "other Gospel" is somehow just not the "whole Gospel," mindful of the fact that our own churches and denominations probably do not grasp the "whole Gospel" ourselves. I may continue to affirm the value of my baptism as an infant, but I have learned much about the necessity of coming to a point of personal commitment to live for Christ and to identify with Christ's mission from my Baptist sisters and brothers, who dramatically display this in the practice of believers' baptism. I have learned much from my Pentecostal sisters and brothers about the supernatural realities of the Holy Spirit at work in the midst of God's church. While

I continue to affirm the importance of personal decision for Chirst, I have learned much from my Reformed sisters and brothers about the sovereignty of God and the importance of God's decision for each person. I daresay that many of my sisters and brothers in more "evangelical" denominations can learn much about God's desire to see Christians engaged in acts of charity, social justice, and witness in the political arena from my Anglican and Methodist heritage. Within the "true Gospel" there is a great deal of room for the various emphases and expressions of Christian denominations, and it is really only in the conversation between these denominations that the "whole Gospel" is heard.

The second of these realities, however, does call us to discern when a body of fellow Christians (and perhaps our *own* body!) has crossed a line and made of the Good News something that it is, simply, not. This most often happens when some single facet of the scriptural witness becomes the central focus of the movement, leading to the distortion of the whole. The "prosperity gospel" certainly began this way, with a few texts about God's promises for prosperity in this life and access to anything we could want through prayer with faith becoming the core of the message. In this instance, a "partial Gospel" crossed the line into "another Gospel, which is no Gospel." The whole counsel of Scripture speaks of God's purposes for Christians quite differently. In sum, God is not out to make us happy as the world measures happiness; God is out to make us more like Jesus, and that's not going to happen without walking in the way of self-denial, dying to our own cravings and urges, and living for what God desires to accomplish *in others* and *for others* through us.[47]

"Other Gospels" tend to appear when more recent texts arise alongside the Scriptures historically received by the people of God (namely, the Old and New Testaments).[48] When the American Joseph

---

47. The "Word of Faith Movement" would be far less objectionable if the verses that it taught its followers to "say" and "receive"—and that it modeled among its leaders—included Mark 8:34–38; Luke 12:33–34; Acts 5:40–42; Gal 5:24; Phil 2:3–8; 3:8–11, 19–21; Col 3:1–17; Heb 10:32–34; 13:12–14; Jas 1:27 and the like.

48. I do not think that the matter of including or excluding the Apocrypha in reference to the Old Testament would come under the heading of this warning, since Christians have been of two minds about their canonical status from the beginning of the church. The antiquity of these texts, their imprint upon the New Testament, and

Smith promoted a collection of texts as something he received on gold plates written in an unknown language from an angel in heaven, he added something to the apostolic Gospel that transformed it into "another Gospel" that is unrecognizable alongside the original. Sri Lankan Christians need to be more wary of what they import from the West (we don't exercise any quality control in what we export *from* the West!).

Paul's example reminds us of the danger of taking on the role of "watchdog" for our tradition. Sri Lankan Christians have to live with pressure from watchdogs from their own pre-Christian traditions, whether Buddhist or Hindu, that keep a wary eye upon the Christian churches. But there is also the danger of becoming watchdogs ourselves for our own particular brand of Christianity, seeing other brands as hostile, as competition. Watchdogs would prefer to see God simply swallow those other Christians up or show them the error of their ways, often taking the lead in this regard themselves. Such was Paul, in regard to Judaism and his fellow Jews who came to faith in Jesus as Messiah, and by such a path Paul found himself opposing God when he most thought himself to be fighting *for* God.

Paul's own teachings, however, should lead us rather to engage Christians who have come to conclusions about faith and practice different from our own in open, constructive conversation in which both sides hold up their views and practices to scrutiny in the Spirit, realizing that now we all see God's truth reflected as if in a distorted mirror (1 Cor 13:12). If Paul could say this about himself and his congregations, how much more should we adopt such a humble attitude in conversation with other Christians! The watchdog—and, in the extreme, the persecutor such as Paul was—stands at the opposite end from humility on this spectrum. Naming "other gospels" stands in tension with working toward Christian unity, or at least Christian cooperation and mutual accountability. It tends, rather, to fuel the formation of new, little denominations, replacing the Body of Christ increasingly with many one-celled organisms. But if we approach the task of challenging "partial Gospels" and "other Gospels" with humility regarding our own constructions,

---

their widespread, positive use during the formative centuries of the Christian church, make them, at the very least, allies of the scriptural witness. See deSilva, *Introducing the Apocrypha*, 20–41.

the humility to listen to one another, and the commitment to raising questions from the shared Scriptures, all parties may hear more of the "whole Gospel" and move toward unity under its banner.

Paul as a Model for Christian Leaders

The reverence in which Paul is held throughout the church naturally inspires us to seek to emulate him. He himself calls his converts to "imitate him" insofar as he himself seeks to "imitate Christ" and embody the mind and heart of Jesus (see 1 Cor 11:1; Phil 3:17). As a Christian leader, Paul also exhibits many qualities and attitudes that we would do well to imitate. But I would also have us be cautious in our imitation of Paul, mindful of—and honest about—the distance that separates our own experience from his. Most of *us* received the Gospel through human teachers in the context of Christian community, and we should acknowledge that and live from that model, rather than from Paul's model of claiming direct revelation from God (1:12). God acted, no doubt, to confirm in our own hearts and lives the Gospel that we received, but we remain thoroughly dependent upon the church throughout the ages for our own reception of the Gospel.

There is therefore all the more need for us to do as Paul did, when he laid out his Gospel before the Jerusalem apostles, to confirm that he had not been running in vain (see Gal 2:1–10). The Christian leader who continually submits his or her message, understanding of the Gospel, and vision for the church to the scrutiny of other leaders—preferably leaders from other denominations, who see more clearly other facets of the Gospel than one's own tradition tends to see—is embodying the best part of Paul's example. As in Paul's case this was not a denial of God working through the individual leader, so it is no denial of our own conviction that we are called by God. It is, however, an acknowledgment in humility that discernment of the truth and of the Spirit belongs to the larger church, and not to ourselves (or even our denomination) alone. Where Christian leaders think that their own experience aligns more fully with Paul's model of having been called directly by God and given a message directly from God, there is all the more need for that leader and for Christians around him or her to "test the spirits" and the Gospel that leader proclaims, to make sure it aligns with the faith handed down once for all to the saints. This was the standard beneath which Paul even set his own authority (1:8–9). Once the apostolic Gospel was proclaimed, it became the standard by which *all* Christian preachers were to be weighed and to which *all* preachers were accountable.

Paul's commitment to seek to please Christ in all things, and never to give in to the temptation to please people when this would compromise his fidelity to Christ and the challenges of the Gospel, is another point worthy of imitation by all Christian leaders and disciples alike. Sri Lankans are not alone in being geared toward pleasing their community or avoiding the conflict that comes from arousing displeasure. In every culture, Christian leaders especially need to examine themselves from the point of view of questions like: Whom am I seeking to please in my ministry? Am I sacrificing pleasing God for the sake of pleasing people—my congregation, other church leaders, forces outside the church—in any decision or practice? Pleasing both at the same time is a good thing, but more often a choice must be made. Paul challenges us to remember that, in every encounter, in every decision, in every intervention, there is One whom we must please, there is One to whom we, as slaves of Christ, are answerable.

If we read 1:16 giving the prepositional phrase "in me" the full force of the locus of God's revelation of his Son, then Paul asks us to consider how we, too, have been chosen by God to be venues for the revelation of God's Son. How does God want to make God's Son known *in and through* me to those around me? One major means in Paul's own experience was through Paul's transformation, and this remains an important means by which God can reveal Jesus as Son through every Christian, whether in leadership or not. The change need not be dramatic in the ways it was for Paul, namely God's transformation of Paul from persecutor to proclaimer of the faith within a few short weeks. But the transformation of a person who lives for himself or herself into a person who lives fully to serve God and others, who gives his or her life day by day unselfishly to accomplish God's good purposes in the lives of the people and the society around that person is no less dramatic, no less a revelation of God's Son "in me."

_Commentary

2:1-10: PAUL'S SECOND VISIT TO JERUSALEM

Then after fourteen years I went up again to Jerusalem with Barnabas, also taking Titus along. ²(I went up in accordance with a revelation.) I presented to them the message of good news that I proclaim among the nations, privately to those of reputation, lest somehow I was running or had run for nothing. ³ But they did not even compel Titus, who was with me and who was a Greek, to be circumcised. ⁴*This issue came up* on account of false brothers who were brought in under false pretences, who slipped in to spy out the freedom that we enjoy in Christ Jesus, in order that they might enslave you. ⁵We did not give in to them in submission even for a moment, in order that the truth of the good news might remain for you.

⁶But from those who had a reputation for being "somebodies"—whatever they were formerly makes no difference to me, since God does not have regard for a person's appearance—those of repute added nothing to me. ⁷On the contrary, seeing that the good news for the uncircumcised was entrusted to me just as *the good news* for the circumcised *was entrusted* to Peter, ⁸since the one who worked through Peter for the purpose of apostleship to the circumcised also worked in me *for apostleship* to the nations, ⁹and knowing the generous kindness that had been shown me, Jacob and Cephas and John—those reputed to be "pillars"—gave the right hand of partnership to me and to Barnabas, in order that we *should go* to the nations, and they to the circumcision. ¹⁰*They added* only that that we should continue to remember the poor, which very thing I was eager to do.

Paul has shaped the narrative thus far to show that his commission and his message came to him independently of the Jerusalem leadership and in complete dependence on God. As Paul recounts at length this private meeting between James, John, and Peter on the one hand, and himself and Barnabas on the other, Paul moves to the next emphasis, namely the Jerusalem apostles' validation of his apostleship and message.⁴⁹

49. For a fuller investigation of this tightrope Paul is walking, see Dunn, "The Relationship between Paul and Jerusalem," 461–78.

He lays out the Gospel he had been preaching (Gal 1:21–24), bringing along an uncircumcised Gentile convert named Titus (Gal 2:1, 3). If the Jerusalem apostles felt the need to correct or supplement any aspect of Paul's Gospel, that would have been the right occasion. Instead, seeing the hand of God to be at work in Paul and Barnabas's missionary endeavors just as in their own (Gal 2:8), and understanding the success of Paul and Barnabas's work to be an outworking of God's favor (Gal 2:9), the Jerusalem apostles affirmed them as partners in mission and "added nothing" to Paul's message (Gal 2:6). Why, then, should anyone be calling for circumcision of Gentiles now? The Galatians should take this as evidence that Paul's Gospel has the recognition of the Jerusalem apostles, whatever the rivals may have said to the contrary.

The selectivity of Paul's narrative is especially evident when one considers that he compresses his fourteen years of missionary work in Syria and Cilicia into a single verse (1:21) but then gives ten verses to a single episode (2:1–10) followed by at least another four verses to a subsequent episode (2:11–14). As mentioned in the introduction, there is some uncertainty concerning whether Paul intends for us to understand the episode of 2:1–10 as happening fourteen years after his encounter with the glorified Christ (1:15–17) or after his first visit to Jerusalem (1:18–20).[50] I tend to agree with those who find the latter to be the more natural reading, but the issue is one on which certainty is admittedly difficult.

Paul asserts that he "goes up" to Jerusalem (the expressions "to go up" and "to go down" are typically used in regard to journeys heading to and returning from Jerusalem, both because Mount Zion is elevated slightly above its surroundings and because of the ideological elevation of Jerusalem on the Jewish map) "in accordance with a revelation" (*kata apokalypsin*, 2:2). We cannot be certain in what form this "revelation" came to Paul, whether as a prophetic utterance in the assembly or as a private prompting of the Spirit within Paul, nor is Paul concerned to elaborate on this. What Paul *does* tell his hearers, he tells them so as to prevent any impression that he and Barnabas went as lackeys of the

---

50. In favor of the former, see Martyn, *Galatians*, 180–82; Longenecker, *Galatians*, 45. In favor of the latter, see Betz, *Galatians*, 83; Schlier, *Galater*, 64–65; Burton, *Galatians*, 68; Robinson, *Redating*, 37.

Jerusalem apostles, either summoned by them to give a report on their preaching and activities or as persons aware of needing to give an account to their superiors.[51] Rather, he went because God—the God who gave him his commission—directed him to do so.

Paul's sense of divine commission and revelation aside, it is important here to note that Paul is aware of the need for agreement and acknowledgment of his Gospel and commission by those who were apostles before him. Despite his certainty of having seen Christ and having correctly understood the significance of Jesus' death and resurrection and so forth, he raises the possibility that he might be, and have been, running "for nothing" (traditionally, "in vain"). Paul understands that failure to receive the acknowledgment of the Jerusalem apostles would have serious consequences for the value of his own mission—at the very least, his efforts to build the one community of Gentiles and Jews in Christ would be undermined, resulting in two separate and divided churches.[52] Perhaps, however, he also realizes the potential for his own human error in discerning the Gospel, and so performs, at God's prompting, this very important "self-check" by going to confer with the Jerusalem apostles about how he has pursued the work of advancing the Gospel and building the church universal.

Paul selects this episode for special focus here in his narrative, further, because he is aware that the Galatians need a standard for discerning the truth of the Gospel beyond either himself or the rival teachers. His narration of the agreement between himself and the Jerusalem pillars accomplishes this: Paul subjected his message to their scrutiny, and they affirmed that it was indeed in line with their understanding of the Gospel and, therefore, with the authentic message of Jesus and about Jesus.[53] The rival teachers cannot now claim otherwise, nor can they claim support of the Jerusalem apostles for their position and mission against Paul's. Paul thus clearly sees a connection between his current situation (his preaching to the Galatians and the current challenge to his gospel) and the "historic" meeting with Peter, James, and John.

---

51. Fung, *Galatians*, 87; Longenecker, *Galatians*, 47.

52. Dunn, "Relationship," 468; Burton, *Galatians*, 73; Fung, *Galatians*, 90.

53. See Bruce, *Galatians*, 35–37.

Paul's intention was to speak "privately to those who seemed to be of repute," namely the Jerusalem leadership (2:2). While this probably rules out an easy identification of this visit with the Jerusalem Conference whose story is recounted in Acts 15 (a meeting clearly public and, indeed, likely intended to be so from the beginning), it also does not appear that Paul entirely got his way in light of the fact that some other parties "sneaked in." The stress on Paul's intentions for a "private" meeting may serve a strategic end, possibly shutting out the rival teachers and others of their inclination as "not in his league" or the "league" of those to whom he considers himself, to some extent at least, answerable. It certainly serves to present the Jewish Christians urging circumcision upon Gentile converts as the ones who are out of alignment with the Jerusalem apostles in their agreement with Paul, still seeking to foster their position against the better inclinations of "those reputed to be pillars."

The impetus toward circumcision and Torah observance, bringing the Gentile converts under the strict tutelage of that outmoded guardian, is to be traced to this third party.[54] Paul describes them in the most unflattering terms. They are "certain false brothers" who pushed their noses into where they did not belong, "weaseling their way in" to the conversation between Paul, Barnabas, and the Jerusalem pillars (2:4). They had no business interjecting themselves into that meeting, and, moreover, they did so with harmful intent, "to spy out our freedom, which we have in Christ, in order to thoroughly enslave us" (2:4). These Jewish Christians are probably the source of the suggestion that Titus, a Gentile convert who had accompanied Paul and Barnabas, needed to be circumcised in order to be fully a member of the new people of God.[55]

---

54. Fee (*Galatians*, 56) suggests that 2:4–5 reveals "the reason for the conference," namely "the insistence on the necessity of circumcision of Gentiles on the part of some Jewish believers." While some people *did* make this *an* issue at this meeting, it is not at all clear that this is "the reason for the conference" as much as a sidebar that arose outside of, and intruded upon, Paul and Barnabas's meeting with James, Peter, and John.

55. Why Paul decided to take Titus along is not entirely clear. Because Paul says nothing here about who Titus is, it can be inferred that the Galatians knew him personally; Titus may, therefore, have been part of Paul's team when he and Barnabas preached in Southern Galatia. Paul might have taken him along to Jerusalem simply

The "slavery" they sought to impose upon the Pauline mission and its converts, to use Paul's loaded image, was the same kind of practice that Paul's rival teachers are now seeking to promote among the Galatian converts (also identified with enslaving and slavery; see 4:1–5, 8–11; 5:1), thus reflecting negatively upon the rival teachers here as well (undermining *their* credibility in the current situation).

Paul, however, firmly resisted their suggestion and any pressure or arguments they might have applied at that time. He emerges from this situation as the champion of the "truth of the Gospel," preserving that truth for the benefit of the whole Gentile mission (2:5). He presents his actions in Jerusalem, holding his own against the false brothers, as a course ultimately undertaken on behalf of all his converts, including those whose conversion was yet in the future, like the Galatians. His steadfastness to the truth of the Gospel and his resistance against voices in Jerusalem akin to the voices of the rival teachers in Galatia brought benefit to them, and should therefore arouse due loyalty and gratitude on their part, rather than defection. Paul also makes it clear that the Jerusalem pillars did not put their weight behind the suggestion of the "false brothers," since, on the one hand, Titus went away uncircumcised and, on the other, the Jerusalem apostles still extended the "right hand of partnership" to Paul and Barnabas.[56]

A comment on the style of Paul's writing at this point is in order. According to the present state of the critical edition of the Greek, Paul starts a sentence in 2:4 that he never actually completes.[57] It remains a

---

because he was a member of the team and, therefore, also involved in the collection of the relief funds they were transporting (if Gal 2:1–10 is a parallel account of the visit narrated in Acts 11:28–30). It is not clear that Paul himself took Titus along as a test case, as if he wanted to bring up the issue of Gentile circumcision or non-circumcision so forcefully himself. This seems, rather, to have been a fruit of the "spying" done at the meeting by the "false brothers." See Longenecker, *Galatians*, 47.

56. Dunn (*Galatians*, 4) praises the "faith and foresight" of the Jerusalem pillars for backing Paul in the face of considerable pressure from the "false brothers."

57. Woodenly, Gal 2:4 could be represented thus: "But on account of false brothers who were brought in under false pretenses, who slipped in to spy out the freedom which we enjoy in Christ Jesus, in order that they might enslave you, to whom we did not give in to them in submission even for a moment, in order that the truth of the good news might remain for you." The grammar has been "cleaned up" for our translation above.

sentence fragment by the end of 2:5, at which point Paul begins another fresh sentence (2:6). Paul does not seem able to finish this sentence in the way he started: he introduces the "pillars" as an object of a preposition at the outset, but then decides just to start over, in effect, by naming these pillars as the subject of the sentence that eventually emerges.[58] These false starts and syntactic bumps suggest, first, a rather high level of agitation or emotional investment on Paul's part, particularly as he recalls the intrusion of the "false brothers" into his meeting with the Jerusalem apostles and the conflict over whether or not Titus needed to be circumcised.[59] Part of this flood of agitation may be, in fact, due to Paul's encounter with similar opposition now in Galatia, when he thought this question had been settled—and that with the full support of the pillars. They also suggest a level of immediacy in Paul's composition of this letter—it is still in "rough draft" form when he sends it, indicating both the urgency of the situation in his opinion and the unlikelihood of his having used a secretary, who should have caught and smoothed out such rough (even incorrect) syntax.

No matter how much the "false brothers" would have wished the requirements of circumcision and Torah observance to be added to Paul's presentation of the Gospel and its requirements, the Jerusalem pillars "added nothing" to Paul. He had presented the message he preached (2:2), and no doubt had spoken of the lifestyle changes he did require (as well as the signs of God's presence and approval that manifested themselves amongst his converts), and the Jerusalem apostles considered all of this to be adequate (2:6).

Paul's aside in 2:6—"whatever they were formerly (*hopoioi pote*) makes no difference to me, since God does not have regard for a person's appearance"—is frequently read as his declaration of not being impressed by the repute of the Jerusalem apostles on the ground that their official status within the church is no basis for genuine authority in God's sight. Paul would, then, be taming, if not undermining, the authority even of the Jerusalem apostles at this point.[60] However, such

58. The grammatical term for this is "anacolouthon."

59. Fee, *Galatians*, 55; Martyn, *Galatians*, 194–95.

60. See, for example, Longenecker, *Galatians*, 53–54; Betz, *Galatians*, 92; Martyn, *Galatians*, 199.

a reading requires taking the *pote* in a rather looser sense (such as a mere intensifier) than its more typical sense of "formerly." According to this latter sense, the *pote* differentiates "what kind of persons they were formerly" (that is, prior to their rising to positions of leadership and oversight in the Christian movement) from what they have now become, people "seeming to be something of substance, of *gravitas*," which Paul respects—all the more, no doubt, because they backed him up on that particular occasion. God's choice of former "nobodies" ("nobodies," that is, compared to the well-connected Paul, if Acts is to be believed on certain points, as, for example, Paul's ability to get a commission from the high priest) to become principal authorities in the Messianic movement is acknowledged to be in keeping with God's regarding the heart rather than outward appearances. Such a reading would be in keeping with the source text for Paul's reference, namely God's selection of David, the young shepherd in the household, over his taller, finer looking brothers (1 Sam 16:7). This would also be in keeping with his own philosophy of not reckoning his own life prior to coming to Christ as anything but "sewage" (*skybala*, Phil 3:4b–8).

As a result of their encounter and of hearing Paul and Barnabas's account of their message and its fruits, the Jerusalem pillars conclude that God has entrusted Paul (and Barnabas, though Paul conspicuously uses the first person singular in 2:8–9) with "the Gospel for the un-circumcised" just as God had entrusted Peter with "the Gospel for the circumcised." These expressions are not meant to indicate two different Gospels (the author of Gal 1:6–9 and 2 Cor 11:4 could hardly applaud that), but rather to affirm that the Jerusalem pillars saw the proclamation and enfleshment of the one Gospel appropriately being conducted among Gentiles by Paul and Barnabas and among Jews by Peter. They recognized that the One God was indeed at work in both missions, extending the deliverance of his Son in both spheres, Jew and Gentile (2:9).[61] Paul speaks of his commission to this apostolic ministry—his "call"—as an expression of God's favor. It is "the gift given" to him by God (see also Rom 1:5; 15:15–16; Eph 3:8), a privilege that has fallen to him in God's kindness. The primary authorities in Jerusalem, named

---

61. Compare the arguments advanced in favor of a mission to the Gentiles—specifically one not involving Torah observance—in Acts 11:3, 15–18; 15:12.

here for the first time in this episode as Peter, James (the Lord's brother), and John, recognize this divine favor operative in Paul's ministry. They offer Paul and Barnabas "the right hand of partnership," agreeing that they are united in a common mission, working for the same Lord and pulling together in the same direction.

Paul refers to these three men as "those who seemed to be pillars." The image of the pillar, a common enough architectural feature in any urban setting in the eastern Roman Empire, was frequently used to speak of key figures supporting a social body of some kind. Hence, sons were held to be the "pillars" of a household (Euripedes, *Iphigenia in Tauris* 57), the patriarchs Abraham, Isaac, and Jacob were the "pillars" of the congregation of Israel (*Exod. Rab.* 15.7); Rabbi Johanan ben Zakkai was a "pillar" of the reconstituted Jewish Sanhedrin after the Jewish Revolt (*b. Ber.* 28b; *Abot R. Nat.* 25.1).[62] Peter, James, and John were reputed to be the "pillars" of the Jerusalem church and its Jewish Christian mission. While it is unclear that 2:6 is meant to show reserve in regard to the authority and reputation of these three persons, it is difficult to read 2:9, "those who *seemed to be* pillars," in any other way. Since Paul will very shortly go on to narrate the failure of one of these three men to walk in line with their agreement, at least in Paul's estimation, it is likely that Paul is expressing some reservation here about people who prove, in Peter's case at least, "shaky" pillars at best.

What exactly was agreed upon at this meeting? Paul believes that the three pillars agreed "that we should go to the nations [or "the Gentiles"], and they to the circumcision" (2:9). Clearly, some kind of division of labor appears to be the focal point of the agreement, but what kind? Some have suggested that Paul believed the division to be geographical, with Judea being the mission field of the pillars and the territories beyond Judea being his.[63] Alternatively, Paul may have understood this in terms of the ethnicity of the people being evangelized: he was to focus on evangelizing Gentiles, while Peter and the other Jewish Christian missionaries focused on taking the Gospel to fellow Jews throughout the Mediterranean and Levant. The second position seems more likely than the first, all the more as Peter was known to have

---

62. Longenecker, *Galatians*, 57; Aus, "Three Pillars and Three Patriarchs," 252–61.

63. See Burton, *Galatia*, 97–99.

evangelized throughout Greece and Rome and James was in touch with Jewish Christians throughout the Diaspora (in his letter).[64] But even this position does not align with the parties' future practice.

If Paul understood the agreement to entail a sharp division as to parties evangelized, agreeing to leave the mission to the Jews to Peter, it is strange to find Paul writing "to the Jews I became like a Jew, in order that I might win Jews; to those under the Law, as someone who was himself under the Law (even though I myself was not under the Law) in order that I might win those under the Law" (1 Cor 9:20). Was the "apostle to the Gentiles" dipping into Peter's pond? On the basis of such evidence, Ronald Fung concludes that the agreement only applied to "the primary direction in which each side was to apply its respective missionary efforts," thus "ensuring that there would be no rivalry and competition between the two sides." [65]

In theory, a Torah-observant mission to Jews and a Torah-free mission to Gentiles could both be affirmed as genuine works of God, and the "right hand of partnership" extended on that basis. It is clear from the events that follow that the implications of this agreement for what should happen when Jews and Gentiles came together in the church were, at the very least, not equally clear to all parties. What is especially strange is that the Antioch church was *already* a mixed congregation of Jewish and Gentile believers, and this issue appears not to have been addressed in this private meeting, leaving the door open for the conflict that would soon arise.[66]

The closing verse in this paragraph really connects with the close of 2:6 rather than the immediately preceding verse: "those of repute added nothing to me—only that that we should continue to remember the poor, which very thing I was eager to do" (2:6, 10).[67] Such a request

---

64. Betz, *Galatians*, 100; Longenecker, *Galatians*, 59.

65. Fung, *Galatians*, 100.

66. Martyn, *Galatians*, 222. Martyn also insightfully observes that the very terms of the agreement—one mission to Jews, another to Gentiles—were framed in such a way as to violate Paul's basic insight that, in Christ, there is no Jew or Gentile (Gal 3:28).

67. This contrasts sharply with Acts 15, where several stipulations, some quite pertinent to the notion of Gentile Christians making concessions to Jewish dietary scruples, are reported to have been added (see Acts 15:19–20, 28–29). Among other

on the part of the pillars, and such a response by Paul, would well suit the context of the visit narrated in Acts 11:28–30, if this private meeting occurred in connection with the delivery of famine relief funds collected in Antioch for the believers in Judea.[68] The pillars would be asking Paul and Barnabas to "continue to do" what they have been doing,[69] and Paul could rightly assert to the Galatians that he had already demonstrated his eagerness to do this very thing without their request. The willingness to make care for the needy in the Judean churches a part of his ministry among Gentile Christians (or mixed congregations) was already a valued sign of the unity of the two missions (the mission to the circumcised alongside the mission to the Gentiles) and would increasingly become a sign of the essential unity of the church, as Paul goes on to make the collection of relief funds for Jerusalem a major focus of his evangelizing work after the meeting with the pillars (see Rom 15:25–31; 1 Cor 16:1–4; 2 Cor 8:1—9:15).

2:11–14: THE ANTIOCH INCIDENT

[11]But when Cephas came into Antioch, I opposed him to his face because he stood condemned. [12]For before certain people came from James, he used to eat with the Gentiles. But when they came, he pulled back and separated himself out of regard for [or even "fear of"] those of the circumcision. [13]The rest of

---

factors, this weighs against an easy identification of the meeting reported in Gal 2:1–10 with the Jerusalem Conference as narrated in Acts 15.

68. Fung, *Galatians*, 103.

69. Longenecker (*Galatians*, 60) correctly observes that the present tense of the subjunctive verb ("that we should continue to remember") has the force of calling for an ongoing activity. This could include an activity that Paul and his team had already started, i.e., in the collection for famine relief. Longenecker (*Galatians*, 60) goes on to read this as a call to Paul and his team to "continue to keep the welfare of the Jerusalem believers in Jesus also in mind," doing nothing in their mission to Gentiles that would jeopardize, by association, the evangelistic efforts among Torah-observant Jews. While Longenecker has certainly hit on an important concern amongst Jewish Christians surrounding the Pauline mission, I do not think that "the poor" is already so well established as a self-designation for Jewish Christians in Judea (though it will become so by the emergence of the Ebionites, the "poor ones") to justify his expansion of the meaning of the call to "remember the poor."

> the Jews were also carried away with him in this charade, with the result that even Barnabas was dragged into their display of play-acting. [14]But when I saw that they were not walking in a straight line toward the truth of the message of the good news, I said to Cephas in front of everybody: "If you, a Jew, live in the manner of the Gentiles and not in the manner of the Jews, how can you force the Gentiles to turn themselves into Jews?"

Paul's narrative concludes with an account of the painful confrontation between Paul and Peter in Antioch, when Paul publically challenged Peter's behavior in front of the assembly. It is entirely possible that the rival teachers brought up this episode first, and did so as a means of discrediting the Pauline practice of encouraging Jewish and Gentile Christians to eat together without concern for all involved keeping kosher, perhaps even as a means of promoting the necessity of Gentile Christians adopting a Jewish way of life for the sake of the unity of the church. Paul does *not* report that his confrontation resulted in either Peter or Barnabas being persuaded to return to their original practice of eating with the Gentile Christians—a glaring omission if Paul had prevailed in that confrontation—which would be another reason to suspect that he must now discuss it to "set the record straight," as it were, about his own ultimate consistency with the "truth of the Gospel."

Paul gives no indication of Peter's purposes in visiting, being interested only in Peter's behavior in Antioch before and after the arrival of "some people from James." Paul must display his own constancy by describing the inconstant behavior of his apostolic colleagues, Peter and, most painfully, Barnabas. Paul tells the story of this incident in such a way as seems to answer the question, "Who really broke the agreement reached in Jerusalem?" In particular, he tells the story in such a way as denies the charge that *Paul* was responsible for breaking the agreement.

From both Paul's description of this incident and Luke's account of the mission both to Jews and Greeks in Syrian Antioch (Acts 11:19–20), it is clear that both Jewish and Gentile Christians were to be found in this church, and they displayed their unity, among other ways, by eating at a common table.[70] Peter himself appears to have understood that such

---

70. Haenchen, *Acts*, 609; Fung, *Galatians*, 107.

an arrangement, though in violation of Jewish purity regulations, was perfectly in keeping with the purity of the new people God had formed from Jews and Gentiles. Indeed, he may have been prepared for this situation himself by his previous experience with the centurion Cornelius and his household in Caesarea (Acts 10:1—11:18), though this would make his subsequent change in behavior all the more disappointing. So Peter himself joined in the practice of the Antiochene church, eating alongside fellow believers in Christ without regard for their ethnicity.[71]

From Paul's point of view, the "truth of the Gospel" (2:14)—the "One Body" fashioned by God out of Jew and Gentile, slave and free, male and female, all of whom are equally acceptable to God on the basis of Jesus' death—was being lived out here as Peter, Paul, Barnabas, Jewish Christians and Gentile Christians all shared the common life of the Spirit and had fellowship at table (perhaps most especially the Lord's Table, in the celebration of the Lord's Supper) as one people, one body. This is the "truth of the Gospel" that was jeopardized by Jewish Christians who wanted to see Gentile Christians circumcised and adopt Jewish practices in Gal 2:3–5, and the "truth of the Gospel" that Peter will himself shortly violate as he moves back to accept Torah's authority to divide Jewish Christians from Gentile Christians, treating the latter as polluting or unclean rather than sufficiently rendered pure by trust in Jesus and reception of the Holy Spirit (2:12–14).[72]

At some point, some men come to Antioch from the Jerusalem church, apparently as a delegation from James.[73] Paul does not name

71. Paul's use of the imperfect tense (*synēsthien*, "he used to eat together with," 2:12) indicates that Peter adopted this practice for some time.

72. See, further, deSilva, *Honor, Patronage, Kinship & Purity*, 280, 283–89.

73. There are signs of some confusion in the early manuscript tradition concerning the number of people who came from James, causing the trouble in Antioch. P[46], our earliest witness, reads "Before a certain person came from James, . . . but when he came . . ." (2:12). Codex Sinaiticus and Codex Vaticanus both support P[46] in regard, at least, to the singular "when he came" in the second half of the verse, though these read "before certain persons came from James" in the first half of the verse. Bruce Metzger (*A Textual Commentary on the New Testament*, 592–93) explains the tendency among some manuscripts, even very early ones, to read "when he came" as opposed to "when they came" as the result of the scribe being influenced by the fact that the three nearest verbs surrounding "when they came" are all third-person singular verbs. Hence "when they came" becomes "when he came" by assimilation

the purpose of their visit, but only the effects of their visit. These Jewish Christians clearly did not approve of Peter's practice of eating with Gentiles, even if they were fellow Christians. From their perspective, and perhaps from James's own perspective at this point, the Gospel did not free Jewish Christians from keeping kosher, whatever else it might mean for their lives. The question that Peter's Jewish Christian colleagues asked of him after the Cornelius episode would become a relevant question in Antioch as well: "Why did you go to uncircumcised people and eat with them?" (Acts 11:3). Unlike the Peter we find in Acts, however, the Peter Paul knows did not offer a persuasive response in defense of such a practice. Instead, Peter yielded to their pressure to return to a more respectable way of life for an "apostle to the circumcision," and he began eating at a separate, kosher table with the emissaries from the Jerusalem church.[74]

Paul attributes this change in behavior to Peter's "fear" of his fellow Jewish-Christian colleagues from Jerusalem, perhaps also involving "fear" of breaking with a position held by James. From Paul's point of view, "fear" kept Peter from continuing to walk in line with what he himself knew to be true about Jews and Gentiles "in Christ," namely that they were all cleansed by faith in Jesus and by reception of the Holy Spirit. From Peter's point of view, however, he was being motivated more by a desire, no doubt, to protect the Jewish mission and even the unity of the larger Christian movement by yielding to the visitors' interpretation of the implications of the earlier agreement.[75] What Paul called "fear," Peter might have called "not making an issue out of it," risking alienation and the splintering of the movement.

Peter's withdrawal from the common table appears to have stung the conscience of the Antiochene Jewish Christians, who then all felt the need to follow Peter's example, giving in to the pressure to observe

(in Greek, this only requires the change of one letter in the verb ending). P[46] would then be our lone witness to the possibility that one individual came from James rather than a team of two or more, hardly strong enough evidence to overthrow the witness of the other manuscripts to a "party" of people arriving in Antioch from Jerusalem.

74. Martyn suggests that he did so out of regard for his own mission to the Jews in Antioch, the people from James having pointed out how detrimental to his witness his non-observant lifestyle would be (*Galatians*, 242).

75. Longenecker, *Galatians*, 74; Fung, *Galatians*, 108.

kosher laws and eat separately from the Gentile converts. Since the celebration of the Lord's Supper involved eating, it is likely that this separation was observed also in connection with this rite.[76] In that context, the physical separation would make an especially poignant statement about the nature of the church of Jews and Gentiles. Paul's break with Barnabas over this issue must have been especially difficult for the apostle to the Gentiles, who stood shoulder-to-shoulder with Barnabas not long before in Jerusalem.

Paul twice refers to this change of practice in terms of "putting on a show": "The rest of the Jews were also carried away with him in this charade, with the result that even Barnabas was dragged into their display of play-acting" (2:13). Paul's point in speaking of their return to a kosher table as "hypocrisy" is that, in their hearts, neither Peter nor Barnabas nor the other Antiochene Jewish believers really believed that the Gentile Christians were still unclean; they were just unwilling to force the issue upon the representatives from the Jerusalem church by making such a forceful statement of their real convictions that "walking in line with the truth of the Gospel" would have required.

Were these "men from James," also described as "those of the circumcision," just Jewish Christian believers who were pressing other Jewish Christian believers to maintain the degrees of separation from Gentiles required by the Torah (and its then-current application)? Or were they "of the circumcision *party*," Jewish Christians who wanted to see Gentile Christians circumcised as part of their full initiation into the new people of God? From Paul's description of the events, the people from James were concerned only about the Christian *Jews'* adherence to Torah, and quite possibly only about Peter's behavior as the most visible missionary to the Jewish people.[77] It was not their intent to make the Gentiles into Jews, and Peter, Barnabas, and the others would no doubt have been confused by Paul's charge that they were "trying to compel the Gentiles to adopt a Jewish way of life" (2:14). They probably did not see what Paul saw with great clarity, namely that their change of behavior sent a clear message to their Gentile brothers and sisters: "you are not really acceptable to God on the basis of your trust in Jesus and your

---

76. Fee, *Galatians*, 74.

77. Bruce, *Paul*, 177.

reception of the Spirit, after all. If you want to find acceptance before God, and enjoy fellowship with God's people, you must make yourselves clean by circumcision and Torah observance."

It is from this perspective that Paul confronts Peter and, in his person, the other Jewish Christians as well, accusing them of not living in line with "the truth of the Gospel" (Gal 2:14). Paul understood that the Christian Jews' action placed an unspoken requirement on the Gentiles, undermining the sufficiency of the saving act of Jesus. Once again (as in Gal 2:3–5), it is Paul who courageously and uncompromisingly stands up for the truth of the Gospel—at a time when even Peter and Barnabas had been pressured by concern for human opinion to depart from walking in line with that Gospel. At this point we reach the climax of Paul's attempt to re-establish his credibility as an apostle: Whom besides Paul can the Galatians trust to tell them the truth of God?

Paul watched as the Antiochene church progressively divided into separate tables for Jewish and Gentile Christians, the resegregation of the One Body of Christ into its former categories of Jew and Greek. The image of the "one new person" in Christ was defaced, and the church reflected once again the divisions between people that belong to this present, evil age and not to the new creation.[78] Therefore, Paul publically confronted the man whose failure of nerve (in Paul's opinion) was directly responsible for this development. Within the honor culture of the ancient Greco-Roman world, Paul publically challenged Peter's honor with this question, trying to bring shame upon him for his action and, thereby, affect the behavior of the other Jewish Christians in the situation. Paul makes no mention of trying to confront Peter on this issue privately first, which might have been more in keeping with his own advice (see Gal 6:1).[79] Nevertheless, the public nature of Peter's actions and its impact upon the whole congregation called for these issues to be addressed publically at *some* point.

Paul opens his challenge with a question: "If you, a Jew, live in the manner of the Gentiles and not in the manner of the Jews, how can you force the Gentiles to turn themselves into Jews?" At the most basic level,

78. Compare Eph 2:11–16, which captures the essence of the Pauline Gospel from this angle.

79. Longenecker, *Galatians*, 79; Martyn, *Galatians*, 235.

Paul is calling attention to Peter's former practice of mingling freely with the Gentile Christians and not regulating his interaction with them in accordance with the hedges that Torah and its then-current interpretation placed around the Jewish people, to keep them separate from the nations. Paul is appealing to this practice as the rule most in line with Peter's own ongoing convictions.[80] If the "people from James" hadn't come, he would still be "living like a Gentile" insofar as he would still not be following the Jewish regulations for keeping separate in regard to foods.[81] Luke's portrait of Peter's early experience with Gentile believers would also lead us to conclude that Peter's personal position would have remained aligned with the heavenly voice that spoke to him within his dream: "What God has cleansed, do not call profane" (Acts 10:15).

That Paul is here appealing to Peter based on Peter's deeply held convictions, temporarily suppressed because of the political considerations of the situation, is reinforced by the immediately following verse: "We who are Jews by birth . . . *know*" (Gal 2:15). In light of the knowledge that Paul and Peter know that they share, Peter's retreat to a Torah-observant life that reintroduces ethnic divisions into the new people of God is inexcusable. Moreover, so is the corollary, namely that, if there is to be a united body again, it would have to be within the narrow confines of Torah observance by *all* parties—thus compelling the Gentile Christians to make Jews of themselves.

The verb "to live," however, is a multifaceted word in Galatians. Even if Paul begins here by referring to matters of daily conduct—whether to regulate one's eating and one's company at the table by Torah or not—he very quickly moves on to speak of "living" in a much greater sense, the sense of "coming alive to God" and to the life of God's Spirit and God's Son living within and through oneself:

---

80. Fung, Galatians, 110; Longenecker, *Galatians*, 78.

81. This was a distinctive mark of Jews throughout the Diaspora, and, indeed, the food regulations were geared specifically toward maintaining Jewish social and cultural identity *through* separateness from non-Jews, especially in largely Gentile areas. See 3 Macc 3:3–4; deSilva, *Introducing the Apocrypha*, 315–17; idem, *Honor, Patronage, Kinship & Purity*, 260–62, 270–71.

> Through the Law I died to the Law, so that I might live to God.
> I was crucified along with Christ. It is no longer "me" living,
> but Christ lives in me. (2:19–20a)

> If a Law had been given that could bring a person to life, then
> righteousness really would come into being on the basis of the
> Law. (3:21)

> If we have come alive by the Spirit, let us order our steps in line
> with the Spirit. (5:25)

Foundational to Paul's opposition to regulating life in the new community in line with Torah (and its intentional reinforcement of the Jew-Gentile distinctions) is the fact that Torah played no role in bringing either the Jew or the Gentile to life in this greater sense. Coming alive to God, to the life that *is* life, all happened through trusting Jesus and receiving the Holy Spirit and, therefore, all happened for the Jew and the Gentile in precisely the same way.

The Antioch incident raised an important question beyond the question of whether or not Gentiles need to be circumcised to be part of God's covenant people in Christ, though that fundamental question had not yet been agreed upon by all parties concerned either. If there was to be "one new people" formed in Christ from Jews and Gentiles, on whose terms would the new people conduct themselves? Paul and the rival teachers that come to Galatia, at least, arrived at different answers to this question. The rival teachers present an alternative solution to the problem of the separate tables in Antioch: we can be "one new people" as long as Gentile converts accept circumcision and take on other defining Jewish practices, so that eating with them would not require Jewish Christians to violate the laws of *kashrut* (i.e., "keeping kosher," "clean" in all one ingests and with whom one ingests it). Paul's solution—which apparently was Peter's solution for at least a short time—was to practice mutual acceptance at the Lord's Table, valuing the cleansing that came upon both Jew and Gentile by faith and the Spirit as sufficiently "kosher" for all parties concerned.

It is likely that Paul was the one who left the field defeated after his argument with Peter.[82] If it were otherwise, he would probably have added that Peter was won back to his former practice against the position of the "people from James." The transformation of the Antioch church into a partitioned church with Jewish Christians placing adherence to Torah in all its particulars ahead of trust in Jesus as sufficient to set the "Gentile sinners" apart for God and for free interaction with God's people may have given the impetus for some believers there to travel to the daughter churches throughout Galatia to promote the new solution to the problem, namely calling for circumcision and Torah observance among Gentile Christians. The rival teachers whom Paul opposes in Galatia may thus themselves have been Antiochene Jewish Christians seeking to clean up after Paul in the churches that fell within the authority and under the auspices of the church in Antioch.[83] They could claim to do so, moreover, with the authority of the "pillars" behind them, though the one pillar, James, would have been sufficiently happy with Jewish Christian observance of Torah and separate tables for the celebration of the Lord's Supper.

The Antioch incident provides a close analogy to the Galatian situation (though the rival teachers are not to be identified with the "men from James" and may not, in the end, even have come from the Antioch church).[84] Paul asserts that the rival teachers, like Peter, seek to uphold the old boundaries drawn around the Jewish people by the Torah because they are afraid to tell their fellow Jews (especially non-Christian Jews) the truth about God's abolition of those boundaries in his new outpouring of favor in Christ. They do not, in other words, "walk in line with the truth of the Gospel." Just as Paul spoke the truth in Antioch—quite possibly to his own hurt in terms of losing that argument—he will speak the truth in Galatia, without consideration for his own advantage or what is politic.

---

82. Dunn, *Galatians*, 12; Martyn, *Galatians*, 236.

83. Dunn, *Galatians*, 14.

84. Witherington, *Grace in Galatia*, 24.

2:15–21: PAUL'S POSITION

[15]We are Jews by nature and not sinners from the Gentiles, [16]and we know that a person is not brought into line with God's righteousness on the basis of the works of Torah except through Jesus Christ's faithfulness [or, "by trusting Jesus Christ"]. So even we have put our trust in Jesus Christ in order that we might be brought into line with God's righteousness through Christ's faithfulness [or, "by trusting Christ"] and not on the basis of works of Torah, since not all flesh will be justified on the basis of works of Torah. [17]But if while trying to be brought in line with God's righteousness in Christ we ourselves are also discovered to be "sinners," then is Christ a servant of sin? By no means! [18]For if I build up again the things I tore down, I turn myself into a transgressor. [19]For I died to the Torah through the Torah, in order that I might live to God. I have been crucified along with Christ. [20]It's not me living any longer, but Christ is living in me. What I'm now living in the flesh, I live by trusting in God's Son, who loved me and gave himself up on my behalf. [21]I do not set aside God's generous kindness. For if righteousness *comes* through Torah, then Christ died for nothing.

In 2:15–21, Paul provides supporting argumentation for the rhetorical question with which Paul introduces this larger statement of his position. If we were to restate 2:14 as a proposition rather than as a question, and fill it out a bit in light of the argumentation that follows, we should probably read: "We cannot impose a Jewish identity and way of life upon Gentile Christians since we Jewish Christians have come to understand that, in Christ, the practices that separate Jews as 'clean' from Gentiles as 'unclean' have no meaning, since Jews and Gentiles are both alike 'cleansed' by faith and the Spirit."

Paul begins his elaboration of his position in a way that plays to Jewish prejudices against Gentiles.[85] To be a "Jew by birth" (literally, "a Jew by nature," hence "born a Jew") carries with it the great advantage of having been born into God's covenant people and under the Torah,

85. Fung, *Galatians*, 112–13; Longenecker, *Galatians*, 83; Martyn, *Galatians*, 248–49.

the gracious provision of God for the ongoing covenant relationship between God and this people. All other ethnic groups, lumped together indistinguishably as "Gentiles," are "sinners" by definition since they live outside of God's Law and covenant (2:15). Gentiles don't even have the *path* to becoming righteous before God, that is, to being anything *but* a sinner. While Paul opens as if embracing this Jewish view of humanity, its divisions, and the ethnic privilege of the Jewish people, he will shortly sweep it all away (much as he will do in greater detail and with greater finesse later in Rom 1:18—3:20).

The sentence in which he sweeps this all away, however, is perhaps the densest and most debated in all of Pauline literature (Gal 2:16). In order to come to a clear understanding of the essence of Paul's position and what is, for him, at stake in the debate in Galatia, we need to grasp what he means in three key phrases, each of which appears multiple times in 2:16 alone: (1) What does Paul mean by "being justified" (*dikaiousthai*)? (2) What does Paul mean by "works of the Law" (*erga nomou*)? (3) What does Paul mean when he speaks of "the faith (or faithfulness) of Jesus Christ" (*pistis Christou*)?

What Does Paul Mean by "Seeking to Be Justified" and "Being Justified"?

Because the question "What is justification?" is a central question in Christian theology, and because Paul's letters (especially Galatians and Romans) are at the center of the scriptural foundation for any theology of justification, I cannot treat the theological question as fully as it merits here. The verb is very much at home in courtroom settings in the classical world, where it is the duty of the court to "give justice," whether to punish or to acquit. In the passive sense, it tends to mean "to be given justice" or "to be acquitted" or "vindicated." Arguably, then, where the context suggests a setting of legal inquiry and examination (e.g., when God comes to judge the world and settle accounts), this set of forensic meanings would come into play, and, in Scripture, usually the positive sense of "being acquitted." The verb also carries the meanings of "to set right," derived from, but of potentially larger scope than, the courtroom meanings. "To set things right" can mean more than to "give justice" or "vindicate." It can include the reordering of a situation such that injustice is undone, disorder restored to order, and the like. It can also be used to mean, "to deem right," in the sense of deeming some action appropriate to take (with that action being provided by a verb in the infinitive).[86]

A forensic setting is not made explicit in Galatians, although Paul's reconfiguration of Ps 143:2 ("do not enter into judgment with your slave, for no living being will be acquitted before you") at the end of Gal 2:16 suggests that God's judgment is very much in the back of Paul's mind. The place of the last judgment in Paul's thought generally (Rom 2:5–11; 3:6; 2 Cor 5:9–10; 2 Thess 1:5–12), as well as the frequent forensic context of the verb "to justify" (in the LXX, *diakaioō*) in the Old Testament scriptures that inform Paul's thought and the literature of near-contemporary Jewish groups, might also allow us to assume this context.[87]

We might provisionally understand "seeking to be justified" (2:16) as investing oneself in that path that would lead to being acquitted before God's judgment seat by virtue of living up to God's righteous standards, or by virtue of being brought in line with God's righteous standards. This would certainly be the motivation of those who turned to "works of the Law" as the revelation of those standards, those behaviors that God would approve and accept. Conforming one's life to the vision for life communicated in the Law was chosen as a path toward being "set right" in God's sight and, therefore, "acquitted" before God at the judgment. An important insight here is that pursuing acquittal by means of works of the Law suggests that acquittal ("justification") is the still-future goal driving an entire lifestyle adjustment, to which lifestyle one commits for the remainder of one's life "in the flesh."[88]

Moreover, this would be the same goal that Paul sees himself and other Jewish Christian believers like Peter pursuing by means of "placing trust in Jesus." Paul promotes "trust in Jesus" as that which opened

86. Liddell, Scott, Jones, *A Greek-English Lexicon*, 429.

87. Schrenk, "*dikaioō*," 211–19, especially pp. 217–18.

88. Longenecker, *Galatians*, 85: "the four uses of the verb in vv 16–17 and the noun in v 21cannot be treated as simply 'transfer terms' [i.e., justification as transfer into the people of God] when the issue at both Antioch and Galatia had to do with the lifestyle of those who were already believers in Jesus."

up for them (and, of course, for all disciples, Jewish or Gentile) a better way to the same end, indeed as *the* way that actually led to that end since "righteousness" does not come through the Law (2:21). It is significant that Paul chooses the noun "righteousness" (*dikaiosunē*) to correspond with the verb "to make right" (*dikaioō*) in this context, as opposed to the noun "acquittal," "justification" (*dikaiōsis*). "Righteousness" (an ethical quality), and not merely a forensic verdict, is that for which the Christian hopes (5:5), something that may not come through the Law (2:21) but, it is implied, can come by virtue of what Jesus secured for his followers by means of his obedient death (or, perhaps better, what God provided—the "favor" or "gift" that Paul refuses to toss aside by now turning back to the Law).

We would add to this puzzle a third piece: the fact that Paul *antici-pates* justification—being acquitted before God—as a result of trusting in Jesus and walking in the new life and the new power of the Spirit that Jesus' death makes available to human beings. At no point in Galatians does he speak of "justification" or "acquittal" as an already-accomplished fact.[89] In Gal 2:16–17, Paul writes about himself and his Jewish Christian colleagues that "we trusted in Christ Jesus in order that we might be acquitted as a result of trusting in Jesus and not as a result of [doing] works of the Law" (2:16). The fact that Paul employed a purpose clause here ("we believed . . . in order to be acquitted"; so also 3:24) is not determinative for this point, but it is interesting that he did not instead employ a result clause, which would have unambiguously placed the experience of acquittal in the past ("we trusted in Christ Jesus *with the result that* we *were* acquitted"). Paul's paraphrase of Ps 143:2 speaks of acquittal strictly in the future tense: "no flesh *will be acquitted* on the basis of works" (2:16). Most telling, Paul speaks about what might happen "while seeking to be acquitted in Christ . . ." (2:17). "Seeking to be justified" describes a pursuit, a quest still in process after any initial response of trusting in Christ. That "seeking to be justified" or "acquit-

---

89. He will speak of "justification" more in terms of forgiveness of sins, and therefore reconciliation with God (that is, more in the terms that we are accustomed to associate with "justification"), when he comes around to writing Romans (see Rom 4:3–8; 5:10–11), though his interest in acquittal at the last judgment remains unabated there.

ted" is a process leading to "acquittal" in the future is reinforced in the following paragraph, as Paul speaks about the importance of finishing the process begun by trust in Jesus (3:3): it is important to Paul that the disciples continue to walk in line with the path opened up for them by trusting in Jesus, specifically so that they can arrive at the end or goal of that path.

In Galatians, then, it would seem that Paul is looking forward to acquittal before God's judgment seat, and that he regards trusting in Jesus—in the efficacy of Jesus' death for his sins, in the efficacy of Jesus' death for redeeming him from the curse of the Law, in the efficacy of Jesus' death for securing for him the blessing promised to Abraham, namely the Holy Spirit, and in the efficacy of the Spirit to bring righteousness to life in him, to nurture within him the fruit that pleases God, to form Christ in him and thus transform him into someone who is righteous in God's sight—as the path to acquittal. The death of Christ, as Romans would develop further but as Paul hints at here when he speaks twice about Jesus' death "for our sins" (1:4; 2:20), certainly means acquittal before God now in regard to past misdeeds, on behalf of which Christ offered his own obedience to the point of death as an act of atonement and reconciliation.[90] But Christ's obedient death also opens the way for us to be deemed righteous at the last judgment on the basis of the transformation God is working within us by means of his Spirit, to whose guidance and empowerment we must yield so that Christ can be formed in us (2:20; 4:19). It is an acquittal, but an acquittal on the basis of setting things right.

"Being justified" is not here limited to what happens *prior to* sanctification, as happens in many constructions of a "systematic" theology. An element of justification happens in Christ's reconciliation of sinners to God such that they may receive God's favor (notably, the gift of God's Holy Spirit, the Spirit of God's Son), but "being acquitted before God" happens finally *after* sanctification and *as a result* of God's sanctifying work in us.[91] This may be how Paul is able to say to believers that those

90. Fee (*Galatians*, 83) defines "justification" thus to mean that "both Jews and Gentiles together have received their pardon and right standing with God through the work of Christ."

91. This suggests "perhaps a greater unity between justification and sanctifica-

who continue in the works of the flesh "will not inherit the kingdom of God" (5:19–21), that is, will not find acquittal, but rather exclusion, and encourage his hearers to keep sowing to the Spirit (and walking in the Spirit, and so forth) so as to reap from the Spirit's increase "eternal life" (6:7–10). All of this remains "God's favor" or "God's gift" (Gal 2:21), rather than opening the door for our attempts to "earn acquittal," since our "being set right" and our "being made over into righteous people" all happens by God's gracious initiative and by God's provision of the means for our transformation from beginning to end.[92]

What Does Paul Mean by "Works of the Law"?

Paul asserts that people will not be acquitted before God on the basis of "works of the Law." We will understand what "works" Paul has in mind here if we take seriously his own qualification of these "works" as "works of the Law," that is, "works prescribed by the Torah, the Law given to the Jewish people." The mutually exclusive alternatives in Galatians are not "faith" versus "works." Paul's polemic against "works of the Law" is not a polemic against "good works," as this is commonly but erroneously understood.[93] Paul certainly expects the Spirit to produce all manner

tion than has often been supposed" (Hooker, "ΠΙΣΤΙΣ ΧΡΙΣΤΟΥ," 342). See also Longenecker's unwillingness to divorce forensic senses of "being justified" from the ethical dimension of becoming "righteous" (*Galatians*, 84–85), as well as Dunn's similar discussion of "righteousness" ("New Perspective," 207–8).

92. This view of "being justified" coheres with Paul's later development of the theme of justification in Romans. First, it takes seriously Paul's declaration that "God shows no partiality" (Rom 2:11). God does not treat Jews (God's chosen people) any differently from Gentiles at the judgment just because they have a special relationship with him (Rom 2:5–10). Any human judge who did so would rightly be called a partial judge, a perverter of justice. Christians should not expect partiality from God at the judgment either. Second, it takes seriously Paul's formulation that "just as through the trespass of one man the many became sinners, just so through the obedience of the one the many will become just" (Rom 5:19). The language in both halves of this verse is the same, such that, if we read the first to say that people *really* became sinners and did what is sinful before God, then we must read the second to say that people will *really* become righteous and do what is righteous before God as a result of living from the life of Jesus, the new Adam.

93. J. D. G. Dunn, *Romans 1–8*, lxvii–lxx; ibid, *Theology*, 354–59, 365; Barclay, *Obeying the Truth*, 82. Or, as Sanders (*Paul, the Law, and the Jewish People*, 159) aptly

of "good works" in the life of the disciple (Gal 5:13–25; Rom 2:6–11; 6:12–13; Eph 2:10), and if "neither circumcision nor uncircumcision has any force in Christ," it is stunning to read what *does* have force: "faith *working* through love" (Gal 5:6).

We should also bear in mind the narrative that provided the context for Paul's exposition of his position, namely the Antioch episode in which practices of Torah were reinstated for Jewish Christians with the result that the One Body was pulled apart again along ethnic divisions at separate tables. In this context, "works of the Torah" particularly signals those practices that had historically set Jews apart from Gentiles (see *Jubilees* 22.16; *Letter of Aristeas* 139, 142; 3 Macc 3:3–4).[94] Remaining "holy" to the Lord entailed remaining distinct and separate from people who did not live by Torah, namely the Gentiles and, quite often, unobservant Jews.

Paul sees a positive function in this, but also sees that Torah was intended to serve that function only for a limited time (3:19–25). With the death and resurrection of Jesus, God had manifested God's desire to extend the promise and the blessing to all the nations, something that "zeal for the Torah" quite thoroughly inhibited. To reintroduce "works of the Torah" like circumcision, dietary regulations, and observance of the Jewish sacred calendar now after the "fullness of time" would be to work against God's purposes for bringing the promise given to Abraham to all people in the new community of Christ, in which the divisions and hierarchies sustained by the labels "Jew," "Gentile," "slave," "free," "male," and "female" are transcended (Gal 3:28). In trying to remain "true" to the Law, non-Christian Jews and Judaizing Christians were, in Paul's understanding, betraying the Law, not observing that its "goal" had been reached in the coming of Christ. Insisting on "works of the Torah" meant trying to re-erect the "dividing wall of hostility" at a time when God had torn it down in Christ and in the outpouring of

states, "The supposed conflict between 'doing' as such and 'faith' as such is simply not present in Galatians."

94. Bruce, *Galatians*, 29; Dunn, "New Perspective," 191–94. Barclay (*Obeying the Truth*, 78) observes most clearly how "the immediate context of the Antioch dispute makes clear that 'works of the law' is equivalent to 'living like a Jew', and Paul's point is that this distinctively Jewish pattern of behavior is not an essential feature of justification, either for Jews or anyone else."

the Spirit (cf. Gal 2:18; Eph 2:11–16), thus acting in open defiance of God. Foundational to Paul's position against regulating life in the new community in line with Torah (and its intentional reinforcement of the Jew-Gentile distinctions) is the fact that Torah played no role in bringing either the Jew or the Gentile to life in this greater sense. Coming alive to God, to the life that *is* life, all happened through trusting Jesus and receiving the Holy Spirit and, therefore, all happened for the Jew and the Gentile in precisely the same way.

While scholars like James Dunn are right to suggest that "works of the Law" such as circumcision, food laws, and Sabbath observance must be foremost on Paul's mind as he remembers Antioch and addresses Galatia, Paul would not exclude other elements of the Torah from among the "works of the Law" that do not lead to acquittal as righteous people before God. Paul considers Torah as a *whole* throughout this letter, pointing out its indivisibility (5:3). The Torah as a holistic system of conduct, with its ethical, ritual, and boundary-maintaining regulations, was a temporary measure in God's economy. Its authority was instituted for a particular people 430 years after Abraham, and its authority came to an end "in the fullness of time" with the coming of faith. Its authority, purview, and promise come to an end for individual people as they accept their adoption as sons and daughters of God, as children rather than slaves in God's household, as "grown-ups" in God (Gal 3:15—4:7).

We need to be cautious lest we continue to allow Paul's rhetoric to make us view Judaism as a "works-based" religion that is somehow "external" and "legalistic." God's giving of the Torah to Moses was regarded as an expression of God's incredible *grace* toward Israel, the gift of a covenant with the One God that God did not make with any other nation.[95] Living in line with the Torah was not typically seen as a means of earning God's grace.[96] It was rather the grateful response to the God

---

95. See Sir 24:1–23; 4 Macc 5:22–26; Dunn, *Galatians*, 16–17.

96. There are some striking passages, of course, that speak of "earning" justification (as acquittal at the judgment) by the doing of works, where the individual earns eternal reward or punishment by doing or transgressing God's law. Fourth Ezra explicitly affirms that having "a storehouse of works" with God brings a reward (4 Ezra 7:77; 8:33). When Ezra claims that God will show his righteousness and goodness by showing mercy to those who "have no store of good works" (4 Ezra 8:32, 36), he is sharply corrected by God (4 Ezra 8:37–40). A text from Qumran, *4QMMT*, explicitly

who had graced Israel with the unique privileges of a covenant relationship, and a means by which to remain within that covenant relationship and enjoy its blessings. Moreover, God had generously made provisions for failure to observe the covenant in the form of sacrifices, so that forgiveness and reconciliation remained available. Such provisions show that "flawless performance" was not expected.

What Does Paul Mean by "the Faith of Christ"?

The Greek phrase *pistis Iēsou* or *pistis Christou* ("the faith of Jesus" or "the faith of Christ") or an equivalent appears at several crucial points in Paul's discussions about how people can pursue justification in God's sight, often set over against "works of the Law" as the rejected alternative (Gal 2:16 [twice]; 3:22; Rom 3:22, 26; Phil 3:9; see also the similar phrase in Gal 2:20). There are two challenges in the interpretation or translation of this phrase. The first is lexical, since *pistis* can have several different meanings. According to three standard dictionaries used in classical and biblical studies, the principal senses are:

LSJM

1. Trust (in others), faith, confidence

2. That which gives confidence (e.g., assurance, proof)

BAGD

1. "that which causes trust and faith," hence "faithfulness," "proof," "pledge"

2. "trust, confidence, faith in the active sense"

3. "that which is believed," "body of faith," "doctrine"

---

claims that doing the "works of the Law" as outlined by the author of this text leads to justification before God "at the end time" (*4QMMT* 30): "It will be reckoned for you as righteousness when you perform what is right and good before Him" (*4QMMT* 31; Vermes, *The Complete Dead Sea Scrolls in English*, 228). Moreover, *m. Aboth* 3:16 declares that "the world is judged by grace, yet all is according to the excess of works." Such a connection between "works" and acquittal at the last judgment is not completely foreign to the New Testament, however. The visions of the last judgment in Matt 25:31–46; Rom 2:5–11; 2 Cor 5:9–10; and Rev 20:12 all say that people will be judged according to their deeds. Paul also speaks of (bad) works resulting in exclusion from the kingdom (e.g., Gal 5:19–21; 1 Cor 6:9–11).

Louw-Nida

31.43 *pistis*[a]

"that which is completely believable," "what can be fully believed," hence "proof"

31.85 *pistis*[b]

"faith, trust"

31.88 *pistis*[c]

"trustworthiness, dependability, faithfulness"

31.102 *pistis*[d]

"[Christian] faith"

31.104 *pistis*[e]

"the content of what Christians believe," hence "the faith, beliefs, doctrines"

33.289 *pistis*[f]

"promise, pledge to be faithful"

In Gal 2:15–16, we are chiefly concerned with two possible meanings: *pistis*[b] ("faith, trust") and *pistis*[c] ("trustworthiness, dependability, faithfulness").[97]

The second issue is grammatical, and concerns what nuance we should understand the genitival relationship between the two nouns to convey from among quite a varied spectrum of possibilities. Nouns in the genitive case generally give greater specificity to, and thus limit, another noun by adding a descriptor. In essence, a noun in the genitive case is set in relationship to another noun (say, "love") to supply an answer to a question like "Whose love?" "What kind of love" "Love for whom?" "Love from what source?" In the phrase *pistis Christou*, this genitival relationship tends to be construed either as "subjective," with the noun "Christ" answering the question "Whose *pistis*?" or as "objective," with the noun "Christ" answering the question "*Pistis* towards whom?" or "*Pistis* whither directed?" A different example of the difference between a subjective and objective genitive can be found in the statement, "The love of Christ [*agapē Christou*] compels us" (2 Cor

---

97. The sense of *pistis*[e], "the faith, beliefs, doctrines," did appear in Gal 1:24.

5:14) Is it love *for* Christ, or Christ's love (for us), that compels Paul and his team to preach the Gospel?

These two sets of variables produce four principal possibilities for the interpretation of the phrase *pistis Christou*:

a. Trust directed toward Jesus, reliance on Jesus

b. Faithfulness or loyalty directed toward Jesus

c. Jesus' trust in God, or his reliance on God

d. Jesus' faithfulness toward God (or possibly toward Jesus' followers)

Almost all modern translation resolve the ambiguity of the phrase in favor of the first of these four options. An increasing number of scholars, however, have been arguing that the phrase would be better translated in line with either the third or fourth of these options.

The issue of how to interpret this phrase is fraught with theological significance for most of those scholars who have engaged this particular debate. One theological concern focuses on the "basis" for justification in Paul, whether that basis should be seen as the person's faith or trust in Jesus or Jesus' faithfulness toward God. In a sort of hyper-Lutheranism, some scholars have ranted against interpreting the phrase as "trust in Jesus" because to do so would, in effect, make "faith" itself into a "work," resulting in just another kind of "justification by works."[98] Resolving the translation in favor of "Jesus' faithfulness," on the other hand, keeps Jesus' own obedience to God to the point of death in focus as the basis for the justification of the believer.[99]

As has not always been clear in the debate thus far, the resolution of the single phrase *pistis Christou* (or its equivalent) in a mere six verses out of Paul's whole body of writing jeopardizes neither theological

---

98. Hooker, "ΠΙΣΤΙΣ ΧΡΙΣΤΟΥ," 321–42, especially 341. Something of the same appears to be operative in Richard B. Hays, "ΠΙΣΤΙΣ and Pauline Christology: What Is at Stake?," 35–60, especially 46, when he writes that reading the phrase as "faith in Christ," that is, as an objective genitive, "verges on blasphemous self-absorption in our own religious subjectivity."

99. Hooker, "ΠΙΣΤΙΣ ΧΡΙΣΤΟΥ," 337–38.

concern—although the theological concerns definitely jeopardize the exegesis of these verses! First, as we have seen above, Paul is not setting "faith in Christ" or "Christ's faithfulness" over against "works" as "any human acts," but rather over against "works of the Law," those acts performed out of an attempt to fall in line with God's righteous standards by conforming one's life to the Torah. "Faith in Christ" will never, then, become a "work" of the kind that concerns Paul (especially of the sort that perpetuates the barriers between Jew and Gentile and the religious hegemony and privilege of the former). If "faith in Christ" is a "work" at all, it is a "work" that aligns with God's purposes for tearing down those ethnic barriers, for the formation of the one people of the One God, the God of Jew and Gentile.

More importantly, however, the "prior question that Paul's antithesis was meant to answer" is not "What has saving power, works or faith?"[100] or "what is the basis on which we are justified?" The question is closer to "what path will lead us toward successfully conforming our lives to the standards of a righteous God, in whose eyes we seek to be acquitted?" There simply is no danger of an objective reading ("faith in Christ") leading to making "faith" a new "work" such that our own believing becomes the basis for our own justification or deliverance. That *basis* is still the beneficent self-giving of Jesus on our behalf and God's gracious provision of the Holy Spirit. This basis, moreover, is explicitly named throughout Galatians quite apart from the resolution of the translation of *pistis Christou* (see Gal 1:4; 2:20–21; 3:10–14), so that this theological concern remains secure as well.[101]

"Faith in Christ" is merely our response of recognizing *that* basis as adequate and recognizing Jesus as a trustworthy and reliable mediator of God's favor and agent of reconciliation,[102] such that we receive their gifts and enter into the reciprocal relationship of grace and response to grace into which God in Christ invites us as the means and venue for our justification (our transformation, by God's Spirit's working within us, into people who reflect God's righteousness). That said, a resolu-

100. Matlock, "Even the Demons Believe," 313.

101. So also, rightly, Martyn, *Galatians*, 271; Watson, "By Faith (of Christ)," 147–63, especially p. 163.

102. So rightly van Daalen, "'Faith' according to Paul," 83–85, especially p. 84.

tion in favor of the "subjective genitive" (i.e., "Jesus' faithfulness") does not diminish the necessary place of "trust" as human response in Paul's theology at all, for the benefits of Jesus' death on our behalf are still only given to those who trust in, or rely on, Jesus ("even we have relied on Jesus in order that we might be acquitted before God," Gal 2:16; cf. Rom 3:22).[103]

The arguments in favor of interpreting the phrase as a subjective genitive, then, are briefly as follows: (1) This reading has the advantage of maintaining parallelism between the "faith of Jesus" (2:16) and the "faith of Abraham" (3:6–9). No one would suggest that we translate the latter as "believing in Abraham." As a fully human being, Jesus, too, needed to have and to demonstrate trust in and reliance on God, especially as the God who raises the dead.[104] Abraham demonstrated trust in God; Jesus, the "seed" of Abraham, demonstrated the same faith or faithfulness toward God; thus the blessing promised to Abraham and to his Seed is secured for all who likewise trust.[105] (2) It also has the advantage of avoiding the redundancy inherent in the traditional interpretation, which, if followed, means that the disciple's trust is mentioned three times in a single verse (Gal 3:22).[106] (3) In regard to the occurrences of the phrase in Rom 3:22–26 it is argued that Paul uses subjective genitives in connection with *pistis* at Rom 3:3; 4:12, 16, and therefore could not expect his hearers to construe the genitive constructions involving *pistis* in the *pistis Christou* constructions in Rom 3:22, 26 as objective genitives.[107]

These arguments, however, are ultimately not strong enough to justify a coup d'état in biblical translation. (1) The example of Abraham points equally well, if not more strongly, in the direction of understanding *pistis Christou* as "trust in Christ," since it is specifically Abraham's

---

103. Hooker, "ΠΙΣΤΙΣ ΧΡΙΣΤΟΥ," 337.

104. Contra James Dunn, *Theology*, 382.

105. Hooker, "ΠΙΣΤΙΣ ΧΡΙΣΤΟΥ," 325–31.

106. Hays, *Faith of Jesus Christ*, 158, 171–72; Campbell, *The Rhetoric of Righteousness*, 62–63; Hooker, "ΠΙΣΤΙΣ ΧΡΙΣΤΟΥ," 322, 329, though she admits that Paul is no stranger to redundancy.

107. Hays, *Faith of Jesus Christ*, 171; idem, "Pauline Christology," 47; Campbell, *Rhetoric of Righteousness*, 66–67; Stowers, *A Rereading of Romans*, 201.

"trust in God" that Paul highlights as the response that led to Abraham's justification (Gal 3:6, 9; Gen 15:6).[108] This is also the sense of Paul's use of Hab 2:4 in Galatians, where Paul has eliminated the word "my" from the original text so as to remove the possibility of a subjective genitive ("my faith," "my faithfulness") and to leave "trusting" God as the alternative to "doing" the Torah (Gal 3:11–12). Hooker's attempt to argue in favor of "Jesus' faith" rather than "faith in Jesus" on the basis of the unlikelihood of translating *pistis Abraham* as "faith in Abraham" is fundamentally flawed insofar as Abraham is *never* explicitly named as a potential object of faith in Pauline discourse (though reliance on Abraham for acquittal before God is conceivable in the first century; see Matt 3:7–9), but Jesus is on numerous occasions (even in this immediate context, Gal 2:16).[109]

(2) Redundancy is the hallmark of Gal 2:16, in particular. Apart from the occurrences of "trust in Christ" (*pistis Christou*) and "we trusted in Christ" (*eis Christon episteusamen*) in this verse, there is a threefold repetition of the verb "to be justified" and of the phrase "works of the Law": "knowing that a person (i) *is not justified* (i) *on the basis of works of the Law* . . . in order that (ii) *we might be justified* . . . not (ii) *on the basis of works of the Law*, because (iii) *on the basis of works of the Law* not all flesh (iii) *will be justified*." The presence of such obvious, triple redundancy in regard to the theme of "justification on the basis of works of the Law" mitigates the force of any objection regarding redundancy of the theme of trusting in Christ. Indeed, the threefold repetition of

---

108. Dunn, *Galatians*, 139.

109. As Barry Matlock ("Demons," 304) appropriately points out, the fact that subjective genitive relationships involving *pistis* are more common in Paul than objective genitives is simply to be expected, and not significant. If the noun accompanying *pistis* is not God or Christ, the possibility of an objective genitive doesn't even arise. Surveying the usage of *pistis* in Plutarch, Matlock ("Demons," 304) found that *pistis* is used in the sense of "faith, trust, confidence" about forty times. Half the time the object of trust is not explicated. When the object is explicitly named, five times it is indicated by the preposition *pros*, once by *peri*, and thirteen times by the object of trust named as a noun in the genitive case. He does not seek thereby to create prejudice *for* an objective genitive reading in Paul, but to provide counterevidence to the trend in the debate to speak of the objective genitive as less natural (or even improbable).

"works of the Law" as well as "to justify" might "just as well be thought to *demand* a threefold repetition of 'faith in Christ.'"[110]

(3) The fact that Paul uses subjective genitives in connection with *pistis* at Rom 3:3; 4:12, 16 does not tip the balance in favor of reading the genitive constructions involving *pistis* at Rom 3:22, 26 as subjective genitives. The context of each fresh occurrence determines which sense of *pistis* will be invoked and what relationship the genitive case will be understood to indicate.[111] The contrast in Rom 3:1–3 between God and the "faithless" or "unreliable" people of God determines the selection of "faithfulness" as the appropriate sense for *pistis* and the selection of a subjective genitival relationship between "God" and "faithfulness" to form an appropriate contrast with Israel's "faithlessness." The context of discussing Abraham (Rom 4:12, 16) as an exemplar of the faith (notably, "faith in God") that leads to justification determines the selection of "faith" or "trust" for *pistis* and the construal of Abraham as the one who is displaying "faith" (hence, a subjective genitive). The question remains, then: what sense of *pistis* and what relationship between the noun *pistis* and the genitive noun *Christou* does the context of Rom 3:22, 26 and, more importantly for this commentary, Gal 2:16 invoke?

To these refutations of the positive arguments in favor of reading *pistis Christou* as a subjective genitive, scholars have added the following arguments in favor of retaining the objective genitive reading:

(4) Christians closer to Paul in terms of linguistic and cultural context—church fathers like Origen and Chrysostom—read the relevant passages as speaking about "trust in Christ," not as speaking about "Christ's faith" or "Christ's faithfulness." In several instances the church father does not gloss or comment on the phrase, leaving it ambiguous (for us). But wherever they give an explanation or gloss that resolves the ambiguity of the grammatical construction, it is consistently in the direction of the objective genitive. Indeed, they give no indication that the subjective genitive reading is even a possible alternative to be weighed.[112] We may even find early interpretations of the Pauline an-

---

110. Matlock, "Demons," 307.

111. Matlock, "Detheologizing the ΠΙΣΤΙΣ ΧΡΙΣΤΟΥ Debate," 16–17.

112. Harrisville, "ΠΙΣΤΙΣ ΧΡΙΣΤΟΥ," 233–41; see also Silva, *Explorations in Exegetical Method*, 29–31.

tithesis of faith versus works of the law (already truncated to faith versus works) in Eph 2:8–10 and Jas 2:14–16. In both instances, "the 'faith' in question is quite unexceptionally that of believers," and not of Christ.[113]

(5) Since "faith toward Christ" and "Christ's faith/faithfulness" are both possible meanings of this phrase, hearers would depend upon the context of the phrase to help clarify which is meant. In the immediate context, the verb *episteusamen* ("we put our trust"), the cognate verb form of *pistis* ("trust/faithfulness"), is used with "Jesus Christ" clearly marked as the object of trust in the middle of two occurrences of the ambiguous genitive phrase "faith of Christ." This should guide the hearers toward resolving the ambiguity in favor of the objective genitive, despite the redundancies within the verse (which, we have already seen, are legion anyway). If Paul had intended for people to hear *pistis Christou* as "Christ's trust [toward God]" or "Christ's faithfulness [toward either God or us or both]," he would have needed to add something that would bring out this nuance more clearly, since the immediate context is working against hearing this sense.[114]

(6) The alternative to *pistis Christou* is *erga nomou*, "works of the Torah," a succinct phrase signifying "doing what the Torah commands." Since this option clearly falls within the realm of human response to God, context again weighs in favor of hearing *pistis Christou* as "trust in Christ," the alternative human response—the response that Paul wants the Galatians to see as incompatible with "works of the Torah," against the rival teachers' suggestion that these two human responses are fully compatible, even integral. Again, the fact that Paul and his fellow Jewish Christians (the imagined conversation partners in Gal 2:15–16) explicitly choose to respond by "trusting in Christ" ("so even we have put our trust in Jesus Christ," 2:16) reinforces hearing "works of Torah" and "trust in Jesus" as two parallel options for human response.[115]

In conclusion, the traditional interpretation of *pistis Christou* as "trust in Christ" in Galatians, at least, seems to be the most probable. This is not to affirm the theological proposition "we are justified by (our)

---

113. Matlock, "Detheologizing," 23; see also idem, "Demons," 306–7.

114. Moule, "The Biblical Conception of 'Faith,'" 157; Dunn, *Galatians*, 139; Matlock, "Detheologizing," 13.

115. Dunn, *Galatians*, 139; Matlock, "Detheologizing," 12.

faith," for, according to Paul, we are clearly justified by Christ's death and rising again to life on our behalf and by the Holy Spirit that Christ sent into the hearts of his followers—and we are justified as we trust in the sufficiency of Christ's provisions for our justification and move forward on that basis toward the manifestation of the life of Christ, the righteous one, within us.

We are now in a position to return, then, to these three concepts in the context of Gal 2:16. Paul presents himself as if he were addressing fellow Jewish Christians, beginning by playing to the general Jewish prejudice according to which God has given the Jews the special privilege of being taken into the Sinaitic covenant and not being left, as were the Gentiles, without Law and thus, *de facto*, "sinners." In his next step, he parts company from non-Christian Jews but still speaks in line with what other Jewish Christians would affirm: "We know that a person is not acquitted before God by conforming his or her life to the requirements of the Torah, except by trusting in Jesus." In Greek, throughout this verse, Paul uses the preposition *ek* ("out of," "from") to introduce "works of the Torah" and "reliance on Jesus." The preposition is most commonly used in a spatial sense, denoting movement out of some space or coming from some space. It is being used here in one of its derivative senses, such as "origin," "cause," or "means." A paraphrase of the verse intending to capture the nuance that this preposition brings to the relationship between "works of the Torah" and "being acquitted" or "being set right" might read: "Conforming one's life to the requirements of the Torah, unless this is joined with trusting in Jesus, does not result in (or does not lead to) acquittal before God."

Paul is not yet presenting "works of the Torah" and "reliance on Jesus" as incompatible paths to acquittal before God, though he is preparing for taking this next step by pointing out that he, Peter, James, the rival teachers, and all Jewish Christians would agree this far: doing the Torah is not sufficient if one hopes to find acquittal at the judgment. All of them alike have put their trust in Jesus as God's Messiah and in his death as, at the very least, an act of obedience that erases past sins under the covenant for those who believe, and thus are seeking to be justified ("acquitted") as a result of relying on Jesus rather than relying on works of the Torah as a sufficient resource. Within these terse phrases—"relying on Jesus" and "conforming one's life to the Torah's regulations"—are encapsulated two processes of transformation. The latter process happens as one becomes an embodiment, on a day-to-day basis, of the stipulations in the Mosaic law; the former happens as one relies on the power and guidance of the Holy Spirit that God has given to make the individual an embodiment of Christ's own spirit. At this point, he is beginning to part company with many of his fellow Jewish Christians, for Paul will now begin to argue that Torah was not sufficient to lead people to justification because, in effect, it was never God's purpose that it should. Thus Jewish Christians who *are* Christians in Paul's mind are now seeking to be acquitted by relying wholly on Jesus and what Jesus, in his death and resurrection, has brought to light, and not relying any longer on conforming their lives to the Torah for this purpose.

The rationale that Paul provides for this claim appears to be an interpretive paraphrase of Ps 143:2 (LXX 142:3). The psalmist prays to God, "do not enter into judgment with your slave, because no living being will be acquitted before you." In the Hebrew text, the psalmist acknowledges his own imperfection in God's sight, asking nevertheless that God would indeed enter into judgment against, and destroy, the psalmist's enemies. Paul alters this in two important ways. First, "no living being" becomes more inclusive: "all flesh will not be acquitted" or "no flesh will be acquitted." Paul looks at humanity here in its frailty, even more specifically its vulnerability to the powers that lead it away from fulfilling God's standards of righteousness toward all manner of harmful self-indulgence (see Gal 5:13–25). Second, Paul limits the scope of the psalmist's declaration of the impossibility of acquittal before God to acquittal that is pursued "by works of the Law." He may be justified in doing so since the psalmist could safely be presumed to have made his declaration in the context of the covenant community, in the context of living by "works of the Law."

Paul's presumption in Galatians is *not* that it would be impossible for a person to live by the Torah. He considered himself "blameless" in his performance of the Torah (Phil 3:6); the near-contemporary Jewish authors of 4 Maccabees and 4 Ezra presumed that it was possible to live by Torah, even though it was difficult and demanding. Paul's presumption is that, now that the fullness of time has come, falling in line with Torah is not the way to fall in line with God, as Paul's own experience had proven. God had now moved salvation history on to a whole new level with the death and resurrection of Christ and the formation of One Body out of divided humanity. Torah was simply never the means by which God purposed to bring "all flesh"—Jews and Gentiles together—to acquittal. Torah's role was more limited in God's plan for the justification of *all* flesh. Indeed, its role was limited to one particular people for the duration of its term, with the "works of the Law" functioning to keep that people separate from the Gentiles. That term being ended with the coming of "the fullness of time," God's provision for setting "all flesh" right again in his sight is now available: the provision of the Holy Spirit for all, Jews and Gentiles alike, who, by trust in Jesus, join themselves to Jesus as the "Seed" of Abraham to whom the promise was given. Paul will provide an elaboration of this point in 3:15–4:7, a confirmation of his rationale here that "no flesh will be acquitted on the basis of works of the Law."

Paul is well aware of the objection that non-Christian and Christian Jews alike raise against his position: if Jews, who have been historically obliged to show their loyalty to the covenant God by observing Torah, now begin to set aside its regulations as they pursue realignment with God on the basis of trusting Jesus and the Spirit-led life, that makes Christ into an agent of sin as sin is defined by Torah (2:17). If Jewish Christians start neglecting the behaviors that keep them set apart from Gentile "sinners"—becoming in this way "sinners" themselves, no different from Gentiles (2:15)—then Jesus has become the excuse for violating the historic covenant and disobeying God through neglect of the Torah.

Paul flatly denies such conclusion, offering an alternative perspective as a rationale (signaled by the particle *gar*, "for," at the opening of 2:18) for his exoneration of Jesus as the "agent of sin" in this scenario: "For if I build up again the things I tore down, I turn myself into a transgressor." The situation in Gal 2:11–14 provides the closest clue within the discourse concerning what is being torn down and rebuilt. If we allow that scenario to guide us, then Paul is speaking here about first tearing down and then reinstating the dividing lines between Jews and Gentiles erected and enforced by Torah (in Antioch, in particular, through its regulations about keeping separate from Gentiles in regard to foods).[116] After eating freely with Gentile Christians, Peter only turns himself into a transgressor when he acknowledges anew the lines that, according to the Torah, should be drawn between Jews and Gentiles, the lines that he had previously transcended in obedience to the leading of the Spirit (and, quite possible, the dream vision of Acts 10). He establishes that he is a transgressor in two important respects: first, insofar as his return to Torah-reinforced separateness amounts to an admission that his previous conduct was a transgression; second, insofar as his return to Torah-reinforced separateness amounts to disobedience to, and denial of, what God is doing *now* in the Spirit-led community of Jews and Gentiles in Christ (as in 3:23–28). Paul will return to this topic more fully in 3:23—4:11 under a different metaphor—that of trying to turn back the clock, as it were, on the fullness of time.

Paul then offers a personal statement as a further elaboration of this rationale (note again the presence of the particle *gar*, "for," at the outset of 2:19), giving us thereby one of the most beautiful expressions of the essence of the Christian life: "For I died to the Torah through the Torah, in order that I might live to God. I have been crucified along with Christ. It's not me living any longer, but Christ is living in me. What I'm now living in the flesh, I live by trusting in God's Son, who loved me and gave himself up on my behalf" (2:19–20). In a mysterious way, Paul's journey away from seeking to be aligned with God's purposes and standards through commitment to the Torah to seeking to be aligned with God's purposes and standards through trusting Jesus and allowing Jesus to come alive within him was itself a journey undertaken in agreement with Torah. His death "to the Torah" happened "through the Torah," in accordance with God's ultimate purposes for the Torah (which Paul will develop in 3:19–25). Torah, as a temporary measure set in place to provide formative discipline for God's people, had to give way to the more powerful means by which God would bring all people, and not just Jews, into alignment with God's righteousness—identification with

116. Longenecker, *Galatians*, 90; Martyn, *Galatians*, 256.

Christ in his death and rising to new life, and the gift of the Spirit to direct and empower righteousness from the heart.

A passage like Gal 2:15–21 causes one to wonder why scholars have so vigorously debated whether "justification by faith" or "participation in Christ" is the "center" of Paul's theology. Both concepts are held together so seamlessly in this statement of Paul's position that it seems truly artificial to divide them and pointless to try to choose between them. Indeed, if we understand "justification" in its fullest sense—God intervening to bring back in line what was out of alignment in human beings and their relationship with the divine—then "participating in Christ," or, perhaps better, "Christ's participation in us" is an essential mechanism of that justification. Paul speaks of Christ's participation in us as the Spirit's activity within and among us (4:6–7; 5:16–25), of "Christ being formed" among the believers (4:19), and of Christ "living" in Paul (2:20). Christ participating in us, changing us to the point that we're not "ourselves" any more because Christ has taken on new flesh in us, is the essential mechanism of the nurturing of that righteousness within us that God seeks in God's people (6:7–10), for which the Christian hopes (5:5), and that the Torah could not effectively nurture (2:21). Paul's interest in God's justifying initiative includes a highly "formational" or "transformational" element.

Being crucified with Christ (2:19) means putting to death the power of the "old person," the "flesh" with its cravings and urges (5:24), so that one can follow the Spirit's leading in all things, manifesting the righteous character and practices that fulfill the Torah's vision for righteousness—becoming the sort of person that Torah would affirm as reflecting God's holiness, even though the Christian arrives at that point by a completely different path than following the Torah's regulations (5:22–23).[117] This "dying with Christ" opened up Paul to a new kind of life before God, one that he characterizes as the freedom of God's mature children, who have the capacity to do what pleases God because

---

117. Longenecker (*Galatians*, 92) captures this quite well: "Crucifixion with Christ implies not only death to the jurisdiction of the Mosaic law (v 19), but also death to the jurisdiction of one's own ego . . . which is antagonistic to the Spirit's jurisdiction." Paul himself returns to this theme of dying with Christ in terms of dying to one's propensity to self-centered living and rising with Christ to the new life of doing what is righteous in God's sight (see especially Rom 6:1–14; Col 3:1–17).

God's Spirit, living within them, guides them.[118] On this side of the cross and resurrection of Jesus—the event that marked the "fullness of time" and the end of Torah's service as "pedagogue" (see on 3:23–25)—all that matters for Paul is cultivating the life of the Spirit within us, or as he puts it here, all that matters is Christ taking shape within, and living in and through, the believer. This is the new creation (Gal 2:20; 4:19; 6:15; cf. 2 Cor 5:16–18) that renders all concern over circumcision or uncircumcision misplaced.

Paul remembers the generous kindness of Jesus, "the Son of God who loved me and handed himself over on my behalf" (2:20b; see 1:4). Jesus displayed the highest form of generosity that any benefactor could, giving not his resources but his very life to bring benefit to others. Such commitment on Jesus' part to those whom he came to benefit ought to awaken an equal commitment to show gratitude to this Jesus and to value his gifts, conferred at such cost to himself, appropriately. One essential component of this response to costly favor is "trust" in and "fidelity toward" such a benefactor, and Paul expresses his own commitment to continue in this response: "What I now live in the flesh, I live by trusting in the Son of God" (2:20).[119] Much of the central argumentative section of Galatians can be read as an attempt on Paul's part to encourage the believers to show more complete confidence in Jesus' ability to bring them into God's household and in the sufficiency of the gifts that Jesus' death has secured for them, most particularly the sufficiency of the Holy Spirit, the blessing once promised to Abraham and now avail-

118. There is an eschatological dimension to the phrase "living to God" as well: Paul may enjoy a new life now before God, but ultimately he embraces the death and life of Christ in his mortal body as the path to sharing in Christ's resurrection, "living to God" for eternity (see Gal 6:8b–9). On "living to God" as a way of speaking about resurrection or post-mortem life, see 4 Macc 7:19; 16:25.

119. While no translation opts to follow these manuscripts, P[46] and Codex Vaticanus actually read "What I'm now living in the flesh, I live by trusting in God and Christ, who loved me . . ." Metzger (*Textual Commentary*, 593) argues that this reading cannot be considered original "since Paul nowhere else expressly speaks of God as the object of a Christian's faith." Paul does, however, speak of the report of the Thessalonians Christians' "faith toward God" (1:8) sounding out across Macedonia and Achaia. The author of Hebrews, whom I take to be a part of the Pauline team, writes of the basic instruction of converts to Christianity including "faith in God" (Heb 6:1). I would still agree with Metzger's conclusion, though not on the grounds of his theological argument.

able to all who trust Jesus (3:14), to lead them to life and righteousness before God (3:21; 5:13—6:10).

Because of the cost Jesus incurred to mediate God's favor, Paul "does not set aside God's gift" (or "generous kindness") manifested in the Son (2:21).[120] For this reason as well, those Christians whom he addressees should also take the greatest care in their present situation not to "set aside God's gift" (or "generosity"). The favor of God lavished upon human beings in Christ and the significance of Christ's death is what is really at stake here for Paul. What is the value of Christ's death, if it is really still through the gates of the Torah that we enter into the people of God? "For if righteousness comes through Torah, then Christ died for nothing" (2:21b). The particle *gar* ("for") here is a sign that 2:21b provides an argumentative rationale for 2:21a. "Setting aside God's gift" or "favor" is precisely what Paul sees happening when one follows the course of action that Paul has rejected, namely building up the dividing walls of Torah once again and returning to the practices that maintain those walls as if that is the path to falling in line with God's purposes for humanity (2:18; 5:2–4). What was the purpose of Christ's self-giving death if Torah already provided the path to righteousness?[121]

Paul sets "grace" in opposition to "Torah" at two key junctures within Galatians: here at the climax of his statement of his position (Gal 2:21) and again in his climactic exhortation not to go as the rival

---

120. The Greek word *charis* can carry any one of three basic meanings: (1) the disposition to help another, hence "favor" or "generous kindness"; (2) the "gift" or help given as an expression of this generosity and willingness to help; (3) the appropriate response to such a generous disposition and gift, hence "gratitude" or "thanks." The context usually makes clear which sense of *charis* is being invoked, though in this particular verse it is difficult to decide between the first two senses. On the everyday social contexts in which "grace" language was at home in Paul's environment, the ethos of "reciprocity" that pervaded those contexts, and the implications for understanding "grace" in the New Testament, see deSilva, *Honor, Patronage, Kinship & Purity*, 95–156.

121. The rival teachers might indeed have had an answer to this: Christ's death was an offering *within* the covenant on behalf of the many transgressions of the many transgressors; his death spares the larger people of God (the Jews), and all the Gentiles who would join themselves to God's people, from God's anger against transgression and gives them all a fresh opportunity to renew their obedience to the covenant. For Paul, however, such an answer would be insufficient.

teachers direct (5:4). This opposition exists for Paul, in part, because Torah was a necessary trapping of human "immaturity," now rendered obsolete by the coming of "the fullness of time" (3:23—4:7). But this is also so because what God has graciously done in Jesus *for all* now makes possible what Torah had not made possible, namely a life lived truly to God, for God, and in the power of God (3:21; 5:13—6:10). Paul's own story is a living example of this premise, for it is precisely when he was most fully engaged in the works of Torah that he was most God's enemy, and it was precisely then that God graciously transformed Paul into an apostle of God's righteousness in Christ. After Jesus' death, a *return* to works of Torah as if these could *add* to what Jesus had done would amount to a repudiation of Jesus' ability to connect us to God and an insultingly low evaluation of the potential of the Spirit, the promised gift won for us at such cost, to transform our lives.

The appearance of the word "righteousness" (*dikaiosunē*) here is significant for at least two reasons. First, it reminds us that Paul's polemic throughout Galatians is not against "doing good works," but against "works of the Torah" performed out of a conviction that the Torah still regulates the life of the people of God. Paul expects the Spirit to produce all manner of "good works" in the life of the disciple (Gal 5:13–25; see also Rom 2:6–11; 6:12–13; Eph 2:10). He understands the Christian hope to entail, in part at least, attaining "righteousness" through the transforming work of the Spirit in the lives of disciples (Gal 5:5). And when Paul has swept aside both circumcision and uncircumcision as meaningless characteristics before God, the only thing left holding value in God's sight is not mere "faith," but "faith working through love" (Gal 5:6). Second, it reminds us that Paul's concern is not simply with "justification" in the sense of "acquittal" or forgiveness of sins, being made initially right with God (*dikaiōsis*), but with "justification" in the sense of being brought fully in line with God's standards of "righteousness" (*dikaiosunē*), which happens as Christ comes more and more alive within and through the believer.[122]

---

122. I would disagree with Fung (*Galatians*, 123–24) when he interprets the occurrence of *dikaiosunē* ("righteousness") here as a noun corresponding to the verb *dikaioō* ("I justify, acquit"), limiting the former by the forensic (or "declarative") sense of the latter. Since Paul *knows* the noun that is truly the cognate of this verb (i.e.,

Will the Galatians appreciate and accept what God has done for humanity in the cross of Christ? Will they trust the efficacy of that single act of costly obedience to join them to the family of Abraham and the family of God, without trying to turn the clock back to a time before Jesus' death? Will they place sufficient value upon the resource God has provided in the Spirit—ever so much more effective and empowering a guide to the heart of God than Torah—to lead them into righteousness? All of these questions are wrapped up in the catchwords "grace" and "trust" that so dominate this letter.

READING GALATIANS 2 WITH SRI LANKAN CHRISTIANS

Authority and Accountability

Despite the fact that Paul fully believed himself to have been called by God to apostleship and to have received his understanding of the Good News from a direct encounter with the glorified Christ, he goes to Jerusalem with his partner, Barnabas, to lay his message before "those who were apostles before" him, who were senior to him, as it were, in God's mission to the world. He understands that, somehow, his efforts would have been in vain, and would continue to be in vain, if they were not in harmony with the efforts and message of these senior partners in the faith.

Paul's activities here stand in stark contrast with the lack of accountability between, and the general contentment with disunity among, churches in Sri Lanka. This is no different, of course, from the state of the Christian church across the globe, but it is especially striking where Christianity as a whole is in such a minority position. Paul's accord with the Jerusalem leaders impresses upon us the importance of seeking cooperation rather than competition, and accountability to one another—particularly, the accountability of the new evangelist on the block, calling from God notwithstanding, to the established church leaders.

---

dikaiōsis, see Rom 4:25; 5:18), I would understand his choice of *dikaiosunē* ("righteousness") to represent an intentional decision to expand the scope of the discussion of God's purposes in Christ for the believer.

While Paul also challenges us to be alert to when we or another Christian preacher or group has lost sight of the core contours on the Gospel and begun to preach "another Gospel," his encounters with the pillars in Jerusalem and, again, with Peter and their fellow-Jewish Christians in Antioch challenge us to look for areas of agreement at the heart of our respective understandings of the Gospel, visions for a transformed life, and calls to mission in our local context. Major denominations in Sri Lanka have far more in common with each other than what is distinctive to each, and what is distinctive is often not in an area that one would call "core." We will have significantly different notions of how the Spirit is at work in God's church and world, but we will agree that the Spirit *is* at work and we will agree that we want to nurture and fall in line with that work. We will have different nuances in our expression of doctrines like justification and sanctification, but we will agree that God is reconciling us, along with the world, to himself in Christ and that God is at work within us and our churches to make us reflect more and more of his holiness and justice. We will practice baptism differently, but we will agree on the transference of allegiances and the transformation of life from the old person to the new person that baptism represents, and will strive after these same ends.

Christians of any one tradition have had a bad habit of stressing the practices and teachings that distinguish them from every other Christian tradition or group at the expense of articulating clearly and honoring appropriately those beliefs, those practices, and that hope that they share with all other major denominations falling within the apostolic tradition. Why we do so is quite understandable: it's the differences that, in the end, are used to justify our meeting in our own church building in our own denomination instead of merging our particular group identity into the larger sea of Christian identity. Every pastor who starts a new church aligned with *no* tradition will be especially tempted to stress how he or she and his congregation "have it right" while their sisters and brothers across Christendom "have it wrong," justifying the boundaries of the new group on that basis. But Paul's example challenges us all to look much more openly and generously at the beliefs, practices, goals, and hopes that are common between us and other Christians— lest we find that we, too, have run and continue to run in vain.

Doing so will enhance the harmony and unity of the whole Body, so necessary if the church in Sri Lanka is to function fully as the church and not as an array of Western cults in competition with one another. It will enhance the witness of the *whole* church, which suffers as long as Christians of so many stripes give the appearance of an utter lack of unity and agreement as to the heart of the Christian revelation. Our Buddhist, Hindu, and Muslim neighbors do not need to hear from us what other Christians have gotten wrong and we have gotten right. They need to hear from us, from members of another Christian group, and from members of yet another Christian denomination what God has done for the world in Christ and what kind of response God seeks. When they hear this clearly from all lips that confess the name of the Lord, then the church will have a reliable witness that they can trust and will have to take seriously. To get to such a place, we need to stop looking upon other Christians as "competition" (such that we keep reminding our denomination as a whole, or just the twenty people we've gathered together around us in a storefront church, how every *other* church has missed the mark, unlike "us") and begin looking upon one another as partners in a common mission, and figure out how we can all join in God's mission throughout Sri Lanka together.

We discover if we've been running in vain as we, as Christian leaders, are transparent with sisters and brothers from other denominations—especially those with deeper roots in the history of the church than our own group's roots—about the Gospel that we preach and that they preach, open to receiving confirmation from them that we have indeed authentically heard God's voice concerning his Son, and open as well to receiving challenges to listen again to God through Scripture, prayer, and Christian conferencing to be sure we're running on track and not self-deceived in some matter. Umbrella organizations like the National Christian Council and the National Council for Evangelical Alliance of Sri Lanka are valuable venues wherein Christians from several different traditions can talk with one another, holding one another accountable, helping on another stay on track. It is greatly to be desired that they do so more and more, and find ways to talk to one another across these two organizations as well.

"They to the Jews, We to the Gentiles"

The programs of the church as a whole are often duplicated and, to some extent, its resources wasted as individual churches try to reach out to the same groups of unbelievers and design their ministries to appeal to the same groups of believers. Often, this is driven by a spirit of competition, whereas the witness of the church in Sri Lanka would be ever so much helped by a spirit of cooperation pervading the various denominations and local churches throughout the island. The gifts of the churches are not being maximized for the growth of the body of Christ in Sri Lanka simply because we have not recognized that each church has a gift or an advantage (i.e., geographical location of the church—urban versus rural, among people groups) for the building up of the national church. For example, there are churches that are more in touch with the grass roots, working among the urban poor in Colombo. There are other churches who are more effective in reaching professionals and even some others who are effectively placed in reaching the elites and decision-makers of the country.

In Jerusalem, the leaders of different missions were able to come to an agreement with regard to the message that was being preached and to which group of people they would be primarily working with. Their model challenges Christian leaders in Sri Lanka to consider how their particular congregations can be most effective in advancing God's mission on the island, being in conversation and even partnership with other churches to assure that each congregation's resources are being maximized and that mission can extend further. Perhaps one church has a very creative and effective ministry in creating summer Bible camp experiences, while some neighboring churches struggle to make such experiences viable for their own youth. They could become partners, pooling their resources and serving all the children of those churches, as well as reaching out more effectively to children outside of those churches, much better than they could do individually. Another church has a strong program in place for equipping laity to provide longer-term pastoral support (programs like the "Stephen's Ministry"). Neighboring churches might have a few laypersons that would commit themselves to such a ministry, but benefit from the training provided at the other church rather than duplicating the same training program in their own congregation with their limited resources. One church may be better positioned to reach out to Hindu families, another to Buddhist families. Such churches could support each other in their particular outreaches, rather than trying to "do it all" themselves.

For such a model to work, once again we need to banish the spirit of competition, to act in good faith toward one another such that there is no fear of any party taking advantage of partnership simply to grow their own church. We also need to look at the stipulation laid upon Paul by the Jerusalem pillars in its most immediate social context: Paul and his team were, simply put, going to have access to converts with a greater wealth than Peter and his team. Partnership and mutual support meant, in part, that Paul's richer diaspora congregations would help support the operations and people in the poorer Judean churches. If one church is better equipped and positioned to minister to the urban or even rural poor, while another is better equipped and positioned to minister to the professional class in Sri Lanka, partnership that allows for each to focus on its particular mission must include the kind of sharing of resources between congregations that was typical of first-century churches—"not that others should enjoy ease and you should endure hardship, but that fairness should be observed" (2 Cor 8:13).

Remembering the Poor

As I have argued in the introduction, it seems likely that the private conversation between Paul and the pillars occurred on the occasion of the delivery of famine relief funds to the elders of the Jerusalem church from the daughter church in Antioch. Mindfulness of the poor was an element of Paul's ministry from first to last, as, indeed, it was on the occasion of his delivery of the grander "collection" taken up amongst his various congregations for the poor in Jerusalem that led to his arrest and the four-year imprisonment that took him to Rome. "Remembering the poor" through acts of real, material support and care is perhaps one of the most constant themes of Scripture—legislated in Deuteronomy, promoted throughout the Prophets (e.g., as the kind of "fast" that God requires, Isa 58:3, 5–7), commended by Jesus as the way in which to lay up treasures in heaven (Luke 12:33; 18:22), affirmed by his closest disciples as the heart of genuine religion and love for God (Jas 1:27; 2:15–17; 1 John 3:16–18). How a Christian encounters a poor sister or brother is the ultimate test of that Christian's commitment to love the neighbor as oneself. Christ's own example in this regard is stunning: Christ didn't empathize with the poor; he *became* poor (2 Cor 8:9).

Despite these scriptural mandates, there is a significant tension in many churches between evangelism and social work, between connecting people with Christ and connecting people with the resources they need for their physical and social existence. Churches are torn apart on the issue of which is more important and tend to "choose sides" rather than hold the two together as inseparable facets of living out their Christian faith both as individual disciples and as communities of faith.

Some churches have taken a step back from helping the poor because of the allegations brought against them by Buddhist and Hindu religious leaders and politicians for using charitable aid as a means of coercing conversion (referred to as "unethical conversion"). These churches have become more cautious about engaging in relief work, focusing instead on preaching the Gospel only, leaving social work to charitable organizations and the social services department. Allegations such as these are perhaps attributable in part to the legacy of colonialism. During the various periods of colonization, better jobs within the colonial administration and its support systems would often be offered to the extent that people converted, and aid might be restricted only to those who converted to that particular denomination from which aid was being sought.

Churches as well as individual disciples are rightly cautioned not to attach conditions to charitable aid. We would also do well, both as churches and individuals, to examine our motives for giving. Even if the only strings attached are spiritual ones (for example, the idea that we gain favor with God by giving to others in need), we would still be guilty of the charge that our giving, like so much non-Christian giving, is ultimately self-interested. Our Buddhist neighbors, for example, similarly seek merit in giving—the merit that accumulates to a better rebirth, closer to the end of the cycle of death and rebirth. We give because Christ gave. We give because it is God's good pleasure that all

God's children be fed, clothed, and share in the dignity of being human, and our highest good is to do God's good pleasure. Because Christ's love compels us and God's word directs us, however, Christians cannot *refrain* from giving, helping lift the destitute up again into the ways that lead to a sustainable life.

Paul will challenge Christians to look in two directions when it comes to benevolence: at the needy in the world at large, and at the needy within the "household of faith" (6:10). When we look at the churches in a city like Colombo, for example, the disparity between the rich and the poor is very obvious. The church as a whole has not yet taken adequate measures to eliminate poverty *within* the Household of Faith, by which we do not simply mean one's own congregation or denomination. Paul would call Sri Lankan congregations both to witness to God's love for all by benevolence toward all and to enact the biblical vision for the people of God, according to which no one among this people is needy (Acts 4:32–35; Deut 15:4–11).

Separate Tables and the Truth of the Gospel

We have spoken of "the truth of the Gospel" being lived out, in Paul's eyes, as Peter, Barnabas, Paul, and other Jewish Christian believers shared a common table with Gentile Christian believers, celebrating together the redemption that both parties shared in Jesus Christ as well as their mutual acceptance before God on the basis of their trusting Jesus and receiving the Spirit of God. They were enacting a facet of the "new humanity" that God was forging out of Jews and Gentiles alike, having restored both to himself through Jesus' death on behalf of their sins and having lavished upon both the promised Spirit (see 3:1–5, 13–14).

This points to what upsets Paul about the direction in which the Judaizers want to take the Gentile Christians in his Galatian churches, as well as what had upset Paul about the change in Peter's and Barnabas's behavior in Antioch, which Paul understands as a movement contrary to God's steering of the churches. By giving in to the pressure of the representatives sent from James of Jerusalem, Peter and Barnabas gave public witness that ethnic boundaries and Torah's regulations had greater value than the shared fact of trusting Jesus and being in Christ.

Paul perceived the message that this would send more clearly, it appears, than Peter did: "If you want to have fellowship with us, you need to become like us," but in ways that ultimately no longer mattered in God's sight.

Paul would challenge us in a similar fashion wherever we say to another group of Christians, "We can't have open fellowship with you, because our mutual reliance on Jesus is not sufficient to protect our own purity before God, though perhaps if you would do the things that would make you more like us, then we could eat at the same table." Painful as it is to admit, the communion table is the most blatant place of violation of "the truth of the Gospel" as Paul sought to defend it in Antioch. Wherever a church restricts sharing at the Communion table to those who belong to its particular denomination, excluding others who have made the same commitment to follow Jesus and received the same Spirit, Paul would challenge that church that "the truth of the Gospel" is at stake in its practice. In recent decades, some mainline denominations have made important progress toward opening up their tables to Christians of other denominations. Paul would have applauded the conversations that led to the practice of inter-communion between Anglicans, Methodists, and Lutherans (as well as discussions about recognizing one another's ordinations), but would urge churches to broaden this conversation more and more.

The question of inter-communion between Catholic, Orthodox, and Reformation churches is far more complex, and inevitably tied up in the history of the church splits that led to this plurality of streams. Nevertheless, generations upon generations of Christians have simply been born into each of these streams, and God has blessed each stream with the presence and movement of God's Holy Spirit. As a result, it is no longer the case that one stream can say to another with integrity, "You are always welcome to share in communion with us, provided you come back into our fold." Paul would hear this as just another echo of the invitation that might have issued forth from the Jewish Christian table in Antioch—the sort of invitation that the Judaizers would eventually extend. Rather, it is now a matter of recognizing the vitality of trust in Jesus and of the indwelling activity of the Holy Spirit in each of these streams, and embracing one another on that basis.

But denominational boundaries are not the only considerations that lead us, in our churches, to the practice of separate tables. As we look around our Communion table or the tables at our fellowship meals, we need to ask ourselves who is present and who is not. We need to ask if we are structuring our congregational (and inter-congregational) life in such a way as leads, intentionally or not, to the practice of separate tables rather than the celebration of the unity that God has bestowed upon us, all together, as the new humanity God is forming in Christ. In urban centers like Colombo, separation by language, which often also entails separation by ethnicity, is a strong possibility in the life of a church. A particular church may offer a service in Sinhala at 9:00 a.m. and a service in Tamil at 10:15 a.m. The goal is entirely admirable: allow persons to worship in their own language and offer the full benefits of a worship service and other events like church school or Bible studies to people in their own language. But the effect is often to raise up two congregations instead of a unified congregation. The Sinhala Christians and the Tamil Christians do not necessarily gather at separate Communion tables, emphasizing their ongoing divisions in terms of how a particular space is arranged at a given time (as in Antioch), but they gather at the same Communion table at *different* times, still bearing witness to their divisions rather than their unity in Christ.

Or a church may offer an English service at 9:00 a.m. and a service in Sinhala at 10:15 a.m. The first actually has the potential to bring Sinhala and Tamil Christians together around a common Communion table, which is exciting indeed! But it also has the capacity to introduce divisions more along class and educational lines, as those with better educations, generally coming from more privileged families in Sri Lanka, are the more likely to seek out a service in English rather than an indigenous language. Nurturing multiple worshiping congregations within a single church based on accessibility of language is an important strategy in the Sri Lankan context both for caring for the household of God and reaching out to the unchurched. Where churches give careful attention for developing common worship experiences, partnership in mission between the "regulars" at the various services, and the like, the benefits of multiple services remain intact while the problem of "separate tables" is avoided. Meeting together once each month for a service of Holy Communion, with hymns and songs available to be sung in both (or all three) languages simultaneously, prayers offered in alternating languages, the sermon kept short for the occasion and translated (or preached in one language and distributed in print in the others), and the character of each community's worship carefully blended together, involves a lot of careful preparation, but it bears witness, both within the church and to the community outside the church, to God's amazing work of reconciliation, breaking down every wall of hostility dividing one child of God from another. Galatians is itself a witness to Paul's passion for nurturing the church's witness to unity in Christ as a more powerful force than the humanly made and cherished lines of separation and inequality that divide one person from another. Conversely, Galatians cautions us in no uncertain terms against building up again those barriers that we have torn down in Christ—or, more so, that *God* has torn down!

God's Purposes in the Gospel

What should we expect from God as a result of our turning in trust toward his Son? There are some voices speaking in and around the church suggesting that we should expect God to pour out material blessings on us in abundance, or to open doors to advancement in the structures and systems of our corrupt world, or to spare us from the experience of pain or sorrow. These voices set their hearers up for not only disappointment, but even apostasy, for when prosperity doesn't come, or prayers to be spared anything unpleasant do not prevent the experience of grief, the individual becomes embittered against God, revokes his or her trust, and turns away.

Paul preaches a different set of expectations: we should expect God to be at work in our lives to form Christ in us, that is, to deepen our capacities for love and other-centered service, to change our hearts from a focus on ourselves and our interests toward a focus on the needs and good of another person, to break us out of our self-centeredness and our immersion in the values of this world so that we will be free to serve and love God as our creator merits. If Paul expected his conversion to faith in Christ and his call to serve Christ to improve his lot in this world, he would have been sorely disappointed. In fact, he lost his prestige, his social power, and, to a large extent, his personal safety and comfort (Phil 3:5–8; 2 Cor 11:21b–33). What he found as a result of his conversion and call was that the power of Christ was coming to life in him, transforming him into a person who pleased God, indeed, refashioning him in the likeness of *the* person who pleased God: "It's no longer me living, but Christ is living in me" (2:20). This transformation was the most important thing he could seek for himself, the thing he wanted most from God, for which he counted the loss of everything else to be just so much trash (Phil 3:7–11).

In contradiction to so much that is preached in Christ's name across the globe, Paul reminds us that God is not out to make us rich. He's not out to make our lives easy or pain free. He's out to make us more like Jesus, able to use everything that comes our way to strip away the old person and form us a bit more into the new person. If the Son learned obedience through the things he suffered and experienced (Heb 5:7–10), how much more should the many sons and daughters prepare themselves to endure rigorous training in this life (Heb 12:5–11), rather than expect ease and prosperity, so as to be fully formed in the image of the Son? Western images of "Christian" life are often very misleading in this regard, reflecting the difficulty Western Christians have divorcing the pursuit of the kingdom of God from the pursuit of the "American Dream," and reflecting as well the very real danger that, in holding onto the latter, we in the West will miss the former. If God brings enough resources our way for us and our families to live on, it is enough. If God brings more material wealth our way than our needs require, it is so that others and their families will have enough to live on by virtue of our sharing with them as conduits of God's gracious provision.

In defining God's purposes as our transformation into Christlikeness or into the "new person," we return to Paul's conception of justification as it comes to expression in Galatians. What Paul seeks is not just forgiveness now, but acquittal before God on the day of judgment. Paul does not expect this acquittal to come on the basis of God's partiality toward those who have made use of his Son's ability to secure special favors for them in the courtroom, but on the basis of God's active investment in believers by means of the working of the Holy Spirit, transforming them into persons who are genuinely aligned with God's righteousness and in whom God's righteous standards are fulfilled. This very transformation is at the heart of God's purposes for the people who have been called together in his Son's name, and represents not our achievement, but God's achievement within us, to which we submit ourselves as people bought back for that very purpose. This has to do, in another sense, with not nullifying or setting aside God's gift (2:21) by neglecting its full purpose and provision.

Integrity: Walking in Line with the Truth

Paul's authority is rooted in the message itself and his faithfulness to that message. Human credentials or authorization by some governing body add nothing to this root authority. Moreover, Paul presents a living example of the courage of the genuine minister of the Gospel, as he refuses to conform the Gospel to the expectations or demands of church or society and as he refuses to avoid confrontation where the truth of the Gospel is not being lived out in the church.

Following Paul's pattern, we are instructed that our own persuasive power and our authority likewise come from our fidelity to that message, and our refusal to accommodate that message to suit the tastes of our congregations or the society around us. That would be to preach a mere human gospel, one that has been circumcised and emasculated of its transformative power. Rather, we are called to preserve the challenge that the Gospel poses to the world and call our constituencies to conform to the Gospel, not vice versa. This is the Gospel that has power from God to transform, to justify, to bring us in line with God's own righteousness.

Finally, if we are to have powerful ministries, we must walk straight in line with the Gospel, conforming our own conduct to the message. Paul consistently measured himself *and* his fellow apostles by whether or not they were walking toward the truth of the Gospel, or behaving in ways that were out of line with that Gospel. Our congregations and constituents will do the same. Nothing can undermine a minister's credibility faster and more completely than merely "talking the talk" while not "walking the walk." There are two main stumbling blocks to integrity at this point: the double-heart that still makes room for the flesh (Gal 5:13–26), and the cowardly heart that shrinks back from living by the Gospel, yielding instead to the expectations and pressures of other people (Gal 2:11–14; 5:11; 6:12–13). Paul's example encourages us that it is always ultimately advantageous to walk in line with the truth of the Gospel, even if this should lead to persecution in some form here.

Paul lives with a vibrant awareness of the presence of God over, and the life of Christ within, his life. He lives and speaks in such a way that God is always present to be called upon as a "witness" to the integrity of Paul's speech and actions. His example is a challenge to us in this regard as well. As we live transparently under God's light—renouncing every behavior or deed about which we would be tempted to lie later, to protect our appearances of honor—we become transparent windows through which the light of God and of Christ is revealed.

3:1–6: PROOF FROM EXPERIENCE— RECEIVING THE SPIRIT

You brainless Galatians, who has put a spell on you, before whose eyes Jesus Christ crucified was openly proclaimed?! [2]I want to learn this one thing from you: Did you receive the Spirit on the basis of works of Torah or on the basis of the message about trust/faithfulness? [3]Are you all so brainless that, after beginning with the Spirit, you are now going to come to completion with the flesh?! [4]Have you experienced such great things for nothing—if indeed it was for nothing?! [5]The one, then, who supplied the Spirit to you and works miraculous signs among you, does he do this on the basis of works of Torah or on the basis of the message about trust, [6]just as Abraham trusted God, and it was accounted to him as righteousness?

With the opening of chapter 3, we arrive at the "proof" section of Paul's address, where Paul will make his case for the truth of his position (2:14–21) on the basis of the addressees' experience of God's Spirit and working in their midst, on the basis of arguments from Scripture, and on the basis of the understanding of salvation history that Paul's reading of Scripture nurtures. The "proof section" (in rhetorical terms, the *probatio*) appears to continue through 4:11, with 3:1–5 and 4:8–11 forming a kind of *inclusio* marking the beginning and ending of the section. Both 3:1–5 and 4:8–11 involve a series of pointed rhetorical questions (using the technique of "interrogation," making clear what the "correct" answers would have to be and leading the audience thereby to a particular conclusion). Both passages also contain direct statements to the audience that are at home in "letters of rebuke" ("You brainless Galatians," 3:1; "I am afraid for you," 4:11).[123] The moral philosophers in the marketplace often called into question the intelligence of passers-by who were not yet taking the "larger view" on life that philosophers promoted, such that Paul's insulting the Galatians' intelligence, while abrupt and attention-getting, was not entirely out of keeping with rhetorical practice.

Paul opens this interrogation by asking "who has bewitched you," using a verb (*ebaskanen*) that generally refers to casting a spell by giving someone the evil eye, hence forming a pun in regard to the next phrase that talks about what the Galatians themselves have "seen" with their eyes.[124] This is a rhetorically charged characterization of the strategies employed by the opponents—not that they actually used magic against the Galatian converts, but that their influence over Paul's converts was exerting a negative force in the congregation.[125] Paul clearly expresses his expectation that the Galatians should have been more critically reflective in their assessment of the truth of the rival teachers' message, and that, if they had exercised their brains more, they would not have come

123. Longenecker, *Galatians*, 97.

124. There are two text-critical issues in 3:1. The later manuscripts upon which the KJV is based contained four extra words that appear to have been introduced here as a duplication from Gal 5:7, hence "who hath bewitched you, that ye should not obey the truth?" (Compare 5:7: "who did hinder you that ye should not obey the truth?") At this point, however, the earliest manuscripts are unanimous in supporting the shorter reading (in KJV language, just "who hath bewitched you?") as the more original. The later manuscripts, and hence the KJV, also add two words in the second part of this verse, "before whose eyes Jesus Christ crucified was openly proclaimed *among you*?" Again, the earliest manuscripts are in agreement against the redundant "among you," identifying this as a later addition.

125. Longenecker, *Galatians*, 100; see Betz, *Galatians*, 131 for examples of the figurative sense of the word in classical literature.

"under their spell" so easily. Had they reflected more on the message about "Christ crucified" that Paul had clearly laid out before them[126] during his first visit to their cities, they would have seen through the rival teachers' false reasoning.

"Christ crucified" is Paul's shorthand expression for the larger proclamation of the Gospel, by means of holding up the most distinctive image and facet of that message (see also 1 Cor 1:23; 2:2). It is also the image that captures most graphically the costliness of this "gift" or "favor" of God that some Galatian Christians are, in Paul's view, in danger of setting aside (2:21). The emphasis on Paul's proclamation of the crucifixion of the Messiah in 3:1 grows organically out of Paul's emphasis on the death of Christ in 2:21 and his conviction that the very value of Christ's death is now at stake in the controversy in Galatia. Taking 2:21 and 3:1 together, we might paraphrase Paul's underlying challenge thus: "We emphasized the redemptive and eschatological significance of Jesus' death on the cross while we were among you: how could you now, then, be so brainless as to begin to entertain the idea that you will fall in line with God's righteous standards by following the Torah?"

Having brought home the significance of his statement of his position (2:14–21) for the Galatians in their current deliberations (3:1), he demands an answer from them in regard to one question: "This *one* thing I want to learn from you" (3:2a). While Paul actually follows this up with four (possibly five, if 3a is treated separately from 3b) questions in relentless succession, these are all foundationally related to a single issue: *how* the Galatians were initially positioned to receive and experience God's Holy Spirit and, therefore, what they should be deducing in their present situation from that one experience. Rhetorical theorists advised that a strong argument, if not the most compelling, should be placed up front in the proof section of one's speech. In this way, the speaker would convince the audience early on, with all following proofs serving to confirm the hearers in their assent. Paul follows this advice

---

126. The verb Paul uses here (*proegraphē*) can mean either "display prominently" or "announce [often in writing] beforehand." In this context, it would appear to carry the first sense (though, of course, Paul is also referring to a previous presentation he had given to the Galatians, at their initial conversion and in their initial instruction), since he speaks of what was laid out there "right in front of [their] eyes." So Fung, *Galatians*, 129; Longenecker, *Galatians*, 100–101.

in Galatians. If he can gain the Galatians' assent concerning this "one thing," he believes that will provide the decisive evidence that settles the issue for the Galatian Christians.[127]

Whether or not the Galatian Christians received the Spirit is really not part of the question in 3:2. Paul assumes that they did, and that they know they did. He asks on what basis (*ek*, "from [what source]") they received the Spirit, and offers them two possible answers from which to choose: on the basis of "works of the Torah" or on the basis of "the report that awakened faith" (or, on the basis of "hearing with faith"). The two options in Greek are *ex ergōn nomou* and *ex akoēs pisteōs*. The first phrase was already encountered in 2:15–16 (three times!). The second phrase is new, and needs careful examination. Indeed, the precise interpretation of the latter phrase has occasioned almost as much debate as "the faith of Jesus"—to which, of course, it is materially related, since it now replaces "trust in Christ" in the antithesis with "works of the Torah."

The noun *akoē* could signify the faculty of hearing or the act of hearing (as it does, for example, in LXX Isa 6:9; Matt 13:14; Mark 7:35; Lk 7:1; Acts 17:20; 1 Cor 12:17; 2 Tim 4:3–4; Heb 5:11; 2 Pet 2:8), or it could signify the thing heard, hence "report" or "message" (as in LXX Isa 52:7; 53:1; LXX Jer 6:4; 30:8; Matt 4:24; 14:1; 24:6; John 12:38; Acts 28:26; Rom 10:16–17; 1 Thess 2:13; Heb 4:2).[128] We are already familiar with the range of senses associated with the second noun (*pistis*), such that the main questions regarding *pistis* concern which of its two principal sense ("trust" or "faithfulness") would be invoked here and, more especially, what relationship between *pistis* and *akoē* the genitive case of the former is trying to signify.[129]

127. Authors who regard 3:1–5 as a digression or interlude (see, for example, Drane, *Paul, Libertine or Legalist*, 24) miss the importance of this passage, as well as the decisive importance of the reception of the Holy Spirit for Paul's theology.

128. Jn 12:38; Acts 28:26; Rom 10:16 are all citations of LXX Isa 53:1.

129. It is tempting to try to resolve the problems by trying to understand each element of *ex akoēs pisteōs* in terms of the parallels in *ex ergōn nomou*, but while the two concepts articulated by these two prepositional phrases are certainly intended by Paul to be seen as parallel, irreconcilable entities, it would be a fallacy to suggest on that basis that every grammatical and syntactical component making up the prepositional phrases is also parallel between the phrases. Two radically different senses of the geni-

The more likely options appear to be (1) "hearing with faith" (the act of "hearing" that is characterized also by "trusting" what is heard) and (2) "a message that awakens faith." Ronald Fung champions the former reading because, first, "hearing" provides a better parallel to the implied "doing" of the "works of the Torah" and, second, it provides a better parallel to the example of Abraham, to whom God announced the promise, and who heard the promise and trusted it.[130] J. Louis Martyn favors the second reading. The strongest argument in favor of taking *akoē* as "message" or "report" would seem to be a statement Paul would make later about the proclamation of the Gospel and the awakening of faith or trust. This is found in Rom 10:16–17, where Paul takes Isa 53:1 as a starting point for arguing that Christ's word is disseminated through the message of apostles like Paul, resulting in the arousal of a response of trust or faith.[131] The genitive case of *pistis* is here understood as describing the "report" in terms of its "direction or purpose."[132] While one should typically have reservations about interpreting an earlier document by a later one, the fact that both Gal 3:2 and Rom 10:16–17 are written by the same author, in documents that clearly have a close relationship with one another, both invoking a similar constellation of topics may be sufficient to allay these reservations. Either reading would be consonant with the earlier antithesis involving "works of the Torah" in 2:16, since either features the response of "trust" directed toward Christ as a result of hearing Paul's initial preaching.[133]

---

tival relationship can exist within the same sentence, as Matlock ("Detheologizing," 16) has shown in regard to Acts 9:31.

130. Fung, *Galatians*, 132. This may also be what Longenecker (*Galatians*, 103) is aiming for when he glosses the phrase as "believing what you heard." Taken at face value, though, Longenecker's particular phrasing would seem to make *pistis* into the head noun of the phrase, supplanting *akoēs*. If this were Paul's meaning, it would seem that the two nouns would need to have been switched, with *akoēs* now describing *pistis* in terms of the object of trust (i.e., functioning as an "objective genitive").

131. Martyn, *Galatians*, 288.

132. See BDF §166.

133. Other possibilities include (1) "hearing about faith" (faith, that is, as a means of being connected to God through Christ's death), reading the second noun as an objective genitive; (2) "hearing about [Christ's] faithfulness," also reading the second noun as an objective genitive, but taking *pistis* in its other principal sense; and (3) the "report" (Paul's preaching) about "faith" (genitive of content). See, further, Hays, *Faith*

It seems, in the end, impossible to know how the audience in Galatia would have construed this phrase, and what variety of interpretations might have existed as they listened to the letter being read to them. We can only wish that Paul had been a bit clearer about his precise meaning. Nevertheless, this much is unambiguous: God had already poured out God's Holy Spirit upon the Galatian Christians because they responded to the message Paul preached with trust regarding the significance of Jesus' death for their connection with God, long before they were considering submitting to circumcision and adopting any part of a Torah-observant lifestyle. Moreover, whether we understand *akoē* as the Galatians' act of listening or as the message to which they listened, it was Paul who spoke in their hearing and Paul's message that awakened their faith, with the result that they received God's Holy Spirit.[134] This, too, should have obvious implications for them in regard to choosing now between trusting Paul and trusting the rival teachers.

If the Galatian Christians can attest from their own religious experience (as Paul believes they should readily be able to do) that they have already received God's Holy Spirit and experienced God's presence in their midst simply as a result of trusting in Jesus and in what his death secured for human beings, they will come to see that (1) they have received the blessing that was promised to Abraham concerning "all the nations" (3:14), (2) they are already sons and daughters of the living God and, thereby, also heirs of God's promise (4:6–7), and (3) they have received from God all that they need to live beyond the power of the flesh and to conform to God's righteous standards, so enjoying God's approval at the end (5:13–25; 6:7–10), all on the basis of having trusted in Jesus and the favor God is showing to the world through Jesus. What more could they possibly hope to gain by turning to performing the works of the Torah? Indeed, if they are actually trying to secure any of

---

of Jesus Christ, 143–49.

134. Paul's description of the Galatians' initial encounter with the Gospel as a combination of hearing the proclamation and experiencing the conviction brought by the Spirit and power of God describes a common feature of the Pauline mission. Paul reminds the converts in Corinth of a similar experience (1 Cor 2:1–5), and the member of the Pauline team who wrote Hebrews reminds his addressees of their experience of God's power and distributions of the Spirit that confirmed the proclaimed word (Heb 2:3–4).

these three things by means of turning to the Torah, what kind of "vote of no confidence" are they offering to Jesus (cf. 2:21; 5:2–4)?

This reception of the Spirit (the religious experience of God's acceptance and gift) on the basis of trusting what God had done for all nations in the death of Jesus is a stronger proof than anything the Judaizers can bring from Scripture, reason, or tradition. Receiving God's Spirit proves God's complete acceptance of the Galatian Christians *as Gentiles* purely on the basis of their commitment to Jesus.[135] Their trust in Jesus was enough to render them "holy" to the Lord, hence allowing the Holy Spirit to rest upon them and dwell among them. There was no need to perform the traditional rites by which Jews had kept themselves "holy" to the Lord and distinct from the Gentile nations.

Paul returns to develop each of these two phrases ("works of the Torah" and "the report that awakens trust") in the next two steps of his argument. "The report that awakens trust" looks forward to Paul's argument from the example of Abraham, whose trust in what God promised to him set the pattern for how one would move toward reception of God's promised blessings and acquittal before God (3:6–9). "Works of the Torah" becomes a central topic in 3:10–13, where Paul argues on the basis of a series of scriptural texts that "works of the Torah" are not the path to alignment with God's righteousness. Paul makes these connections clearer by speaking explicitly of "those who are characterized by trust" (3:9a) and "those who are characterized by works of the Torah" (3:10a), keeping the mutually exclusive alternatives before the congregation's eyes.

Paul follows up this question with a second, related question. Assuming that his audience would answer "of course, Paul, we received God's Holy Spirit on the basis of responding to your proclamation of Christ crucified with trust in this Jesus and what he was able to do to connect us with God," Paul asks further: "Are you all so brainless that, after beginning with the Spirit, you are now going to come to completion with the flesh?!" (3:3). Paul assumes that the congregations will share his evaluation of the "Spirit" as far more positive and valuable a force than the "flesh." This is a rather safe assumption given the wide-

---

135. A similar point is made by the extensive episode of Cornelius and its interpretation in Acts 10–11, 15.

spread devaluation of "flesh" (as "physical body") below "spirit" (as a person's "non-physical essence," like a "soul," or as divine spirit indwelling and leading a person) in Greco-Roman philosophical writings and, no doubt therefore, in speeches in the market place of every city. Paul does not share in this general devaluation of the "body," since he clings to the hope of the resurrection of the physical body in *some* sense, insisting on *some* connection between one's future, eternal body and the physical body of our mortal life (see 1 Cor 15:35–58; 2 Cor 5:1–4). But he does capitalize on this hierarchy from the outset of his argument, even as he will refine his audience's understanding of both "flesh" and "Spirit" as the letter progresses to its close.

"Flesh" (as "body," "physical existence") is certainly less powerful than "Spirit" when it comes to pursuing the life of righteousness that God seeks in God's people. Paul will later develop the concept of "flesh" as a kind of collection of drives within the individual human being, and even in the midst of human community—that is, not limiting "flesh" to the physical aspects of being human, but also to our internal and our social existence. Hence the "works of the flesh" include the ways in which we rebel against God's righteous standards with our bodies (lust, gluttony, drunkenness, and the like), but also with our minds and in our relationships (enmities, factions, anger, envying, and the like). In Gal 5:13—6:10, Paul will make it clear that "flesh" as a power in our midst that turns us away from God's righteousness and Christ's example of self-giving love is not the same as "flesh" as the soft tissue covering our bones.

At this point, however, Paul is content to play on the generally accepted evaluation of "flesh" as that which participates in our mortal weakness. When Paul denies that he conferred with "flesh and blood" after his divine commission (meaning the apostles who had accompanied Jesus, 1:16–17), he expects his hearers to understand with him that "flesh and blood," being of a lower order and possessing a weaker insight than God, could add nothing of value to what he had already received from God and his experience of the glorified Christ. He uses the term again when he speaks of the impossibility of "all flesh" (meaning "all humanity") being justified, or brought in line with God's righteous standards, by means of the Torah (2:16). He uses the term more neutrally in 2:20 when he speaks of the life he now lives "while in the flesh," but this is "neutral" rather than negative because Paul lives within the relationship of trust or faith with Jesus, such that Jesus is coming to life within Paul, living through him, giving him a new life that is beyond the limitations of "flesh" on its own or even "flesh" aided by the guidance and guardianship of Torah.

Here in 3:3, Paul consigns Torah itself essentially to the realm of "flesh" and thus the realm of that which is impotent to help bring human beings to where God wants them to be. Since circumcision represents the cutting of the covenant into the "flesh" of each Jew or Gentile proselyte, the term "flesh" works especially well here (as also in 6:12–13). Paul's argument works by reducing his rivals' position to absurdity: if the Galatian converts already have experienced the Holy Spirit of God working in their midst collectively and in their lives individually, what could they possibly think that cutting around the flesh of their foreskin would add? If they had begun their journey in the power of the Spirit, how could they possibly think they could make greater progress now by turning to the "flesh" (both as attention to the physical alteration of the penis and as a collection of commandments that were concerned about such things as circumcision, what foods a person ate, and what one did to rinse pollution off the body)?[136] They have already made a good beginning in the Spirit, and can only make progress now by heeding the Spirit (hence the attention to this topic in 5:13—6:10, especially 5:16–25), not by submitting to something of merely fleshly power.

Paul's next question suggests that, were the Galatians to turn now to circumcision and other works of Torah as a means of making progress in their life before God, they would betray everything with which God had graced them up to that point: "Have you experienced such great things for nothing—if indeed it was for nothing?!" (3:4). The verb *epathete* is properly translated here as "you experienced," and not "you suffered."[137] The verb is often used to speak of painful or otherwise nega-

---

136. The unflattering linking of Torah with "flesh" continues in 4:21–31, as Paul connects Ishmael, the child born of the "flesh" (4:23a, 29) as opposed to the child born of "promise" (4:23b) or of "Spirit" (4:29), with those people who remain under the covenant of Sinai, that is, the Torah (4:24–25).

137. Burton, *Galatians*, 149; Fung, *Galatians*, 133; Longenecker, *Galatians*, 104.

tive experiences, and so "suffered" is generally an appropriate rendering. Here, however, Paul is referring to the Galatians' experience of the Spirit and of God's power working in their midst, asking if it was all for nothing—clearly positive experiences. "Have you suffered" was a fine translation in 1611, when "suffer" meant "passively experience" something, and not just "experience painful things," as it does in contemporary English. Paul had already hinted that turning now to the Torah would amount to repudiating God's generous kindness (2:21), and will again raise this alarm in 5:2–4 as part of his climactic appeal on this topic.

So important is it to Paul that the Galatians reflect on their own, firsthand experience of God's favor and acceptance on the basis of their having responded to Paul's announcement of the Gospel with trust in Christ that he essentially asks the question first posed in 3:2 again in 3:5: "The one, then, who supplied the Spirit to you and works miraculous signs among you—does he do this on the basis of works of Torah or on the basis of the message about trust, just as Abraham trusted God, and it was accounted to him as righteousness?" What is new in this iteration is the introduction of the historical example of Abraham in 3:6. This verse is almost universally taken as the beginning of a new paragraph or thought, despite the fact that, as it stands, it is an incomplete and therefore dependent clause. It is better construed syntactically as introducing a comparison (in the form of a historical precedent or case study) guiding the resolution of the rhetorical question of which it would now form a part.[138] Nevertheless, as the verse also effects a smooth transition to 3:7–9, we will consider it in connection with the following verses.

3:7–9: PROOF FROM EXAMPLE—ABRAHAM

[7]You all know, then, that these people—the ones who exhibit trust—are Abraham's sons and daughters. [8]For the Scripture, perceiving in advance that God would bring the Gentiles in line with his righteousness on the basis of trust, announced the message of good news ahead of time to Abraham that "All the nations will be blessed in you." [9]So then, those who exhibit trust are blessed along with Abraham, who exhibited trust.

138. So Fung, *Galatians*, 128.

Abraham was regarded as the ancestor of the Jewish people, the people of God. To be a child of Abraham, then, was to be part of God's people and an heir of the divine promises given to Abraham. It is likely that Paul has to discuss Abraham here in Galatians because the rival teachers had already promoted their own position on the basis of Abraham's story.[139] Abraham was, in Jewish tradition, the exemplary convert. He began life as a Gentile and a worshiper of idols in the house of his father Terah, but he left these idols behind in his quest for the living God who created heavens and earth.[140] God choose him, therefore, to be the vehicle of blessing for all nations, and to make of him a great nation. To "seal the deal," as it were, Abraham accepted the sign of circumcision upon himself and upon every male in his household in perpetuity (Gen 17:9–14). The rival teachers had, in Abraham, a strong argument in favor of circumcision, insofar as this was prescribed in Scripture as the prerequisite for being part of Abraham's family and thus an heir of the promise. For Paul, however, it was Abraham's trust in God and not his circumcised flesh that made him the recipient of God's promise and resulted in his being accounted "righteous" in God's sight. In this way, Abraham could indeed become the ancestor of many nations, the vehicle for God's blessing "all the nations" (Gal 3:8). Circumcision marked one as a Jew; trust marked one as an heir of Abraham, whether Jew or Gentile.

Paul introduces the example of Abraham by reciting LXX Gen 15:6 almost word for word (Paul uses "Abraham" rather than "Abram": this episode precedes God's changing of Abram's name). This text gives Paul a warrant for claiming that trusting God's word of promise is in itself something that God considers a righteous response to God's initiative. Paul would later develop this in Rom 4:3–8, in conjunction with Ps 31:1–2, in terms of God's forgiveness of sin: the phrase "it was accounted to him for righteousness" (Gen 15:6) is interpreted by the

---

139. For a creative attempt to reconstruct the kind of sermon the rival teachers might have preached on Abraham, see Martyn, *Galatians*, 302–6.

140. Stories of Abraham's pre-conversion involvement in idolatry, questioning of the validity of idolatrous worship, and prayer that the real God would reveal himself were popular in the intertestamental period. See *Jubilees* 11–12; *Apocalypse of Abraham*; Josephus, *Antiquities* 1.7.1.

psalmist's words, "blessed is the person whose sin the Lord does not hold in his account" (Ps 31:2). Paul will also develop in Rom 4:9–11 the significance of Scripture speaking of Abraham's trust and God's response of considering Abraham to be "right with God" in an episode several chapters prior to Abraham's circumcision (Gen 17:9–14).

Here, however, Paul exploits neither of these possibilities. Rather, he goes on immediately to define those who constitute Abraham's descendants, the children of promise: it is those who exhibit the family resemblance of "trust" in the announcement of God's promise ("these people—the ones who exhibit trust—are Abraham's sons and daughters"). This argumentative move is supported implicitly by the context of the verse Paul quotes in Gal 3:6 (Gen 15:6). God had just promised Abraham descendants as countless as the stars of the sky, assuring Abraham that he would have heirs from his own "seed" (Gen 15:5). Paul uses *huioi* in Gal 3:7 ("sons and daughters") rather than *sperma* ("seed," "offspring"), the word used for "offspring" in Gen 15:5, as he will take the interpretation of that particular term in a very different direction in Gal 3:15–18. Nevertheless, it is clear in Gen 15:5 that numerous descendants (and not one particular descendant, one particular "seed") are the substance of the promise at that point. Paul will return to this topic in 4:21–31.

Paul now cites a second word of promise spoken by God to Abraham: "all the nations will be blessed in you" (3:8). Paul blends together God's initial word of promise to Abraham ("all the tribes of the earth will be blessed in you," Gen 12:3) with a second utterance spoken by God within himself about Abraham ("all the nations will be blessed in him," Gen 18:18). Paul retains the direct address of the first, but uses the phrase "all the nations" (*panta ta ethnē*) from the second, as it better underscores God's purposes for the Gentile nations as well as the Jewish nations within the scope of God's promise. Paul interprets this phrase as "Scripture" (meaning "the Author of Scripture," referring to the composer by the composition) announcing well ahead of time God's intention of making the Gentile nations righteous. Paul is thus specifying the content of the rather general "blessing" that is promised to the nations through Abraham, and doing so in line with what Abraham himself received by trusting God's promise: righteousness (Gen 15:6). Abraham thus remains indeed the prototype, but not just for Gentile proselytes. Rather, he is the prototype showing how all people—Jew or Gentile—will fall in line with God's righteousness and find acquittal together at the judgment: "those who display trust (*oi ek pisteōs*) are blessed along with trusting Abraham" (3:9).

The rhetorical force of the repetitions of "blessing" ("will be blessed," 3:8; "are blessed," 3:9) in close association with the response of "trusting" God ("Abraham trusted," 3:6; "those who display trust," 3:7, 9; "on the basis of trusting," 3:8) will not be fully felt until Paul arrives at 3:10, where he introduces the major alternative course, "works of the Law" ("as many as occupy themselves with the works of the Torah," 3:10), in close association with "curse" ("under a curse," "cursed," 3:10). This double contrast between "blessing" and "curse," associating the former with "trust" and the latter with "works of the Torah," continues to force apart as incompatible what the rival teachers are promoting as complementary and mutually completing.

3:10–14: DEDUCTIVE PROOF FROM SCRIPTURE

[10]For as many people as align themselves with the works of the Torah are under a curse, for it is written: "Cursed is everyone who does not remain in all the things written in the book of the Torah, to do them." [11]It is clear that no one will be brought in line with God's righteousness by means of Torah in God's estimation, because "the one who is righteous on the basis of trust will live." [12]And the Torah does not involve operating on the basis of trust, but "the one doing these things will live by means of them." [13]Christ redeemed us from the curse of the Torah, having become a curse on our behalf (as it is written: "Cursed is everyone who hangs upon a tree"), [14]in order that Abraham's blessing might come to the nations in Christ Jesus—in order that we might receive the promised Spirit through trust.

Paul advances his argument by creating a matrix of contrasting, irreconcilable pairs. Abraham's trust became the vehicle for God's blessing for all people who joined themselves to Abraham by exhibiting the same trust toward God and God's promise (Gal 3:8). The Torah, on the other hand, was a vehicle for "curse." Paul connects Torah and curse by reciting Deut 27:26: "Cursed is every person who does not persevere in all the things written in this book, to do them." In its original context, this verse is the climactic curse of twelve curses to be pronounced by the Levites after the twelve tribes have crossed over the Jordan. The first eleven curses are pronounced specifically in relation to the violation of a particular commandment—setting up an idol, failing to honor parents, moving a boundary marker, misleading a blind person, failing to give justice to orphans, widows, and aliens, various kinds of incest and bestiality, murder, and taking a bribe. The "words of this law" in the twelfth curse may have been intended, in the first instance, to refer to the encapsulation of the ethical commands in Deut 27:11–26. Paul has given it its broadest application, however, by replacing "all the words of this law" with "all the words written in the book of the law." Those who, like Israel, place themselves under this covenant place themselves also under the threat of its curse.[141] This text would more naturally be read to promote Torah obedience, threatening the curse upon those who neglect its decrees. Indeed, it may have been introduced into the debate by the rival teachers, and not by Paul, to serve that very purpose. Paul uses it, however, to assert Torah's essential character as "curse" rather than "blessing," which in any case belongs to the promise and to trust.

Does Paul assume that those who rely on works of the Law are "under a curse" because it is categorically impossible for anyone to do all the commandments without misstep? Scholars frequently assert that this is Paul's underlying rationale for his claim.[142] This flies in the face, however, of the testimony of other Jews in regard to observance of Torah. Deuteronomy itself asserts the feasibility of keeping the covenant sufficiently: "Surely this commandment that I am commanding you today is not too hard for you, nor is it too far away" (that is, "out of reach," Deut 30:11 NRSV). Jews did not appear to understand Torah as a collection of laws that they had to fulfill perfectly or else fail to attain

141. Bruce, *Galatians*, 158; Fung, *Galatians*, 141; Longenecker, *Galatians*, 117.

142. See Kim, *Paul and the New Perspective*, 141–43; Burton, *Galatians*, 164–65; Longenecker, *Galatians*, 118; Fung, *Galatians*, 142.

God's favor.[143] Rather, the commandments of Torah constituted the way of life they were to embody in response to God's favor, and the sacrificial system was God's provision for imperfect people trying to live out this pattern of life. The "curse" of the Law did not fall on those who failed to do everything perfectly, but on those who sinned willfully, committed idolatry, or otherwise turned away from the covenant God. Some rabbis may indeed have thought that failing to keep one commandment would result in the curse, or in death. Rabbi Gamaliel was said to have wept at the implications of "he that does them shall live," that one must do *all* the commandments in order to live, and not just one (*b. Sanh.* 81a). But Rabbi Akiba would later retort that in doing each one, individually, is life. The author of 4 Maccabees assumes that, if a commandment is given, that is proof enough that it can, in fact, be kept (2:5–6). And while the author of 4 Ezra would stagger before the daunting requirement of keeping the commandments in the face of the power of the "evil inclination" if one is to attain to the age to come, and lament the fact that the majority of humankind would be lost, it remains possible for the person who applies himself or herself to this contest to keep the commandments and enter into life (7:45–60, 70–73, 127–131).

By broadening Deut 27:26 as he does, Paul may be thinking beyond the performance of individual commandments and considering the observance of the entirety of the Torah. This would include heeding the prophet whom God would "raise up" after Moses (Deut 18:18, understood in early Christian discourse to refer to Christ, as in Acts 3:22–23), as well as the model of Abraham, whose trust in God the readers of Torah are taught to imitate. Through their zeal for the Torah, and their resistance to what God was doing in Christ in the new phase of salvation history, Israel had made itself an enemy of God (Rom 10:2–4; 11:28, 31), refusing to submit in obedience to God. As such, their "doing" of Torah was only partial and misguided, so that they did not in fact "observe and obey all the things written in the book of the law" (Deut 27:26; 28:58, as given in Gal 3:10). In trying to keep the Sinai covenant alive after Christ in the way that was appropriate before Christ, they actually turned away from the covenant and fell under the curse. Paul's assessment of his own standing before God prior to his conversion—zealous for Torah, yet the

143. So Nock, *St. Paul*, 30.

enemy of God's Messiah—would plausibly have led him along such a train of thought. We should also bear in mind that Paul understands life in the Spirit to be qualitatively different than, and superior to, life under the Torah, as freedom is to slavery. He has discovered, by virtue of encountering Christ and receiving the Spirit, that "life" that Torah was intrinsically unable to provide (Gal 3:21).[144]

Trust is, therefore, associated with blessing and with righteousness; Torah with curse and failure to fall into alignment with God's righteousness. Paul asserts that "It is clear, then, that no one is accounted righteous in God's estimation through the Law," adding a rationale that incorporates a quotation from Hab 2:4: "because the righteous person will live on the basis of trust."[145] The Hebrew Bible and Greek Septuagint differed in regard to whether or not a person would live by "his (or her) faith" or by "my (i.e., God's) faith." Paul omits any personal pronoun whatsoever, putting the entire focus on "trust" or "faith" as the path that brings the righteous person to life before God. He now seeks to drive a wedge between Torah and trust. Following the Jewish exegetical principle of *gezera shawa*, whereby the meaning of one verse is drawn out by means of interpreting it in light of another scriptural text containing the same key word or words, Paul brings Lev 18:5 into the conversation: "But the Law is not done on the basis of trust, but rather 'the one who performs these things will live by means of them'" (Gal 3:12). The structural parallels that would recommend these two texts (Hab 2:4; Lev 18:5) as related and mutually interpreting go far beyond the occurrence of a shared word:

Hab 2:4	Lev 18:5
"the one who is righteous"	"the one who does these things"
"will live"	"will live"
"on the basis of trust"[146]	"through them"

144. Martyn, *Galatians*, 310.

145. Paul, the exegete of Scripture par excellence, brings together in 3:10–14 the only two texts from the Jewish Scriptures that combine a focus on "trust" and "righteous/righteousness" (Gen 15:6; Hab 2:4). See Sanders, *Paul and Palestinian Judaism*, 483–84.

146. This parallelism is one reason I prefer to align with those scholars who un-

In this juxtaposition, being "righteous" is linked only with the first path, the path of trust. This aligns with Abraham's experience and Paul's interpretation of the promise given to Abraham that all nations would be blessed (that is, made righteous) insofar as they walked in his example of trust (Gal 3:6–9). Since doing the Torah is based on something other than this trust, it cannot lead to becoming righteous. If one hopes to be a "righteous person," then, one is compelled to look to the path opened up by trust in Jesus and by the gift of the Spirit.

The verb "to live" (*zaō*) appears here again, now in such a way as suggests that it carries the more special sense of "to gain life before God," a special quality of life resulting from God's blessing upon the person. This is certainly how the Palestinian *targumim* interpreted Leviticus 18:5: the life of which it spoke was "everlasting life" or "the life of eternity" (*Tg. Onq.* And *Tg. Ps-J.* Lev 18:5).[147] For Paul, trusting God in Christ brings a person into the life of the "new creation," which is ultimately "eternal life" (2:19–20; 6:10).[148]

Relying on works of the Torah, or putting oneself under the yoke of Torah on this side of the Christ-event, is ultimately contrary to God's purposes in Christ—purposes achieved only at the greatest and grisliest cost to Jesus himself. "Christ redeemed us from the curse of the Torah, having become a curse on our behalf, as it is written: 'Cursed is everyone who hangs upon a tree'" (Gal 3:13). Paul quotes an excerpt from Deut 21:22–23, a regulation originally governing the limits of the amount of time an executed criminal's body could be put on display to further degrade the criminal and serve as a warning to others. The regulation stipulated that the body of the deceased criminal was to be buried before nightfall, so as not to defile the land of Israel. Presumably,

---

derstand the phrase "on the basis of trust" to describe the verb "will live" rather than to describe the manner in which "the righteous" became such. It is not the case, as Fung (Galatians, 146) suggests, that the two scriptures Paul cites (Hab 2:4; Lev 18:5) can be read to answer the question "Who shall enter into life?" as opposed to "How will one enter into life?" Because the Leviticus text includes the element "by means of them [i.e., the commandments performed]," it can only answer the question "How?" and, therefore, it seems reasonable to read Habakkuk as addressing that question as well.

147. Longenecker, *Galatians*, 120. The *Targumim*, notably, were affirming that the doing of Torah was, in fact, the way to attain this life.

148. So also Martyn, *Galatians*, 315.

the curse upon the person derived not from the fact that the body was displayed on a gibbet of some kind, but from the fact that he or she had been a transgressor of such a kind as merited capital punishment and beyond. Nevertheless, by the first century the verse was applied also to those who were executed by crucifixion or hanging.[149]

This text was no doubt an important factor in non-Christian Jewish rejection of Jesus as God's Messiah, including Paul's own rejection of the same.[150] How could the Messiah die accursed under the Law (indeed, specifically "cursed by God," according to Deut 21:23)? Surely it was slanderous even to suggest such a thing! Jewish Christians, however, convinced of Jesus' resurrection, were convinced thereby that God had personally vindicated Jesus as righteous and not as accursed, overturning the verdict of the Jewish authorities, the Roman enforcers, and the Torah itself. Paul had denied the reality of this reversal until he encountered the glorified Jesus, which brought home to him the reality of the resurrection and, thus, God's vindication of Jesus. As a result, Torah itself appeared to have been ranged against God and God's Messiah by virtue of pronouncing the latter "cursed by God"[151] when, in fact, he was the first human being to experience the ultimate blessing of resurrection from the dead.

Paul answers the question of how Jesus, God's Messiah, could come under Torah's curse by connecting this passage with the scripture that places everyone who is under Torah under a curse. The principle of *gezera shawa* is again operative in the selection and juxtaposition of Deut 21:23 and Deut 27:26. Christ became accursed under the Torah in order to redeem all those who had been born under Torah's curse (see also 4:4–5).[152] One facet of the significance of his death by crucifixion

149. See Fitzmyer, "Crucifixion in Ancient Palestine," 493–513.

150. Hengel, *The Pre-Christian Paul*, 83.

151. Paul, however, judiciously omits the phrase "by God" when he quotes Deut 21:23, thus heightening the sense that the *Torah* may curse the one hanged upon the tree, but *God* would not therefore necessarily curse such a one (Martyn, *Galatians*, 320).

152. Paul is speaking here specifically about the eschatological redemption of the people of Israel, a prelude to the blessing of all the nations, Jewish and Gentile, together. See Donaldson, "The 'Curse of the Law' and the Inclusion of the Gentiles," 94–112, especially pp. 94, 100; Betz, *Galatians*, 148; Hays, *Faith of Jesus Christ*, 113;

was that he had become an "exchange curse"[153] for the Jewish people, freeing them from living under the threat of curse and bringing the authority of Torah to an end.[154] With the term of Torah—that which separated Jew from Gentile—over, God would now deliver the blessing, promised through Abraham, to "all the nations," Jewish and Gentile alike (3:14).

Belleville, "'Under Law,'" 53–78; against Schlier, *Galater*, 136–37; Fung, *Galatians*, 148–49.

153. Longenecker, *Galatians*, 121. The exchange theme occurs frequently throughout the New Testament, as for example in the following texts: "He made him who did not know sin to become sin on our behalf, in order that we might become God's righteousness through him" (2 Cor 5:21); "You know the generous kindness of our Lord Jesus Christ, that, though he was rich, he became poor on account of you, in order that you might become rich through his poverty" (2 Cor 8:9); "Christ suffered for sins once for all, a just person for the unjust, in order to lead us back to God" (1 Pet 3:18).

154. To be sure, Jesus' death redeems Gentiles as well, though Paul will speak about Gentiles more in terms of being formerly enslaved to the "elementary principles of the cosmos" (*ta stoicheia tou kosmou*) than to the Law specifically. Torah is, for Paul, one of these "elementary principles," but functions thus for the Jewish people in particular, not for all peoples. Nevertheless, noteworthy scholars have stressed, counter to the position espoused here, that Paul means to say that Jesus redeemed all people, Jew and Gentile, from the curse of the Law: since its curse falls upon non-observance of the Torah, it must fall *de facto* upon all Gentiles (Martyn, *Galatians*, 317). I would agree with Martyn that Paul does not observe a consistent distinction between the "we" of Galatians as Jewish Christians and the "you" of Galatians as the Gentile Galatian converts, such that the "we" in 3:14 would be all-inclusive (Martyn, *Galatians*, 334–36). But it is certainly the case that the "we" is not *always* all-inclusive (as in 2:15–16), and we must decide on a case-by-case basis who would have been heard to have been included or excluded by a "we." Paul speaks of Gentiles elsewhere as being "without Law," not "under Law." He speaks here of all people enslaved to the *stoicheia tou kosmou*, but makes a distinction again between those who are enslaved or imprisoned "under the Law" and those who are enslaved or imprisoned "under [other] *stoicheia tou kosmou*" (4:3) which involves "being enslaved to beings that are not, by nature, gods" and thus being alienated from the One God (4:8–9). Martyn (*Galatians*, 336) regards the identification of Torah as a *stoicheion* as a sign that "before the advent of Christ humanity was an enslaved monolith," while "in Christ humanity is becoming a liberated unity." I would agree that Paul regards all people as enslaved prior to Christ's coming, but not as a "monolith." They were all in prison, but in separate cells. Only now in Christ are the various prison doors opened, so that Jews ("under Law") and Gentiles ("under [other] *stoicheia*") mix in a single body in freedom.

Two purpose clauses close this segment of Paul's argument: Christ redeemed the Jewish people from the curse of the Torah "in order that Abraham's blessing might come to the nations in Christ Jesus—in order that we might receive the promised Spirit through trust" (3:14).[155] The two clauses express the same spiritual reality, the second giving clearer definition to the first. The Holy Spirit *is* the content of the blessing of Abraham that was promised to the nations, the promised gift (Gal 3:14).[156] On what basis could Paul make this identification? First, in the experience of the early church, the Spirit came upon all who trusted in Jesus, whether Jews or Gentiles. It was as universal in scope as had been the promise to Abraham: "in you all the nations will be blessed" (Gen 12:3; Gal 3:8). Second, the Spirit signified the believers' adoption by God as sons and daughters (Gal 4:6–7). The phenomenon of being filled with the Spirit led the early Christians, who thenceforth called upon God as "Abba, Father" (Gal 4:6), to understand this as a spiritual begetting by God's own self, making them spiritual children of Abraham (Gal 3:26–29; 4:21–28) just like Isaac was the spiritual child of Abraham, having been born on the basis of God's promise rather than the deeds of flesh.

The Holy Spirit is the God-given resource for our transformation into people who are indeed righteous before God, people in whom the "Righteous One," Christ himself, comes to life and through whom he lives. The Spirit is the God-given means by which those who have trusted in Jesus, whether Jew or Gentile, are "set right," or "brought in line with God's righteous standards." Sending the Spirit into the hearts and lives of believers was the way in which God would "justify the nations" (3:8), empowering them to find acquittal on the day of judgment. Paul will say more about *how* the Spirit intervenes to empower the fulfillment of God's righteous requirements in 5:16—6:10, proving his claim that the Spirit—the gift bestowed on the basis of trust in Jesus—is indeed sufficient not only for the beginning of the disciples' journey, but

---

155. A few early witnesses, notably P[46], read "the blessing of the Spirit" in place of "the promise of the Spirit." In Greek, the two words begin with the same letter, end with the same three letters, and share yet another two letters in their stems, making it likely that this early scribe simply misread the text at this point.

156. Martyn, *Galatians*, 323.

for bringing them to the completion of their transformation without the disciples relying on "works of the Torah." At this stage, it is sufficient for Paul that he has demonstrated to his converts that they had already received the blessing promised to and through Abraham, and thus their response of trust toward God was sufficient to join them to Abraham without any need for circumcision or other "works of the Law."

3:15-18: PROOF FROM ANALOGY—TESTAMENTARY LAW

[15]Brothers and sisters, I am speaking at a human level here. Be that as it may, no one sets aside or adds to a person's testament once it has been ratified. [16]The promises were spoken to Abraham and to his "seed/descendant." It does not say "to seeds/descendants," as concerning many, but as concerning one, "and to your seed/descendant," which is Christ. [17]And I say this: The Torah, coming into existence 430 years later, does not nullify a testament previously ratified by God, so as to make the promise void. [18]For if the inheritance comes on the basis of Torah, it is no longer on the basis of a promise— but God graced Abraham with a promise.

The promise given to Abraham and the fulfillment of that promise in the pouring out of the Spirit upon all who are "in Christ" (Gal 3:14) make the promise, and not the Law, the focal point for Paul's model of salvation history. In this new section, signaled by the fresh address of the audience as "brothers and sisters," Paul will seek to establish the ultimacy of the promise and its fulfillment "in the fullness of time" (Gal 4:4) in God's plan for redeeming humankind, with these two events—promise to Abraham and fulfillment in Christ—forming a pair of parentheses around the Torah, which has a much more limited (and limiting) function in God's plan.

To pursue this line of argument, Paul seeks to draw an analogy between the common practice among people of drawing up wills or "testaments" (*diathēkē*) and the effects of the giving of the Law on a previous "testament" ratified by God. The Greek word *diathēkē* can refer to a variety of legally binding agreements. In addition to the "covenant" struck between two parties by mutual agreement (such as the covenant made at

Sinai), it is very commonly associated with the practice of drawing up a document granting one's property to designated heirs upon one's death, hence the "testament" or "will." The facet of testamentary law upon which Paul wants his hearers to focus is the fact that once a person's will is made and ratified no one else can attach additional provisions to it.[157] A person may typically change his or her will prior to dying, such that wills tend to be "revocable" in the ancient world, though Paul and his hearers would also have known of a kind of "irrevocable" will whereby a person actually passes on possession to other parties while he or she is still living, with the provision that he or she will continue to enjoy the use thereof until death.[158]

Difficulties arise when we try to press Paul's analogy beyond the level of precision that he himself employs and beyond its capacity to "fit" the dealings of an immortal deity and human beings.[159] Paul, however, admits at the outset that his analogy is not perfect, speaking as he is "at the human level" (*kata anthropon*, "in a human fashion," "at the human level," perhaps even "from human experience).[160] The practice of testamentary law is merely a means by which he seeks to illustrate the relationship between the promise to Abraham and the Torah (3:15–18), as well as the qualitative difference between these two kinds of arrangement between God and God's people (3:19–22).

In a manner, then, analogous to that of a human being's "last will and testament," God made promises "to Abraham and to his 'seed'" (Gal

157. Bruce, *Galatians*, 171; Fung, *Galatians*, 154. Paul uses a word here (*epidiatassō*) that is not found elsewhere in extant Greek literature, though its meaning can readily be deduced from its component parts (*epi* + *diatassō*). See Longenecker, *Galatians*, 128.

158. Longenecker, *Galatians*, 129–30.

159. The author of Hebrews will try to "solve" this problem in his own way by speaking of the death of Jesus as the necessary death upon which the provisions of a will take effect (Heb 9:15–17), though this introduces problems of its own as, now, it is the mediator of the will/covenant, and not the benefactor making the will, who dies. Both Paul and the author of Hebrews clearly assume that their hearers will grant them some degree of looseness in using the analogy of wills and testaments in regard to the divine.

160. The word *homōs* that introduces the statement about no one nullifying another person's will also has a concessive nuance, being translated "nevertheless, notwithstanding, for all that," and the like (so *LSJ* s.v. ὅμως [*homōs*]).

3:16). Here Paul offers a stunning interpretation, based on a close examination of the Genesis text. He notices that the word "seed" (*sperma*) is in the singular, and not in the plural (*spermata*, "seeds"), deducing from this that God had in mind a particular descendant of Abraham's as the recipient of the promises, and not all the natural descendants of Abraham. The word "seed" in the relevant passages in Genesis (see Gen 12: 7; 13:15; 15:5–6, 13; 16:10; 22:17–18) is typically—and rightly—read as a collective noun, much as the English word "offspring" can refer to a single child or all of one's natural descendants (even through the generations). God's promise to Abraham in each of these passages clearly has in view a great multitude of offspring or descendants, as God regularly tells Abraham that his "seed" will be in number comparable to the stars of heaven or the sand by and in the sea. The Aramaic paraphrases of the Hebrew Bible (the *targumim*) also tend to explain the singular, collective "seed" (Heb, *zerah*) as "sons and daughters" or some other plural noun.[161]

The history of the Jewish people could easily have led Paul to reject the collective understanding of "seed" (*sperma*), since the promise of God's blessing all the nations had not come to pass through the nation of Israel at any point, though now, in his experience, it was coming to pass where the Gospel was proclaimed and the Holy Spirit poured out upon people from any nation who trusted God's promises in Jesus. Paul also appears not to have been entirely alone in this reading of Abraham's "seed": other Jewish authors are known to have applied the promises to Abraham and David concerning their "seed" to the figure of the Messiah.[162]

Paul does not, moreover, simply ignore the element of God multiplying Abraham's seed (Gen 13:16; 15:5; 16:10; 22:17–18). However, the means by which God will multiply the heirs of the promises is quite unlike anything foreseen by other Jewish interpreters of those passages. If the "Seed" in view is singular, namely Jesus, the Messiah, the promise of God multiplying Abraham's seed comes to pass as people are incorporated into the Seed, clothing themselves with Christ in their baptism, joining themselves not to Abraham's "seed" in the form of the Jewish

161. See Wilcox, "The Promise of the 'Seed,'" 2–20.

162. See ibid., 16.

people, but to Abraham's "Seed" in the form of Jesus the Messiah. Paul sees God's promise resulting in far more numerous descendants than a few million physical descendants (the Jewish people). Rather, countless millions would become Abraham's seed by means of joining themselves to the Seed that is Christ (Gal 3:26–27, 29). For this reason, Paul also regards the prophesy of Isa 54:1 to be fulfilled as Sarah's spiritual progeny (those born "in trust" and "on the basis of God's promise) are multiplied through the proclamation and reception of the Gospel across the Mediterranean (see Gal 4:26–28). All who are in Christ, therefore, are incorporated into the promise quite apart from Torah's stipulations.

We arrive here at the relevant point that Paul had in mind when he asked his hearers to consider the common practice among human beings of making "wills," legal dispositions of goods to which no one could add any further provisions or make any alterations after the will had been legally made: "The Torah, coming into existence 430 years later, does not nullify a testament previously ratified by God, so as to make the promise void" (3:17).[163] The figure of "430 years" comes from Exod 12:40, where it is given as the length of time "that the Israelites had lived in Egypt."[164] The time between Abraham's reception of the promise and the migration of Jacob and his family to Egypt would, of course, have added substantially to that tally, but Paul is simply using a well-known biblical number associated with the exodus rather than trying to provide a precise calculation of the time elapsed between the promise being given to Abraham and the Torah being given to and through Moses. Paul stands starkly against the contemporary Jewish tradition of the eternity of the Torah here. The second-century BCE book *Jubilees*, for example, retells the stories of the patriarchs in a way that depicts them following and teaching their descendants the precise stipulations of the Torah during their lifetimes, long before Torah was revealed to Moses

163. The "Majority Text" adds two words: "a testament previously ratified by God *for Christ*" (hence the King James Version [KJV], "the covenant, that was confirmed before of God in Christ"). The earliest manuscripts (P[46], Sinaiticus, Vaticanus, and Alexandrinus), however, are unanimous in their witness that these two words are a later addition, another result of later scribes attempting to clarify the meaning of the text they received.

164. Compare Gen 15:13, where the time of Israel's bondage in Egypt is given as 400 years.

on Mount Sinai. This is one means by which Jews gave expression to their conviction that the Torah had always and would always regulate the relationship between, and practice of, God and God's people.[165]

Paul's point is that the giving of the Torah in no way changes the terms of the original promise (which was like a "testament" or "will") that God made to Abraham and to Abraham's "Seed," namely Christ and all those who would join themselves to that Seed. Since God had already bequeathed his inheritance to Abraham and his "seed," the Torah that was added 430 years after the fact could not be understood even as an amendment to that promise, let alone a legal arrangement that replaces the promise regarding who may inherit the blessings promised to Abraham, or on what basis inheritance may take place (3:18).[166] It must have some other, more limited role (which Paul will explore in 3:19–25). This paragraph introduces the very important concept of "inheritance" into the fabric of Galatians, a concept that will remain prevalent throughout the letter (Gal 3:29; 4:1, 7, 30; 5:21), continually reminding the hearers of the priority of God's promise to Abraham and the Seed (Christ) over the Torah.

3:19–22: HOW DOES TORAH FIT IN?

[19] Why, then, the Torah? It was added for the sake of transgressions, until the seed/descendant to whom the promise was made should come. It was established through angels by the hand of a mediator. [20]The mediator is not *a representative only* of one, but God is One. [21]Is the Torah, then, against the promises [of God]? By no means, for if a Law that had the ability to give life had been given, then righteousness would indeed have been on the basis of that Law. [22]But the Scripture has consigned all things under sin, in order that the promise

165. See also the rabbinic texts *Gen. R.* 1:4; *Pes.* 54a; *P. Aboth* 3:14.

166. Paul makes a similar point when he returns to these topics in in Rom 4:13–14: "The promise to Abraham or to his seed, that he should be the heir of the cosmos, is not through Law but through the righteousness that springs from trust. For if the inheritance were on the basis of Law, trust would be nullified and the promise made void."

might be given on the basis of trusting Jesus Christ (or, Jesus
Christ's faithfulness) to those who exhibit trust.

Having raised the problematic nature of Torah's "intrusion" into God's
plan in 3:15–18, Paul must now explain what role the Torah in fact served,
if not as the God-given means of aligning oneself with God's righteousness. His answer, unfortunately, is quite cryptic: "it was added for the
sake of transgressions (*charin parabaseōn*), until the Seed, to whom the
promises were made, should come" (3:19). What is clear from Paul's answer is that the Torah was introduced as a temporary measure, to serve
some function for the limited time between God's making promises to
Abraham and the "fullness of time" when the promised blessings would
be delivered in Christ (for example, the bestowing of the Holy Spirit
as the agent of bringing people in line with God's righteousness, 3:14).
What is not clear, however, is the precise sense of the Law being "added
for the sake of transgressions."

The ambiguities in that terse phrase can lead to significantly different understandings of the role of Torah in God's economy:

1. Torah exercises a limiting or restraining force against
   transgressions.

2. Torah provides a means of dealing with transgressions (e.g.,
   punishing offenders against God's righteousness and/or making
   amends by means of the sacrificial system), though perhaps not
   eliminating transgression.

3. Torah provokes transgressions.[167]

4. Torah brings an awareness of transgressions and, thus, of the
   distance between human behavior and God's righteousness.[168]

It is difficult to choose between these options on the basis of the context of Galatians alone, though the first seems least likely on account
of Paul's crediting of the Spirit with this restraining, even overcoming,

---

167. Martyn (*Galatians*, 354–55) favors this sense, on the ground that, since
transgression is technically a violation of a law, the law must be given and known
before there can be any transgressions.

168. Longenecker (*Galatians*, 138) favors this meaning.

power. Paul addresses this topic in greater detail in Romans, where the last two options seem particularly to be developed. There, the Law brings "knowledge of sin," the recognition of certain patterns of behavior as being contrary to God's standards of righteousness and holiness (Rom 3:20), but it also gives an opportunity for Sin, as a supra-personal power wreaking havoc in the lives of human beings, to provoke people's impulsive desires to move in directions contrary to God's law. The very command "do not covet" gives Sin an opportunity to provoke covetousness in all directions in the human heart (Rom 7:7–8). This may name the same inner-personal reality or dynamic that Paul speaks of under the label "flesh" in Gal 5:13—6:10. Perhaps, again, Paul is not trying to be nearly as precise as commentators would like to think, such that all he is trying to accomplish here is forging a link between Torah and transgression, countering the link between Torah and righteousness that the rival teachers are promoting and that Paul is opposing (as, in the immediate context, in 3:21).[169]

Paul says that the Torah was "instituted by angels, by means of a mediator." Moses' role as a mediator of the Law—the agent through whom God revealed, recorded, and instituted the Torah and the covenant based thereon—was well established in the Pentateuch (as early as Exod 20:18–22a). While Moses is not called a "mediator" in the Pentateuch, he is called by this term in first-century Jewish texts.[170] The role of angels in the giving of the Law, however, is not so apparent from the beginning. Recollections of the appearance of God at Sinai, however, increasingly depict God coming with his angelic retinue (as in Ps 68:18), with the result that angels were commonly associated with the giving of the Law—indeed, providing a link in the chain of the giving of the Law—by the first century CE (see *Jub.* 1:27–29; Heb 2:2; Acts 7:38, 53; Philo, *Somn.* 1.140–44; Josephus, *Ant.* 15.136).[171]

While most Jewish authors spoke of the appearance of angels at this event to increase the significance and magnificence of the revelation of the Torah, Paul views the scene negatively—certainly as a sign of

---

169. Longenecker, *Galatians*, 139.

170. See *Testament of Moses* 1.14; Philo, *Vit. Mos.* 2.166; Callan, "Pauline Midrash," 549–67, especially p. 555

171. Callan, "Pauline Midrash," 551; Longenecker, *Galatians*, 140.

the inferior origin of the Torah, perhaps even of its failure to align with the most central creed of Judaism: "The mediator is not *a representative only* of one, but God is One (*ho de theos heis estin*)." The second part of this statement quotes the opening of the *Shema*, the compilation of texts recited twice daily by pious Jews: "Hear, O Israel: the Lord our God, the Lord is one" (*ho theos . . . heis estin*, Deut 6:4 LXX). By opposing the involvement of multiple parties (hence requiring a mediator) in the giving of the Torah to the essential oneness of God, Paul distances God from the giving of the Torah, and hence calls into question the absoluteness of Torah as the revelation of God's will and God's covenant.[172] Indeed, God's distance, if not absence altogether, from the giving of the Torah in Paul's account here is striking. Torah appears, at first glance, to be a matter of a negotiated treaty between angels and Hebrews, with Moses functioning as the "go-between." As an agreement struck between multiple parties, moreover, the Sinaitic covenant depends upon the ongoing performance of obligations by both parties in order to remain in force, and in order for the benefits of the covenant to be enjoyed (and for the negative consequences of failing to remain in the performance of the same to be avoided). Torah is a mediated treaty, whereas the promise given to Abraham is an absolute word spoken personally by the One God, guaranteed to the Seed (Christ) and all those who join themselves to the Seed by trust.

Israel's collective experience down to the time of Paul (and all the more in the decades after!) is a testimony to the Sinaitic covenant essentially ensuring a fairly consistent state of "curse" for Israel due to its collective failure to keep the covenant. Failure to keep the covenant

---

172. The involvement of a mediator at all means that God is operating at a greater distance in giving the Torah than previously in giving the promises to Abraham, with the result that the latter is the more reliable. See Betz, *Galatians*, 171–73; Callan, "Pauline Midrash," 555–67. Awareness of this perception is reflected also in rabbinic texts that, contrary to the increasingly popular tendency to view the Law as given "through angels," affirms instead that God spoke the Torah directly to Moses and not through any angels or intermediaries (*Sipre Deut. 42* [on 11:14]; 325 [on 32:35]; *Abot R. Nat. B 2*; see Goldin, "Not by Means of an Angel," 412–24; Longenecker, *Galatians*, 136–37). There is also a more subtle problem inherent in the Torah—whose effect was to set Jews apart from Gentiles—in regard to the One God who is God both of Jews and Gentiles (cf. Rom 3:27–30), whose oneness is to be reflected in the oneness of the people of God, as will eventually come to pass in Christ Jesus (Gal 3:26–28).

resulted in the Assyrian invasion and deportation of the Northern Kingdom; in the Babylonian invasion, deportation of Judean elites and destruction of the first temple; in Persian, then Greek, then Egyptian (Ptolemaic), then Syrian (Seleucid) domination; in the desecration of the temple and desolation of Jerusalem under the Seleucid monarch Antiochus IV; and, finally, after temporary independence under the Hasmonean family, in the establishment of Roman domination. How much, really, did Israel ever see the blessings of the Sinaitic covenant in its collective life? "Righteousness" thus did not come through the Torah (3:21), and the people therefore did not experience the blessings of the Torah, but only its curse.

The kind of covenant (*diathēkē*) represented by Torah is a qualitatively different kind of arrangement from the covenant God made with Abraham, which is more like a bequest or a will (also *diathēkē*), depending on the generous kindness of one party toward the beneficiaries, who only need to trust that the one who promised will accomplish what he promised—the gift of righteousness through the working of the Holy Spirit among and within all those who have joined themselves to *the* Seed, which is Christ. Paul will return to this contrast between the two "covenants" and their qualitative differences in Gal 4:21–31.

It is not that the Torah was opposed to God's promises (Gal 3:21).[173] Paul knows that God was behind the giving of the Law, and would be much more openly affirming of the holiness of the law itself in Romans (7:12). The Torah was simply not part of God's plan to deliver the promised blessings: it had no power to "give life," since it had no power to make righteousness take root amongst the people, righteousness being the prerequisite to finding "life" before God. The verb "to make alive" (*zōopoiēsai*) does not denote the bestowal of merely physical life, since Paul (and the Torah) addresses people who already breathe and move and conduct their affairs. Torah cannot "make alive" in the

---

173. Codex Sinaiticus, Codex Alexandrinus, and the Majority Text read "the promises of God" in Gal 3:21, and thus the phrase "of God" is included in most translations. These words are absent, however, from P[46] and Codex Vaticanus. It is more likely that these two words were added by scribes wishing to make clear what promises were meant by Paul (hence, a scribal "improvement" of the text) than that two very early witnesses omitted the words, for which there would be no motive (or easy explanation of accidental oversight).

sense of opening its adherents up to living a new kind of existence in the here and now and living an eternal life beyond death, beyond God's judgment, beyond the consequences of our first parents' disobedience that brought death into the world (see Rom 5:12–21).[174] This was never its purpose. The Spirit, however, brings people alive in this way, opening them up to the life of Christ taking on flesh within them (Gal 2:19–20; 4:19) and, ultimately, to eternal life (Gal 6:7–10).

In Paul's estimation, the Law that was given was not able to give life; it was not able to bestow righteousness before God. On the contrary, "the Scripture has consigned all things under sin, in order that the promise might be given on the basis of trusting[175] Jesus Christ [or, on the basis of Jesus Christ's faithfulness] to those who exhibit trust" (3:22). "Scripture" again appears somewhat strangely as the subject of a sentence (see 3:8), but not as though it were itself an independent force, but as the revelation of the purposes of God, whose movements and actions Scripture reveals. God has consigned all things under sin; Scripture simply makes this fact known. Some scholars suggest that Paul has a particular scriptural text in mind here, specifically, again, Deut 27:26, which had placed all those who live on the basis of works of the Law "under a curse."[176] This would presume, however, a reading of Gal 3:10–14 that understands Jews and Gentiles alike to labor under Torah's curse, while it seems more probable that Paul is conceptualizing Jews and Gentiles as living out their servitude under different *stoicheia* (see, further, 3:23–25, 4:1–11). Other scholars regard the reference to "the Scripture" here as "Scripture in general," the general witness of Scripture to the failure of all human beings to live in line with God's righteousness.[177] The promise of "righteousness" and of "life" would be given not through Torah, but on the basis of God's promise to Abraham

---

174. On the fuller sense of "life" here, see also Fung, *Galatians*, 162–63.

175. "On the basis of trust" (*ek pisteōs*) is an adverbial prepositional phrase qualifying how the promise "will be given" (*dothȩ̄*). So, rightly, Fung, *Galatians*, 165.

176. Burton, *Galatians*, 195–96; Longenecker, *Galatians*, 144.

177. See, for example, the string of quotations from Scripture that Paul later brings together in Rom 3:10–18 to establish the point that "all—both Jews and Greeks—are under sin" (Rom 3:9); Schlier, *Galater*, 164; Fung, *Galatians*, 164.

and to Abraham's Seed, and thus received as one joins oneself to that Seed in trust.

Galatians 3:22 is one of the key verses that could speak of the importance of Christ's faithfulness *and* the disciple's trust as essential elements of receiving the promise and, thereby, justification. The promise will be given:

(a) "on the basis of trust in Jesus Christ"
  or "on the basis of Jesus Christ's faithfulness"

(b) "to those who display trust."

The role of a trusting response to God's promise is already present in the second element (b). The question concerns, as in Gal 2:16, the phrase *pistis Iēsou Christou* in the first element. If contextual indicators are any guide, we would once again have to resolve this in the direction of the "objective genitive," wherein "Jesus Christ" is the object of trust, despite the apparent redundancy.[178] Jesus Christ's faithfulness toward those he came to redeem, however, remains an essential, if not *the* essential, element in the narrative of redemption, captured in such verses as Gal 1:4; 2:20; 3:13.[179]

3:23–29: PROOF FROM ANALOGY—
LIFE IN THE HOUSEHOLD

[23]Before faith came, we were being guarded under Torah, penned up unto the faith that was about to be revealed, [24]with the result that the Torah has been our pedagogue until Christ, in order that we might be brought in line with God's righteousness on the basis of trust. [25]But now, with faith having come, we are no longer under a pedagogue. [26]For you are all sons and daughters of God in Christ Jesus through faith: [27]for as many of you have been baptized into Christ have put on

178. According to Fung (*Galatians*, 165), the genitive phrase provides the objective basis for God's delivering the promise (the basis of trusting Jesus) and the second phrase the subjective basis on which the promise is received by human beings.

179. Jesus' faithfulness to God is also amply attested in Paul, as, for example, in Phil 2:5–8.

Christ as one would put on one's clothes. [28]There is no longer
Jew nor Greek; there is no longer slave nor free; there is no
longer 'male and female'—for you are all one in Christ Jesus.
[29]And if you are Christ's, then you are seed/descendants of
Abraham, heirs in accordance with a promise.

Paul turns to an analogy from the life of children growing up in households of more-than-moderate means, that is, households that could
afford to own several slaves. Children moved through several stages of
care—first nannies or "wet nurses," then pedagogues, then teachers—
before reaching maturity, the age at which they become adult children
within the household and participants in the life of the city. Paul likens
the period of the Torah's authority over the Jewish people to the authority of the pedagogue over the children in a household, and the coming
of "faith" to the "coming of age" of children in the household. Paul will
continue to develop this analogy in 4:1–11, where the implications for
the Galatians' current situation are drawn out. Just as the child who has
come of age cannot (and should not want to!) turn back the clock to
return to the time that he or she was under the discipline of the pedagogue, so those who have come to know Jesus and his gifts cannot now
turn back the clock to the period before Christ's coming, so as return to
live under the Torah or any of the other enslaving powers that people
lived under before "the fullness of time."

Paul has been arguing that the Torah's authority extended until
the coming of Christ and the possibility Christ's coming opened up of
joining oneself to Abraham's Seed in trust, imitating Abraham's own
response to God's promise (3:15–19, 22). We might expect him to write
"before Christ came" in 3:23 and "with Christ having come" in 3:25,
but instead he speaks of "the faith" or "faith" coming at these points. In
so doing, he is focusing on the kind of response to God that is called
for after a certain point, or, better, after a certain development in God's
salvation story. This shift is warranted as it is precisely the appropriate
response to God that is at issue now in Galatia, whether trusting God's
provision in Jesus (and walking forward and growing in what God has
provided) is the sufficient response from beginning to end, or if taking
on the "works of the Torah" is a necessary component of this response.

"Faith" or "trust" is, by this point in Paul's address, a term loaded with meaning and connections:

> We received the Holy Spirit on the basis of trusting the effectiveness of Jesus' death and resurrection (3:2, 14).

> Abraham exhibited trust, which was counted as righteousness before God (3:6).

> Those who trust, like Abraham, share in the blessing promised to Abraham (3:9, 22).

The temporal scheme of "Promise—(Torah)—Coming of the Seed/ Christ" is also well established by this point (3:15-17, 19). The "coming" of "faith" stands parallel to the arrival of Christ, the Seed whose "coming" signaled the end of Torah's term of authority (3:19), and to God's sending his Son in the "fullness of time" (4:4).[180] "Before faith came," then, could be heard as shorthand at this point in Paul's letter for "Before the possibility came of exhibiting Abraham-life trust toward God in regard to what God was making available through Jesus Christ," or "Before the necessary events took place (i.e., Christ's coming, death, and resurrection) that would allow us to be aligned with God's righteousness on the basis of trusting the effects of Jesus' death and the power of the Holy Spirit that would be shed abroad in our hearts."

Prior to the hinge point of God's salvation history, Paul claims, the Jewish people were "being kept under guard under Torah, penned up and corralled toward the object of trust and the possibilities of trust that were about to be revealed in Christ" (3:23).[181] The images Paul uses are those of confinement, but confinement in a certain direction, "towards the faith" (*eis . . . pistin*) that was "about to be revealed." This is the only positive function Paul assigns to the Torah and its effects upon the

---

180. Martyn, *Galatians*, 361–62.

181. The fact that Paul writes "law" and not "*the* law" at this point does not mean, as Fung (*Galatians*, 167) asserts, that Paul has now switched his focus to "the general principle of law." Paul reverts immediately in 3:24 to speaking of "the law," signaling that his focus has not left the Jewish Law, the Torah, and the predicament of the Jewish people prior to the coming of the Messiah. The experience of the Jews under the Torah, however, is paradigmatic for the experience of all peoples under the other *stoicheia*, as Paul develops in 4:1–11.

Jewish people in Galatians. It pointed their noses in the right direction, with the result that, when Christ did come, there was a core of Jewish people who saw what God was doing, saw how texts throughout their Scriptures were pointing in this direction, and thus trusted in Jesus as the Jewish Messiah (cf. Gal 2:15–16). To be sure, most Jews in Paul's time never left the corral of the Torah to enter into the fields of freedom in Christ, a fact most grievous to him (cf. Rom 9–11).

The confining and guarding function of the Torah suggests to Paul that the "pedagogue" set over young children in a household was an apt metaphor: "thus the Torah has become our pedagogue until Christ,[182] in order that we might be aligned with God's righteousness on the basis of trust" (3:24). In English, "pedagogue" and "pedagogy" are words associated with the education of children. The latter, in fact, concerns the methods used in the classroom to teach children and youths. In the ancient (elite) household, however, this was not typical. The "pedagogue" (*paidagōgos*) is clearly distinguished from the "teachers" (*didaskaloi*) that educate the child.[183] He was the disciplinarian and babysitter wrapped up into one, the person who made sure the child didn't misbehave and who gave him a serious scolding or smack if he did.[184] Neither Torah nor the other *stoicheia* (see Gal 4:1–11) are seen from the point of view of having a positive, educating and formative function, but performing more a negative function of keeping the unruly in line. Torah served this function, moreover, not in order to provide the means by which to be aligned with God's righteousness—that role belongs to trust and to the promised gift that is bestowed upon those who trust (3:24b).

Paul's view of the Torah is here quite different from that of Jewish authors nearly contemporary with him. The author of 4 Maccabees, for example, very much viewed the Torah as the "instructor" (*paideuta*,

---

182. The preposition *eis* here could have a directional or temporal sense, thus "unto Christ" or "until Christ." In the context of Paul's sharp division of periods of time—one in which Torah had authoritative force, and a subsequent one, commencing with the advent of Christ, in which it no longer had force—the temporal sense seems far more appropriate here. See, further, Longenecker, *Galatians*, 148–49.

183. See Plato, *Lysis*, 208C; *Laws*, 7.808D–E; Xenophon, *Laced.* 3.1. These and other texts are recited and discussed in Longenecker, *Galatians*, 146–47.

184. Thus Young, "*Paidagogos*," 150–76, especially pp. 157–65; Longenecker, "Pedagogical Nature," 53–61, especially pp. 53–56; Martyn, *Galatians*, 389.

5:34) and not merely the "pedagogue." The aged priest Eleazar praises the education that Torah offers: "it teaches us self-control, so that we master all pleasures and desires, and it also trains us in courage, so that we endure any suffering willingly; it instructs us in justice, so that in all our dealings we act impartially, and it teaches us piety, so that with proper reverence we worship the only real God" (5:23–24 ESV). The language throughout this passage links Torah with *paideia*, the formative education that made children into virtuous and competent adults. It is quite possible that the rival teachers tapped into this kind of tradition, promoting Torah as God's trainer for virtue and for rising above the power of the passions of the flesh, such that Paul responds by demoting Torah to the function of the pedagogue and asserts that the Spirit is alone sufficient to tame the passions and desires of the flesh and to bring forth the fruit of virtue in a person's life and relationships (5:16—6:10).[185]

"Now that faith has come," however, "we are no longer under a pedagogue" (3:25). Paul returns to the claim he had already made in 3:19: that Torah had a temporary role in God's plan, one that came to an end with the coming of Christ and the means Christ opened up for people to be aligned with God's righteousness through trust and all that trust receives. The analogy of children who pass on from being under the authority of the pedagogue to young adults who enjoy greater liberty and answer to the internal norms of virtue makes Paul's salvation-historical claim seem more natural, and thus more persuasive. It also reinforces the notion of a decisive transition point in a person's (or, in this case, in a people's) life, calling for leaving behind one stage (the stage of being "under law" as "under a pedagogue") and entering a new stage (being "in Christ," enjoying a new freedom while being accountable to the Spirit). Jesus' death and resurrection mark a kind of rite of passage, a rite of collective "coming of age," from which there is no turning back.[186]

185. Certainly, Paul would not have advocated for Torah as an effective check on the passions and desires of the flesh (*contra* Lull, "The Law Was Our Pedagogue," 495).

186. This would include the freedom of Jews to continue to live a Jewish lifestyle (as in Rom 14:1—15:7), where this did not violate the greater principle of the unity of all people who have been baptized into Christ—a greater principle that was being violated when Paul spoke up in Antioch (Gal 2:11–14).

Theologians from the Alexandrian school of the second and third centuries through the Protestant Reformation and Catholic Counter-Reformation of the sixteenth century have divided the Torah in to the "moral law" and the "ritual law" (John Calvin further differentiated the "civil law," the regulations that applied to the polity of ancient Israel), teaching that the "ritual law" is fulfilled in the sacrificial death and on-going mediation of Christ, but that the "moral law" remains binding on Christian disciples. Paul himself advocated a more radical position in Galatians, something that John Chrysostom appears to have discerned in his rejection of the Torah as an ethical guide.[187] While the Torah as "the first five books of Scripture" would continue to have educative value for the believer, as Paul amply demonstrates in Galatians and throughout his letters (see, notably, 1 Cor 10:1–14), Torah as "legal code" has no ongoing role in the believer's life.

We arrive at this point at one of Paul's most marvelous declarations of the change that has happened in human existence because of Christ and wherever people join themselves to Christ and, in Christ, to one another:

> For you are all sons and daughters of God in Christ Jesus through faith: for as many of you have been baptized into Christ have put on Christ as one would put on one's clothes. There is no longer Jew nor Greek; there is no longer slave nor free; there is no longer "male and female"—for you are all one in Christ Jesus. (3:26–28)

By joining themselves to God's Son in trust, the many have also become God's sons and daughters, sharing in the Sonship of Christ, to whom they have united themselves in trust and who is taking shape himself within them, changing them from the inside out to become righteous in God's sight (2:20; 4:19), so that all are moving towards reflecting the family resemblance of the righteousness of God shown in Jesus. Many English translations render 3:26 as "you are all sons and daughters of God through faith in Christ Jesus." This obscures the likelihood that Paul intends the two prepositional phrases—"through trust" (*dia tēs pisteōs*) and "in Christ Jesus" (*en Christǫ Iesou*)—to be understood separately, in

---

187. See his *Commentary on Galatians* 3:25–26; Longenecker, *Galatians*, li.

parallel fashion ("you are God's sons and daughters by means of trust" and "you are God's sons and daughters in Christ Jesus"). He goes on in 3:27 specifically to develop the meaning of being "in Christ Jesus" and how being "in Christ Jesus" changes personal identity and social relationships within the Christian assembly. Moreover, if Paul had intended to communicate "faith directed toward Christ" here, it is more likely that he would have continued to use the phrase *pistis Christou*, as in 2:16 and as recently as 3:22. [188]

Paul draws on the powerful image of the ritual of baptism, asserting that in that ritual Christ covered them like a garment, and former distinctions no longer held any value or significance. It is quite possible that, in 3:27–28, Paul is reciting a formula already in use among the Christian assemblies in connection with the rite of baptism. Only the first pair in 3:28 ("neither Jew nor Gentile") is relevant to the situation in Galatia. Paul does not deal with social relationships between slaves and free persons in Christ in any way throughout the letter (though he will use the image of slavery and freedom), nor will he engage the question of the roles and relationships of males and females in the church. Moreover, similar formulas appear elsewhere in Paul's letters, both times in connection with baptism (see 1 Cor 12:13; Col 3:10–11).[189] Paul is thus reminding the Galatians about what happened to them, in some sense objectively, as they underwent the Christian rite of initiation.[190]

The symbolism of baptism by immersion, as it was no doubt most commonly practiced in the early church, is powerful indeed. Paul could liken it, in effect, to drowning, such that one dies with Christ in baptism

188. So Fung, *Galatians*, 171–72. If Paul had meant for "in Christ" to describe "trust," he would ideally have written *dia tēs pisteōs tēs en Christō*, though the rule about including the second article (*tēs*) to indicate adjectival use was not hard and fast in Koine Greek.

189. In the latter text, association with baptism is seen in the language of putting off the garment of the old person and putting on the garment of the new person, as here in Gal 3:27. See also Rom 10:12, though not in the context of statements about baptism or the baptismal transformation of the person: "There is no distinction between Jew and Greek. The same Lord is Lord of all, pouring out riches upon all who keep calling upon him."

190. Schlier, *Galater*, 174–75; Betz, *Galatians*, 181–85; Longenecker, *Galatians*, 154–55.

to one's former life and its connections and is born to a new life when emerging from the water (Rom 6:1–14). Here the image of the rite is harnessed to stress the joining of the convert to Jesus, the intimate and complete association of the two together, as if to say "you were submerged into Christ; Christ engulfed you, covered you over, enveloped you like a garment.[191] What we see now when we look at each other is Christ in us, over us, surrounding us" (3:27). Baptism into Christ provides another image by means of which Paul can speak of "communion with Christ in the most intimate relationship imaginable."[192]

If all disciples are thus submerged into Christ, while Christ also lives within them and takes shape within them, they form an essential unity. What they share is exponentially more important than what divided them while they were living as part merely of the old creation and not the new creation. The lines that divide humanity and that protect systems of inequality no longer have force in the church, where all are "one in Christ Jesus." The lines that differentiated Jews on the one hand from Greeks (Gentiles) on the other, slaves on the one hand from free persons on the other, male persons on the one hand from female on the other,[193] are transcended by the identity that all believers share—people clothed with Christ, people in whom Christ lives. Christians are thus no longer to relate to one another based on the divisions and prejudices inherent in these divisions. Rather, these oppositions and dyads have been resolved in Christ, with whom each Christian has been clothed, so that "Christ's own" becomes the only term of significance to define the identity and belonging of each.

191. The imagery of garments and changing garments is a powerful one in early Christian discourse to capture the thorough transformation that God is seeking to effect within and among us. See Col 3:5–17 for a striking ethical application.

192. Longenecker, *Galatians*, 154.

193. The parallelism of the "neither . . . nor" pattern in the first two pairs is broken in the "not . . . and" of the third due not to any special distinction Paul is making in regard to the third of these pairs, but to the fact that he is drawing on the exact phrasing found in Gen 1:27, where God made humanity "male and female," the prototypical dyad transcended in the new creation. Each of these three pairs reflects the racism and chauvinism that pervaded the ancient world, though, from the Greek perspective, the first pair would be given as "Greek and barbarian," with Jews included with all other non-Greeks in the pejorative second term of that pair. See Longenecker, *Galatians*, 157.

Paul's declaration that "you are all one in Christ Jesus" ultimately answers the claim that "God is One" (Gal 3:20) and the objection to the Torah as somehow violating the very Oneness of God that it announced (Deut 6:4). Torah was the warden that cordoned the Jewish people off from all Gentiles, even though God was not the God of the Jews only, but also the God of the Gentiles—since God is One (Rom 3:29–30). The Oneness of God would at last be reflected in the new humanity coming together in Christ, in freedom from the Torah and the other *stoicheia* that created lines of differentiation to serve as barriers and boundaries on human interaction and potential.[194]

We need to return for a moment here to the little word *gar* ("for") at the opening of Gal 3:26. This word suggests a logical connection between this verse (and thus all of 3:26–29) and Paul's declaration in 3:25 that "we"—specifically Jewish Christians—"are no longer under a pedagogue." Torah functioned to keep Jews separate from all other people groups: the "confinement" of which Paul spoke (3:23) was very much along ethnic lines, and that most intentionally.[195] While all people might have been shut in under sin, they were not all in the same pen, as it were. With the ending of the pedagogue's term of authority, there is no longer any reason for the separate confinement of Jews and Gentiles. Jews have received adoption as sons and daughters (4:5); the Gentiles who have trusted God's promises in Christ are also all sons and daughters of God (3:26). They have all together—Jew and Gentile—joined themselves to Christ, clothed themselves with Christ, become newly alive with Christ's life within them. When they descended into the waters

---

194. Paul's meaning is well captured in Eph 2:14–16: "[Christ] himself is our peace, he who made the two one and destroyed the enmity—the wall that divided them—in his flesh, having set aside the Law consisting of commandments in decrees. He did this in order that he might create out of the two one new humanity in himself, making peace and reconciling the two to God in one body through the cross, killing enmity upon it."

195. This is reflected theoretically in Lev 20:22–26, where Israel is called to be separate from the nations and to make careful distinctions between "clean and unclean" in imitation of God's making distinctions between Israel as "clean" for God and the nations as "unclean" and, therefore, not God's own. It is also reflected practically in 3 Macc 3:4, where observing the dietary laws of Torah causes the Jews to keep clear lines of separateness from people of other races. See, further, deSilva, *Honor, Patronage, Kinship & Purity*, 260–62, 269–74.

of baptism, the rite of initiation into the Christian assembly, they died to the powers of the cosmos that had drawn the lines of division and inequality that kept human beings apart and limited the possibilities for human existence. When they rose up out of the waters of baptism, they put on a new self like a new garment—the garment of Christ, the new creation coming into being in each of them individually and all of them collectively, in a new community in which the labels and lines of "Jew as opposed to Gentile," "slave as opposed to freeborn person," "male as opposed to female" no longer had power to constrain relational and individual possibilities and potential.

This is directly relevant to the situation in Galatia, where rival teachers are trying to extend the authority of Torah not only over themselves and Jewish Christians on this side of their "coming of age" in God's timing, but over the Gentile Christians who were never "under Torah," never "under *this* particular pedagogue" before, presumably so that the Gentile converts could become true sons and daughters of Abraham, heirs of the covenant blessings, and "clean" partners for Jewish Christians in the common life of Christian assembly.

Paul now comes full circle to answer the question under debate in Galatia: who are the heirs of the divine promises? Paul has been addressing this question from the outset of chapter 3, first calling the Galatian converts to remember their actual experience of receiving the Spirit and of God's working in their midst (3:1-5)—in other words, to remember that they had already received *what* was promised (3:14). He went on to demonstrate from Scripture that "those who exhibit trust," following Abraham's example, receive the blessing promised through Abraham (3:6-9), while those who rely on the "works of the Torah" labor under a curse (3:10-12). He demonstrated from a close reading of the promises themselves that God bequeathed his blessing on Abraham and a *particular* offspring of Abraham, and not Abraham's descendants generally, such that those who joined themselves to that particular Seed (Christ) joined themselves to the heir, to share the inheritance (3:15-18). He returns to this point as a mathematician signs "Q.E.D." at the conclusion of a mathematical proof: in baptism, the Galatian converts joined themselves to Christ, becoming one together in Christ. They are therefore, collectively, the Seed of Abraham to which God gave the promise, and the true heirs of God's promise of the Spirit and of the righteousness and, thereby, life that the Spirit is given to nurture and bring to completion (3:29).

READING GALATIANS 3 WITH SRI LANKAN CHRISTIANS

The Importance of the Experience of the Living God

Paul's argument in Galatians stands or falls depending on his converts' awareness of the Holy Spirit in their hearts, and their awareness of the Spirit's work within them and between them (Gal 3:1–5). Paul's descriptions of the involvement of God's Spirit and power in his initial proclamation of the Gospel, and the important of an encounter with God's Spirit to effect conversion,[196] resonate with the role played by "power encounters" in the conversion of Buddhists, Hindus, and others in Sri Lanka. In our endeavors to "know" the truth and make it "known," Paul reminds us not to neglect the surpassing importance of the experience of the Holy One. This is the bedrock of Paul's proof, and it is often the bedrock of our personal perseverance in faith. It is ultimately not the "facts" we know or even the "faith convictions" that we have, but the experience of a relationship with God and the awareness of God's Spirit at work within us that provides a center for our faith and that, at times, keeps us "in the faith." In the face of the challenges posed to faith throughout the course of a life, faith must be more than doing the right rituals and knowing the right doctrines: it must be grounded in a living, ongoing relationship with God through the Spirit.

Paul's reliance in Galatia upon the converts' awareness of this Spirit urges us to value the experience of God in our times of worship and to help our fellow disciples cultivate an awareness of God's presence and of God's hand at work in their lives. Pastor and parishioner, counselor and counselee, teacher and student alike must be able to find the irrefutable signs of God's love, acceptance, and favor in their lives, and our life together as a Christian community should be directed, at least in

---

196. See also Paul's description of his preaching in Corinth (1 Cor 2:1–5) and the author of Hebrews' reminder to his audience of their "power encounter" with God, confirming the word spoken to them (Heb 2:3–4).

part, toward cultivating transforming encounters with the living God. Without the active presence of God's Spirit in our lives, we lack, in Paul's view, the very inheritance promised in Christ and the key to our transformation into the likeness of Christ.

While Paul's attention to nurturing an awareness of the presence and power of God is a strong point for our imitation in our ministries, Paul's pastoral technique in 3:1–5 might call for considerably more reserve and finesse. Paul dares to use shaming in confronting the Galatians (1:6–7; 3:1–5). Paul has the authority to use this kind of speech. Paul gave birth to these churches: indeed, Paul first brought the Gospel to that region (a claim that no one living today in Sri Lanka could make). His investment and involvement in them from the outset gives him that authority. Pastors may be presumptuous to scold congregations as a parent would his or her children, if they haven't invested in those parishioners as parents do in their own children.

Christ, Bearer of Our Shame

Paul speaks of Christ taking upon himself the curse that hovered above those who were under Law (3:10–14). Sri Lankans are familiar with curses, being cursed, and anxiety about the removal of curses, and so this statement of the good news may resonate well in this setting, perhaps even more than Christ "taking our sin upon himself." The threat of any supernatural force ranged against a person has been disarmed by Jesus, who interposed himself in his death upon the cross. But another potent expression of Jesus' actions on our behalf would be that Jesus has taken our shame upon himself and clothed us with his honor. Sri Lanka is a shame-oriented culture. Shaming is a powerful force in power politics, in the ethnic distinctions that have been exacerbated by three decades of civil war, in the gender roles and inequalities that are typical of Asian societies, and in the class and caste systems that rank the worth of individuals and ascribe honor or lack of honor accordingly. The message that Jesus bore our shame, and celebrating the honor that Christ has bestowed on each individual joined to his body, offers a powerful path to reconciliation within the Christian community across all of these lines of inequality. Believing in the Jesus who embraced and carried all of our shame in the shameful death of crucifixion offers a way to overcome the effects of shame in our lives and our society, as we honor one another in Christian community as people whose shame has been lifted, and upon whom the glorious honor of adoption into God's own family has been granted.

Reviving the Curse among the Heirs of Blessing?

Paul's description of life under the Torah as an existence "under a curse"—an existence from which Jesus went to and through great pains to redeem people—challenges us to exercise care lest we create an ethos of "living under a curse" within the Christian community rather than helping fellow Christians experience life in Christ as freedom and blessing (blessing, that is, in terms of the enjoyment of the Spirit's guidance and empowerment and in terms of knowing God as our Father). Our minds are so stamped by the "elementary principles of the world" that, once one taskmaster and set of rules is lifted, we immediately rush in to create another rather than allow the Spirit to fill that vacuum.

Wherever a church's culture is characterized by a "do this and be damned, do that and be damned" mentality, the reign of the curse is being renewed and the Gospel polluted. Yes, there are ethical dangers that seriously jeopardize our forward progress in "Christ being formed in us," and which are therefore to be avoided (Gal 5:19–21), but churches and their leaders cannot create new Torahs (in this setting, not even given by angels, but just formulated by mere human beings) in order to confine their congregations under the protective custody of human-made regulations, hedging them in and imposing authoritarian rule over them. Under the pretext of guiding their flock in the straight and narrow way, pastors of such cult-like Christian groups often end up using such bodies of rules to exercise their *own* totalitarian rule over their enslaved congregations, using the threat of curse and damnation to coerce submission and guard against defection. There are even now many captives in Sri Lanka to be liberated from being treated like minor children by domineering pastors and cultish leaders.

Wide-open spaces are scary for people who ultimately trust in walls. The freedom that God's sons and daughters are meant to enjoy requires responsible use of that freedom, as Paul will develop at great length (5:13—6:10), but ultimately Spirit-directed freedom is God's will for God's people in Christ. New Torahs, while having the appearance of nurturing obedience, in fact constitute *dis*obedience to God's purposes for us and a repudiation of Christ's death to bring us that freedom.

When All Are Clothed in Christ, and Christ Lives in All

A major thrust of Galatians is to demonstrate that the social lines of division created by the labels "Jew" and "Gentile," and enforced by the regulations of Torah for keeping the two groups separate, are transcended as people are baptized into Christ, and thus into a new identity, and as people receive the Holy Spirit, given to all who trust (and not just to those who conform to Torah's regulations for holiness as "Jewishness"). Paul goes on to include, however, two other pairs reflective of social divisions and vast inequalities: there is also "neither slave nor free, not 'male and female," where people have clothed themselves with Christ. The first of these is especially bold under the system of Roman imperialism, which depended upon slavery for its economic health, and within which one in four persons was a "living tool," to use the words of Aristotle's definition of the slave. The second is perhaps even more daring. While one might compare a slave and a freeborn person and conclude that there really are no differences by nature, but only by social usage and convention, this would not be the case when setting a male and a female side by side. Indeed, the distinctions, and hence the division of humanity into "male and female," are inherent in nature and perhaps even in God's design for creation itself (Gen 1:27).

But Paul is not interested in the order of the old creation. He is interested in seeing the order of the "new creation" come to life within the communities of those who have been baptized into Christ, who have put on Christ, and in whom Christ is being formed. Indeed, "neither circumcision nor lack of circumcision is anything, but a new creation!" (Gal 6:15). In this new creation, the dividing walls of ethnicity are torn down, social prejudices are neutralized, and gender inequalities and male chauvinism are negated.

Many barriers across the landscape of Sri Lankan society divide people from one another. The importance of ethnic and religious identity, generally in the combinations of "Sinhalese Buddhists" on the one hand and "Tamil Hindus" on the other, undermines any sense even of national identity as Sri Lankans. These lines have been more deeply etched by three decades of civil war, and by lingering prejudice and inequities across these particular divides. Socio-economic divisions between rich and poor are also sharp and glaring. Sri Lankans who speak English enjoy numerous advantages over those who speak only indigenous languages, presenting the possibility of looking down upon fellow Sri Lankans who don't speak English.

The caste system, which is closely linked to one's ethnicity, still exercises power in Sri Lankan social relationships. From the outset of the postcolonial period the caste system has been gradually breaking down. Particularly in rural areas, however, it still shapes and constrains relationships—both in Sinhala and Tamil communities. When it comes to the marriages of their children, parents may scrutinize the backgrounds of prospective brides or grooms. A family from a higher caste will consider choosing a bride or groom from a lower caste to be injurious to their dignity. The fear that relatives and society at large would look down on the union—the fear of social stigma—overrides the factors of the potential spouse's character and integrity.

Lines of gender inequality also pervade Sri Lankan society, as in many other Asian countries where the woman has been traditionally considered as having a lower status than the man. Again this is manifested more strongly in the rural and village settings. In village communities, a wife might not sit with her husband in a public setting and might be expected to stand up when she sees the husband coming into the house. At mealtime, a wife might not eat with her husband, but might rather be expected to serve food and wait on her husband while he eats his meal. Sometimes a wife may have to eat her meal by herself, relegated to the kitchen and eating whatever is left after feeding husband and children. Travelling through rural areas, one might see a couple walking down the road—the husband walking ahead empty handed while the wife walks behind her husband balancing a heavy bag of goods on her head. This mindset can even invade the bedroom, with the wife being used as the vehicle for childbirth by a husband who does not attend to giving her the pleasures of intimacy.

Does Christian practice perpetuate these divisions and the social inequalities they inscribe, or does Christian practice challenge them, witnessing to the "new humanity" being formed in Christ in their communities, where Christ is all and in all? In baptism, we have all put on Christ—God clothing us with a fine, new garment as in a festival season, or as draping a lovely robe over a poverty-stricken person wearing only a loincloth, covering his shame. To what extent does the life of Christian community and the quality of relationships between Christians reflect the celebration of this festival of our new honor and unity in Christ? To what extent do we continue to ignore the garment of Christ draped around each one of us, peering again under another's robe to see and treat that person according to the old garments of this world's divisions?

A number of Christian churches held, and continue to hold, bilingual services in Tamil and Sinhalese, bringing members of both major ethnic groups together in worship and around the communion table. In this setting, they were able to practice the command to "welcome one another as Christ welcomed us" (Rom 15:7), and provided a valuable witness particularly during the decades of the civil war to the power of Christ and the Holy Spirit to reconcile people one to another. This witness continues where churches give intentional thought to bringing Christians from both ethnic groups together, nurturing an environment of mutual acceptance, honor, and partnership in mission in Sri Lanka (even if fully bilingual or trilingual services are more sporadic). But where in the life of the church does a person's identity as a Sinhala or a Tamil trump his or her identity as a Christian? Where does the former prevent us from treating someone fully on the basis of our new identity in Christ? Latent ethnic divisions can surface when two young people in the church, one Tamil and one Sinhalese, begin to think seriously about marriage, a union that even Christian parents might resist. Similarly, the prejudicial structures of the caste system surface in the church when it comes to marriages—where two people from two different castes fall in love and intend to get married. Even Christian leaders have objected to their son or daughter marrying a person from a different caste or ethnic background.

However, when a Tamil Christian marries a Sinhalese Christian, and they build their relationship upon the principles of mutual love and service, their happy home challenges the ethnic divisions and the depreciating of marriage that plague Sri Lankan society. It is encouraging to note that a growing number of Christian parents are blessing marriages between children of different ethnic communities, heralding the church's increasingly healing impact on the nation. That young people who harbored racial prejudice before coming to Christ have experienced transformation and gone on to marry partners of a different race or caste is also evidence of this.

The socially prescribed lines of inequality in gender roles can intrude upon Christian homes, with the husband still taking his "superiority" for granted. For example the husband may demand that his wife "serve" him and "submit" unquestioningly. On the other hand, if a wife converts to Christianity and the husband remains non-Christian, the wife may be censured as being unsubmissive. Domestic violence even in Christian circles is sadly not uncommon. Often pastors have to deal with couples where the husband has used violence to enforce his supposed authority. While the physical differences between men and women are inherent in creation, the expectations that relegate females to a supporting role at best, and often to an inferior status, are not. These are, instead, inherent in the fall and the curse (see Gen 3:16c). A Christian husband and wife, however, are challenged by Paul to relate to one another first as fellow Christians and fellow heirs of the gift of life (cf. 1 Pet 3:7), and to bestow *mutual* honor, and to extend *mutual* submission, on that basis (Eph 5:21).[197] This extends, of course, into the larger life of the Christian community, which is to become a place where one's immersion into Christ and one's responsiveness to the Holy Spirit—and not one's gender—guide how one will contribute, and be valued as a contributor, to the life of the church.

In a society divided along ethnic and caste lines, the church invites people from all castes and ethnic groups to come under one roof to worship God beneath the cross. Where this eventuates in acceptance and

---

197. If your Bible introduces a section heading to separate Eph 5:21 from Eph 5:22, scratch that heading out: Eph 5:21 leads into 5:22 as part of the same sentence, even sharing a single verb in the Greek!

reconciliation, the church witnesses to the power of God's Spirit and the reality of God's plan to reconcile all things in God's Son. Paul challenges us to continue to examine our hearts and our practice along these lines, asking continually, "What would life in the Christian community look like if Christians approached all such issues from the position articulated in Gal 3:26–28 and committed themselves to live out fully this facet of the baptismal life, the new creation?"

4:1–7: ARGUMENT FROM ANALOGY, RESUMED

And I say, for the extent of time that the heir is a minor, he or she differs in no way from a slave, even though he or she is master of all, [2]but he or she is under guardians and stewards until the time set by the father. [3]In this way, we also, when we were minors, were enslaved under the fundamental principles of the cosmos: [4]But when the fullness of time came, God sent his son, coming into being from a woman, coming into being under Torah, [5]in order to redeem those under Torah, in order that we might receive adoption as children. [6]And because you are sons and daughters, God sent the Spirit of his son into our hearts, crying out "Abba, Father!" [7]The result is that you are no longer slaves, but sons and daughters—and if sons and daughters, then also heirs through God.

Paul returns to develop further the analogy he had introduced in 3:23–25, namely "coming of age" in a household. The plight of the underage heirs in the household is now described in even bleaker terms: "for the extent of time that the heir is a minor (i.e., not yet of legal age), he or she differs in no way from a slave, even though he or she is master of all." The minor child has no right to dispose of the property that he or she will inherit; the child likewise does not have authority over his or her own person or actions. Being governed by others in respect of person, property, and action, the minor child's life resembles more the life of a slave than the life of a free person.[198] Paul here introduces the language

198. A similar comparison of the pedagogue to a prison warden, and of the children placed under the care of such a guardian as no better off than slaves, appears as early as the writings of Plato (see *Laws* 7.808D–E).

of "slavery" that he will use to great effect throughout the remainder of the letter: the state of "slavery" versus the event of "adoption" that makes people sons and daughters in the household of God; "slavery" to the rules and powers of this age versus the "freedom" for which Christ liberated people, a freedom people are to defend against every enticement to fall back into bondage to this world's rules and ruts, but a freedom also not to be misused to cater to one's self-centered drives and desires.

Here the "pedagogue" of 3:24–25 is expanded to "guardians and stewards"—those who have effective control over the person and property of the underage heirs in the household.[199] The minor heir lives out his or her life under the authority of these masters "until the time set by the father" for the minor child to enter into his or her inheritance and the accompanying authority over his or her own person and property. Scholars have diligently sought out the background for Paul's imagery in actual Roman, Greek, or Greco-Phrygian (that is, local Galatian) legal practice.[200] In favor of Greco-Phrygian practice is the fact that local law allowed the father some flexibility in terms of the setting of the age of coming to "majority," whereas this age was standard in Roman and Greek law.[201] Nevertheless, identifying a particular background—even demonstrating that Paul was reflecting a particular legal practice—is not necessary to hearing Paul's point or following his argument. He is using sufficiently familiar categories (the oversight of underage children, a change of legal status and authority over self and goods at a certain age) to be understood by people accustomed to a variety of specific, local legal practices and, indeed, may just as easily be adapting actual legal practice somewhat to better parallel his understanding of salvation history and the coming of the "fullness of time" in the Father's own good time.[202]

199. Belleville, "Under Law," 63; Martyn, *Galatians*, 388. The word *epitropos* refers to the guardian of a minor, even entering Hebrew as a loan word from the Greek (Taubenschlag, *The Law of Greco-Roman Egypt in Light of the Papyri*, 123–24).

200. Ramsay, *Galatians*, 391–93; Betz, *Galatians*, 202; Schlier, *Galater*, 189; Longenecker, *Galatians*, 162–63.

201. Longenecker, *Galatians*, 163.

202. Fung, *Galatians*, 180.

In 4:3–7, Paul applies this domestic analogy to the location of the Galatian converts, as well as other Christian groups, in the timeline of salvation history. Just as the underage children in the analogy, "we also, when we were minors, were enslaved under the fundamental principles of the cosmos" (the *stoicheia tou kosmou*, 4:3). Two questions need to be considered in regard to this and the following verses: who is included among the "we," and what are the *stoicheia tou kosmou*?

It becomes increasingly difficult, as Galatians proceeds, to make hard and fast distinctions between the "we" (as Paul and other Jewish Christians) and the "you" (as Galatian converts and other Gentile Christians) in terms of ethnicity, although this was easily done in 2:15–16. This is appropriate, as, in Paul's view, God was working in Christ and in the sending of the Spirit to erase those hard and fast distinctions between Jews and Gentiles in the new people of God.[203] Burton and Betz regard the "we" as inclusive here, speaking of both Jews *and* Gentiles living as slaves under *ta stoicheia tou kosmou*.[204] Longenecker reads the "we" as a more specific reference to Jewish Christians, as in 2:15–16; 3:23–25, since Paul goes on almost immediately to talk about those who are "under the *stoicheia tou kosmou*" (4:3) as those who are "under Law" (4:5).[205] What we can say with certainty is that Paul would never speak of Gentiles as being "under Torah" in any sense: being "under Torah" specifically preserved the boundary between Jew and Gentile. Gentiles were "without Torah" or "outside the Torah" (Rom 2:14; 1 Cor 9:20b–21), their lives constrained and limited by other *stoicheia*. Thus "those under Law" in 4:5 are the Jewish people, and the "we" of 4:3 must at least include Jewish Christians. Whether or not Paul includes Gentile Christians along with them in the "we" of 4:3, Paul clearly goes on to speak about the Galatian Christians (as typical of Gentile Christians) as also having been enslaved to the *stoicheia tou komou* prior to their conversion (4:8–9), and in danger of reverting to such a state of slavery again, this time under the *stoicheion* of the Torah. It is perhaps not so important to determine who is included among each "we" as to notice what is included among the *stoicheia tou kosmou*—both the Torah, the

203. Martyn, *Galatians*, 391, more particularly in reference to 4:6.

204. Burton, *Galatians*, 215; Betz, *Galatians*, 204.

205. Longenecker, *Galatians*, 164.

pedagogue of the Jewish people, and the idol-centered ideologies that drove and determined Gentile pre-Christian life.[206] This is a stunning thing for a Jew to consider, let alone say. The divine origin of Torah, which clearly separates it from every other religion or religious body of law, is quite muted in Galatians.

What, then, are the *stoicheia tou kosmou*, these enslaving powers from which Christ redeemed the Galatians, and which therefore constitute an essential element of Paul's worldview and what is amiss with humanity apart from Christ? The term could refer to a series of things lined up in a row, hence the alphabet, and in an extended sense to "the ABCs" of some body of teaching, even the "ABC's" of human and institutional logic as this has taken shape in our rebellion against God.[207] Paul would not be using the term to speak positively about some elementary teaching serving as a preparation for the Gospel, but more as a set of rules, ideas, values, prejudices, and divisive categories (like "slave versus free," "male versus female," "Greek versus barbarian," "Jew versus Greek") that imprison and constrain those who grow up knowing nothing else and nothing better. In this sense, Paul would be speaking about slavery to "the way the world works," however the society in which a person is born and bred defines the rules and sets the parameters on life.[208]

The best-attested meaning for *stoicheia* and especially *stoicheia tou kosmou* in the first century and before is the elements out of which the natural world was believed to have been made, namely earth, water, air, and fire.[209] These elements were often divinized, whether in and of

206. Bruce, *Galatians*, 30; Longenecker, *Galatians*, 181; Martyn, *Galatians*, 393. Barclay (*Obeying*, 210–11) suggests that the polemic situation in which Paul finds himself, and within which he is hammering out his theology of Torah's limited role in the overall plan of God, leads Paul to make more extreme statements here. His view becomes more balanced, and more positively inclined toward Torah, by the time he writes Romans (that is, when the heat of controversy on this topic is passed).

207. Burton, *Galatians*, 510–18; Belleville, "Under Law," 67–68; Young, "Paidagogos," 172.

208. Martyn (*Galatians*, 389) insists on this negative evaluation of the *stoicheia* and their impact on a person's experience of life, community, religion, and so forth.

209. For lexical data, see Blinzler, "Lexicalisches zu dem Terminus ta stoicheia tou kosmou," 427–43, especially pp. 439–41; Rusam, "Neue Belege zu dem *stoicheia tou kosmou*," 119–25. Martyn (*Galatians*, 395) cites Philo, *Heres* 134; Wis 7:17; 19:18; 4 Macc 12:13; 2 Pet 3:10, 12.

themselves, or in connection with a particular deity associated with each element, a fact to which Jewish authors drew attention. Philo, for example, observed that Gentiles "call fire Hephaestus . . . air Hera . . . water Poseidon . . . and earth Demeter" (*Vit. Cont.* 3; see also *Decal.* 53), while the author of Wisdom of Solomon wrote that Gentiles "were unable from the good things that are seen to know the one who exists, nor did they recognize the artisan while paying heed to his works; but they supposed that either fire or wind or swift air, or the circle of the stars, or turbulent water, or the luminaries of heaven were the gods that rule the world" (Wis 13:1–2). In this reading, slavery to the "elements" would communicate much what Paul and other Hellenistic Jews communicate elsewhere as they speak of Gentiles worshiping facets of the created order rather than the Creator himself.[210]

The term could be applied to the heavenly bodies—the sun, moon, other stars and planets—that exercised influence over people, whether as indicated by Jews' interest in watching them to discover the times for particular observances in a religious calendar, or by Gentiles' obsession with horoscopes, astrology, and divination through reading the stars' and planets' movement. In the mind of the ancients, these heavenly bodies were connected with spiritual beings or powers, often hostile toward humans and, thus, needing to be heeded and observed. Evidence for the use of *stoicheia* specifically to refer to these phenomena outside Paul is lacking until the second-century Christian author Justin Martyr (*Apol.* 2.5.2; *Dial.* 23.3), but the immediate context of Galatians (see 4:8–11) does point in this direction.[211]

One often overlooked clue concerning Paul's conception of the *stoicheia tou kosmou* is that he considers the Torah to be a representative of this group of constraining, enslaving forces. Torah had a dimension of spiritual power—it was given by angels (3:19), and represented a means by which angelic beings exercised control over a particular people. It had a cosmic dimension, instructing those under it to observe particular signs in the sky and regulate their lives accordingly (that is,

210. *Stoicheia* comes to be used to speak of actual gods, daemons, and other spirit beings, but not until the third or fourth century CE (as in Pseudo-Callisthenes, *Alexander Romance* 1.1). Bruce, *Galatians*, 193–94; Martyn, *Galatians*, 395; Moore-Crispin, "Galatians 4:1–9: The Use and Abuse of Parallels," 203–23, especially p. 211.

211. Betz, *Galatians*, 205; Bruce, *Galatians*, 204; Martyn, *Galatians*, 395.

by observing sacred days and seasons, and setting these apart from ordinary days on which to attend to other business). And, of course, it had
a dimension of "fundamental instruction" regarding the way the world
worked, clothing this instruction with an aura of divine legitimacy (as
did every Greek or Roman or other pagan construction of "how the
world worked").

The *stoicheia* under which other nations labored and by which
their lives, relationships, and knowledge of the divine were limited
and dominated may themselves be seen to reflect the multiple facets of
Torah. Pagan religion was linked with worship of the *stoicheia* as "building blocks of the physical world," but this religion also permeated the
social, political, and cultural world, so that worship of the *stoicheia* had
far-reaching implications for the ordering of society, for the identification of what would be valued within society (e.g., military strength
[Ares], sexual gratification and pursuit of beauty [Aphrodite], wealth
[Pluto/Hades], and so forth), and for the social structures that would divide people into haves and have-nots, into elites and peasants and slaves
("living tools," in Aristotle's definition). There was a cosmic dimension
to the *stoicheia* as well, seen in the pagan counterparts to Jewish observation of the stars and moon as the taskmasters who separated days of
work from days of rest, as well as the slavery of Gentiles to astrology and
omens. And the *stoicheia* had a dimension of superhuman power, as the
rules of "the way the world worked," the idol-permeated structures of
society, and the astral powers confronted the pagan as irresistible forces
calling for submission without question.[212]

Even though Greek-speaking Gentiles would probably understand
ta stoicheia tou kosmou first to mean the four elements of which the
cosmos is composed (air, earth, water, fire), Paul is more interested
in the *kosmos* as "this present, evil age" (1:4) to which he has himself
been crucified and which has been crucified to him (6:14). The *stoicheia*
are the guiding powers and principles of this age, the building blocks
from which the present, evil age is composed—which have contributed
to perverting and corrupting the present age. The term *stoicheia* denotes that which guides, limits, and constrains human beings in their

---

212. Caird (*Principalities and Powers*, 51) links these with the "principalities and
powers" (cf. Col 1:16).

thoughts, behaviors, and interactions, keeping them in a form of ideological and systemic bondage. They include, especially, all that contributed to the internal and external divisions among human beings, the power differentials across those divisions, the ideologies that sustained those divisions and power structures, and so forth: "The formula of Gal 3:28—with its announcement of liberation from enslaving pairs of elemental opposites—constitutes a key part of the context in which, in 4:3–5, Paul explicitly speaks of liberation from the enslaving elements of the cosmos."[213]

The "time set by the father" for his minor children's accession to authority over their own persons and property corresponds to the time set by the Father in heaven for the removal of the spiritual and social pedagogues, guardians, and custodians—the ending of the time of Torah's authority to constrain the Jewish people and maintain the separation of the same from "all the nations"—and for the coming of all peoples, Jews and Gentiles, into the possession of the inheritance promised to them. Paul has already spoken of this inheritance as receiving the Holy Spirit (3:14), which would lead Jew and Gentile alike to become righteous and obedient from the heart (5:5, 16), and which would bring to life within them the very life of Christ, the "righteous one" (2:20; 4:19). The Spirit would succeed where the Torah had failed, empowering victory over the impulses of the flesh and bringing righteousness to fruition in the lives of Christians individually and corporately (5:13—6:10).

When the time was right (from God's perspective—Paul and other Christians came to know this "time" only by hindsight), "God sent his Son" to redeem the slaves and make them sons and daughters (4:4–5).[214] Paul departs in a significant way here from his opening analogy. Paul began with the image of a natural-born child living the life of a slave under guardians and coming of age and coming into his or her own.

---

213. Martyn, *Galatians*, 404.

214. While James Dunn (*Christology in the Making*, 39–40) sees in this verse merely a reflection of Jesus' own tendency to speak of himself as "son" and as "sent by God" (as in Mark 9:37; 12:6), the phrase seems to presume the preincarnate life of the Son, building perhaps on early identifications of the Son with the figure of Wisdom (Longenecker, *Galatians*, 167). Paul and the members of his team clearly believed in Christ's preincarnate existence, as evidenced by 1 Cor 8:6b; 10:4; Phil 2:5–8; Col 1:15–17; Heb 1:1–4.

Now he shifts to the image of adoption, whereby those who were not part of the family (and, indeed, were slaves to second-rate masters) are made part of the family and, thus, heirs in the family by the action of the *paterfamilias* (here, the action of God). It wasn't *just* a matter of anyone coming of age in the fullness of time. The coming of the Son, the unique Seed of Abraham (3:16, 26–29), redeemed the slaves so that God could give them—Jews as well as Gentiles—the gift of adoption into the family of God. This radical shift from slave to son or daughter is a witness to the experience of Jewish Christians like Paul, who discovered for themselves a new quality of relationship with God, described in the intimate terms of becoming God's children and knowing God as Parent.[215]

The Son was "born of a woman," thus sharing our humanity; he was, further, "born under the Torah," sharing in the particular experience of the Jewish people, to redeem them, allowing the blessing promised to Abraham thence to flow forth to the Gentile nations. The argument here in 4:4–5 repeats from another angle the significance of Christ's coming to redeem those who were "under a curse" in 3:13–14. Once again, the redemption of the particular people (the Jewish people, living under the *stoicheion* of the Torah) was prerequisite to making the Spirit, and the adoption into God's family that the Spirit brought about, available to all people (enslaved as they were to various other *stoicheia*).

It is significant that, from Paul's point of view, Jews had to receive adoption as sons and daughters just as Gentiles needed to receive this adoption, and this became real through the sending of the Holy Spirit into the heart of the one just as into the heart of the other (3:13–14; 4:6–7). All were slaves to various *stoicheia* before Christ without distinction, and now, in Christ, all can receive adoption into God's family without distinction:

> And because you are sons and daughters, God sent the Spirit
> of his son into our hearts, crying out "Abba, Father!" The result
> is that you are no longer slaves, but sons and daughters—and
> if sons and daughters, then also heirs through God. (4:6–7)

The importance of the early Christians' experience of the Holy Spirit again comes to the fore (as in 3:1–5). Paul points the Galatians to their

215. Longenecker, *Galatians*, 172.

own experience of entering into a new relationship with the One God, whose Holy Spirit within them has enabled them to call upon this God as "Abba, Father," even as the Son addressed God as "Abba" during his lifetime (Mark 14:36).[216] They have acquired experiential knowledge of God (see also 4:8–9) that should give them all the evidence they need of their acceptance by God and their place in God's family.

The appearance of the Aramaic term *Abba* here is striking (as again in Rom 8:15). In order for it to be a meaningful part of Paul's argument, it probably reflects the actual practice of using this foreign term among Diaspora Gentile congregations, even as the phrase *maran atha* (Aramaic for "Our Lord, come!") came into usage in Greek-speaking congregations, as seen in the eucharistic prayer in the *Didache* (10.6).[217] Whether this practice was introduced into Diaspora Christian congregations by Jewish Christian evangelists like Paul in imitation of the Lord, or as an actual manifestation of the Spirit moving Jewish and Gentile converts to address God using a foreign term (corresponding, supernaturally, to the actual practice of Jesus and Judean Christians), cannot be known.

We have tried to pay close attention to Paul's use of pronouns throughout this letter, asking whether or not his shifts from "we" to "you" carry significance. In some instances, the significance has been clear. In Gal 2:15–16, for example, Paul is clearly addressing fellow Jewish Christians and including them in the "we," but not the Gentile Christians who would overhear this part of the speech (whether in Antioch or in Galatia). In these verses, Paul's alternations between "you" and "we" seem confused: "in order that *we* might receive adoption as

---

216. See Jeremias, *The Prayers of Jesus*, 11–65. Paul will return to this topic in strikingly similar terms in Rom 8:14–17: "For as many as are led by God's Spirit, *these* people are God's sons and daughters. For you did not receive a spirit of slavery leading again into fear, but you received a spirit that conferred adoption, by means of which we cry out 'Abba, Father'. This spirit bears witness along with our spirit that we are God's children—and if children, then heirs, heirs of God and fellow-heirs with Christ, if indeed we suffer with him in order that we may be glorified with him."

217. The *Didache*, the short title for the "Teaching of the Twelve Apostles," is an early church manual on ethics, baptism, the Eucharist (or Communion), discerning the true prophet from the false, and other such topics. It may date from the late first or early second century, and derives from Jewish-Christian circles in Syria or Palestine.

sons" (4:5); "because *you* are sons and daughters, God sent the spirit of his Son into *our* hearts" (4:6); "so *you* (singular) are no longer a slave, but a son or daughter" (4:7). The Greek textual tradition behind the "Majority Text" (upon which the KJV was based) reads "God sent the Spirit of his son into *your* hearts" rather than "*our* hearts," in an apparent attempt to regularize the use of pronouns. The earliest manuscripts, however, are unanimously in favor of "*our* hearts" being the original.[218] The careful distinctions between an "us" (as Jewish Christians) and a "you" (as Gentile Christians) breaks down here—perhaps intentionally, perhaps subconsciously—as Paul delves deeper into the common plight of Jew and Gentile under the *stoicheia* and their common adoption into God's family through trust in Jesus and their reception of the Spirit.

Receiving Christ's Spirit made the Galatian Christians to be numbered among Abraham's seed, gathered together around and united with the one Seed that is Christ.[219] Paul repeats the fact that being made thus a son or daughter also makes the Galatian convert an "heir through God" (see also 3:29),[220] returning to the overarching debate: "Who is

218. Greek forms of "your" and "our" or "you" (plural) and "we" are often confused in the manuscript tradition, since they differ in Greek only in the opening vowel, and since these opening vowels (upsilon and eta) came increasingly to be pronounced alike in the Byzantine period.

219. Fung (*Galatians*, 187) observes, "4:1–7 implies a close connection between justification by faith, sonship to God, and reception of the Spirit." However, he also argues that "sonship logically precedes the gift and operation of the Spirit, which in turn attests the reality of sonship. Sonship is not the result of the operation of the Spirit, but is attained through faith (3:26)" (Fung, *Galatians*, 184). This does not appear to be the full testimony of Paul. Am I a "son" or "daughter" *before* and *apart from* God's bestowal of the Holy Spirit? Romans 8:9, 14–16 suggests otherwise. Without the Spirit, we are not Christ's own. We have received the Spirit as "a spirit of adoption." We are sons and daughters because the spirit of God's Son lives in us. It is better, with Longenecker (*Galatians*, 173), to be content to say that, "for Paul, it seems, sonship and receiving the Spirit are so intimately related that one can speak of them in either order" (comparing Gal 4:6–7 with Rom 8:15–17).

220. The "Majority Text" (hence the KJV) reads "an heir of God through Christ" rather than the shorter "an heir through God" (hence most modern translations). The shorter reading is again supported unanimously by the earliest manuscripts (P[46], Sinaiticus, Vaticanus, and Alexandrinus). The longer reading appears to be the result of a scribe's attempt to clarify and emphasize Christ's role in our becoming heirs at this climactic point in Paul's argument.

the heir of the divine promises?" God's children and, therefore, heirs are those who have been made such by reception of "the Spirit of God's Son," who have entered into a new quality of relationship with this God, relating in alignment with the norms of the new age, the new humanity formed in Christ, the norm of the Spirit's guidance and empowerment rather than the pedagogues of this present, evil age.

4:8-11: IMPLICATIONS OF ARGUMENT FROM ANALOGY—IS REVERSION TO SLAVERY DESIRABLE?

[8]But formerly, not perceiving God, you were enslaved to things that were not gods by nature. [9]And now, knowing God—and, what is more, being known by God—how can you turn back again to the weak and impoverished elementary principles, to which you desire again to submit yourselves afresh as slaves?! [10]You are observing days and months and seasons and years! [11]I am afraid for you, lest somehow I have labored over you for nothing!

Paul had been speaking about life under the *stoicheia* from his own point of reference—living under the Torah and being redeemed thence by Christ. Now as he addresses the Galatian Christians directly, he speaks differently of their experience of their former life under the *stoicheia tou kosmou*. As Gentiles, their preconversion life was marked by ignorance of the one, true God. Paul stands alongside other Hellenistic Jewish authors on this point: "All people who were ignorant of God were foolish by nature; they were unable, on the basis of the good things that are seen, to know the One who is" (Wis 13:1). Gentiles failed to move from contemplation of the created order to the discovery of the Creator, falling instead into serving "things that are not divine in nature" (Gal 4:8): "Those who call 'gods' the products of human hands—gold and silver items carefully sculpted, images of animals, a useless stone worked by someone's hand long ago—are pitiful, setting their hopes on dead things" (Wis 13:10). Paul would include idolatrous religion as a facet of the *stoicheia* that dominated and limited Gentile life in society (as in 1 Thess 1:9), but he was looking beyond it to the larger issue of how

Gentiles, like Jews, were slaves to the ideological and social structures around them.[221]

The Galatian Christians had, however, moved out from that state of ignorance of God and bondage to "no-gods" into a new state of knowing God as a father (4:9a) and being known by God as God's sons and daughters (4:9b). They have the testimony of the Spirit to this fact in their inner person. Thus Paul asks, hardly hiding his exasperation with them, "how can you turn back again to the weak and impoverished elementary principles (*stoicheia*), to which you desire again to submit afresh as slaves?!" (4:9b). How could they return to slavery to inferior powers and structures, when they have been received by the Most High God as daughters and sons? Just as the adult cannot again be a child, the person who drinks deeply of God's Spirit cannot again look backward to any of the *stoicheia*, Torah or otherwise, for the way forward. More insidiously, turning back to the *stoicheia* would mean repudiating the freedom, the new and glorious status of "heir" and "son or daughter," that Christ won for the believer at such great cost through his death "under the Torah" (Gal 4:4–5).

No doubt the Galatians were not looking at their choices in such terms, and so this is part of Paul's rhetorical strategy. Indeed, it is quite possible that the rival teachers had themselves discussed the *stoicheia* in their presentation to the Galatian Christians, contrasting the Galatians' slavish worship of the elements themselves (in the form of their idolatrous worship of created things instead of the Creator, as well as in their own calendrical observances based on their observation of the stars) with the possibility they now have of worshiping the one and only God aright, and observing the calendar that God himself enjoins upon people, having given the heavenly bodies as indicators of that calendar (and not objects of veneration in their own right). Abraham would continue to serve as a model here of the ideal proselyte who moves from idolatry

---

221. Bruce (*Galatians*, 30) comments on the essential difference between Torah as a *stoicheion* and the *stoicheia* to which Gentiles were enslaved: "According to Paul, pagan worship was always culpable because it involved idolatry and the vices which followed from idolatry; Jewish worship in the pre-Christian stage of God's dealings with humanity was far from being culpable—it was divinely instituted—but it had the character of infancy and immaturity as compared with the coming of age into which human beings were introduced by faith in Christ."

to correct observance of the One God's calendar. While the Genesis account does not suggest that Abraham observed the Sabbath and other such religious days, Jews began to retell the story of Abraham and the other patriarchs with a view to showing how even they, long before Moses, observed the Torah before it was given in written form (see, for example, *Jubilees* 16).[222]

Paul's response is to put the Torah on a par with the *stoicheia tou kosmou* that had regulated the life of the Gentiles apart from Christ. Both equally enslaved human beings, and the binding power of both was equally broken by the coming of Christ to give the gift of adoption as sons and daughters.[223] Because of this, Paul can speak of the Galatians' move toward taking on some of the works of the Torah (which they had *not* practiced before converting to Christ) as essentially a *return* to slavery to the *stoicheia tou kosmou* (others of which they had served, as idolaters and products of their upbringing in Greco-Roman society, before converting to Christ). Here again we see how Paul drives a wedge of incompatibility between two facets of practice that the rival teachers are presenting as completely, even necessarily, complementary (namely, faith toward Jesus and observance of the requirements of Torah).

One of the indications of this return to slavery for Paul was the fact that some of the Galatian Christians, at least, had begun to observe a particular calendar of religious festivals—"you are observing [special] days and months and seasons and annual festivals" (4:10). Paul is probably referring here to the adoption of the Jewish religious calendar among his converts as an initial step toward conforming their lives to Torah's regulations, as the rival teachers were urging.[224] The language of this verse specifically recalls the language of Gen 1:14 (in the Septuagint translation), where the stars and other astronomical bodies are created to serve "for signs and for seasons and for days and annual festivals." These are precisely the same terms as found in Gal 4:10 (with the ad-

222. Martyn, *Galatians*, 397–400.

223. Vilehauer, "Gesetzesdienst und Stoicheiadienst im Galaterbrief," 543–55, especially p. 553; Bruce, *Galatians*, 202; Longenecker, *Galatians*, 181; Martyn, *Galatians*, 393.

224. Paul similarly links the observance of holy days and regulations concerning pollution through contact and ingestion, apparently referring there also to Torah-based practices, with servitude to the *stoicheia* in Col 2:16–17, 20–23.

dition of "months" or "new moon" festivals).[225] The Galatians were beginning to observe the Sabbath days, the new moon festivals (see Num 28:11–15), and could be expected, then, to observe the seasonal feasts (feasts lasting more than a day, like Passover and Tabernacles) and annual commemorations, like the New Year.[226] The observance of the Sabbath, together with circumcision and the distinctive dietary practices, were the most obvious and most universally well-known "works of the Law" that set Jews apart from Gentiles.

In submitting themselves to the Jewish ritual calendar, however, the Galatian Christians were submitting themselves to the authority of the stars and other heavenly bodies that determined the timing of the holidays and, thus, regulated the lives of Jews "under Law" (see *Jubilees* 2:8–10 and *1 Enoch* 82:9). Giving sun, moon, and stars such authority over one's life and practice amounted, for Paul, to a return to idolatrous service to things that were not in themselves divine. They were also submitting themselves to the authority of the custodian who had kept Jews and Gentiles corralled in separate pens, drawing back from the work of Christ creating the one, new humanity out of the two. If they are all now part of one family (3:26–29; 4:5–7), and that on the basis of the action of the Holy Spirit within them, there is no value in continuing to adhere to (or take up) practices that were in force while they were not family—either with God or with each other. Whether they reverted to their pagan past practices or reverted to Paul's own pre-Christian practice (the close observance of Torah), as was immediately the case, it was all the same to Paul: they were throwing away the freedom that Christ had died to give them, and moving against the Holy Spirit of God that was at work sanctifying one people together for God. The seriousness of the situation in Paul's eyes is underscored by his exclamation of fear that his work among them might turn out to have been all for nothing (4:11)!

4:12–20: MAKING THE ARGUMENT PERSONAL

[12]I beg you, brothers and sisters, become like me, because I myself became like you. You did me no injury. [13]You know

225. Fung, *Galatians*, 192–93; Bruce, *Galatians*, 205–6.
226. Longenecker, *Galatians*, 182.

that I proclaimed the message of good news to you the first time on account of a sickness of the flesh, [14]and you neither scorned nor rejected the trial you endured in my flesh, but rather you received me as a messenger (or, an angel) of God, even as Christ Jesus. [15]What happened to your earlier conviction that I was a person specially favored by God? For I testify to you that, if it were possible, you would have dug out your eyes and given them to me. [16]Have I, then, become your enemy by being truthful with you? [17]They are not courting you with noble intent, but they desire to shut you out in order that you might begin courting them. [18]It is a noble thing always to be courted in a noble pursuit, and not only while I am present with you. [19]My children, with whom I am again in labor pains until Christ takes shape in you: [20]I keep wishing that I could be present with you even now and to change my tone, because I am at a loss where you're concerned!

Having shared his deeply personal fear that his work among them may prove to be all for nothing (4:11), Paul continues to write in a more personal vein throughout this next paragraph, specifically recalling his former connection with the Galatians, forged during his earlier time with them. After much argument, Paul begins to turn to exhortation: what should the Galatians *do* in light of all that Paul has said in 2:14—4:11? He urges them first to "become like me," since he himself had also become as they were. Paul will from time to time set himself forward as a positive example of how to respond to Christ, an example of discipleship to be imitated particularly insofar as Paul successfully imitates Jesus (1 Cor 11:1; Phil 3:17). Here, however, Paul's exhortation is not based on his own imitation of Jesus, but on his correct understanding of the significance of Jesus' death and the gift of the Spirit for how Jews were to treat the old regulations that kept them separate from the Gentiles, whom God was also calling to be God's people.

What Paul means when he says that he had also become like the Galatians is perhaps best illumined by 1 Cor 9:20b–21: "to those under Torah I became as one under Torah, though not being myself under Torah, in order that I might win those under Torah. To those without Torah, I became as one without the Torah—not being without God's

Torah but rather keeping within Christ's law—in order that I might win those without Torah."[227] Paul went to the Gentiles on their turf and on their terms, interacting and eating freely with them, all to share Christ and to demonstrate what it now meant that God was bringing Jews and Gentiles alike into God's new people in Christ. His example was the polar opposite of the policy of the "men from James" who had gone to Antioch, whose behavior told the Gentiles, in effect, "become as we are, because we're certainly not to become as you are" (compare Gal 2:14). Paul was willing to behave like someone who was dead to the Torah—to count himself as a "former Jew," in effect—for the sake of connecting the Gentile Galatians with their inheritance in Christ. He calls here for some reciprocity from his converts. They, too, should consider themselves dead to the Torah as to any and all *stoicheia tou kosmou* for the sake of holding onto that inheritance, and for the sake of remaining true to their good friend who had so well and so genuinely served their interests during his earlier times with them.

In 4:13–14, Paul recalls his first visit to the Galatians and does so, as we have already explored in the introduction, in terms that are quite different from any accounts of Paul's activity in Galatia (whether South or North) in Acts.[228] But here we have a firsthand remembrance of that evangelistic visit, the details of which are likely therefore to be far more reliable than those reconstructed by Luke several decades later. Paul appears not to have planned to spend any significant time in the region of Galatia at all. Perhaps it was his original intent to go directly to the ma-

---

227. Each instance of "Torah" here is represented in the Greek by the word *nomos*, which simply means "law." Paul clearly has a particular legal code in mind here, however, namely the Mosaic Law, the Torah.

228. Paul refers to this evangelistic visit as *to proteron,* either meaning "the first" (i.e., "original") visit or "the former" visit of two such visits. Reading *to proteron* in the second sense, scholars have made much of how the two implied visits line up either with the two visits mentioned in Acts 16:6; 18:23 (and thus, possibly, with a North Galatian destination and later date for the epistle, though see the introduction on this point) or with the two visits recounted in Acts 13:13—14:28 (the second being briefly related in 14:21–23). Moulton and Milligan (*The Vocabulary of the Greek New Testament,* 554) have shown on the basis of their study of Roman-period papyri and their examination of uses of the word in the New Testament that *to proteron* more likely carries the looser meaning of "originally" or "previously" rather than the more precise meaning "the first time of two or more."

jor centers of Asia (Ephesus) and Greece, from which the word would spread in all directions, including back into less-developed Galatia. Paul's body, however, did not cooperate. There is no way of knowing the nature of Paul's illness or infirmity, though there has been no shortage of theories. All we know is that it slowed Paul down considerably. Paul, however, turned an annoying setback into an opportunity for proclaiming the Gospel.[229] Finding the people in Galatia receptive, he apparently changed his plans so as to spend more significant time in the southern cities of that province.

Paul's physical condition was such that he might have expected the Galatians to turn away from him in contempt and reject anything he might have had to say. After all, how could a person who was so obviously *not* enjoying the favor and protection of the gods claim to be speaking on behalf of one of them? He might have been more readily seen to be the object of the gods' disfavor at the moment. And what kind of spiritual power could he have, or could this Christ give, if Paul, Christ's ambassador, could not gain the upper hand over his own sickness or infirmity? Or perhaps he had himself been overcome by the evil spirits by means of which he worked his magic?[230] While the Galatians would have had several culturally conditioned reasons for despising Paul, they did not let his condition—nor the evident inconveniences it caused them[231]—stand in their way of hearing the Gospel and warmly embracing its messenger. So enthusiastic, indeed, was their response as Paul recalls it that he likens it to the kind of response they might have shown had an angelic being or even Christ Jesus himself appeared in their midst to announce the good news of God's acceptance. At that time, they indeed did him no wrong (4:12b).

229. Franz Mussner, *Galaterbrief*, 307. See also Paul's attitude in regard to his imprisonment in Phil 1:12–14.

230. Fung, *Galatians*, 198; Martyn, *Galatians*, 421.

231. The manuscript tradition is divided on whether we should read 4:14 as "you did not scorn or reject *your* trial in my flesh" or "*my* trial in my flesh." Sinaiticus, Vaticanus, and Alexandrinus favor the first; P[46] and the Majority Text favor the second. The question concerns whether Paul is specifically calling attention to the burden his physical condition made him to the Galatians ("*your* trial in my flesh") or not. The early manuscript evidence weighs somewhat more heavily in favor of the first reading.

Paul was aware throughout his ministry of the need to allow his hearers to encounter not just a persuasive speaker, but the very power of God. He did not want anyone's faith to rest on the strengths of the human messenger, but on the convert's experience of the living God and God's Spirit:

> When I came to you, brothers and sisters, I announced God's mystery to you not with flowery speech or rhetoric, for I decided to know nothing among you except Jesus Christ—and him crucified. I was among you in weakness and apprehension and great fear, and my speech and my proclamation was not executed with well-crafted and strategic words, but with a demonstration of Spirit and power in order that your trust might not be grounded in the cleverness of human beings but in God's power. (1 Cor 2:1–5)

> We do not announce ourselves, but we announce Jesus Christ as Lord and ourselves as your slaves on Jesus' account. The God who said "let light shine out of darkness" shone his light into our hearts to shed abroad the light of the knowledge of God's glory in the face of Christ. But we have this treasure in clay pots, in order that the abundance of power might be God's and not our own. (2 Cor 4:7–12)

God showing up to work wonders and to send his Spirit into the hearts of those in Galatia who heard the weak and ailing Paul was very much in line with what would become Paul's conscious philosophy of evangelism and ministry.[232]

Paul holds before the Galatian converts the gulf between the way they received Paul, thought of Paul, and clung to Paul formerly and the way they are now allowing themselves to come under the spell of teachers who are taking them in a different direction from the course he originally set out for them. This might indeed serve to make the Galatians feel ashamed of how they have proven less than reliable in their relationship with Paul. Their change of course is a clear signal that they have been entertaining second thoughts about Paul's reliability. So after

---

232. See deSilva, *Introduction to the New Testament*, 586–89; Martyn, *Galatians*, 421.

remembering their open arms and open hearts to him and his message, he asks, "What happened to your earlier conviction that I was a person specially favored by God?" Paul uses the Greek word *makarismos* here to speak of the way in which the Galatians viewed and esteemed him. A *makarismos* is, according to Aristotle, a pronouncement of a person or group to be "divinely favored," "privileged," "honored."[233] This kind of pronouncement is common throughout Scripture, seen throughout the Psalms, Prophets, and New Testament, wherever someone or some group of people is pronounced "blessed." The Galatians formerly looked upon Paul that way.[234] Paul speaks hypothetically of their willingness to pluck out their own eyes for him, not giving us thereby a clear indication that it was his own eyes that were the source of his troubles, but rather using this graphic image to remind them of how much they cared for Paul and how much they would have sacrificed to make him better.[235]

What, he asks, had he done to change their opinion of him? The "truth of the Gospel" has been a prominent topic in Galatians, and Paul has maintained that he has consistently spoken and acted in line with this truth, even defending it in the course of the developing Christian mission (2:5, 14). He brought this truth to the Galatians, but the rival teachers appear to have called Paul's message and motives into question, perhaps suggesting that he wasn't such a good friend to the Galatians after all, withholding the critical information about the ongoing authority of Torah and circumcision as the seal of the covenant.[236] Paul has by this point spent several chapters demonstrating that he did indeed proclaim the true message of God's actions in Christ, recalling twice now the Galatian converts' own experience of acceptance by God in their receiving God's Holy Spirit. On this basis he asks ironically how he can

233. Aristotle, *Rhetoric* 1.9.34. See, further, deSilva, *Seeing Things John's Way*, 274–76.

234. See Fung, *Galatians*, 198: a *makarismos* is "an act of declaring or counting as blessed or happy." Since Paul had just been speaking about the Galatians' regard for Paul and their awestruck reception of him, this sense of *makarismos* seems far more likely than the sense put forward by Longenecker (*Galatians*, 192), who reads this as referring to the Galatians' former state of blessedness, a state that has now come to an end.

235. Fung, *Galatians*, 199; Longenecker, *Galatians*, 193; Martyn, *Galatians*, 421.

236. Martyn, *Galatians*, 420.

be considered now to be their enemy,[237] as if he did not have their best interests at heart and did not deal truthfully with them about God's plan for their inclusion in God's family, since he had indeed brought them the genuine Gospel as their experience of the Spirit decisively proved. If anyone should be treated like an enemy in this situation, it is not Paul but the rival teachers, as Paul goes on immediately to assert.

Paul accuses the rival teachers of showing interest in the Galatian Christians motivated essentially by self-interest: "they are not courting (*zēlousin*) you with noble intent, but they want to shut you outside so that you'll begin courting (*zēloute*) them" (4:17). The Greek word *zēlos* and related forms generally had to do with the feeling of "emulation," admiring someone with a view to imitating them and acquiring thereby the good reputation or success that they had also enjoyed. Here, however, it carries the sense of "making a big deal of someone," "showing earnest interest in someone," hence "courting."[238] The verb is so used both to speak of the behavior of men and women pursuing one another and of the relationship of teachers and students (both of the teachers' quest for followers and of followers' attachment to their teachers).[239] Paul's allegation here is that the rival teachers are showing a great deal of interest in the Galatians, but not to the latter's advantage. Instead, the rival teachers' goal is to shut the Galatians back outside of the people of promise (i.e., by convincing them that, as Gentiles, they have no place in the people of God) so that the Galatians will attach themselves to these teachers and eagerly follow their instructions about how to pass through the gate into the people of God (i.e., through becoming Jews themselves).[240]

---

237. Longenecker (*Galatians*, 193) suggests that 4:16 is more properly read as an indignant exclamation: "So, then, I have become your enemy by telling you the truth!"

238. Liddell, Scott, and Jones, *A Greek-English Lexicon*, 755; Martyn, *Galatians*, 422. Paul uses the verb also in this sense in 2 Cor 11:2, where he presents himself as courting the Corinthian Christians on behalf of Christ, wishing to present them to him as a pure bride.

239. Bruce, *Galatians*, 212; BDAG, s.v. *zēloō* 1.b; Longenecker, *Galatians*, 193–94; Plutarch, *De virtute morali* 448E.

240. The rival teachers' goal of "shutting the Galatians out" does not focus, strictly speaking, on alienating the Galatian Christians from Paul, as Longenecker (*Galatians*, 193–94) suggests, but from the people of promise, so that the Galatians will be put in

Paul appears to quote a proverbial saying at this point: "it is always a noble thing to be courted with noble intentions."[241] This holds true, Paul adds, not only when he is present with them, but also in his absence. On the one hand, Martyn may be correct to say that Paul is indicating by this that his annoyance at the rival teachers does not spring merely from jealousy or an awareness that his "turf" has been violated. Paul would have thought it a fine thing for other teachers to come along after him, if their interest in his converts ended up working for the good of his converts (compare 1 Cor 3:4–15; Phil 1:15–18).[242] The way Paul has phrased this, however, may serve more primarily as an assertion that Paul had courted the Galatians with noble intentions while he was with them, namely the full formation of Christ within them,[243] with perhaps two implications to be drawn: the rival teachers, regrettably, did not court them with noble intentions in Paul's absence; in his absence, Paul is still courting the Galatians with noble intentions, unlike the rival teachers who are now present among them.

Paul's noble intentions for courting the Galatians is clearly stated in 4:19: he has sought from the outset that Christ take shape in them, that they be transformed fully into the image of Christ, God's righteous one. Paul expresses clearly here the essential formational element of justification, namely God's desire to restore his image within us by conforming us to the likeness of Jesus, his Son, the perfect human bearer of that image. In this process of transformation, we *become* righteous (hence, are justified, brought into alignment with God's standards and

---

a position to try to re-enter the people of promise by courting the rival teachers and following them as disciples (rightly, Martyn, *Galatians*, 423).

241. Burton, *Galatians*, 247. Longenecker (*Galatians*,194) translates this maxim as "good is always to be courted in a good way," taking *kalon* as the subject of the infinitive *zēlousthai*. While this translation is not impossible, the opening *kalon* is far more likely to have been heard as the impersonal "it is good," or "it is a noble thing," *kalon* and *aischron* being very common openings for maxims, coordinating some attitude or behavior with the "noble" and the "shameful," the primary axis of value in the Hellenistic-Roman world. Additionally, if Paul had meant for *kalon* to be heard as the subject of the infinitive, he would likely have introduced it with the article, *to kalon* ("the good").

242. Martyn, *Galatians*, 423.

243. Fung, *Galatians*, 202.

heart) as we *become* more like God's Son, who comes to life within the believer by the action of the Holy Spirit. Whether Paul speaks of Christ taking shape in and among the believers (4:19), or of Christ living in the believer (2:20), or of believers being shaped into Christ's likeness (as in Phil 3:8–11; 2 Cor 3:18), such transformation is the passionate heart of Paul's Gospel and theology.[244]

Paul's passion for seeing this transformation continue unimpeded in his converts' individual and collective lives comes through clearly in the images he chooses to capture the pitch of his emotional and personal investment in the process: calling the hearers his "children," he claims to be "again in labor pains until Christ takes shape in you" (4:19). Although he usually addresses his converts as "brothers and sisters," Paul occasionally addresses them as his "children" when he wants to draw attention to the fact that he has been the active agent—their "spiritual father"—in bringing them to the new birth of the faith (see, for example, 1 Cor 4:15; Phlm 10). Here, however, the role of the "father" simply does not suffice. Such is his personal investment in, and his anguish over, the successful "birth" of the Galatians into the new life of Christ that he identifies more with the birth pangs of a mother in labor for her children.[245] Paul's metaphor is more complex, however, since ultimately it is Christ who is the one being born ("taking shape") in the midst of the Galatian community, and so Paul is casting the Galatian Christian community itself as a kind of womb, in whom—individually and collectively—Christ, like the fetus, is taking shape.[246] The work of the rival teachers has put this process of formation in jeopardy, and Paul is in anguish to get his converts back on track.

This anguish, no doubt, has led to the severity of the letter from the outset (e.g., 1:6; 3:1–5; 4:11), a fact that Paul appears to realize at this point as he expresses the wish not to be writing from a distance, but

244. See also Martyn, *Galatians,* 425, 430–31.

245. The idea of being in labor pains a second time to "give birth to children for immortality" appears in 4 Macc 16:13, where a mother endures watching her seven sons tortured to death—even spurring them on to continue to resist the tyrant, despite the heart-wrenching grief if causes her—as a second round of labor pains to give them "rebirth for immortality." On Paul as a "mother figure," see Gaventa, "Our Mother St. Paul," 29–44; idem, "The Maternity of Paul," 189–201.

246. Longenecker, *Galatians,* 195; Schlier, *Galater,* 214.

to be present with his converts instead, so that, face to face, he might have reason not to write so harshly. Such a tone—and the developments in the situation that have led to his taking this tone—is not what Paul would have chosen in regard to his dear converts. He has, however, just communicated quite clearly where his annoyance, angst, and anger come from: he believes that the formation of Christ within them and in their midst is in jeopardy of being stalled, even stillborn, and he is in anguish over that possibility.

4:21–31: PROOF FROM ALLEGORICAL READING OF SCRIPTURE

[21]Tell me, you who wish to be under Torah, do you not listen to the Torah? [22]For it is written that Abraham had two sons, one from the slave woman and one from the free woman. [23]But the one from the slave woman has been born in accordance with the flesh, and the one from the free woman *has been born* through a promise. [24]These things have a symbolic meaning, for these women are two covenants. The one was born from Mount Sinai into slavery, which is Hagar. [25]And Hagar is Sinai, a mountain in Arabia. She corresponds to the present Jerusalem, for she is enslaved along with her children. [26]But the Jerusalem above is free, and she is our mother, [27]for it is written: "Rejoice, barren woman who is not giving birth; writhe and cry out, you who are not in labor, because many more are the children of the barren than of the woman who has a husband." [28]And you, brothers and sisters, are children of promise in the manner of Isaac. [29]But just as the one born in accordance with flesh at that time persecuted the one born in accordance with Spirit, so also now. [30]But what does the Scripture say? "Cast out the slave woman and her son, for the son of the slave woman will by no means inherit along with the son of the free woman." [31]Therefore, brothers and sisters, you are not children of the slave woman, but of the free woman.

Paul concludes his proof from scriptural arguments with an allegorical reading of the Sarah and Hagar episodes of Abraham's story (Gal 4:21–

31), thus returning to the theme of Gal 3:6 (Abraham "believed God" with regard to God's promise of offspring) and to the question of who is the heir of the divine promises. It is somewhat surprising to find Paul returning to an argumentative mode after making such an earnest and personal appeal in 4:12–20. This troubles scholars who try to make neat divisions between the "argument" and the "exhortation" of Galatians. Richard Longenecker, for example, argues that Paul's exhortation begins in 4:12, and that 4:21–31 therefore "should be seen not as part of Paul's argumentative *probatio* but as part of his appeals and exhortation."[247] The allegory of 4:21–31 clearly supports the exhortations of Galatians, as does all the argumentation or exposition in the letter, but it is itself expository and not hortatory. We find, then, that Paul uses an interlocking structure whereby 4:12–20 would indeed begin the exhortation in earnest, leading into 5:1—6:10, but where 4:21–31 closes off the arguments based on Scripture. The blurring of the lines of transitions between sections (where does argument end and exposition begin?), rather than a more formulaic and abrupt transition from *probatio* to exhortation, is a sign of Paul's artistry and facility in rhetorical form.

Paul opens this new paragraph with a direct address, challenging those among the hearers who "want to be under Torah" with an interpretation of an episode from the Torah that should convince them that Torah itself—rightly understood—would counsel them not to heed the rival teachers' advice, but to continue in the way that Paul had taught them. Paul gives us another indirect indication that the Galatian Christians have not yet fully taken the plunge into a Torah-observant lifestyle (including circumcision, the seal of the covenant), as he described them as not yet "under law," but "wanting to be under law."[248] Paul also bears witness to the ambiguity of "Torah" or "the Law" in the era after Christ's death. The term is being used two ways in this verse. In the first instance, it refers to the enslaving power of the Mosaic Torah, Israel's pedagogue and custodian from which Christ liberated those who would respond in trust. In the second, Paul uses the term to refer to the text of Scripture as an ongoing witness to God's purposes, as a

247. Longenecker, *Galatians*, 199.

248. Longenecker, *Galatians*, 206–7.

collection of oracles to which Christians should pay attention and that they should heed.[249]

Paul draws their attention to the relevant segment of the Torah (as Scripture) with the formula, "It is written." Normally this formula is reserved for introducing a specific quotation; here it introduces a summary of a scriptural story instead. The way Paul introduces the story suggests that he expects the audience to be quite familiar with it. He doesn't mention any proper names in 4:22–23, expecting his hearers to know who he means by "the handmaid," "the free woman," and their respective sons, as well as the general contours of the story (at least those elements found in Gen 15:1–6; 16:1–16; 21:1–14). It is quite possible that the rival teachers had used this very story to advance their own interpretation of how one becomes an heir of Abraham. Paul's use of words and expressions at this point in Galatians (Jerusalem as "mother," "Sinai") and elsewhere in the letter (such as "seed of Abraham") that he does not use anywhere else in his writings is one indicator that these topics were introduced into the situation by another party, and that he is taking up those topics and expressions to give them a different interpretation or application.[250]

If the rival teachers had spoken of this story in their preaching, they could have advanced their cause by means of a quite literal reading. Abraham fathered Ishmael with his wife's female slave, Hagar. Thirteen years later, he fathered Isaac by his own wife, Sarah. Only the descendants of Isaac were counted as Abraham's heirs and the people of the promise (and, indeed, only the descendants of Isaac's younger son Jacob would be counted as heirs as well). Only the Jews—and those who join themselves to the Jewish people by submitting to circumcision and adopting the distinctively Jewish way of life spelled out in Torah—are Abraham's heirs. The blessing that comes to the nations is the invitation issued through God's Messiah to join the historic people of God, and thus to share in the inheritance of God's promises. Paul will draw radically new lines through this story, wreaking havoc with the ethnic lines

---

249. Martyn, *Galatians*, 433.

250. Martyn, *Galatians*, 437; Barrett, "The Allegory of Abraham, Sarah, and Hagar," 1–16, especially p. 9.

drawn by the emphasis on physical descent from Sarah through Isaac and Jacob when it comes to defining the "children of promise."

Paul claims that the story of Hagar and Sarah reveals something beyond what the narrative communicates at face value: "These things have a symbolic meaning" or "communicate something else (*estin allēgoroumena*)" (4:24a). Indeed, Paul's language indicates that he is about to engage in an allegorical reading, though it is not clear whether Paul himself understands the story to be "allegorically spoken" (thus, originally written with the intent of communicating something more) or that the story is to be "interpreted allegorically." In 1 Cor 9:9–10, Paul attributes allegorical *intent* to the author of the particular law prohibiting the muzzling of an ox while it treads out the grain, claiming that the lawgiver was not himself concerned about oxen but revealing a principle applicable to human workers' access to the fruit of their own labors and right to sustenance for their labors.[251]

Paul's "allegory" is worth comparing to Philo's allegorical interpretation of the same story. In Philo's reading, Sarah represents moral virtue and Hagar the "preliminary studies," that is, the course of formal education, whether formally or informally pursued. "We are not yet capable as yet of receiving the impregnation of virtue unless we have first mated with the handmaiden, and the handmaiden of wisdom is the culture gained by the primary learning of the school course," or "the lower branches of school lore" (*De Congressu Eruditionis Gratia* 9–10, 14). In Philo's hands, the story really does "communicate something else," something quite divorced from the historical dynamics of the narrative. Paul's allegorical reading is much more reserved, insofar as he is not seeking to eliminate the historical specificity of the story in favor of some timeless philosophical principle.[252] Rather, he has discovered a principle at work specifically within the world of the story of Sarah and Hagar (expressed indirectly in 4:23), applying this then to the larger story of God's fulfillment of the promises given to Abraham.

That principle concerns the way in which God's promises come to fulfillment. They do not come about on the basis of "flesh," that is, what human beings can manage for themselves on their own strength

251. Longenecker, *Galatians*, 209.
252. Hanson, *Allegory and Event*, 82–83.

and with their own resources. Rather, they come about through what the Spirit works among and within human beings, empowering them beyond their own capacity. Paul's substitution of "according to the Spirit" (4:29) for "through promise" (4:23) in describing Sarah's child and children in contrast to those born "in line with the flesh" shows that "Spirit" is primarily in Paul's mind here, in keeping with the identification of the Spirit as the promised inheritance (3:13–14) and looking ahead to his discussion of the Spirit's empowerment of the human being to rise above the power of the flesh and live a righteous life before God (5:13—6:10). The applicability, then, to the situation in Galatia becomes immediately apparent: circumcision of the physical flesh and the adoption of at least some of the works of the Torah are all things that human beings can manage on their own in an attempt to align with God's righteousness, but God has decreed that the promise of righteousness will be attained on the basis of trusting Jesus and trusting the Spirit's guidance and empowerment (3:11).

Rather than stay at the level of physical descent from Abraham through Isaac and Jacob as the criterion of being an heir, Paul moves to another level of meaning—"these women are two covenants" (4:24), one a covenant based on the flesh and perpetuating slavery, another a covenant based on promise and the Spirit, introducing freedom. Paul's hearers can already plot where Paul is heading, for he has already connected living under the Torah (hence, the Sinaitic covenant) with living in a state of slavery (4:3–5), and being born a child and heir with the action of the Spirit (4:6–7).

Hagar was a young and fertile woman, with whom Abraham could have children on the strength of their mutual reproductive capabilities alone. Paul therefore connects the path promoted by the rival teachers— the path of submitting to circumcision and some portion of the works of Torah—with Hagar, since "they are engaged in a human, religious exercise that no more involves the power of God than did the arrangement (via Hagar) by which Abraham and Sarah got Ishmael."[253] The Sinaitic covenant (the Torah), thus, is connected not with Sarah, the free woman, but with Hagar, the slave woman. This connection is supported by the geographical reference to Mount Sinai being in the territory of

253. Martyn, *Galatians*, 436.

Arabia, with which Hagar was also associated. Though originally from Egypt, Hagar ended up settling somewhere in Arabia (traditionally in the area of Petra) after her expulsion from Abraham's camp.[254]

Hagar thus "lines up (*systoichei*) with the present Jerusalem, for she is in slavery along with her children" (4:25). The verb *systoicheō* was originally used to speak of soldiers lining up in columns or rows.[255] It is used appropriately here as Paul is creating, in effect, two rows of columns and asking the Galatians to find themselves lined up with one row rather than the other. [256] In one column, Paul is lining up "Hagar," the "Sinaitic covenant," Paul's contemporary "Jerusalem" and all who look to Jerusalem as their "mother," and "slavery" and being born into slavery. In the other column, Paul will line up "Sarah," the "promise/Spirit," the "Jerusalem above" and all who look to that city as their "mother," and "freedom" and being born into freedom. In so doing, he has radically rewritten the genealogy of the Jewish people, who trace their lineage naturally from Isaac, not Ishmael. Paul contends, however, that the lesson to be learned from the story is that those who are born on the basis of God's promise and the Spirit are the ones who inherit the blessing of Abraham (Gal 4:30–31): in the immediate situation, this would include the Gentile Galatian Christians, but *not* the rival teachers, who still labor in slavery and seek to enslave the converts as well.

In a post-Holocaust world, scholars have raised some questions concerning who it is that Paul has in mind when he writes about "the present Jerusalem" that is "in slavery along with her children." Does he make a pronouncement thereby on all Jews outside of the Christian movement?[257] Or does Paul limit his allegory to the two Jewish Christian missions directed toward Gentiles—one promoting Torah observance as a condition of conversion and membership, and one proceeding free

254. McNamara, "'To de (Hagar) Sina oros estin en tē Arabia,'" 24–41, especially p. 36. There is some discrepancy among manuscripts, even among the earliest ones, whether Hagar is actually named in this verse ("And Hagar is Sinai, a mountain in Arabia") or not ("And Sinai is a mountain in Arabia"). In neither case is an essential element in the allegory lost, since Hagar's correspondence to Sinai is already established in 4:24. Martyn (*Galatians*, 438) favors the longer reading.

255. Burton, *Galatians*, 261–62.

256. Martyn, *Galatians*, 438, 449–50.

257. So, for example, Fung, *Galatians*, 209.

of the Torah (i.e., Paul and his team, and other Jewish Christian missionaries sharing his position)? J. Louis Martyn has argued especially strenuously in favor of the latter.[258] It is appropriate to affirm that Paul is not particularly targeting non-Christian Judaism, and thus that he has the kind of mission represented by the rival teachers more in mind. For Paul, and in the midst of the argument in Galatia, "Hagar" and "the present Jerusalem" that is now in slavery includes especially the Torah-observant Gentile mission and is meant to speak primarily about their exclusion from the freedom of the promise.

But what indication does Paul give that he limits "the present Jerusalem" to the Torah-observant Jewish Christian mission? What clues does he give that he would not place all non-Christian Jews also among the spiritual descendants of Hagar, and thus among the children of "the present Jerusalem" in his allegory? All the clues he *does* give point, rather, to his lumping together of rival teachers and non-Christian Jews within this group. Paul ranks *all* who are "under Torah" as slaves (4:3–5). Given Paul's assessment of his own former life, and even the essentially non-Christian character of the rival mission as he perceives them (if they lead people to be cut off from Christ, Paul could not affirm them to be "in Christ" themselves), Paul could only affirm all non-Christian Jews to be "in slavery" along with, and as part of, "the present Jerusalem."[259]

Paul looks, however, to "the Jerusalem above," the Jerusalem that is "free," as the mother of those who are children of promise, who are born by the working of the Holy Spirit (4:28–29).[260] The Christian hope

---

258. Martyn, *Galatians*, 457–66; idem, *Theological Issues in the Letters of Paul*, 191–208.

259. Martyn (*Galatians*, 38) does concede that Galatians "does contain an *implication* with regard to Judaism: Paul's zealous observance of the Law failed to liberate him from enslavement to the elements of the old cosmos. That liberation came through God's apocalypse of Jesus Christ, not through any religion, including that of Judaism."

260. The earliest manuscripts read "our mother" (P[46], Sinaiticus, Vaticanus); Alexandrinus, along with the Majority Text (hence the KJV), reads "the mother of us all." In Greek, the issue concerns the addition of a single word for "all." The shorter reading is probably the more original, with scribes explicitly broadening Paul's inclusivity.

is no longer bound up with the future of an earthly city, even one with so distinguished a pedigree in the acts of God as Jerusalem. Instead, "our citizenship is in heaven" (Phil 3:21), and we look for "a better, that is, a heavenly homeland" (see Heb 11:11–16; 13:13–14; Rev 21:1—22:5) rather than setting our sights on any disputed stretch of land in the Middle East. This affords a rare glimpse into Paul's eschatology. While the earthly Jerusalem is bound up with the history of a particular ethnic people (the Jewish people), Paul looks to a heavenly city as an appropriate future dwelling place for the multinational, multiethnic people of God formed in Christ.

At this point, Paul cites Isa 54:1–2 as an authoritative text that provides confirmation of his reading of the Hagar and Sarah story, introducing this quotation with the customary formula: "For it is written, 'Rejoice, barren woman (*steira*) who is not giving birth; writhe and cry out, you who are not in labor, because many more are the children of the barren than of the woman who has a husband'" (Gal 4:27). Does Paul rip this verse out of context? By the standards of the modern study of the Old Testament, Paul may fail to read Isa 54:1 first as a word to the returning exiles from Babylon. By first-century standards, however, Paul handles this text as a responsible and well-trained exegete with a high level of sophistication.

Paul connects Isa 54:1, which addresses the "barren woman" (*steira*), with the story of Sarah, who is also called "barren" (*steira*, Gen 11:30 LXX) in Scripture. Paul was following a practice of biblical interpretation known as *gezera shawa*, whereby two texts sharing a common term or phrase are brought together to interpret one another. Moreover, Sarah did "shout for joy" giving birth to Isaac (Gen 21:6–7), and Isaac's descendants became more numerous than those of Ishmael. Paul applies this promise from Isaiah, then, to the (Torah-free) Gentile mission, which was in fact making many more spiritual descendants for Abraham (born through promise by means of the Holy Spirit) than proselytism to either Judaism or Torah-observant Christianity (born into the family on the basis of the flesh, that is, through circumcision of the flesh).[261]

261. Fung, *Galatians*, 211.

Paul may be reading Isaiah even more closely that this, however. The verse that he recites (Isa 54:1) follows immediately after the famous Servant Song (Isa 52:13—53:12), in which the righteous one bears the sins of many, ransoms many, makes many righteous, and sees his offspring despite being cut off from the land of the living—indeed, engenders offspring precisely in being offered up for sin. Jesus, the Messianic servant who brings blessings to many who are then accounted his offspring, permits this flourishing of offspring for the barren one, multiplying endlessly the children and heirs of Abraham through the Torah-free Gentile mission.

The Galatian Christians resemble Isaac in the most important respect: they, like Isaac, were born into the family of Abraham in line with God's promise, specifically through their reception of the promised Holy Spirit (4:28).[262] Paul does not specify the second of the two covenants, the one represented by Sarah (4:24), but given the prevalence of the language of promise and the focus on Abraham, he may well be thinking here in terms of the promise given by God to Abraham (3:15–18), which was also given in terms of a covenant. In other settings, of course, Paul would speak more in terms of the "new covenant" instituted by Jesus (see, e.g., 1 Cor 11:25).

Again looking to the story of Sarah and Hagar for a historical precedent to the situation of the Torah-free Gentile mission, Paul claims that "then, as now, the one born after the manner of the flesh persecuted the one born after the manner of the Spirit" (4:29). Genesis, however, does not speak of Ishmael's hostile intent towards Isaac. Sarah, after observing the two boys playing together, tells Abraham to send Hagar and Ishmael away so that the latter will not inherit alongside her own child (Gen 21:9). Later retellings of the story attempt to justify Sarah's rather cold-hearted command by suggesting that Isaac was in some danger

262. The earliest manuscripts are split between reading "and *you*, brothers and sisters, are children of promise" and "and *we*, brothers and sisters, are children of promise." One of the more common kinds of variant in New Testament manuscripts in general involves this switch from "we" to "you," which differ in the Greek only in the initial vowel (and these vowels came to be pronounced in an increasingly similar fashion). In this instance, it is more likely that scribes were influenced to replace an original "you" with "we," conforming this verse to the "we" statements that surround it in its paragraph (4:26, 31). Metzger, *Textual Commentary*, 597.

(see, for example, *Gen. Rab.* 53:11; *Tg. Ps.-J.* Gen 21:10; *Tg. Onq.* Gen 21:9; Josephus, *Antiquities* 1.215),[263] and Paul appears to have been familiar with these developments of the original story and to have valued them insofar as they helped to cement his point that what happened long ago was paradigmatic for what was happening in the immediate situation of his mission to the Gentiles.

Whom would Paul have considered to have been persecuting the children born of the Spirit in his own setting? Some scholars have understood Paul to refer to the activity of the rival teachers themselves, their dogging Paul's steps and putting new pressure on Paul's converts, as "persecution."[264] Indeed, Paul has regarded certain Jewish-Christian parties as hostile to himself (as seen, for example, in 2:3–5), and might even begin to have seen their activity as "persecution." However, the other four explicit references to persecution in Galatians are used in the context of non-Christian Jewish opposition to the Christian movement. Paul twice refers to his own former activity as persecuting the church while still "in bondage" himself (Gal 1:13, 23). He also refers to the persecution that he alleges the rival teachers to be themselves avoiding by promoting circumcision (Gal 6:12), and that Paul could have hoped to avoid were he to do likewise, but doesn't (Gal 5:11).

There is more contextual evidence, therefore, for regarding 4:29 at least to include non-Christian Jewish persecution of the Christian movement. This persecution bears most directly on Jewish Christians who appear to go beyond the pale of Torah or speak against the central pillars of the Mosaic covenant (see, for example, the circumstances surrounding Stephen's murder in Acts 7–8 and Paul's former activity as a persecutor), but makes itself felt among Gentile Christians as well. The rival teachers are troubling the Galatian churches on account of a desire to avoid persecution themselves by persuading Gentile converts to Christianity to become circumcised, thus making the whole Christian movement essentially an effort of Jewish proselytism.[265] They have thus aligned themselves also with Ishmael.

263. Callaway, "The Mistress and the Maid," 94–101.

264. Martyn, *Galatians*, 445; Longenecker, *Galatians*, 217. Fung (*Galatians*, 213) allows for this possibility.

265. Schlier, *Galater*, 227. Fung (*Galatians*, 213) prefers this scenario.

The fact of persecution is taken as a sign of the true identity of each party in the allegory. Those doing the persecuting are enacting the role of Ishmael, "the one born in accordance with the flesh"; the Jewish Christians involved in the Pauline mission (and others of similar mind) are cast in the role of "the one born in accordance with the Spirit." The children of the Spirit, and hence the children of promise, are those who align themselves with the latter group (hence with Paul and his Gospel, against the rival teachers and theirs).

The response to God being promoted by the rival teachers is not, for Paul, simply an alternative route to justification, not even an inferior route to justification. It is, simply, *no* route to justification at all. God's promise cannot be attained in a fleshly manner, but only by the power of the Spirit. To bring this home, he follows the story of Ishmael to its end in the Genesis narrative. While Ishmael was raised in Abraham's tents for thirteen years, he was destined to be disinherited. Paul recites the words of Sarah to Abraham as the very words of Scripture passing sentence on those who seek to attain God's promises by trusting in physical descent, circumcision, and joining the covenant of Moses: "Throw out the slave girl and her son, for the son of the slave girl will by no means share in the inheritance with the son of the free woman" (4:30; see Gen 21:10).[266] Paul has changed the quotation slightly, substituting "the son of the free woman" for "my son Isaac," thus extending its applicability beyond the historical situation of Sarah and Hagar. Paul has already proven that the Galatians *have* inherited what was promised through Abraham, namely the Holy Spirit (3:1–5, 13–14; 4:6–7), and so concludes that he, his team, and all those who have come to Christ through his mission (including the Galatians) "are not children of the slave girl, but of the free woman" (4:31). While not Sarah's physical descendants,

266. Though spoken by Sarah, God confirms the course of action for which Sarah called (Gen 21:12). It was only after this that Abraham consented. It is quite possible that the Galatians would have heard in the recitation of Gen 21:10 an invitation to break off relations with the rival teachers, which would no doubt have pleased Paul. Paul himself, however, seems to be more interested in the second half of the quotation, in which "Scripture" declares the rival teachers and all those who remain "under Torah" with them to be outside of the inheritance, and declares only those who have been born in the freedom of the promise and the Spirit to be God's heirs. This is the part of the quotation on which he actually comments in 4:31.

and while not joining themselves to the community of Sarah's physical descendants (i.e., the Jewish people), the Galatian Christians are nonetheless Sarah's genuine descendants because they, like Isaac, have been born into God's family by the action of the promised Spirit.

READING GALATIANS 4 WITH SRI LANKAN CHRISTIANS

The Stoicheia in Sri Lanka

The *stoicheia* are spiritual forces exercising authority over the human race. They represent the power of the basic principles of the world's way of doing things, the domination systems that we take for granted and cannot dream of living without. They represent the ideologies of nation, of militarism, of economics (whether capitalism, socialism, or communism), even of religion and how far the sphere of religion is permitted to extend, and the ways in which these ideologies shape our society and control and constrain us.

Sociologist Peter Berger describes how people are programmed from birth ("socialized") in their society's self-preserving values, ideals, and behavioral norms, so that each individual member of society will do his or her part to keep that society functioning more or less without question.[267] Indeed, our programming tends to prevent us from even raising questions. This socialization limits the options we perceive for our responses, our relationships, even our ambitions. Paul insightfully described our condition as human beings in society as a kind of slavery, or as that of children under various disciplinarians and guardians (Gal 4:1–11). He challenges us to discern how these *stoicheia*, which we could think of somewhat glibly as the "-isms" in our social context, have been operative in our lives *and* in the life of the church, so that we may become ever more free to respond to one another and to the world from the ideals and values taught by God. The importance of the Spirit here cannot be overestimated: only by hearing and following the Spirit, often in conjunction with studying the Scriptures, can we break out of the prisons our society constructs around our minds and aspirations from birth.

267. Berger, *The Sacred Canopy*, 3–52; idem, *Invitation to Sociology*, 66–121.

Sri Lankan culture has been forged, and continues largely to be shaped, by a majority Sinhalese Buddhist community and, secondly, the Tamil Hindu community. In practice, both religions foster a culture steeped in the worship of idols, the performance of particular rituals and deeds (for example, the emphasis within Hinduism on reciting hymns, confessing the creeds, visiting holy places, bathing in the holy rivers, chanting mantras, piercing one's body, and giving alms as means to attaining salvation), and attention to superstitious practices (for example, using horoscopes and astrology to determine auspicious times for particular undertakings).

These beliefs have such control over people—leaders, educators, and street sweepers alike, in rural and urban settings alike—that they submit their plans for both major life decisions and day-to-day activities to such practices. Auspicious times are sought for setting the time and date for weddings or the opening ceremonies of particular programs in the hope that such timing will bring success and good fortune. Certain days are avoided for these events fearing it will bring misfortune. Even burying the dead might have to wait an extra day. Politicians may cancel appointments because the "time was wrong" or the horoscopes were bad. A bride and groom will choose an auspicious day and time even though it may be very unpractical and inconvenient. A black cat crossing one's path or a certain type of bird flying over your head could be a bad omen. Babies are given a pottu depicting a third eye to ward off evil spirits. At every stage of life people are bound by these practices and the worldview that supports them.

Paul declares that Christ came and the Spirit was given to free human beings from all such bondage to superstitious constraints. The favor of the One God was freely available, not constrained by "the proper time" nor thwarted by alleged "bad signs." Human beings are invited into a new quality of relationship with Deity—the relationship of sons and daughters with their Father. This is a distinctive image of the divine-human relationship not found in other religions in Sri Lanka, even as "Abba, Father" is a distinctive image of God.

Paul poses a double challenge in this regard to the Christian community. First, the Christian convert must work to embrace this freedom by releasing superstitious practices that deny the reality of the availability of God's favor, to be dispensed as God desires. Christians are often found resorting to horoscopes and auspicious times for important events; it seems difficult for them to distance themselves from superstition such as belief in omens of good and bad luck and the beneficial or evil influence of the planets on their lives. In times of desperation and difficulty often they are tempted to turn to these worthless practices that lead to bondage.

But the second challenge is that Christian communities must work hard not to create new forms of bondage for their adherents through their own construction of new bodies of rules and sets of practices that replace the leading of the Spirit with a new law code. This is a danger faced in the popular practice of Roman Catholicism, whereby a convert from Hinduism might approach weekly attendance at Mass, reciting the Rosary, lighting candles to saints, rigorous fasting, and visiting shrines with the same attitude and understanding that she formerly brought to her Hindu practice. It is equally a danger faced in the practice of many evangelical Christian groups, which might emphasize the need to perform baptism in a particular way or with the recitation of particular words, or might seek to enforce a particular code of conduct in regard to days for worship, forbidden beverages, and proscribed activities, when Paul himself would relegate such matters to the status of "indifferent things" wherein a Christian could honor God by eating or not eating, drinking or not drinking, observing one day for worship or another.

It is important, at the same time, that Christians distinguish mythology and superstition from harmless cultural practices that are not offensive to God. Early Western missionaries often did not encourage such careful distinctions, but rather introduced elements of Western culture to replace what they thought were linked to pre-Christian religious belief and practice. Traditional cultural practices that could, and perhaps should, have been retained were thus totally eliminated from the lifestyle and liturgy of converts to Christianity. In Sri Lanka this has resulted in Christianity being branded as a Western import, an enemy of indigenous culture outright. Sri Lankan Christians are challenged to struggle together to discern where they need to distance themselves from inherited, indigenous practice as incompatible with being "Sri Lankans *in Christ*," and where they may embrace the same as fully compatible with being "*Sri Lankans* in Christ." Embodying the Gospel has, in every place, required both the careful sifting of pre-Christian customs and practice and the new embodiment of Christian practice in indigenous cultural forms.

The "elementary principles of the world" enslave Sri Lankans in other respects as well. The *stoicheia tou kosmou* include the worldly, unredeemed ways of thinking, values, socio-political categories and systems—in short, all that encounters us from "outside" as we are growing up in this world, and that finds its way "inside" us as we internalize the logic, the values, the practices, and the boundaries that we are taught and observe.

- The ideology of ethnicity—the formation of personal identity grounded in belonging to a particular ethnic category, the regulation of relationships on the basis of remaining associated with people of one's own ethnic group, the belief that members of one's own ethnic group are superior in some way, or have superior claims in some regards, than members of another ethnic group—has been a powerful *stoicheion* in Sri Lanka over a long and violent history.

- The bond between Buddhism and nationalism is an operative *stoicheion*, seen for example in the erecting of statues of the Buddha throughout the north—that is, in predominantly Tamil and Hindu areas—in the aftermath of the civil war as an alleged "symbol of unity."

- The overemphasis on education, especially in cities, by which children are driven to excel, valuing success more than life (witness the instances of suicide among children who don't make the cut for entering university) and certainly more than the enjoyment of a less stressful childhood, is a powerful principle enslaving and controlling many lives. As a corollary, it teaches competition for a limited good (seats in university) as a primary mode of social interaction, rather than cooperation with a view to expanding access to this good.

- As residents of a developing country, Sri Lankans are attracted to Western culture, dress, foods, entertainment, and values. Political colonization has, in many ways, given place to cultural and economic colonization. The formerly colonized continue to act out the script that the colonizers had pressed upon them: "Look to us, imitate us, what we have is good, what we have is better than what you can gain by following your own path." Thus international schools in Sri Lanka offer Western education with the goal of helping Sri Lankans get into university and proceed to find foreign jobs rather than dedicate their skills and energies to the development of their native land (Sri Lanka has the second largest expatriate population per capita in the world). Thus also Sri Lankan Christians continue to live within a largely "colonized Christianity"—even when its services are offered in Sinhala, for example, the music is often a Sinhalese translation of a Western hymn or praise song. Instances of this mentality are vestiges, in many ways, of Sri Lankans' *literal* experience under guardians and custodians, an experience that has produced a mindset (a *stoicheion*) that has long outlived formal colonialism.

- Patriarchy is a pervasive feature of the "elementary principles of the world," seen at work in many cultures. Gender becomes determinative for a person's potential, value, role, and access to power—and this in every sphere, domestic, social, and political. With men and women relegated to different spheres of life, each sphere potentially suffers from the loss of balance that the complementary virtues and instincts of the two genders could bring to those spheres.

- Militarism—the belief that violence can actually produce peace, and the corollary that the suppression of resistance means that concerns regarding justice and peace have been addressed—is a *stoicheion* that has carved deep ruts in the human consciousness, having exercised its logic and indoctrinated generation after generation into its logic since prehistory.

- The belief in karma-samsara deeply infiltrates individual thought and social interaction in Sri Lanka, as in other countries where

Hinduism and Buddhism have been major forces shaping social consciousness. Responsibility for poverty, suffering, and pain lies with the individual, who pays for the lack of merit acquired in a past incarnation. This, in turn, relieves those who witness poverty, suffering, or pain of the responsibility to help (except insofar as they might gain merit for themselves and their own progress in the cycle of samsara), and potentially spares the social structures much-needed scrutiny in regard to the systemic problems and failures that perpetuate poverty and suffering among part of the population.

An essential component of the "good news" of the Gospel is that we have been liberated from continuing to live out our lives in servitude to these ideologies and structures. A new Spirit has been poured into our hearts, driving out the spirits of this age, so that we can apply ourselves to building our lives around the teachings and example of Christ, the guidance of the apostles, the counsel of fellow Christians—trying to discover together what authentic life free from the domination of these *stoicheia* will look like.[268] If our liberation is to become real, we need to attend to the long process of discovery of those areas in which we (as individual disciples and church bodies) continue to act upon what we have internalized from these *stoicheia*, discarding these practices, and inquiring into what Christ-formed practices could take their place.

The Buddha Was Our Pedagogue?

Prabo Mihindukulasuriya has suggested that Paul's model of passing from the tutelage of the "pedagogue" (3:23–25), the "custodians and stewards" (4:2), and the "elementary logic of the world" (4:3) into the state of being mature heirs in the household of God provides the means by which Sri Lankan Christians, particular those who come from Buddhist backgrounds, can look constructively back upon their

268. There are many books that help us think about the "powers and principalities" that constrain human society, the foundational logic of the world-gone-astray from God. I would list the following among the most helpful: White, *Making a Just Peace*; Wink, *Naming the Powers*; idem, *Unmasking the Powers*; idem, *Engaging the Powers*; Ramachandra, *Subverting Global Myths*.

Buddhist heritage and even integrate it into their Christian world view.[269]

Mihindukulasuriya makes several observations on the basis of his study of Gal 4:8–9 and Col 2:8, 20–23, the places where Paul speaks of *ta stoicheia tou kosmou*. First, the *stoicheia* function among the Gentiles in a manner comparable to the way Torah functioned among Jews. The Gentiles' cultural and religious traditions served as the "ethical counterpart" to the Torah among Jews (though Mihindukulasuriya recognizes that Paul regarded the Torah to be qualitatively superior to Gentile traditions; see Rom 2:20; 7:12; 9:4–5). Second, Paul casts these "elementary principles" in a rather positive role when he sets them in parallel to Torah, Israel's "pedagogue." This "custodial function over human societies" would have included "inculcating ethical virtue, spiritual piety, existential wisdom, and community bonding" as well as "restraining, to an extent, humanity's propensity for collective evil." Finally, the *stoicheia* are only called "weak and poor" (4:9) in light of the surpassing value of the freedom of becoming God's sons and daughters.

Our analysis above disagrees with that of Mihindukulasuriya in a few respects. Paul speaks of life under the *stoicheia*—including the Torah—as slavery and confinement. It is a state from which liberation is desperately required (3:23; 4:1, 7–9), and to which one should not consider turning back for a moment. Moreover, the "pedagogue" does not serve an educative role in the Greco-Roman world. The pedagogue is not the teacher. He may accompany the child to the teacher. He may stand over the child to make sure the child completes any lessons assigned by the teacher. But he does not serve an educative, formative role.[270] Finally, I think one would have to grant that Paul regarded the *stoicheia* as "weak and poor" in an absolute sense, and not just in comparison with the freedom of life in Christ. We also have to reckon with the fact that Paul is here at his most negative in regard to the Torah: it is,

269. Mihindukulasuriya, "Without Christ I Could Not Be a Buddhist," 83–110. The material on Gal 4:8–9 appears on pp. 102–4.

270. In this regard, the Jataka tales that use the motif of the Buddha spending time under a teacher before returning home to father and throne, cited by Mihindukulasuriya, differ in an important way from Paul's model of the authority that the pedagogue wields over the heir for a time since, again, the Greek pedagogue is *not* a teacher or guru.

for the moment at least, *just* another *stoicheion*. That is to say, we should probably not read Paul's more positive statements about the Torah in Romans back into Paul's image of the pedagogue in Galatians.

Nevertheless, all exegetical sour grapes aside, Mihindukulasuriya's model is contextually relevant and fruitful, and well grounded in early Christian practice. It is in keeping with the willingness of Paul and other early Christian leaders to draw upon the wisdom of the sages and teachers of other cultures to contextualize their message, and even to support their message.[271] It is especially in keeping with the venerable tradition of the *preparatio evangelica* of the ante-Nicene and Nicene-period Christian writers, who looked to Greek and Latin philosophers and religious practices for the hints and prefigurations of what was later to come into the world in Christ and the proclamation of the Gospel. As Mihindukulasuriya rightly comments on this point, "if the Greek and Latin Fathers could express gratitude to God for the wealth of their Pagan heritage,[272] Christians of Buddhist culture can celebrate with at least as much enthusiasm. For surely, the discerning enjoyment of the wealth of Buddhism is part of the 'all things' for which Christ has matured and entitled us (cf. Gal.4.1, 7)."[273] A Christian rereading of Buddhist texts is also very much in keeping with the practice of the Jewish wisdom tradition (the compilers of Proverbs, Yeshua Ben Sira, and the like) and their openness to the wisdom of non-Jewish peoples.

Sri Lankan converts from Buddhism or Buddhist families are invited by these paradigms within the Jewish and Christian traditions to return to the familiar writings of the Buddha and to explore them anew from their place in Christ so as to integrate their own past religious experience and formation into their new formation in Christ. The Buddha perceived many of the important problems besetting human life and

271. See, for example, Acts 17:23, 28–29; 1 Cor 15:33; Heb 2:14–15 (which praises Jesus' accomplishments in terms directly reminiscent of philosophers' praise of Socrates dying in such a way as to free people from the fear of death); Heb 12:11 (which paraphrases a familiar Greek proverb, "the roots of education [discipline] are bitter, but its fruits are sweet").

272. For Justin Martyr, Clement of Alexandria, Tertullian, and Augustine's assessments of their own philosophical tradition, see McGrath, ed., *The Christian Theology Reader*, 4–6.

273. Mihindukulasuriya, "Without Christ," 103–4.

human community, and Jesus and his apostles had much to say to address these problems as well. In one sense, then, the Buddha still offers helpful diagnoses, even if we turn to Christ for the treatment and cure. In other respects, the Buddha's counsel resonates with Christian counsel at many points—his admonitions against certain vices and "cankers" provide an outrigger to the canoe of Christian discipleship.[274] In yet other respects, those who have experienced life in Christ may be able to say, with respect, that the Buddha did not see some aspects of human existence, or of the interest and investment of the Divine in human affairs, as clearly as we have been enabled to see by God's Holy Spirit. Like Virgil in Dante's *Divine Comedy*, the Buddha can only guide a person so far, after which it must fall to someone who has experienced that life of the Spirit that Virgil (or the Buddha) had shut out.

By attending to sifting through classical Buddhist literature from the perspective of *preparation evangelica*, Sri Lankan Christians coming from Buddhist backgrounds need not reject their heritage outright. This might also help allay the sense that converts to Christianity from Buddhism are (or will become) antagonistic toward Buddhism and agents of Western imperialism. Throughout the remainder of the commentary, we will give due attention to some of the fruitful points of connection and conversation between the Buddha and Paul, and hence between the devotees of both.

Checking Our Motives for Mission

There were indeed theological disagreements that led to the formation of two Jewish-Christian missions to Gentiles, but Paul suggests that theology was not the sole motivation behind the fragmentation of mission in the middle of the first century. Indeed, as one moves on from the conflict in Galatia around 50 CE to the multiplication of missionaries and competition between missionaries in Corinth and in the place from which Paul writes Philippians in the late 50s, theological rationales tend to recede more and more behind the less noble motives for competing missions (rather than cooperative ventures). In Galatia, Paul suggests that the rival teachers are motivated also by a desire to preserve or in-

274. Ibid., 83.

crease their own reputation (that is, they want the Galatians to show interest in them and to follow them as the gatekeepers to the kingdom) as well as to preach a Gospel and shape a congregation in a way that will be more readily accepted by non-Christians (particularly, the non-Christian Jews whom the rival teachers do not wish to provoke). Indeed, the rival teachers' *theological* motives might be seen as putting a pretty face on their desire to maintain their ethnic privilege and superiority as members of God's historic people, the Jews.

Even the mission of the early church was hindered by parties looking out for their own interests and pursuing their own agendas, not caring for the health of the larger cause of God or the spiritual health of the people they were supposedly serving. It is not surprising, then, to find such ills besetting the contemporary church in every setting, including Sri Lanka. The explosion of the number of churches in a major city like Colombo calls us to self-examination in regard to this fragmentation, which is a major stumbling block to the credibility of Christianity in this country. To what extent are we, as members of one church or another, pursuing our smaller group's agenda and pursuing the interests of our smaller circle, rather than pursuing God's agenda for Sri Lanka? We are hurting God's cause here whenever we break off to form a new church, often a new "denomination" of a single congregation, rather than finding new ways to work together for God's larger purposes as a united church, united despite all our variety. We have seen some pockets of change as pastors have left their differences and competitiveness aside to create authentic partnerships that go beyond simply uniting for a time of prayer and getting together to discuss key issues and to foster unity in the name of Christ.

Can we be as brutally honest with ourselves as Paul is in regard to his rivals? Or can we even go so far as to listen to what our rivals might say critically about us, to test whether or not there is something self-centered rather than God-centered about the way we are pursuing our ministry or mission? We take for granted that Paul's rivals ought to have listened to him and to have stopped contributing to the fragmentation of the early church. To whom ought we to be listening? Such questions need also to be asked of our engagement in particular missions and relief work. Are we interested in people for the right reason, and for their benefit? Or are we pursuing them, or pursuing certain ministries, to build up our own reputation, to ingratiate ourselves with certain bodies, and the like? Do we invest in relief work out of a heartfelt desire to "remember the poor" or because it is a path that gains greater favor from those in power and offers access to greater resources, foreign and national?

Paul poses another challenge to us as we consider his approach to mission vis-à-vis the approach taken by the rival teachers. The Judaizers are one example of a Christian mission coming into foreign territory with an agenda to impose upon the people in that territory. They have "the answer" that the church (and converts yet to be won) in Turkey and beyond "needs" in order to become better Christians. They do not stop to ask the converts in Turkey what resources they feel they need in order to grow more in discipleship and extend their own mission in their own region. Perhaps out of their own lack of confidence in their discipleship or in their own discernment in the Spirit, the Galatians seem all too willing to accept whatever program the Judaizers have to offer them. A similar dynamic may be seen in relationships between Western Christians and churches in the developing world. Vinoth Ramachandra identifies this dynamic when he writes that "those who live in the poorer South[ern Hemisphere] are constantly at the receiving end of 'packaged' gospels, discipleship courses, leadership seminars, church-growth 'gurus', even sermons and 'worship' DVDs from rich churches abroad. The latter have no desire to learn from others and, ironically, have little impact in their own societies. There is no shortage of local people who volunteer to be appointed as the 'national representatives' of these churches and organizations from the North[ern Hemisphere] and to promote their subsidized wares."[275]

These imports rarely threaten "the truth of the Gospel," though occasionally we find even such threats (such as materials and programs that promote the "prosperity gospel," which is really nothing more than the importation of the "American Dream" under the guise of religion). But it is also rare to find our sisters and brothers from the West engaging

---

275. Vinoth Ramachandra, "Authentic Partnerships," n.p. [cited 14 June 2011]. Online: http://vinothramachandra.wordpress.com/2010/10/01/authentic -partnerships.

in serious dialogue with us about what our churches need or how we would see them offering help in the best ways for Sri Lanka, as opposed to simply exporting what worked for them in their context. This one-way flow continues the trend of making Christianity in Sri Lanka look like Christianity in the Western world, rather than helping Christianity fully take on flesh within this native context.

Paul has approached the Galatians in a very different manner. Paul, the Jew from Cilicia, can urge the Galatian converts to become like him, because he first became like them, fully contextualizing himself in the life of the Gentile Galatian community and stripping himself of the culturally-bound practices of his own ethnic and religious background. He sees far better than the rival mission what is at the core of the transformation God wants to work in the lives of human beings, and therefore is focused on helping the Galatians to discover how to be Spirit-led Christ-followers *as Gentile Galatians* rather than being focused on making them Jewish Christians. He does have a message to preach, and he does have boundaries to mark out on Christian practice and belief, but he does not import a program of imposing one form of the contextualization of the Gospel (how Christianity takes shape in a Palestinian Jewish context) on another group in another context where the "Jewish" elements would be culturally and even religiously out of place.

But the onus was on the Galatians, not on Paul and not even on the rival teachers, to discern what was contextually appropriate and what was in keeping with their own experience of God through the Spirit of God's Son. Paul blames them for not exercising their responsibility and not sufficiently trusting their own experience and discernment of the Spirit. They knew enough about God, and had sufficient experience of God working in their midst, to recognize that the Judaizers' program for "how to be a real Christian" was not for them. And so, perhaps, Paul would also place the responsibility on Sri Lankan Christians to ground themselves more solidly in their knowledge of God as their own Father, to find the confidence that comes from recognizing and learning to follow God's Spirit, and thus not to be tossed to and fro by every strange wind that blows in from the West or from other quarters. It is a fine thing to learn about church growth strategies that seem to be working in the West, but before adopting and imitating those practices Sri Lankan Christians need to ask some contextual questions. Whether or not Americans should be building "mega-churches," is the model of the "mega-church" really right for Sri Lankan Christianity? Or is the progress of the Gospel and of growth in discipleship better served by many smaller congregations working together, but providing the person-centered and relationship-centered matrix that is so vital a part of Sri Lankan culture? Is "church growth" an appropriate goal in the Sri Lankan context, or is the multiplication of a network of small churches more appropriate? Or should a focus more explicitly on "Christian growth" in terms of growth in discipleship and service be at the center in Sri Lankan churches, and let the numbers go where they will?

Sri Lankan Christians, who have come into maturity in the Spirit and are no longer under pedagogues (including the colonial pedagogues of the West), need to ask many such questions even of current practices so that Christ takes on Sri Lankan flesh as he ought. I cannot refrain from pointing out two egregious examples. First, the phenomenon of "King James Bible only" Christianity in Sri Lanka is an astounding triumph for colonialism in the church. A translation made in the land and in the language of the British colonizers is promoted in some Sri Lankan Christian circles as the "only" reliable Bible. Far better a translation into Tamil or Sinhala undertaken by Sri Lankan scholars working in Sri Lanka on the basis of the Hebrew, Aramaic, and Greek originals, and far better the realization that *any* translation into *any* language will stand at some distance from the meaning communicated by those originals. Second, the tendency of so many churches to look to the musical compositions and styles imported from the West for their own expression of faith, worship, and commitment to Christ should raise questions, at least. *Can* Christ be worshiped in a Sri Lankan manner? What expressions would Sri Lankan Christian poets and composers give to their faith, and how would this elevate facets of Christian experience, hope, understanding, and mission of far greater relevance and importance in the context of Christian worship? It is fine to select hymns and songs composed by Western sisters and brothers for use in worship in Sri Lankan churches, but not at the expense of Sri Lankan hymnists and songwriters finding their own voice and adding their "new song" to the praise of God and the Lamb.

Justification Is Formation

"My children, over whom I am again in labor pains until Christ takes full shape in and among you!" If we were to ask Paul what the Gospel is all about, or what God really wants to make happen within, among, and through Christians, he would probably *not* answer in terms of typical Protestant statements about "justification." Paul's Gospel has formation at its center; formation is at the center of justification itself, and of Paul's understanding of God's work in our lives and communities of faith. Sri Lankan Christians do not need to entangle themselves in Western-spawned arguments concerning whether justification is "forensic," "imputed," or the like, leftovers as these are from Reformation and post-Reformation debates. Nor do Sri Lankan Christians need to accept the tendency of Western Protestants (and especially evangelical Protestants) to privilege such statements as the core or heart of the Gospel.

Even now biblical theologians in the West are caught up in debates surrounding the "New Perspective on Paul," defending the old lines of the old perspective, arguing about justification in terms that still reflect the battle lines drawn in the sixteenth century.[276] We have the opportunity to take statements such as Gal 4:19; 2:20, along with all that Paul has to say about transformation into Christ-likeness (all the *morph-* and *symmorph-* words in his letters), as seriously as Paul did—for it is when he talks about transformation of the whole person into Christ-likeness, or about Christ coming to life in the disciple, that he is at his most passionate and personal.

In the midst of his fullest sharing of his own example, his own passion as he pursues discipleship and mission, Paul writes: "I want to know [Christ] and the power of his resurrection and the fellowship of

---

276. See, for example, on the one hand, Dunn, *The Theology of the Paul the Apostle*; Wright, *What Saint Paul Really Said*; and, on the other hand, Kim, *Paul and the New Perspective*; Stuhlmacher, *Revisiting Paul's Doctrine of Justification*; Carson, O'Brien, and Seifrid, eds., *Justification and Variegated Nomism*, vols. 1–2.

his sufferings—to be refashioned in his fellowship into the likeness of his death if, somehow, I might arrive at the resurrection from the dead" (Phil 3:10–11). The immediate context suggests that this transformation is Paul's description of what "the righteousness that comes by faith" more precisely means and looks like (Phil 3:9). This is the passion and direction that he wants for his friends in Philippi to internalize as they, too, seek to embody more and more the "mind of Christ" shown in his other-centered and God-serving approach to death (Phil 2:1–11). The Spirit has removed the veil over the eyes of believers, such that "we, gazing at the Lord's glory with unveiled faces are being transformed into the same image, from glory to glory, as the Lord, the Spirit, enables" (2 Cor 3:18). With many other such images, like the putting away of whatever belongs to the old self and the nurturing of the life of the new self (Col 3:1–17), or dying and rising to new life with Christ as slaves of righteousness (Rom 6:1–14), Paul puts the transformation of the inner person and the outward practice of the disciple front and center in God's interest and purposes for us. This is ultimately, for him, what the Gospel is all about, and therefore his example recommends that we be most passionate about this as well.

The Jerusalem above Is Our Mother

While many Old Testament texts fix the reader's eyes on the city of Jerusalem in the land of Judah as the focal point of the hope of God's people and as a site of eternal concern to the Almighty, early Christian leaders tended to look beyond the capital city of a particular nation and ethnic group when looking for the home of the new people of God drawn from "every tribe and language and people and nation" (Rev 5:7). For the author of Hebrews, John the seer, and the author of 2 Peter, earthly Jerusalem is merely a part of the visible, manufactured cosmos whose elements will be consumed with fervent heat (2 Pet 3:5–6, 10) or shaken and removed so that the way into our heavenly homeland will be revealed (Heb 12:26–28). All of these leaders point us away from any earthly city toward the city of God as the place of our citizenship and the focal point of our hope (Heb 11:11–16; 13:14; 2 Pet 3:13; Rev 21:1–22:5).

Paul might therefore find himself quite perplexed at modern Christians' interest, and especially more evangelical Christians' investment, in the affairs and in the promotion of the interests of earthly Jerusalem and the modern state of Israel. Gal 4:21–31 is decidedly *not* a Zionist text! Zionism itself appears to be largely another Western import into Sri Lankan Christianity, learned from American conservative evangelicals who have lobbied in their own country for support for Israel against the nations and peoples surrounding it. Some evangelical churches continue to embrace the pro-Zionist stance modeled by Western rightwing believers, and their insensitivity to the Palestinian cause has brought disrepute to the church in Sri Lanka. Non-Christian Sri Lankans tend to be more interested in establishing a homeland for Palestinians.

In this particular matter, non-Christian Sri Lankans may have something important and healthful to communicate to evangelical Sri Lankan Christians—the God of Jew and Gentile is interested in peace with justice for all peoples, not the one-sided privileging of any people at the expense of another. Paul's redefinition of who constitute Abraham's seed and who are the people of promise needs to be more fully processed by the church and applied to the international political scene. As Christians ourselves, our first allegiance should be not to the state of Israel, but to Israeli and Palestinian Christians, even as our allegiance here should not be defined first in terms of our particular ethnic group, but in terms of our Christian family, whether Tamil, Sinhalese, Burgher, or any other ethnicity.

5:1–6: PAUL'S CENTRAL EXHORTATION AND RATIONALES

Christ freed us to live in freedom: Stand firm, then, and do not again bear a yoke of slavery. [2]Look: I, Paul, am saying to you that, if you get yourselves circumcised, Christ will benefit you nothing. [3]I am testifying again to every person who is getting circumcised that he is obliged to perform the entire Torah. [4]You were cut off from Christ, you who are being brought in line with God's righteousness by means of Torah; you fell from

favor. [5]For we are awaiting the hope of righteousness by Spirit
on the basis of trust. [6]For in Christ Jesus neither circumcision
nor uncircumcision has any force, but rather faith working
through love.

We have read Galatians as a specimen primarily of deliberative rhetoric,
a communication aimed at having an impact on what course of action
the audience will take in a particular situation. Paul's deliberative goal
is stated most clearly in Gal 5:1, as Paul directly appeals to the Galatian
converts to choose *against* the course of action that the rival teachers
promote: "Christ freed us to live in a state of freedom; stand firm, therefore, and do not again shoulder up a yoke of slavery."[277] This is not just
a transition verse,[278] though it accomplishes this goal admirably as well
by displaying the connection between the "indicative" of what God has
done for the Galatians (the subject matter of 3:1—4:7; 4:21–31) and the
"imperative" that the Galatians must now live out in light of God's favor
and gifts (preserving their "freedom" as children of God and heirs of the
promised Spirit, and as people who have been redeemed from slavery to
the principles and powers of this age). More than this, however, it is the
principle exhortation toward which all of the preceding argumentation
has been leading. Above all, Paul wants the Galatians to hold onto their
freedom and not put their necks under Torah's yoke or the yoke of any
other *stoicheia* ever again.

Paul picks up on the language of freedom and slavery from the
preceding allegory of the Sarah and Hagar story (4:21–31), though slavery has also been thematic since 4:1–11. Representing the Greek text
more woodenly in English, we would read "Christ freed us for freedom,"
the phrase "for freedom" here representing the Greek *eleutheria* in the
dative case. In this instance, the dative case is indicating that "freedom"

277. This is how the earliest manuscript evidence (Sinaiticus, Vaticanus, and
Alexandrinus) reads. The Majority Text reads, somewhat less forcefully and elegantly,
"In the freedom, then, for which Christ freed you, stand firm and do not again bear a
yoke of slavery" (hence the KJV, "Stand fast therefore in the liberty wherewith Christ
hath made us free"). The sense of the verse remains consistent in both readings,
though the unanimous witness of the three major, early codices argues strongly in
favor of the reading given in the main text above.

278. Against Burton, *Galatians*, 270; Fung, *Galatians*, 216.

is the destination or purpose behind Christ's liberating action.[279] Adolf Deissmann found this expression used in documents recording "sacral manumission," a procedure for freeing a slave in which a slave was freed from bondage to his or her human master, with "ownership" passing to a particular god.[280] Hence, Paul is saying that Christ freed us from bondage to the *stoicheia* in order to allow us to live as free persons. The corresponding obligation, then, is that we must protect and preserve this state of freedom that was conferred on us at such personal cost to Christ ("who gave himself for us," 1:4). Paul understands this obligation as the logical consequence—"Stand fast, *therefore*"—of having received so costly a gift, and the argumentation that follows in 5:2–4 shows clearly that, for him, this gift and this obligation go hand in hand.

Jewish authors used the image of the "yoke" to speak about their submission to the Torah (*m. Ber.* 2:2). Wisdom teachers like Ben Sira and even Jesus use the same image as they invite people to learn wisdom from them (Sir 51:26; Matt 11:29). In Ben Sira's case, "wisdom's yoke" is the equivalent of Torah's yoke (see Sir 24:1–23 for the identification of Wisdom with "the book of the covenant of the Most High God"). In all such instances, the "yoke," while signaling submission, is nevertheless beneficial. Paul uses the image negatively, however, as a burden that brings no benefit and, more specifically, as a burden that God does not wish for people to continue to bear (to the extent that he sent his Son to die to redeem people from every "yoke of slavery"). It would not be going too far to say that Paul himself is thinking here of Torah's yoke as a yoke of slavery, in strong contrast to his Jewish contemporaries' assessment of Torah's yoke as a privilege and as a path to living wisely before God. When Paul exhorts the Galatians not to "bear *again* a yoke of slavery," he is signaling once more his equation of the Torah that dominated Jews with the *stoicheia* that formerly dominated Gentiles: the Galatians formerly bore the enslaving yoke of the latter; for the Galatians to turn to the Torah is to return "again" to an enslaving yoke.[281]

279. See Smyth, *Greek Grammar*, §1531 on the "dative of place whither"; Barrett, *Freedom and Obligation*, 55; Longenecker, *Galatians*, 224.

280. Deissman, *Light from the Ancient East*, 326–28.

281. Longenecker, *Galatians*, 225.

Paul's position on the Jewish law code as enslaving would resonate with popular Stoic philosophy. The philosopher and statesman
Dio Chrysostom, who was born about the time Galatians was written,
defined freedom as "the knowledge of what is allowable and what is
forbidden, and slavery as ignorance of what is allowed and what is not"
(*Or.* 14.18). Freedom is not autonomy, or absolute license to do what
one wishes in every situation (*Or.* 14.3–6), but rather an opportunity
to conform to the absolute law of God. Slavery, on the other hand, con-
sists in being unclear of the laws God has laid down for humankind,
and in being bound instead by ever-multiplying human-made laws (*Or.*
80.5–7). For Dio, following local, ethnic, national laws while remaining ignorant of "the ordinance of Zeus" is "the grievous and unlawful
slavery under whose yoke you have placed your souls" (*Or.* 80.7). Paul
now classes the Torah with such second-rate law codes, calling it also a
"yoke of slavery," relegating it to the period of humanity's ignorance of
the law of God written on the heart by the Spirit.

What follows in 5:2–12 supports this exhortation. Gal 5:2–4 outlines the consequences of failing to heed this exhortation; 5:5–6 reaf-
firms the positive consequences of walking in line with their trust in
Christ and with the Spirit, and the lack of value in being either circumcised or uncircumcised; 5:7–12 returns to questions about the credibility of those who have been urging the Galatians differently. Paul will
begin a supplementary, and more constructive, exhortation in 5:13: if
the Galatians do keep themselves from Torah's yoke, how will they attain mastery of the passions without the discipline of Law?

Paul begins 5:2 most emphatically, both with the attention-getting
command ("Look!") and the underscoring of Paul's personally addressing the Galatians ("I, Paul, myself am saying to you"; compare 2 Cor
10:1). He wants to have their full attention as he lays out what is at stake
in the decision they have been contemplating: "if you get yourselves
circumcised, Christ will benefit you nothing" (5:2). In this and the following two verses, Paul is drawing a stark line dividing "grace" from
"Law." One has to choose whether to rely on Torah for aligning oneself
with God's righteousness *or* on the favor that God has shown in the
Messiah's ransoming death and in the gift of the Holy Spirit, and thus

also on the sufficiency of the Spirit to bring righteousness to life within and among the Christian disciples.

It is important to bear in mind that Paul is not talking about Jewish Christians whose circumcision was decided for them on their eighth day of life, nor about Jewish Christians who continue to circumcise their infants for cultural reasons, but about those currently on the verge of undergoing the procedure because they have been convinced that trusting Christ and receiving the Spirit are not enough. "If you let yourselves be circumcised" (5:2) addresses adult Gentile Christians about to make a decision based on an assessment of the sufficiency or insufficiency of the Holy Spirit. Similarly Paul's words "to every person undergoing circumcision" (5:3) speak about those now in the process of making that decision, not those for whom that decision had been made. The consequence of accepting circumcision on the terms of the rival teachers is that "Christ will not benefit you" (5:2). Christ will cease to act as the personal patron of the converts, and all the gifts bestowed because of his generous favor will cease to be operative. He "gave himself to ransom them from this present, evil age" (1:4), but that would do them no good if they put themselves back under the power of this present, evil age. Paul wants to emphasize that the Torah is a complete "package deal," even as Christ's death and provision of the Spirit is a complete "package deal." Christ and his gifts and Torah and its stipulations are not all laid out buffet style for the consumer to select so many items from this cart and so many items from that cart. Paul had already hinted at this "all or nothing" requirement of Torah in 3:10, when he quoted the words of Deut 27:26: "Cursed is everyone who fails to live by *all* the things written in the book of the Law, to do them." Paul reinforces this with a clever parallel in wording: Christ will not "benefit" or "be obliged to" (*ōphelēsei*, 5:2) those who, by accepting circumcision, make themselves "debtors" or "people obligated to" (*opheiletēs*) the whole Law (5:3).

We also need to remember that, at this time, the sacrificial cult prescribed by Torah was active and well. The Jerusalem temple was bustling with the activity of people bringing sin/guilt offerings, purification offerings, and well-being offerings, not to mention the twice-daily *tamid* offering. Trusting in Torah means going back to trusting in—and having to perform—those sacrifices as the means of mediation between

God and the community of God, the means of sustaining and repairing the relationship between God and the person. One can't hold to Christ's death as the fulfillment of a portion of Torah (the cultic aspects of its ritual law) while clinging to the validity of other portions (the ritual part, as far as circumcision, keeping kosher, and observing Sabbaths are concerned). Thus, if the Galatian Christians submit to circumcision, they commit themselves to the whole ritual-cultic system of dealing with God and to its relative slavishness. Christ's death "will not benefit" them.

Those who are "aligning themselves with the standard (*dikaiousthe*) of the Torah" (Gal 5:4), trying to "bring themselves in line with God's standards" by performing circumcision and observing other "works of Torah,"[282] have grossly undervalued God's gift of the Spirit and not preserved Christ's gift of freedom. These affronts to the Giver stand behind Paul's dramatic language of the breaking off of the "grace" relationship between the believer and Christ: "you are cut off from Christ, . . . you have fallen from favor" (5:4). Paul creates an intentional contrast in 5:4–5, underscoring this contrast again by careful parallelism in phrasing and wording, between "those who try to make themselves righteous by Torah" and "we who await the hope of righteousness by Spirit on the basis of faith." These verses contribute to developing a larger picture of justification as transformative process rather than a forensic, declarative act.

"Righteousness" (*dikaiosunē*, a word closely related to the verb *dikaioō*, "to make righteous," "to justify") remains God's goal for the believer (Gal 5:5), but lining oneself up with Torah (5:4) does not make one righteous before God, in large measure because doing so continues to maintain the boundaries that God has obliterated in Christ. God "justifies" people—God makes people righteous, or brings them in line with

---

282. The person who is *dikaios* ("righteous") is righteous in regard to a particular standard of what defines righteousness. The present tense of the verb *dikaioo* is being translated accordingly here as "lining up with a standard so as to be 'just' in regard to that standard." The form used in Gal 5:4 could be taken as a passive voice ("you who are being aligned") or a middle voice ("you who are aligning yourselves"). Both the historical and literary context—where the hearers are taking steps themselves to bring themselves in line with what the rival teachers say God requires—suggest that we understand the middle voice here.

his standards—through the Spirit. Indeed, Paul will go on to explore at length how this process of "lining up with the Spirit" (5:25) leads to genuine righteousness in 5:13—6:10. God sends the Spirit into Jew and Gentile alike to bring all who believe into conformity with God's character and will, transforming them into the image of the Righteous One, Jesus himself (Gal 4:19; 2:20) and causing the people of God to reflect the unity of the One God (3:28). "Righteousness" is something that Paul and his faithful converts look forward to in hope as the outcome of this transformative process: "we, by the Spirit and on the basis of trust, await the hope of righteousness" (5:5).[283] Paul is not talking here about merely being "declared righteous" while not actually *being* righteous in God's sight. The Christian hope as he expresses it is nothing less than total transformation into Spirit-led and Spirit-empowered people who do and are what pleases God (again, see 5:13—6:10). Because this transformation depends entirely upon the action and empowerment of God's Spirit, it remains fully "justification on the basis of faith" and on the basis of what "faith" has received from God, namely the promised Spirit.[284]

Paul rounds out his support for his exhortation with a statement that serves as an effective summary of his entire argument:[285] "For in Christ Jesus neither circumcision nor lack of circumcision has any force, but rather faith working through love" (5:6).[286] This is offered as a rationale supporting what Paul has said in 5:2-5, and recalls the climac-

283. In an awkward and somewhat desperate attempt to avoid the ethical focus of Paul's language in 5:5-6, Ronald Fung (*Galatians*, 226) tries to find a way to construe "righteousness" as a subjective genitive. He argues that 5:5 should be understood as "we look for that which righteousness (= the righteous) hopes for" or "the hope to which the justification of believers points them forward." In either case, the reader is having to import a great deal more semantic material than reading the noun simply as a genitive of content specifying what we are hoping for, as also in the Pauline phrases "the hope of glory" (Rom 5:2; Col 1:27) or "hope of deliverance" (1 Thess 5:8).

284. On this point, Rudolf Bultmann was quite correct (see his "Das Problem der Ethik bei Paulus," 123–40, especially p. 140).

285. Longenecker, *Galatians*, 228.

286. "Working" here represents the Greek middle participle *energoumenē*. The form could technically also be construed as passive, but the absence of any "agent" responsible for the action tips the scales against this. The verb was typically used in the middle voice to show the investment of the subject in the action, hence "faith investing itself in working through love."

tic remark in Gal 3:28 to the effect that, "in Christ there is neither Jew nor Greek," circumcision and lack of circumcision being defining physical marks of the distinction between Jew and Greek and the *value* in God's sight of that distinction. It also recalls the arguments in 3:15—4:7 that proposed that Torah, with circumcision as its starting point, had a defined term limit that was now expired. In this regard it supports Paul's claim that "the hope of righteousness" belonged to those who relied on the Spirit rather than those who tried to align themselves with the stipulations of the expired Torah.

Paul does *not* write that "the only thing that counts is faith." Rather, he qualifies what kind of faith "counts" before God,[287] and this is "faith investing itself through love." This is the formula for righteousness (*dikaiosunē*) under the new covenant and the Spirit's guidance and empowerment. Such love is only possible, of course, because of God's gift of the Holy Spirit, which brings its fruit to maturity within us and in our lives (as Paul will go on to develop in 5:13–25). Love (*agapē*) will become a keyword in Paul's positive discussion of the life that is aligned with God's Spirit, as love for neighbor represents the core command of the Torah (such that the person who loves the neighbor essentially *fulfills* the Torah without *doing* Torah; 5:13–14) and is the primary fruit of the Spirit (5:22).

5:7–12: PUTTING DISTANCE BETWEEN THE GALATIANS AND THE RIVAL TEACHERS

> [7]You were running well. Who cut in on your lane, preventing you from continuing to obey the truth? [8]This conviction is not from the one calling you. [9]A little yeast leavens the whole lump. [10]I myself am confident concerning you all in the Lord that you will not think otherwise, but the one who is disturbing you will bear the judgment, whoever he is. [11]But as for me,

---

287. Fung, *Galatians*, 229. Fung (*Galatians*, 230) is himself interested in affirming that this does *not* mean that love such as we show plays any real role in justification, as this would suggest some kind of synergy of God's action and ours. It is sufficient for me that faith that *fails* to express itself in works of love is not any kind of faith that brings one in line with God's righteousness, and hence does not lead to justification before God.

brothers and sisters, if I still were proclaiming circumcision, why am I still being persecuted? In this case, the scandal of the cross would be made void. [12]I wish that those upsetting you would cut off their own parts!

With this paragraph, Paul moves away from giving attention primarily to *logos* (sustained, reasoned argument in support of his position and against the position of the rival teachers) to giving more direct attention to *ethos* (creating connections with the hearers, and breaking connections between the hearers and the rival teachers) and *pathos* (arousing strategic emotions in the hearers, particularly toward the rival teachers). In both language and rhetorical focus, it resonates strongly with 1:6–9, forming something of an *inclusio* around the main body of the letter.[288]

Paul commends his converts for the progress that they had made prior to the rival teachers' intrusion into their community. He uses the image of running a race as a metaphor for pursuing a particular course of life, as he had done when referring to his own missionary activity in 2:2. The image allows him to cast the rivals' intrusion in a particularly negative light: like people cheating in a footrace, they cut in on the Galatians' lane, tripping them up and breaking their stride (5:7). Even as Paul nurtures his connection with his converts by praising their former progress, he also seeks to arouse feelings of enmity toward the rival teachers with the suggestion that they have done the Galatians wrong, getting in the way of their steady, continued obedience toward the truth of the Gospel.[289] The rival teachers' interference has put the Galatians' progress toward alignment with God, and hence "righteousness," in serious jeopardy. Paul frames this allegation in the form of a question ("Who has cut in on you?"), much as he did as he began his argument

---

288. With Gal 5:8, "from the one who called you," compare 1:6, "the one who called you"; with 5:10, "the one troubling you," compare 1:7, "those who are troubling you"; with 5:10, "he will bear the judgment," compare 1:8–9, "let him be accursed."

289. Paul uses a present infinitive when he speaks of "obeying," which indicates that his focus in on their ongoing obedience, which was interrupted, hence the translation "preventing you from continuing to obey the truth" rather than simply "preventing you from obeying the truth," which would have been the sense had Paul used an aorist infinitive at this place.

("Who has bewitched you?" 3:1), even though Paul knows full well *who* is responsible.

Paul continues to call his rivals' credibility into question by asserting that following the rival teachers means moving in a direction away from "the one who called you" (5:8), a phrase that would recall Paul's opening allegation against the Galatian converts ("I am astonished that you are so quickly deserting the one who called you," 1:6). The rivals' persuasive influence ("this conviction")[290] does not come from a divine source (an assertion that Paul has sought to establish in his lengthy argument against their position), and should therefore be rejected. Paul applies a bit of proverbial wisdom to demonstrate that the rival teachers and their influence represent a danger to the entire Christian enterprise in which the Galatians are engaged: "a little yeast leavens the whole lump" (5:9). The proverb is effective since everyone would be familiar with how a teaspoon of yeast or a small amount of "leaven" (in effect, a sourdough starter) gets worked into the whole lump of flour and makes the whole lump puff up equally (transferring the smell of fermentation also equally throughout the lump). Paul uses this same proverb in 1 Cor 5:6 to talk about the corrosive effects of one shameless sinner on the moral fabric of the entire community. A little shamelessness in regard to sin in one small pocket of the community has the power to erode the entire community's sensitivity to sin and God's ethical standards. So here, being persuaded by the rival teachers on a small point (e.g., the necessity just of circumcision, let alone obeying the whole Torah) or allowing their influence to take hold in a small pocket of the church would lead to the reintroduction of slavery to the whole.

Paul next offers an even stronger statement of confidence in the Galatians, showing that Paul still bears them good will and holds them in high esteem, expecting the best for them and from them (5:10a). He reflects here a common strategy for rendering an audience "well-disposed" toward the speaker (see Aristotle, *Rhetoric* 1.8.6; 2.1.3, 5). His confidence in their good decision is matched by his confidence that the

---

290. The Greek word *peismonē* appears here for the first time in Greek literature (Longenecker, *Galatians*, 230). We must be very careful, therefore, in assuming too much in regard to its connotations. It appears to be a noun formed from the verb "I persuade" (*peithō, peisomai*), hence "persuasion" or "conviction."

"one troubling" them will have to answer to God for what he or she has done in their midst (5:10b). There is rhetorical weight in Paul's identifying the rival teachers as "the one troubling you"—as agitators, troublemakers, people who are disturbing the peace of the community (see 1:7, where Paul describes the rivals using the same expression, though in the plural).[291] The rivals are creating turmoil and division, not acting with a view to the health and harmony of the Christian community. They are, in effect, enemies of the peace, and, according to Paul, answerable to God for the damage they are doing among God's churches. Such claims may help the hearers dissociate themselves from the rival teachers. Who wants to be allied with those who stand under God's judgment?! Once again, Paul avoids giving any hint that he knows—or even cares—about their identity ("whoever he is"), which is a typical way for orators in the Greco-Roman world to speak about their rivals or enemies, not even giving them the honor of being named.

The next verse introduces a new topic rather abruptly: "But *I*, brothers and sisters—if *I* were still promoting circumcision, why am I still being persecuted?" (5:11). We can readily understand how Paul's mind jumped to this, since the rival teachers whom he has been undermining in 5:7–10 were primarily "promoting circumcision." This reminds Paul of what appears to have been a charge made about Paul by the rival teachers: "Paul still promotes circumcision, elsewhere at least if not among you." The charge must have been made (or, at least, Paul must believe the charge to have been made against him to the Galatians) for 5:11 to make sense as it stands: Paul does not explain the charge, since he knows that his hearers know all about it; indeed, it only comes up because someone else (thus, probably, the rival teachers) had brought it up earlier, and Paul now needs to explain himself.

Where would the rival teachers get the idea that Paul promoted circumcision? There is no evidence that Paul ever preached a Torah-observant Gospel, since he himself grounds his learning of the Torah-

---

291. Paul uses a singular expression here in 5:7 ("the one troubling you"), but this appears to be a "generic singular" (Longenecker, *Galatians*, 232) representing any member of the group of teachers who have come into the Galatians' midst, for Paul more regularly refers to them in the plural ("the ones troubling you," 1:7; "those who are upsetting you," 5:12).

free Gospel—*his* Gospel—in his encounter with the risen Christ (Gal 1:11–17). From the beginning of his Christian preaching, he would have preached a Torah-free Gospel. If he ever "preached circumcision," it was most likely in his pre-Christian zeal for the Torah.[292] The rumor that Paul here opposes might, alternatively, have arisen from his policy of allowing circumcision among Jewish believers and their families— letting Jews remain Jews, but also still letting Gentiles remain Gentiles. The rival teachers were probably arguing as follows: "Paul supports circumcision elsewhere, so in his heart he clearly believes it is the right thing to do. For some reason, he was reluctant to share this conviction with you, perhaps because he thought he'd have better success among you if he left that part out."

Paul, however, can instantly refute this charge and, thus, affirm his absolute consistency: if he still promoted circumcision as part of his mission, he would not continue to be persecuted by his fellow Jews (see Acts 13:50; 14:2, 19–20; 2 Cor 11:24) because his Gospel would no longer be a threat to the Mosaic covenant and to the loyal obedience of all Jews (whether or not they claimed Jesus as Messiah) to that covenant.[293] If Paul promoted circumcision, he would remove "the stumbling block of the cross," that is, the offense inherent in the proclamation of the crucified Messiah.[294] How could God's Messiah die accursed under God's Law? The conclusion that finally impressed itself upon Paul after his encounter with the vindicated Jesus—that Torah itself was judged to be out of line with God's purposes in the Messiah, and therefore the Torah's authority was shown to have come to an end—would certainly be a stumbling block to Paul's fellow Jews.

292. Lightfoot, *Galatians*, 207; Burton, *Galatians*, 286; Fung, *Galatians*, 238–39; Longenecker, *Galatians*, 232–33.

293. Fung, *Galatians*, 238. Longenecker (*Galatians*, 233) thinks that Paul is pointing here to persecution at the hands of people like the rival teachers. The fact that the rival teachers are promoting circumcision themselves to avoid persecution, however, alongside the fact that Paul has suffered physical punishments as a result of his obedience to Christ (6:12, 17), points to persecution by the non-Christian Jewish community, which apparently had the authority in certain localities, at least, to administer discipline among their own.

294. I take "of the cross" here as a "genitive of definition" supplying the specific content of the "stumbling block" (following Fung, *Galatians*, 240).

Paul concludes this series of remarks with a snide comment about castration, expressing the wish that the rival teachers who are so eager to circumcise the Galatian Gentile Christians would "go all the way" with themselves instead. It is striking that Paul now locates circumcision (the sign of the covenant) along the same spectrum as castration: both are mutilations, differing only in degree. A similar statement is found in Phil 3:2, where Paul refers to Judaizers as "the mutilation party" instead of "the circumcision party" (*katatomē* instead of *peritomē*). In this, Paul appears to be playing on Greek sensibilities in regard to the Jewish rite of circumcision, which was regarded by them as an incomprehensible bodily mutilation.

5:13–26: THE SPIRIT'S SUFFICIENCY
TO NURTURE RIGHTEOUSNESS

13For you were called to freedom, brothers and sisters—only not freedom as an opportunity for the flesh. Rather, through love serve one another as slaves. 14For the whole Torah has been fulfilled in one word: "You will love your neighbor as yourself." 15But if you bite and eat one another up, watch out lest you be devoured up by one another!

16But I say, keep walking in the Spirit and you will certainly not fulfill what the flesh desires. 17For the flesh yearns against the Spirit's leanings, and the Spirit against the flesh's leanings, for these stand opposed to one another in order that you may not do whatever you want. 18But if you are being led by Spirit, you are not under Torah. 19And the works of the flesh are clearly evident: sexual immorality, uncleanness, self-indulgent debauchery, 20idolatry, drug-induced spells, enmities, strife, emulation, wrathful outbursts, rivalries, divisions, factions, 21envying, drunken bouts, gluttonous parties, and other things like these. Concerning these things I tell you in advance, just as I warned you before: Those practicing such things will not inherit the kingdom of God.

22But the fruit of the Spirit is love, joy, peace, patience, goodness, kindness, faithfulness, 23forebearance, self-control. Against such things there is no Law. 24And those who are

> Christ's have crucified the flesh along with its passions and desires. [25]If we live by Spirit, let us also fall in line with Spirit. [26]Let us not become conceited, challenging one another, envying one another.

Scholars have had widely varying understandings of the role of 5:13—6:10 in the letter, given its straightforwardly ethical character. J. C. O'Neill considered it to be a later interpolation of Pauline ethical instructions into Galatians, having no particular connection to the problem Paul addresses in Galatia.[295] Martin Dibelius thought it belonged originally to Galatians, but also saw no connection between these paragraphs and the situation in the churches there or Paul's argument in the rest of the letter.[296] Others have regarded it as both integral to Galatians *and* related to the situation in the churches there, but not the same aspects of that situation that Paul addressed in Gal 1:1—5:12.[297] Hans Dieter Betz was able to see this situation, and thus Galatians, in a more fully integrated fashion. The Galatian Christians were attracted to the Torah in the first place, in part at least, because it gave them a concrete and regimented guide to ordering their new lives and identifying clearly what God expected from them. Galatians 3:3 gives a strong indicator that the Galatian converts were indeed seeking to make progress in their moral transformation—to move on to "perfection"—by means of Torah, which Paul labels "flesh," playing on the obvious concern with the "flesh" of the foreskin that is the target of circumcision, the initiation rite into the life of Torah. Paul therefore has to do more than argue against turning to Torah and circumcision. He must show how what the Galatians have already received from God in Christ is sufficient to help them identify and deal with moral failure and the power of their lower drives and tendencies (the power of the "flesh"),[298] the problem that the rival teachers were able to exploit (if they did not raise it themselves).

295. O'Neill, *The Recovery of Paul's Letter to the Galatians*, 65–71.

296. Dibelius, *From Tradition to Gospel*, 239.

297. Among these would be the theories of W. Lütgert, *Gesetz und Geist*; and J. H. Ropes, *Singular Problem*, both of whom suggest that Paul is combating a libertine perversion of the Gospel in 5:13–6:10, after combating the Judaizing movement in 1:1—5:12.

298. Betz, *Galatians*, 8–9, 273–74. This understanding of Gal 5:13–6:10 is elegant-

"Libertinism," a tendency toward self-indulgence born of the conviction that traditional morality does not apply, is probably not a real problem among the Galatian Christians (as it would be among the Corinthian churches).[299] Paul would have been clear about the ethical contours of the new life to which the Spirit had given them birth, and the Galatians would have been clear that any libertine tendencies in their culture had no place in the new community of faith. It is more likely that the Galatians' openness to the rival teachers' message about the Torah sprang from their own desire to find all the help they could to overcome the cravings and impulses of their "old selves" so as to live more closely in line with the ethical ideals taught by Paul.

Galatians 5:13 is a well-crafted resumption of 5:1. Both begin from the same premise: "Christ freed us to live in freedom" (5:1); "you were called to freedom" (5:13). In 5:1, Paul moved from this premise to the conclusion that the Galatians must not now submit again to any yoke of slavery such as belonged to the pre-Christian revelation (whether Torah or their old systems of Gentile *stoicheia*). Now Paul moves forward from the same premise to give them positive instruction on how to live in that freedom so as not to remain in another kind of slavery—slavery to the power of the passions and desires of the "flesh." The gift of "freedom" is not to be misused against the good intentions of the Giver, but used fully aligned with the intentions of the Giver, intentions that can be known through the leading of the Spirit. This freedom is not an opportunity for the "flesh" to take over, leading a person deeper and deeper into vice, but an occasion for the Spirit to guide the believer into all virtue.

By "flesh," Paul does not simply mean the "meat" of our physical person, as Origen thought (*De Principiis* 1.3.4; 3.2.3; 3.4.1–5; *Contra Celsum* 8.23).[300] It is not a "lower nature" that is irrevocably part of who we are as human beings, in contrast to some "higher nature" within us.[301] It is not the whole person, and it is not even the part that is the person in the truest sense (that part that can assent to the flesh or yield to the Spirit). It is a powerful force at work within human beings that

---

ly refined and developed in Barclay, *Obeying the Truth*, 68–72, 106–77.

299. Against Longenecker, *Galatians*, 235.

300. Cited in Longenecker, *Galatians*, xlvii

301. Fung, *Galatians*, 244.

can manifest itself in thought, word, and deed, in the yearnings of mind and soul as well as body.[302] It is "the influence of an 'era' and its human traditions and assumptions" that has invaded human beings,[303] established a forward command center close to the center of the human will, seeking to claim us as slaves for the powers of this age. It manifests itself in those impulses, desires, and cravings that tend toward self-gratification and self-advancement at the expense of others, of the harmony of community, or of the accomplishing of the purposes of God in our lives, communities, and world.

The power of the flesh is probably what makes the removal of the bridle of Law (in some form) all the more frightening and risky. What is to save us from being swallowed up by our own desires, passions, and impulses, if not rules and regulations carefully laid out? Paul's answer will be "the Spirit" (5:16), the divine Spirit poured into our hearts. Regulations could never tame the passions of the flesh, but the Spirit of God can. Yielding to this Spirit in each new moment is now the divinely-prescribed path to righteousness. The absence of Torah's restraining rules and discipline does not mean that the flesh will go wild and unchecked, resulting in "ethical chaos," as the rival teachers might well have warned.[304] It does not mean that God's purposes for human community will fail to be served. Rather than allow their freedom to become "an opportunity for the flesh" to have its own way, Christians may use their freedom in service to one another out of love. Paul now introduces the image of "slavery" in a startlingly positive sense as the genuine expression of Christian freedom: "through love, serve one another as slaves," "offer one another loving service as people who are bound to one another" (5:13b).

Is it really that simple? Does other-centered, loving service really capture adequately God's standards for human behavior in community? Paul claims that it is this simple, asserting that "the whole Law" is fulfilled "in a single word," that is, in a single commandment: "You will

---

302. Hellenistic Jewish authors were also able to speak of "the passions" as applying both to the soul and to the body, to be equally resisted and brought into submission. See 4 Macc 1:13—2:23.

303. Barclay, *Obeying*, 213.

304. Martyn, *Galatians*, 27.

love your neighbor as you love yourself" (5:14, reciting Lev 19:18). Paul was likely aware that Jesus himself had identified this commandment alongside the command to "love the Lord your God with all your heart and with all your being and with all your understanding" as the two most important commandments (Mark 12:28–31; Matt 22:36–30; Luke 10:25–28). It was also the basis for Hillel's summary of the Torah: when approached by a Gentile who promised to convert if Hillel could teach him the whole Torah while he stood on one foot, Hillel responded, "What you hate, do not do to your neighbor; that is the whole Torah, and the rest is commentary" (*b. Shabb.* 31a).[305] Paul himself would provide a more detailed argument in support of the claim that this one commandment encapsulated the intent of the whole Torah in Rom 13:8–10:

> Owe no one anything, except to love one another, because the one who loves has fulfilled the other portion of the Law. For the commands "You will not commit adultery," "You will not commit murder," "You will not steal," "You will not covet," and any other commandment, are summed up in this word: "You will love your neighbor as yourself." Love does nothing wrong to the neighbor; therefore love is the fullness of the Law.

It might seem strange that Paul would refer positively to a commandment of Torah in Galatians, having gone to such pains to demonstrate that Torah had a limited role for a limited time in God's purposes for God's people. Here we bump up against the dual nature of Torah for Paul. As a legal code to be followed in all its particulars as a sign that one belongs to God's people, or as a way of trying to align oneself with God's righteous standards, Torah's role is over. To be "under Torah" on this side of the cross is to be in slavery when God's purpose is freedom; it is to reaffirm the special value of being a Jew when God has brought Jew and Gentile together in Christ and broken down "the dividing wall of hostility." However, Torah still bears witness to God's purposes, God's plan, and God's standards of righteousness.

Several theologians have hit upon an important distinction in this regard: Torah is not something to be "done" by Christians, but Torah is

305. See also *Tg. Ps.-J.* Lev 19:18, which appends this negative form of the "Golden Rule" to the commandment, "You will love your neighbor as yourself."

"fulfilled" by Christians.[306] Jewish authors normally speak of "doing," "keeping," or "guarding" the Torah, having in mind the obligation to perform the various commandments given by Torah. Paul avoids all these verbs, using instead "fulfill," a verb that is rarely used in relation to Torah by Jewish authors and *never* in relation to Torah in the Old Testament (either in the Greek Septuagint or the original Hebrew).[307] In the words of Stephen Westerholm, "'doing' the law is what is *required* of those 'under the law'; 'fulfilling' the law is, for Paul, the *result* of Christian living,"[308] the requirements of which are laid out in terms of following the Spirit, walking in the Spirit, ordering our steps by the Spirit. Those "under the Law" are debtors to do the whole law in all its particulars (Gal 5:3); those who walk by the Spirit fulfill the whole Law in the course of loving service. Paul can thus speak of the Christian realizing in his or her own life all that the Torah sought to bring about in the lives of those who lived under it, without speaking as if the Christian is obliged to "do" Torah in any sense. Insofar as it is the revelation of the righteousness of God, that righteousness emerges in the lives of the believers—but by an entirely different route, namely, "faith working through love" (5:6) or "ordering one's steps in line with Spirit" (5:25).

Paul colorfully captures the ugliness and consequences of failing to focus on "loving service" as the core ethos of Christian community by presenting a contrary scenario: "if you bite and eat one another up, watch out lest you be gobbled up by one another!" (5:15). "Serving one another through love" stands at the polar opposite from a "dog-eat-dog" approach to social, business, and political interactions—an approach that is all too pervasive in any society. The consequences of this approach is, of course, that a lot of people get chewed up in the course of satisfying other people's hunger for power, getting ahead, or gratifying other cravings. Despite the fact that the whole ethical section is composed with the Galatians' situation in view, we should not assume that every vice Paul names was rampant in the congregation, nor that every virtue he promotes was missing, nor that every positive command sug-

306. Betz, *Galatians*, 275.

307. Barclay, *Obeying the Truth*, 138.

308. Westerholm, "On Fulfilling the Whole Law," 229–37, especially p. 235; see also Fung, *Galatians*, 247; Barclay, *Obeying the Truth*, 142.

gests a situation in which that course of action was not being pursued already.[309] Nevertheless, the subject matter of 5:15 is reinforced twice in this section, first in the listing of several overlapping "community" vices amongst the "works of the flesh" ("enmities, strife, emulation, wrathful outbursts, rivalries, divisions, factions, envying," 5:20–21) and second in the attitudes and behaviors specifically warned against as the opposite of falling in line with the Spirit's leading ("Let us not become conceited, challenging one another, envying one another," 5:26). It is quite plausible that the rival teachers—to whom Paul does refer as "troublemakers" and "agitators"—have stirred up divisions, arguments, and some personal hostilities among the Galatian Christians as a result of their meddling.[310] At the very least, we can say that Paul shows a particular concern throughout this section with promoting the kinds of behaviors that produce harmony, cooperation, and other-centered investment and service among the Christian communities he addresses.

Paul now introduces the solution to the problem of the power of the "flesh" over the human being who desires to live a life of righteousness before God: it is the same Spirit that God gave to the Galatians when they responded with trust in Jesus' giving of himself for them (3:2–5), that bore witness within them that they had entered into a new and intimate relationship with the living God (4:6–7) after their lives of serving things that were not divine by nature: "I say, continue to walk in the Spirit and you will certainly not fulfill what the flesh desires" (5:16). Paul introduces the topic of the mastery of the passions (not fulfilling "the impulsive desire of the flesh")[311] as if this is an agreed-upon good. Indeed, it was a common topic among ethical philosophers—including those preaching in every market place in the Hellenistic world—that "reason" and "the passions" were opposed to one another, and that a person would only attain virtue to the extent that he or she followed "reason" and gained mastery over the "passions," which included desires, emotions, and physical sensations. Where the passions gained the upper hand, however, a person would fall into vice of one kind or another (whether the experience of fear or pain leading a person to

---

309. Barclay, *Obeying the Truth*, 217–18.

310. Burton, *Galatians*, 297; Hays, "Christology," 289.

311. Martyn, *Galatians*, 479.

cowardice, or the experience of anger or envy leading a person to some act of injustice, or the experience of sexual cravings leading a person to immoderate or illicit sexual encounters).[312]

Hellenistic Jewish authors like the author of 4 Maccabees or Philo would promote close observance of the Torah as the God-given discipline that would help a person master the passions and walk in line with the dictates of virtue, and it is reasonable to suppose that this line of argumentation played into the preaching of the rival teachers as well. For Paul, however, Torah could not empower the individual to resist the flesh, nor consistently empower victory over the force of the "impulsive desire of the flesh." The Holy Spirit, however, could. Thus he urges the Galatians to "keep walking in the Spirit,"[313] where "walking" is a typical Jewish idiom for "conducting one's life," "living day to day."[314] Paul makes an astounding promise: those who keep themselves centered on the Spirit and allow the Spirit to guide and empower their day-to-day actions "will certainly not bring to completion what flesh desires" (or, "will certainly not fulfill the desires of the flesh").[315] Paul chooses here to use a particular Greek construction (an "emphatic future negation") reserved for the strongest assertions about consequences that will never, ever come to pass. Paul sees the desires of the flesh moving in a direction very similar to James's understanding of the same. The desires of the flesh lead to sin (Jas 1:15), expressed in Galatians as "works of the

312. For a fuller discussion, see deSilva, *4 Maccabees: Introduction and Commentary on the Greek Text of Codex Sinaiticus*, 67–78; idem, *4 Maccabees*, 51–58. Against the background of popular ethical philosophy (which permeated Hellenistic Jewish literature and thought as well), it could not be said that the "words rendered 'passions' and 'desires' are in themselves neutral" (Fung, *Galatians*, 274).

313. The imperative "walk" appears in Greek in the present aspect, indicating that the command involves being ongoingly involved in the action prescribed.

314. The Hebrew verb *halak*, "to walk," is the root on which the noun *halakha*, "a legal prescription," is formed. It was the goal of the pious Jew to "walk" in line with the Torah, hence the Torah (and further regulations deduced from the Torah) provided the instructions on "how to walk," how to order one's "steps," figuratively speaking. See Longenecker, *Galatians*, 244.

315. Translations like the Revised Standard Version (RSV) that render this as "do not gratify the desires of the flesh" have gotten the Greek wrong. This half of the verse is a promise related to the command in the first half of the verse, not a second command itself.

flesh" that exclude a person from the kingdom of God. The full crop of sowing to the flesh is "death" (Jas 1:15), expressed in Galatians as "corruption" (i.e., decaying as a corpse in the grave) as opposed to "eternal life" (6:8). "Continuing to walk in the Spirit" (5:16), "ordering our steps by the Spirit" (5:25), or "continuing to sow to the Spirit" (6:8) is the path that God has laid before the Galatians to come to the full possession of their inheritance in God's kingdom.

How can Paul make such a strong claim as he does in 5:16? He seems to sense himself that this assertion requires some explanation, and so he continues: "For the flesh yearns against the Spirit's leanings, and the Spirit against the flesh's leanings, for these stand opposed to one another in order that you may not do whatever you want" (5:17). Paul creates a picture here of the individual person caught in the struggle of two powers as they push in different directions from one another, preventing that individual from doing "whatever he or she might wish." This is not, however, a picture of stalemate between two equal forces, nor of the individual's paralysis in the midst of their push and pull.[316] If it were, 5:17 would hardly provide evidence in support of the claim made in 5:16! The Spirit and the flesh are not equal powers.[317] God has given his Spirit to the believer as a means of keeping the believer from doing whatever it is that he or she might wish *under the influence of the flesh*. The Spirit gives us the leverage we need against the flesh and its passions and cravings.

> The Galatians have been called to freedom (5:13) but the Spirit ensures that this is not a *carte blanche* for 'doing whatever you want' . . . The flesh would certainly exploit this absolute freedom (5.13), but the Spirit provides a counteracting force which motivates and directs them to *exclude* the flesh. In other words, the Galatians are not in the dangerous position of being free to 'do whatever you want' because, as they walk in

---

316. Against Longenecker (*Galatians*, 246; so also Burton, *Galatians*, 302), Gal 5:17 does *not* "set out in rudimentary fashion what is later spoken of more fully in Rom 7:14–25."

317. Barclay, *Obeying the Truth*, 115.

the Spirit, they are caught up into a warfare which determines their moral choices.[318]

Martyn makes the important observation that this is the Spirit's war against the "impulsive desire of the flesh," not the believer's war. The Spirit is not a resource that can help us in our battle; rather, we have been drafted to fight in the Spirit's battle, to "fall in line" with the Spirit as with a commander (Gal 5:25).[319] It is a battle that the Spirit cannot lose, if we do so fall in line, and thus Paul's assurance in 5:16 is a reliable one. Those who are "led by the Spirit are not under the Torah," not only for the reasons already given by Paul in 3:10—4:11, 21–31, but also because the "Spirit provides all the necessary guidance in the fight against the flesh."[320] Rather than a list of exercises by means of which to get in shape before God, we have a personal Trainer. The fact that Paul opposes being "led by the Spirit" with being "under Law" here also shows that he has the Galatians' situation and the rival teachers' position still in view as he composes this ethical section.[321]

As Paul weaves together topics of freedom and slavery, flesh and Spirit, he creates a discourse that is very much at home in Hellenistic Jewish ethics. Philo, for example, also regarded "flesh" and "Spirit" as two guiding principles that competed for the allegiance of human beings: "the race of humankind is twofold, the one being the race of those who live by the divine Spirit and reason; the other of those who exist according to blood and the pleasure of the flesh. The latter species is formed of earth, but the former is an accurate copy of the divine image" (*Who Is the Heir of Divine Things* 12.57). Like Paul, Philo understood "freedom" to be realized as one lived according to the divine Spirit and leading of God, which puts "a check upon the authority of the passions," while "slavery" exists wherever "vice and the passions have the dominion" over the person (*Every Good Person Is Free* 17). A major difference between the two authors is the role of Torah: for Philo (as also for the author of 4 Maccabees), the study and doing of Torah was the path to

318. Barclay, *Obeying the Truth*, 115.
319. Martyn, *Galatians*, 530–31, 534–35.
320. Barclay, *Obeying the Truth*, 116.
321. Fung, *Galatians*, 252.

freedom; for Paul, the death of Jesus and the gift of the Spirit made this freedom possible apart from Torah.

Lists of vices and virtues were a common literary form in ethical literature of the Greek, Hellenistic, and Roman periods. The form appears to have been developed by Stoic authors, continuing to appear frequently in the writings of authors from that school of thought and of those influenced by Stoic philosophy (for example, Hellenistic Jews like Philo of Alexandria and the authors of Wisdom of Solomon, 4 Maccabees, and the *Testaments of the Twelve Patriarchs*). It is not surprising also to find lists of vices and virtues commonly in the literature of the early church, as Christian authors were similarly interested in the moral formation of their people. [322]

Paul creates a vice list to illustrate "the works of the flesh," the kinds of attitudes, behaviors, and consequences that result when "flesh" gains the upper hand and directs the lives of human beings. That he intends his list to be representative rather than comprehensive is clear from the way he ends it—"and such things as these" (5:21). [323] His introduction ("the works of the flesh are obvious," 5:19) suggests that this is a matter of common knowledge, and because of the work of popular philosophers he is no doubt accurate. Greeks, Romans, and Jews all had adequate witness to what kinds of behavior were noble and praiseworthy in the sight of the gods (or God) and all people of quality, and what kinds of behavior merited shame.

Paul's sample list begins with "sexual immorality (*porneia*), uncleanness (*akatharsia*), self-indulgent debauchery (*aselgeia*)." *Porneia* seems to have originated as a term for the buying and selling of sexual

---

322. For a more detailed discussion and extensive references to primary literature, see Longenecker, *Galatians*, 250–51.

323. Betz, *Galatians*, 284; Longenecker, *Galatians*, 253; Fung, *Galatians*, 260. There was a tendency among copyists of the New Testament to expand this vice list to include vices that were present in other New Testament vice lists, making Paul's list of "works of the flesh" thereby more comprehensive. By the time of the Majority Text, "adultery" was firmly in place before "sexual immorality" (more traditionally, "fornication") in 5:19 and "murders" followed "envying" in 5:21 (compare especially Rom 1:29), hence these two vices are included in the KJV of 5:19–21. These particular vices are not included in this list in the earliest manuscripts (Sinaiticus, Vaticanus, and Alexandrinus), which probably better represent Paul's original, hence their absence from modern translations of this list.

favors, though it came to be used to refer to a variety of sexual practices outside of marriage. "Uncleanness" (*akatharsia*) is a term originating in the context of the purity codes of ritual and sacred spaces, where special care is shown for approaching the divine in a state of "cleanness" (for example, by not touching certain things or persons) rather than "uncleanness," bringing some pollution into contact with the holy. The term is frequent in the Greek translation of Leviticus. Here it carries a strongly ethical dimension, referring to moral impurity rather than merely outward impurity (for example, through touching a corpse). The third term, *aselgeia*, goes beyond the first two in that it connotes a certain shamelessness in regard to vice or sin. Not only does one indulge one's flesh, one does it "without regard for self-respect, for the rights and feelings of others, or for public decency."[324]

"Idolatrous acts" would not appear in any Greco-Roman authors' vice lists, since worship of the gods was considered an essential facet of justice, giving to each his or her due. The word itself appears only in Jewish and Christian literature,[325] a combination of the Greek word *eidōlon* ("image") and *latreia* ("service, worship"). This is in keeping with the tendency of Jewish and Christian authors to focus on the idol itself as the object of worship, and thus something ridiculous (see Ps 115:3-8; Isa 44:9-20; Jer 10:2-15; Letter of Jeremiah; Wis 13:1—15:19), whereas Gentiles regarded the idol as a means of access to a spiritual reality behind and beyond the image itself.

The Greek word here translated "drug-induced spells" is *pharmakai*, which gives us our English word "pharmacy" and "pharmaceuticals." The word generally refers to the use of drugs as medicines, with two major negative connotations: poisoning and using drugs in the context of practicing sorcery. Paul probably has the latter in view, as does John the visionary (see Rev 21:8; 22:15). Drugs could be used to manipulate one's state of consciousness, opening one up to the spirit world; drugs (or "potions") could be used to manipulate one's situation or other people in one's situation. The modern drug scene is not far removed from the aims and practices of ancient "sorcery" in these

324. Bauernfeind, "*Aselgeia*," 490. See also Barclay, *Flesh and Spirit*, 31; Burton, *Galatians*, 305–6; Longenecker, *Galatians*, 254.

325. Longenecker, *Galatians*, 255; Fung, *Galatians*, 256.

regards. All such attempts at spiritual manipulation are antithetical to, and incompatible with, walking by the Spirit, going where the Spirit leads, seeking what the Spirit desires for us.

If there is any particular emphasis in Paul's list of vices, it is on those attitudes and behaviors that lead to the disruption and fragmenting of community (see also 5:15, 26): "enmities (*echthrai*), strife (*eris*), fanaticism (*zēlos*), angry outbursts (*thymoi*), self-promotion (*eritheiai*), dissentions (*dichostasiai*), factions (*haireseis*), envying (*phthonoi*)." Most of these need little comment since they—and their liabilities to community—are indeed "evident." The word here translated "fanaticism" can also be translated "zeal" (*zēlos*), and it can have both positive and negative senses. Positively, it is used to name the feeling of "emulation." This is what virtuous people feel when they see someone like them achieve great and noble things, and want to achieve such things themselves. This is a virtuous emotion because people who feel it make themselves better people and achieve better things because of it. "Zeal" also has several negative sides. The first is "jealousy," a feeling that divides and creates hostility (rather than friendly competition). The second is "'intense devotion' or 'anger' arising out of devotion."[326] It is what drove Phinehas to plunge a spear through an Israelite and his concubine (Num 25:6–13), Mattathias and his sons to kill apostate Jews and forcibly circumcise their boys (1 Macc 2:23–28), and Paul to persecute the Christian movement (Gal 1:13–14; Phil 3:6). Paul could have had either of these two senses in mind when he named *zēlos* as a "work of the flesh." Jealousy obviously supports enmity and divisions within a community; fanaticism objectifies and makes an enemy out of those who practice their faith differently, rather than patiently conversing and, perhaps, converting (or, in humility, being taught a better way oneself).

Eritheiai was used to talk about gathering support for oneself to get elected or named to an office, or about working for a wage.[327] It names here that attitude of self-seeking and self-promotion that is the opposite of the other-centered, other-serving attitude that the Spirit seeks to bring to life among Christ-followers.

---

326. Longenecker, *Galatians*, 256.
327. Fung, *Galatians*, 258; Longenecker, *Galatians*, 256.

Unlike its close relative, *zēlos*, *phthonos* is always a wicked emotion. It denotes "envy," the pain one feels when a deserving person gets what he or she deserves, all because one wants such for oneself (even if one has no claim to enjoy it). There is nothing redemptive about "envy" since it focuses its energy purely on wishing the other person did not enjoy the happiness he or she has attained and merited, whereas *zēlos*, at least, motivates a person to go out and do what is necessary to earn those rewards for himself or herself.[328]

Paul closes the list of examples with overindulging in drinking wine or eating ("drunken bouts" and "gluttonous parties," *methai*, *kōmoi*), such that one loses control of oneself rather than keeping a clear head, thereby handing over the reins to the passions, or eats beyond the needs of the body to the detriment of the body (and to the neglect of those who are hungry and lack even the necessities).

Paul follows this list with a severe admonition: "I warn you, even as I warned you before: those who continue to practice such things as these will not inherit God's kingdom" (5:21). The previous warning about the necessity of leaving behind the "works of the flesh" or, as he would put it elsewhere, the "works of darkness" (Rom 13:12) or "your earthly aspects" (Col 3:5) or "the old person with its practices" (Col 3:9), was probably a facet of Paul's instructions to his converts while he was with them in person.[329] Paul's solemn pronouncement ("I am warning you"), together with his recollection of having spoken along these lines before ("as I warned you previously"), is meant to get his hearers' full attention and underline the seriousness of what he is about to say: a transformed life is not optional, but *essential!*[330] Paul will underline this yet again in 6:7–10 when he speaks about sowing and reaping. Investing oneself in fulfilling one's fleshly impulses leads to death; investing one-

---

328. Commentators frequently cite Jas 4:5 as an exception, since there, according to them, "God yearns jealously (*pros phthonon*) for the spirit that he has caused to dwell within us" (thus, for example, Longenecker, *Galatians*, 257). This is a misconstrual of the Greek of Jas 4:5, however, which should be translated: "the spirit that he has caused to dwell in us (i.e., the human spirit) inclines toward envy."

329. Longenecker, *Galatians*, 258.

330. Or, as Fung (*Galatians*, 283) well puts it, "the new life (with the Spirit as its source) must become evident in the new conduct (under the Spirit's direction) and cannot exist without it."

self in following the Spirit's leading leads to eternal life. Taking part in God's kingdom at the consummation means submitting to God's rule over one's life now (or, in the language of Galatians, "walking in step with the Spirit").[331]

The picture is ugly where the impulses of the flesh direct individual and community life. Quite different is the quality of the person and the community of persons where the Spirit leads: "the fruit of the Spirit is love (*agapē*), joy (*chara*), peace (*eirēnē*), patience (*makrothymia*), goodness (*chrēstotēs*), kindness (*agathōsunē*), faithfulness (*pistis*), forebearance (*prautēs*), self-control (*enkrateia*)" (5:22–23). These virtuous qualities will naturally result where the person who has received God's Spirit allows the Spirit to control and guide him or her. The "fruit" of the Spirit is the "harvest" not of following rules and regulations, but "of the self-forgetfulness that looks away from itself to God."[332] This harvest, nevertheless, calls for conscientious and constant investment on the part of the believers: Paul will soon speak of "sowing" to the Spirit, even as the person who continues in rebellion against God's reign "sows" to the flesh (6:7–8).[333] The disciple is responsible to keep himself or herself oriented toward God and God's Spirit, so that the Spirit can produce this harvest.

That "love" (*agapē*) should head the list is no surprise. "Love" is the common element in Jesus' selection of the two most important commandments, as, indeed, it is Paul's own choice for the most essential virtue (1 Cor 13:13) and the verb in the commandment that sums up, for Paul, the whole Torah (Gal 5:14; Lev 19:18). *Agapē* was rarely used by pagan authors, though they did occasionally use the verb form (*agapaō*). They preferred to speak of "love" using three other terms: *philia*, the term for the love that exists between friends; *storgē*, the term for affection, especially as the love that exists between family members; and *erōs*, the love and attraction between men and women. *Agapē* and its related verb form appear in the Septuagint, often to denote the "love" that human beings are to show God and one another (hence the appearance of the verb in Deut 6:4 LXX; Lev 19:18), though not exclusively so (it is

---

331. Fung, *Galatians*, 261–62.

332. Barrett, *Freedom and Obligation*, 77; Fung, *Galatians*, 262.

333. Longenecker, *Galatians*, 259; Betz, *Galatians*, 287; Ridderbos, *Galatians*, 207.

also used for sexual desire in 2 Sam 13:15 LXX and frequently in Song of Songs).[334] Probably because it was not in common use (hence "available" to take on special, "Christian" meanings more easily than *philia* or the others), and because it was associated with the "love commands" of Scripture, *agapē* becomes the prominent word for "love," especially that quality of other-centered, self-giving love that Christ demonstrated and we are called to imitate, in early Christian culture.

The "joy" of which Paul speaks is rooted in the pleasure of knowing God, of experiencing the friendship of the Holy Spirit, of being assured of one's place in God's people and God's good future. It springs from an awareness of God's love and beneficence toward the believer, and from mindfulness of God's gifts in the midst of all circumstances. Unlike the joy that we all know, believers and unbelievers alike, as a result of the experience of good fortune, pleasant circumstances, and other such external goods, this joy is not fragile, liable to being dashed and dispelled by a sorry turn of events. Indeed, early Christian leaders often specifically identify the persistence of this joy under adverse conditions as its hallmark (see 2 Cor 7:4; 8:2; Col 1:11–12; 1 Thess 1:6; Heb 10:34; Jas 1:2; 1 Pet 1:6–8).

"Peace" is not merely a negative quality (the *absence* of strife), but a positive one—the result of enjoying "personal wholeness and beneficial relationships."[335] The Hebrew concept of *shalom*, the enjoyment of solid and edifying connections with others throughout the community and beyond, cannot be far in the background. The impulses of the flesh lead to strained or broken relationships; the Spirit, by contrast, leads us to take the initiative in working toward healing and restoration. It moves us to act as peace-makers in a world of bruised relationships, even where that carries a significant cost to our own well-being or security.

"Patience" (*makrothymia*) has two commonly used senses. In the first, it denotes gentleness in the face of others' failures or slights, a slowness to take offense and, especially, to take vengeance. It is a quality often attributed to God in the Scriptures, beginning with God's self-revelation to Moses on Sinai (Exod 34:6). It is also used, however, to speak about perseverance under hardship, as throughout *Testament of Job* and Jas

---

334. See Longenecker, *Galatians*, 260.

335. Longenecker, *Galatians*, 261; so also Ridderbos, *Galatians*, 207.

5:7–11. In this sense, it bespeaks the courage of the disciple, both in the face of the rigors of discipleship (e.g., resisting temptation, seeking steady and sure growth toward the likeness of Jesus) and in the face of the hostility of unbelievers. In the present context, being surrounded by relational and other-centered virtues that build up community, Paul more likely has the first sense in mind.

"Kindness" may be described as the disposition to treat someone well, to help them if possible, to be a harbor for them in the midst of a stormy life. Kindness helps the other person to feel "love's touch," providing a safe haven from interpersonal injury.

"Goodness" carries overtones of "generosity," as in the contrast between the "good" landowner and the envious workers in the parable of the laborers (Matt 20:1–16).[336] The disciple's experience of God's goodness and generosity overflows into the lives of others, arousing a genuine benevolence toward others. When we see a need, we must respond to it in the compassion of Christ, uplifting the quality of people's lives around us.

Again in the context of interpersonal virtues, *pistis* denotes the ethical quality of "faithfulness," "reliability," and "loyalty."[337] It is the quality that leads those around us to feel safe in relying on us (hence, to experience *pistis* as "trust"). It is the social counterpart of God's own reliability, bearing each individual believer aloft in the safety net of the community.

The Greek word *prautēs* is often translated as "meekness," though this English word tends to have negative qualities (a failure to be assertive or display appropriate strength). Aristotle defines this virtue as the mean between excessive anger and the inability to get angry (*Eth. Nic.* 2.1108A). It speaks of proper restraint of anger or power, out of consideration for the other person, thus "forbearance" may capture its essential meaning more accurately. Paul will show us this virtue in action in 6:1, where believers are urged to follow the Spirit in restoring fellow-believers "in a spirit of forbearance" rather than in a harsh, judgmental manner. "Forbearance" is able to confront difficult issues or behaviors,

---

336. Fung, *Galatians*, 268.

337. Burton, *Galatians*, 316; Bruce, *Galatians*, 254; Longenecker, *Galatians*, 262.

but to do so in a way that allows the confrontation to be received as an expression of love, care, and commitment.

Self-control (*enkrateia*) closes Paul's list, where it would probably open a list of virtues in other authors' discussions of the mastery of desires and passions. "Self-control" involves the mastery of the passions, and is often seen as the foundation for all the virtues since the passions of the flesh are the primary hindrance to every virtue (as in 4 Macc 1:30b-31). Its appearance at the close of Paul's list is probably not an indication of its unimportance, but it may reflect Paul's essential position that being "other-centered" is the ultimate guiding principle of life in the Spirit or of having the mind of Christ (hence "love" and other relational virtues are listed first), whereas "self-control" is focused on "self" (though self-control is a necessary prerequisite to showing genuine love and the other virtues).

People in whom this fruit is abundant are people whom the Law would never condemn; indeed, *no* law would condemn such people and, where it did, it showed a failure in that law itself. The expression "against such as these there is no law" recalls a statement by Aristotle. Speaking about people who exhibited greater moral excellence than the common lot, Aristotle said that "against such people as these there is no law" (*Politics* 3.13.1284A).[338] Aristotle's point, and probably Paul's as well, is that people in whom such virtue is so well formed are exactly the sort of the people that a good and just body of laws would have sought to form.[339] Paul would add, however, that no external body of laws, however holy and just and good, could effectively form such virtuous character within the person. This is the good news about the sending of the Holy Spirit, and why the Spirit is so important a gift that Paul sees it as the inheritance promised to all people in Abraham: the Spirit *can* empower and guide such inner transformation as will make people righteous according to God's standards.

338. Cited by Longenecker, *Galatians,* 264.

339. Longenecker, (*Galatians,* 267) observes that, "while we might have expected such items as alms-giving, evangelism, social service, care for the widows and orphans, etc. to appear in the list [of the Spirit's fruit], Paul enumerates, rather, such items as 'love, joy, peace, patience, kindness,' etc. Again, it appears that Paul is not so concerned with precisely how each of these matters works out in practice, but with the underlying orientation of selfless and outgoing concern for others."

Flesh and Spirit are incompatible powers, as Paul has already affirmed by drawing attention to their mutual and perpetual antagonism (5:17). The death of Jesus becomes, by means of the Spirit, something in which the believer can participate. Paul declares that he was "crucified together with Christ," with the result that Christ now lived in him (Gal 2:19–20). Similarly, the disciple who belongs to Christ voluntarily and actively crucified the power of "the flesh with its passions and desires," so as to be mastered by them no longer (Gal 5:24). With Paul, they were crucified to this present, evil age, and the power of the present, evil age was crucified to them (Gal 6:14), and they came to life as part of the new creation of God.

The past tense of "crucified" (5:24) is significant here, something that Paul would affirm again in Romans as he spoke about baptism as a death to sin and a rising to new life in Christ (Rom 6:1–14). Paul is well aware, however, that it takes time for that new "fact" of existence to take shape in the thick of experience. Paul's "talk of crucifying the flesh suggests a decisive break with such influence on the part of all those who enter the new creation. But since the old aeon continues as the sphere in which the Christian life must be lived, there is always the danger that the Christian will be lured by its false human-centered perspective."[340] Thus Paul will also speak of continuing to cooperate with the Spirit, so that the Spirit can live within him or her—or, to return to Paul's earlier terminology, so that "Christ may be fully formed" in the believer, or so that the believer's life lived in this mortal flesh may become Christ living in him or her (4:19).

Jesus' crucifixion, particularly as crucifixion "for us," releases a new power that allows human beings to rise above the domination of the "flesh" in favor of giving themselves over to domination by the "Spirit." One component of *how* this happens is the relationship of "grace," of mutual favor and obligation, into which God invites human beings in Christ. The experience of being loved by the one who "gave himself over for our sins" (1:4; 2:19) weighs in against our natural (fallen) tendency to live for ourselves, awakening in our hearts the possibility of loving as Jesus loved, of "living no longer for ourselves but for him who died and was raised on our behalf" (2 Cor 5:15), specifically by "looking out

340. Barclay, *Obeying*, 213.

not for our own interests, but for the interests of others" in imitation of Jesus' self-giving (Phil 2:3–11). Jesus' death was an act of love that breaks the self-seeking, self-protective, self-reliant power of the flesh, initiating a new cycle of showing love and other-centered concern on the basis of having experienced such amazing love and other-centered concern as Jesus has shown the disciple.

Paul's paired pictures of life driven by the flesh and life driven by the Spirit lead Paul to issue a pair of summary exhortations in 5:25–26. The first exhortation looks chiefly to the list of the Spirit's fruit: "If the Spirit has given us life, let the Spirit also direct our steps," or, a bit more woodenly, "If we live because of the Spirit, let us also order our steps (*stoichōmen*) by the Spirit" (5:25).[341] With the first verb (*zōmen*), Paul is referring to a special quality of life, or kind of life, and not just our physical life as animal beings. Appropriately, he speaks first of a kind of death in the previous verse, death to who and what we were as "the old person," the person (mal)formed after Adam's likeness. Corresponding to that death is this new life that the Spirit has given us, the life that has the potential to grow fully into "the new person" that is Christ living in us (see Gal 2:19–20), Christ "fully formed" in us (4:19).

Paul's second verb was carefully chosen: *stoichōmen* (5:25) cannot fail to recall *ta stoicheia* (4:3, 9), those principles and powers with which the Galatians formerly fell in line before they experienced Christ's liberation. Having been freed from the domination of the *stoicheia*, the believers are now to fall in step (*stoicheō*) with the Spirit. As they fall in line with the Spirit, like soldiers marching according to the orders prescribed by their General, they find the power of the flesh nullified and the fruits of righteousness multiplied in their lives (Gal 5:16, 18–23, 25). The Spirit provides the answer to the question raised in 3:3: "having begun with the Spirit, are you going to reach completion by things that

341. This brief exhortation provides an excellent example of a genuine chiasm, which was known and promoted in the Greco-Roman world as a structuring device at the level of the sentence or a pair of sentences. "If we have life (*ei zōmen*, A) by the Spirit (*pneumati*, B), by the Spirit (*pneumati*, B') let us also order our steps (*kai stoichōmen*, A')." The exhortations in 5:25–26 look back in reverse order to the lists of the works of the flesh in 5:19–21 and the Spirit's fruit in 5:22–23, but this would be rather an instance of *hysteron proteron* (taking up the last-mentioned issue first, and working backwards) than of chiasm proper.

pertain to the flesh?" No, the journey of transformation begun in the Spirit will only be completed in the Spirit, by the Spirit's leading and in the Spirit's power.

Just as the "fruit of the Spirit" is both positively defined and defined against its opposite ("the works of the flesh"), so the positive exhortation to fall in line with the spirit is given additional definition by contrast with its opposite: "let us not become conceited, challenging one another, envying one another" (5:26). If this exhortation is meant specifically to reflect the "works of the flesh" (that is, by urging the hearers to avoid those works), it is significant that Paul focused on the interpersonal or community-health dimension of those works. The exhortation, in other words, calls attention to that large group of "works of the flesh" in the middle of the list, rather than the more obvious vices related to sex and partying at the beginning and the end. Again, due to the repetition of these sorts of problems throughout 5:13–26 (and to some extent also in 6:1–6), these might actually reflect issues in the Galatian congregations that Paul sought specifically to remedy. The Spirit's fruit stands in stark contrast to these attitudes and interpersonal behaviors. Where there is envying, provocation, and challenging one another (probably with a view to gaining something at the other's expense, if they fail to answer the challenge), there is greater need to "put to death the leanings of the flesh" and yield further to the Spirit's leading.

READING GALATIANS 5 WITH SRI LANKAN CHRISTIANS

Do We Trust the Spirit or Our Rules?

Circumcision as a rite of joining the people of God is no longer a prominent issue among Christian churches. Indeed, the practice of circumcision itself is meaningful only among Muslims in Sri Lanka. Nevertheless, Paul's stern warning about the incompatibility of trying to align ourselves with God's righteousness by means of following the Spirit in faith and by means of following external regulations, whether based in the Torah or created within Christian culture, remains an important reason to examine our practice and the practice of our churches in this regard.

The historic Torah as external code to be followed still plays an important role in several Christian denominations. It does so, moreover, in ways that serve as boundary markers between those who are "in" and those who are "out," just as it did in Paul's situation. One example would be the role of the Sabbath among Seventh Day Adventists or the Worldwide Church of God, where it is ultimately a badge of "belonging" to the circle of God's "real" followers. Where Christians practice the observance of the Sabbath as an expression of their own commitment to honor God (the God who created the heavens and the earth and rested on the seventh day, the God of the exodus who gave rest to oppressed slaves), Paul would affirm their practice. Where Christians practice the observance of the "Lord's Day" as an expression of their own commitment to honor God (the God who vindicated Jesus as the Christ on the first day of the week, the God who gives life to the dead), Paul would affirm their practice. Where Sabbath-observant Christians tell other Christians that they are breaking God's Law and outside of God's will because they worship on Sunday, or where Sabbath-observant Christians harbor in their hearts the notion that they are more acceptable to God because they observe Saturday rather than Sunday as their day of worship and rest, Paul would take serious issue. (Indeed, he does take serious issue with this specifically in Rom 14:1–12). The question of observing one day or another reflects a persistent use of Torah to create divisions again between the "true people of God" and "second-rate Christians" or, in some instances, "non-Christians" (the most extreme example I've encountered interprets Sunday worship as the "mark of the beast").[342]

We have already touched on several other human-made rules that are frequently imposed upon Christians in an attempt to replace Christian freedom in the Spirit with hard-and-fast regulations. Many denominations insist upon total abstinence from alcohol, condemning even the moderate use of alcohol and those "looser" Christians from other denominations who permit such practice. We should pay attention here to the fact that Paul condemns drunkenness as a work of the

---

342. One could go on to examine the use of other Torah-based practices as "litmus tests" of one's true standing in the people of God, such as the practice of tithing (with the strict accounting of the 10%).

flesh, not drinking beer or wine in and of itself (which, indeed, he promotes on one occasion as a treatment for Timothy's stomach problems). Some churches forbid social dancing as if the practice is in and of itself always contrary to Christian holiness.

Paul would insist that we cannot legislate the behavior of our fellow Christians in such matters (indeed, if we can't insist on the set of rules found in the Torah, how much less can we insist upon rules of our own devising!). Outside of Galatians, he returns to this topic and point again most clearly in Colossians:

> Let no one, then, judge you in regard to food or drink or a festival or new moon celebration or Sabbath day. . . . If you died with Christ to the elementary principles of this world's order, why do you put yourselves, as though living within this world's order, under rules and regulations—"Don't participate in this; don't eat that; don't touch this" (all with reference to things that don't outlast the using of them)—in line with human rules and teachings. (Col 2:14, 20–21)

We cannot legislate the Christian life; we *can*, however, invoke the presence of God's Spirit and invite our fellow Christians to examine whether or not their practice is fully consonant with walking in the Spirit rather than gratifying the flesh, but we also have to be ready to accept their answer in such indifferent matters. If the cardinal difference between works of the flesh and the Spirit's fruit has to do with self-centered versus other-centered behavior, we should bear in mind that really good dancing is one of the most other-centered activities in which we might engage. Moreover, if one's goal in going out to dance is to give one's husband or wife an enjoyable evening and thus to promote marital health, this would more surely fall in the column of Spirit-inspired behavior rather than indulgence of the "flesh."

Christian freedom and Christian responsibility requires, however, that we also be honest with ourselves and with our sisters and brothers if our practice is challenged. Are we using alcohol as a painkiller when we should be taking that pain to the Lord? Are we going out to clubs seeking flesh-indulgent encounters? Christian freedom is not "license," and the consequences of our misuse of this freedom (and, thus, our misuse of God's gift of the Spirit, given to guide us into the healthful use of our freedom) are harsh and inescapable (see 6:7–8).

The same principle applies both to our attempts to lay out inviolable "don'ts" and inviolable "dos." One student related a story about a woman who converted from Hinduism to Christianity being pressured to eat meat at a discipleship training center. Some Hindus are vegetarian, and the idea of eating meat is repulsive. It seemed as if, at this particular center on this particular occasion, the teacher in charge was insisting that she eat meat as, in effect, a sign of completely leaving Hinduism behind. Viewed through Galatians, this situation looks like a Christian leader or community requiring adherence to a new set of food regulations for the sake of having table fellowship, requiring the Hindu convert to eat meat along with Buddhist converts or people born into the church, for whom meat is simply a part of the diet, as if "real Christians eat meat." This was a situation in which, perhaps, the ethic of 1 Corinthians 8 and 10 ought rather to have been applied, with established Christians foregoing the eating of meat for the sake of the newer Hindu convert, and certainly not pressuring her to eat meat at *any* point in her walk of faith.

Paul's representative catalogs of "the works of the flesh" and "the Spirit's fruit" are given, in part, as diagnostic tools. Are arguments among Christians leading to the division of a group of Christians into factions around some issue? Is the harmony of a Christian body being broken because of some issue? This is a sign that "flesh" is at work somewhere in the equation—and more than likely on *both* sides. It is a sign that all parties need to stop, take a step back, and pray for the Spirit to illumine what is really going on in their situation and in their hearts. It is a call to recommit as a united body to discerning the Spirit's guidance in unity, and laying down all personal agendas to that end. But such cannot be legislated. Rules like "don't argue" or "don't address the difficult issues because this might lead to division" can't achieve God's purposes in the church.

The stakes and risks of really trusting the Spirit rather than rules remain very high. The absence of written laws, however, does not mean that we can "fool" God, using the freedom from Law as an opportunity to "sow to the flesh," finding room for self-indulgence and the temporary pleasures of sin (Gal 6:7–10). Those who abuse their freedom to indulge the flesh (whether in terms of indulging our bent toward strife and divisiveness in community, our bent toward sexual indiscretions, and all such things) "will not inherit the kingdom of God" (Gal 5:19–21). There is no room in our lives for indulging the "flesh" in any of its dimensions. In the absence of the "guard rails" of Torah, the life of the Spirit calls for complete honesty with ourselves, with our Christian family, and with God, if we are truly to follow the Spirit and move forward into the righteousness that God would form in us. It requires a heart that wishes to go where and as the Spirit directs, that does not resist the Spirit in order to protect some areas of fleshly indulgence.

The risks of such a walk are the risks that attend maturity. In our childhood, our guardians keep us from danger and make many moral decisions for us; as adults, we must find that moral faculty fully formed within us, and be responsible before our own conscience for our actions. So now, Paul's analogy would affirm, Christians are entrusted by God to be responsive to the Spirit and responsible to the Spirit. They no longer need to be hemmed in by rules like children, but are free to seek righteousness in the context of their mature relationship with God through the Spirit. This corresponds to the "writing of the Law on the hearts" of God's people that was the burning hope of prophets like Jeremiah (Jer 31:31–34), and to the "circumcision of the heart" (Deut 10:16; 30:6; Jer 4:4) that symbolized obedience from the inner person in response to God's favor and fellowship.

The Works of the Flesh in Christian Community

For Paul, neither "sin" nor "holiness" is just a matter of the individual's heart and practice. Sin and holiness, the works of the flesh and the Spirit's fruit, are very much social phenomena as well. Paul's list of the works of the flesh focuses, insofar as it has any focus, on sins within the community, not just individual sin and defilement. This is reinforced by Paul's particular interest in dispelling attitudes and behaviors like "biting and nipping at one another," "provoking one another," and "envying one another" (5:15, 26) as particularly antithetical to walking together in the Spirit. The Spirit's fruit—love, peace (with others), patience (toward others), kindness (toward others), generosity, faithfulness, and forbearance—is largely expressible only in community, rather than as virtues of the private individual.

Paul would take a keen interest in disunity within a church and among churches, calling us to account wherever we act on the basis of competition, rivalry, self-interest, or protecting one's own agenda. Even if the venue for such action is Christian mission, it is still driven by the "flesh" rather than the Spirit! Internal divisions among Christians are a mark against Christian presence in Sri Lanka. Our disagreements with other Christians on matters of belief and practice, and our tendency to form ever new "denominations" on the basis of these disagreements (or merely on the basis of a desire to "do church" our own way and for our own egos), proclaim that Christians are themselves unclear about their message and way of life, preferring to squabble amongst themselves to really living out a clear witness to the Lordship of this "Christ."

A competitive spirit appears to be at work here and there motivating ministry and relief work in Sri Lanka. Where this is the case, it is a manifestation of the flesh rather than the Spirit, a manifestation of the spirit of the agitators, who are looking to establish their own work and reputation for the same (cf. 6:12–13). Churches compete with one another, trying to build the biggest church in Sri Lanka, to sign on the highest number of members, or to organize the most programs. Competition is evident in theological education: cooperation could lead to far greater effectiveness in providing Christian leaders in every corner of the island with the support of educational equipping, whereas competition leads to institutions duplicating each other's efforts in the same area. Competition is evident even in relief work. When a large, international relief organization brings its efforts to Sri Lanka, it tends to establish its own presence and programs rather than coordinate with and support efforts already in place locally. Because of its superior funding, it can offer better-paying jobs to those with experience in local relief work, thus sapping the strength of personnel (the few with experience and/ or training here) from local relief organizations. If I am interested first in "my ministry" rather than simply ministering and advancing God's causes, I will tend to duplicate efforts already in place, doubling overhead in proportion to actual relief, rather than designate some funds for the support of that particular relief work as already practiced within "others'" ministry and reserving new overhead for new ventures.[343]

Where the Spirit directs ministry, we are selfless in regard to the "ownership" of that ministry. We are invested in seeing ministry flourish, but not in seeing "our" ministry flourish over against, or in comparison with, "another's" ministry. Within a local congregation, similarly, we are invested in seeing the church discover and get behind what the *church* discerns God to be doing and desirous of doing in their midst and through them. We are not invested in seeing the church get behind what *we* think God is calling the church to do. The latter attitude leads to divisions, dissension, factions, even enmity and strife. The Spirit-led alternative lays down all self-directed and self-protective interests in favor of allowing the Spirit to make God's interests known, and to get behind those interests together in one, harmonious body.

Where the church is so God-centered that the Spirit produces such fruit, the church becomes a vital witness to the reality of the claims of the Gospel. Such God-centered and other-centered harmony becomes our best witness to the fact that God indeed sent Jesus into the world (John 17:20–23), to the fact that God is unstoppably at work in the Christian movement for the deliverance of believers (Phil 1:27b–28), and that the Spirit is indeed real and able to bring God's vision for human community to pass in "real life."

Desire, the Dhamma, and the Gospel

Paul's diagnosis of the human problem has an important point of contact with the Buddha's assessment of the same. Both locate the essential source of suffering and distress in the "passions of the flesh," to use Paul's language, or the "desires" or "cravings," to use the Buddha's.

343. I am particularly grateful to Mrs. Karin Ramachandra for her insights here. Her counsel for people thinking about engaging in some ministry is very astute: If God is calling you to work with children in Colombo, go and find out who's working with children in Colombo and see how you can work *with* them, rather than setting up "your own ministry," reinventing the wheel, making all the same mistakes that someone else has already made and learned from and grown past. She challenges us to manifest the unity of Christ and the Christian church by working together, working smarter, collaboratively.

According to the Buddha, "the entangling and embroiling craving" is the thing most to be eliminated (*Dhammapada* 180) and "desire is the bane of humankind" (*Dhammapada* 359). Paul is more specific about the class of "desires" or "cravings" that lead to suffering among humankind in the present and in the future, speaking more narrowly about "the desires that spring from the 'flesh,'" which, when acted upon, produce the vices listed as "works of the flesh" in Gal 5:19–21. The Buddha would have read Paul's list with approval, identifying as "fetters" to be renounced or uprooted many of the same inner-personal and inter-personal manifestations of self-centered desire, including anger, pride, jealousy, selfishness, deceit, hatred, lust, and hypocrisy (*Dhammapada* 221, 262–263, 407): "Just as a storm throws down a weak tree, so does Mara overpower those who live for the pursuit of pleasures, who are uncontrolled in their senses, immoderate in eating, indolent, and dissipated" (*Dhammapada* 7).

The Buddha nourished both the commitment and the discipline required to destroy the "cankers," so that the individual "whose senses are subdued like horses well trained by a charioteer" might become "pure as a deep pool free from mud" (*Dhammapada* 93–95), a person characterized by patience, freedom from anger, and self-control, which are the marks of the true "holy person" (*Dhammapada* 399–400). Paul also identifies "cankers," calling for ethical purification by cultivating the fruit of the Spirit while checking the works of the flesh (Gal 5:13–25). The person who is fully formed in the Spirit would manifest many of the characteristics prized in the Buddha's vision of the *arahat*.

One of the most significant differences between Paul's vision and the Buddha's, and hence between Christianity and other religions, is that Paul proclaims that God provides us with the Holy Spirit to enable us to perform God's will. Christianity presents the Holy Spirit as a means by which to be free from the cycle of sin and from the power of desire (as well as anger and delusion) so as to love fully and in a truly other-centered way. Other religions leave us at the mercy of our own effort and power, teaching that God will accept us in proportion to how we overcome sin or evil. The cross of Jesus Christ presents a "stumbling block" to Buddhism in regard to its rejection of self-reliance and relying on the power and guidance of God's Spirit instead. In this, however, Paul's doctrine of crucifying one's self along with its desires in union with Christ's crucifixion is in a way more faithful to the Buddhist doctrine of *anatta*. Buddhists rely on their own efforts for deliverance from the wheel of samsara while, ostensibly, there is no "self" on which to rely. Christians understand a "self" to exist, but deny that it is sufficiently stable or powerful to effect deliverance from the power of desire, anger, and delusion.

While compassionate love for others is a central focus of both Christian and Buddhist ethics, as it is, indeed, an essential teaching of most every religion, there are some noticeable differences in the conceptualization of the ideals of *agapē* and *metta*. Both are other-centered ideals, but the Buddha cautioned against allowing compassion to turn into endearment and connection: "From endearment springs grief, from endearment springs fear. For him who is wholly free from endearment, there is no grief, whence then fear?" (*Dhammapada* 212). *Metta* is quite different from Christian love in that Christians can risk love and endearment because hope in the resurrection answers grief and fear, and takes away the sting (the *dukkha*) inherent in and brought by death. *Metta* remains detached, "universal" compassion expressed now towards this individual, now towards that. *Agapē* is very much an "attached" compassion and love felt toward the "particular" human being toward whom one shows compassion.

Agapē is the focal point of the Spirit-led ethic, and Paul depends upon the power of the Spirit to nurture this love. Following the Spirit, the Christians will be transformed into a community of mutual investment, care, and support, rather than one characterized by mutual hostility and detraction (Gal 5:15), where members are poised against one another in pride, envy, and provocation (Gal 5:26). It leads to the quality of relationships between people that leads outsiders—even those who are hostile to the presence of Christianity in their midst—"Look how they love each other, . . . and how they are prepared to die one for the other" (Tertullian, *Apology* 39.7).

6:1–10: PRACTICAL WAYS TO WALK IN THE SPIRIT

Brothers and sisters, if a person is overtaken in any transgression, you who are Spirit-led are to restore such a person in a spirit of forbearance, each of you watching yourself lest you also be tempted. [2]Carry one another's burdens, and in this way you will fulfill the Law of Christ. [3]For if anyone thinks himself or herself to be something, when that person is nothing, he or she is deceiving himself or herself. [4]But let each person test his or her own work, and then he or she will have his or her boast in/to himself or herself alone, and not in/to the other person. [5]For each person will carry his or her own load. [6]Let the one who is instructed in the word share in all good things with the one who gives instruction. [7]Don't deceive yourselves: God is not mocked. Whatever a person sows, that shall he or she also reap: [8]the one sowing to his or her flesh will harvest decay from the flesh, but the one sowing to the Spirit will harvest eternal life from the Spirit. [9]Let us not grow tired of doing what is noble, for we will reap the harvest in its own season if we do not give up. [10]As long as we have a season, then, let us work what is good towards all, and especially towards those who belong to the household of faith.

Paul is not beginning to formulate a new Torah in these chapters, but focuses rather on giving a few specific examples of how the Spirit transforms human community, what the signs are of the Spirit's work in producing a community where the ideal of love is realized, and what the symptoms are when the "flesh" exerts its power again. Love shows itself where the sinner is gently reclaimed, where believers invest in one another enough to "bear one another's burdens" (Gal 6:1–2); love shows itself where believers refuse to regard a sister or brother as a spiritual trophy of any kind, as if the conversion or transformation of another person could become a claim to honor for oneself (as the rival teachers are doing, in Paul's mind; Gal 6:4–5, 13). Love manifests itself in the sharing of resources between believers who bring more of the truth of God to light for one another (Gal 6:6). Where love is made real, God's transforming Spirit is truly at work, bringing believers into conformity with God's righteousness. The liberty of the Spirit may seem dangerous in terms of a person's ability to fool himself or herself, or a person's ability to try to "get away with" feeding more of the flesh than he or she might have been able to do under the yoke of Torah. The integrity of the life of the Spirit, however, is guaranteed by the omniscience of God, "unto whom all hearts are open, all desires known, and from whom no secrets are hid" (*Book of Common Prayer* 1979). There is no fooling God, and thus Christian freedom can never be misused without consequences.

Addressing the hearers afresh as "brothers and sisters" in 6:1 indicates at least a minor break and new beginning after Paul's more general pictures of the flesh-led and the Spirit-led life in 5:13–26.[344] Paul knows that the "flesh" will not go down without a fight, and that disciples will not always be able to keep in step with the Spirit. There will be occasions of stumbling, of falling back into sinful, self-centered patterns of thought and behavior. What kind of response does the Spirit call for in regard to brothers and sisters who lose a battle with a particular impulse of the flesh? "If a person is overtaken in any transgression, you who are Spirit-led are to restore that person in a spirit of forbearance, each of you keeping an eye on yourself, lest you also be tempted" (6:1). One of the safeguards against "flesh" or "the deceitfulness of sin" (to borrow a phrase from Heb 3:12) misleading and overpowering the individual disciple is the community of faith. In the absence of the road map of a written code like Torah, the community's discernment of what is "of the Spirit" over against what is "of the flesh" provides the guard rails to help the individual believer stay on track in regard to "keeping in step with the Spirit."

Being "overtaken by a sin" suggests falling into sin through error, neglect, lack of vigilance, or sheer weakness rather than willful transgression, though it is difficult to exclude even the latter if there is the possibility also of willful repentance. Those who are themselves led by the Spirit ("you who are spiritual" or "in-Spirited," *pneumatikoi*)[345] are

---

344. Longenecker, *Galatians*, 265.

345. Paul is probably not using this term ironically or with any degree of biting sarcasm (against Schlier, *Galater*, 270). Rather, he is appealing to those brothers and sisters who are indeed walking in step with the Spirit that they have received as heirs of the promise, as in 5:16–25 (Bruce, *Galatians*, 260; Barclay, "Mirror-Reading," 82, 92n28; Fung, *Galatians*, 285; Longenecker, *Galatians*, 273).

to invest themselves in restoring the wayward, rather than using it as an opportunity to honor oneself at the other's expense. They especially have the opportunity to manifest a particular facet of the Spirit's fruit while doing so—"forbearance" or "gentleness" (*prautēs*). They are not to approach the wayward in a spirit that would beat down or alienate, or that would bring shame, but with the humility and sympathy born of knowing one's own vulnerability to temptations to sin. There is no room inside the disciple's heart for secretly or openly preening himself or herself on not falling into the sin that has ensnared another believer—only for vigilance against the inroads that the impulses of the flesh would make into their own hearts. While Paul elsewhere prescribes shunning as a means of community discipline, presumably *until* the offender repented and returned to an acceptable mode of life (see 1 Cor 5:11; 2 Thess 3:14),[346] this was an extreme step to be taken only after other, gentler steps had not produced repentance.

Helping one another discern and stay in step with the Spirit, especially investing in restoring a brother or sister who has strayed back into following the "flesh," is one way in which believers must "serve one another in love" (5:13), or, as Paul renews that directive here: "Carry one another's burdens, and in this way you will fulfill the Law of Christ" (6:2).[347] In the immediate context, "burdens" refers to the moral and personal failures from which individual disciples need restoration, but Paul would no doubt also include as "burdens" the trials that life simply sends each person's way, in the face of which each person needs the support, love, and often material help of others.[348] Carrying another person's burden was the work of a slave, when one was available; voluntarily

---

346. In the latter case, shunning explicitly comes only after the offenders had not heeded Paul's (by this point repeated) warning.

347. Early manuscripts are divided between reading "fulfill" as a command (Sinaiticus and Alexandrinus, followed here by the Majority Text) and "you will fulfill" as a future tense verb (P[46] and Sinaiticus). In the Greek, the difference is a matter of a single letter in the verb ending. Text critics tend to favor the latter (so Metzger, *Textual Commentary*, 598), since scribes might be more likely to assimilate a stray future indicative ("you will fulfill") to the mood of the imperatives that dominate this paragraph rather than the reverse.

348. Burton, *Galatians*, 329; Betz, *Galatians*, 299; Barclay, *Obeying the Truth*, 132; Fung, *Galatians*, 287; Longenecker, *Galatians*, 274–75.

doing so, particularly in regard to the burdens that make life oppressive or that erode a person's walk in the Spirit, is the work of love.

By claiming that such mutual burden-bearing is the way to fulfill "the Law of Christ," Paul recalls his claim that "the whole Torah has been fulfilled in one commandment: 'You will love your neighbor as yourself'" (Gal 5:14; Lev 19:18). Mutual burden-bearing is a practical expression of loving one's neighbor as oneself, since one takes up the neighbor's burdens as also one's own. By "the Law of Christ," Paul is not referring to the eschatological "Torah of the Messiah" imagined in rabbinic circles, that is, the Torah as interpreted and taught by the Messiah.[349] Nor does it seem likely that Paul is referring to the body of Jesus' teachings as a new Torah for the Christian disciple.[350] The closest parallel expression in Paul's own writings appears in 1 Corinthians, where Paul speaks of the person who is "under the law of Christ" (*ennomos Christou*), who is neither "under Torah" nor "without God's Law" (1 Cor 9:20–21).[351] Such a person falls into neither category that defined people before and apart from Christ, namely "Jews" (those "under Torah") and "Gentiles" (who are "sinners" by definition since they are "without Torah," as in Gal 2:15). Instead, they are being normed by Christ, patterned into the mind and example of Christ, by the work of the Spirit within them. "Love for neighbor" is also what Jesus himself exemplified to the full when he showed his love for Paul (Gal 2:20) and for all (Gal 1:4) by giving himself on their behalf.[352] The "Law of Christ" holds together both Jesus' identification of the heart of the historic Torah (Lev 19:18) and Jesus' exemplary obedience to that one command in which the whole is fulfilled. Christ's other-centered, self-giving love *is* their Law, and mutual burden-bearing is a day-to-day expression of living by the norm of Christ.

Paul supports the command to "carry each other's burdens" with a proverb-like saying presented as a rationale: "for (*gar*) if anyone thinks himself or herself to be something, when that person is nothing, he or

---

349. Davies, *Setting*, 109–90.

350. Davies, *Setting*, 341–66; Fung, *Galatians*, 288; Dodd, "*Ennomos Christou*," 134–48.

351. Barclay, *Obeying the Truth*, 126–27.

352. Barclay, *Obeying the Truth*, 133; see also Beker, *Paul the Apostle*, 105.

she is deceiving himself or herself" (6:3) If other-centered service, seen in the willingness to bow down, figuratively speaking, to help someone shoulder their burden is the measure of progress in discipleship, then the conceitedness that makes people think they are more important than, and above, the struggling sister or brother is empty self-deception. The person who is "puffed up" with self-importance is still just a novice in the faith,[353] whereas the person who thinks his or her struggling sister or brother to "be something," such that that person invests time and self into helping the sister or brother bear some burden, is taking on the shape and role of the Master.

The attention given to the practice of one's fellow disciple must be matched—indeed outmatched—by the attention one gives to the critical examination of one's own practice, to make sure it is Spirit-led and affirmed by the presence of the Spirit's fruit: "But let each person test his or her own work, and then he or she will have his or her boast in (or 'to') himself or herself alone, and not in (or 'to') the other person. For each person will carry his or her own load" (6:4–5).[354] Paul urges believers to avoid self-deception, whether on the basis of comparing oneself favorably against another who has fallen into some transgression, or on the basis of comparing oneself competitively with another's positive achievements, as if it was the tally that justified and gave cause for pride and honor, rather than the transforming work of the Spirit.

The sense assigned to the preposition *eis* ("in" or "to") in 6:4 is important. Is it a question of a person holding onto a claim to honor based on his or her own actions (and thus not dependent on what another person is doing)?[355] Or is it a question of keeping one's claim to honor to oneself rather than waving it in front of another person, with the

353. The Buddha was also keenly aware of the danger of self-deception in regard to one's intelligence, achievement, or importance: "Fools who know their foolishness are wise at least to that extent, but fools who think themselves wise are fools indeed" (*Dhammapada* 63).

354. P[46] and Codex Vaticanus omit "each" in "but let each person test his or her own work," with the result that the person envisioned in 6:3 remains the subject of the commands in 6:4 (hence, "let such a one test . . ."). This verse becomes, in these manuscripts, even more clearly a prescription against the inflated self-opinion warned against in 6:3.

355. Fung, *Galatians*, 290; Longenecker, *Galatians*, 276.

result that Paul's instructions here are geared toward reducing rivalry and competitive boasting?[356] The majority of translations major the first understanding, though the second is the more typical for *eis*. Moreover, Paul has tended throughout Galatians to use *epi* or *ek* to express the source or basis for something (e.g., "faith," "works," "promise"), which would also favor the second reading. It is also difficult to imagine Paul countenancing any kind of boasting within the congregation (whether on the basis of one's own progress in discipleship or Spirit-led works, or on the basis of one's superior achievements in comparison with another's), all of which leads to competitive rivalry, divisiveness, and general conceitedness. The man who claims that he will only boast in the cross of Jesus Christ is, therefore, probably urging people to find their ground for self-respect in their own rootedness in the Spirit's leading, and then to keep that "boast" to oneself. Richard Longenecker aptly captures the import of Paul's exhortation: "Christian feelings of exultation and congratulation should spring from one's own actions as seen in the light of God's approval and not derive from comparing oneself to what others are or are not doing."[357]

At first, Paul may appear to be contradicting himself when, after urging disciples to "carry one another's burdens (*barē*)," he then declares that "each person will bear his or her own load (*phortion*)." There is a balance between individual responsibility and community support, with the community charged with doing all in its power to help each individual member remain within the boundaries of the proper and fruitful exercise of his or her freedom as a Christian. The weight of the "burden" is to be shared among Christians in the assembly; the ultimate responsibility for a life cannot be shared, even if one would wish.[358] This is true not only in regard to shortcomings, but also successes. There will be no reward on that Day for having done *better* than another believer, only for what one has done oneself in God's sight and God's estimation.

356. Barclay, *Obeying the Truth*, 160–61; Martyn, *Galatians*, 550.

357. Longenecker, *Galatians*, 277. The Buddha had similarly advised his students to pay strictest attention to their own works and their own room for growth and improvement: "Let none find fault with others; let none see the omissions and commissions of others. But let one see one's own acts, done and undone" (*Dhammapada* 50).

358. Barclay, *Obeying the Truth*, 162; Fung, *Galatians*, 291.

In this sense the saying ties in most directly with 6:4. The self-examination and the self-testing that Paul urges is to be done with a view to discovering what, in our own progress and practice, will have positive value before God when everyone stands in front of Christ's judgment seat, "in order that each may receive the due reward for what was done while in the body, whether good or ill" (2 Cor 5:10).

The next exhortation seems to introduce a completely new topic: "Let the one who is instructed in the word share in all good things with the one who gives instruction" (Gal 6:6). The distinction between the "instructed" and the "instructors" implies the beginnings of a specialized ministry within the church, with particular individuals entrusted with the instruction and edification of the community and all its members, devoting time to this task that is taken away from the work of providing for oneself.[359] In a spirit of reciprocity, those who benefit from the commitment of the instructors are to share their material resources with them for their sustenance, so that they can continue in their work on behalf of the community. Paul may be especially concerned that the men and women to whom *he* had entrusted this work among the congregations continue to have the support and allegiance of the communities of faith in South Galatia, as the rival teachers were their rivals as well and may well have sought to alienate them and their influence along with Paul's among the Galatian churches. This exhortation also provides a further example of mutual burden-bearing: some within the body bear the burden of equipping the saints for a fully informed faith and effective ministry; others bear the burden of financially supporting these individuals so that they may continue that equipping ministry.

Christian freedom brings with it great responsibility. Having been freed from being "under Torah," we are freed *for* God's purposes, not free to do anything that we might want, impelled by our self-centered cravings. Paul assures his hearers that, even though they are free from the rigorous demands of the Torah, they are not "getting away" with anything or "getting off the hook" in regard to God's high expectations for humanity in community. The absence of Law does not mean the absence of consequences or accountability before the One who searches our inmost intentions and thoughts:

359. Longenecker, *Galatians*, 279; Martyn, *Galatians*, 552.

Don't deceive yourselves: God is not mocked. Whatever a
person sows, that shall he or she also reap: the one sowing to
his or her flesh will harvest decay from the flesh, but the one
sowing to the Spirit will harvest eternal life from the Spirit.
Let us not grow tired of doing what is noble, for we will reap
the harvest in its own season if we do not give up. As long as
we have a season, then, let us work what is good towards all,
and especially towards those who belong to the household of
faith. (6:7–10)

The foundation for Paul's closing exhortation is a common maxim.
It would be familiar both within Jewish and Greco-Roman discourse.
Just within the former, one finds, for example, the following:

Whoever sows injustice will reap calamity. (Prov 22:8)

Those who plow iniquity and sow trouble reap the same. (Job 4:8)

Sow for yourselves righteousness; reap steadfast love. . . . You have
plowed wickedness, you have reaped injustice. (Hos 10:7–8)

Do not sow in the furrows of injustice, and you will not reap a
sevenfold crop. (Sir 7:3)[360]

The maxim captures an undeniable truth of agriculture, proven year after year, crop after crop, applied throughout the Jewish Scriptures (and
here by Paul) to ethical behavior and its consequences. The truth of the
natural order supports, by analogy, Paul's claim about the moral order
of God's economy.

The Buddha applies the similar image of fruit ripening, applying
this to the consequences of good and evil deeds coming to full "fruition":

Fools of little wit are enemies unto themselves as they move
about doing evil deeds, the fruits of which are bitter. Ill done
is that action of doing which one repents later, and the fruit of
which one, weeping, reaps with tears. Well done is that action
of doing which one repents not later, and the fruit of which
one reaps with delight and happiness. So long as an evil deed

360. See also Plato, *Phaedrus* 260 C; Aristotle, *Rhetoric* 3.3.4; Philo, *Conf.* 21; *Mut.*
268–69, cited in Longenecker, *Galatians*, 280.

has not ripened, the fool thinks it as sweet as honey. But when the evil deed ripens, the fool comes to grief. (*Dhammapada* 66–69)

It may be well with the evil-doer as long as the evil ripens not. But when it does ripen, then the evil-doer sees [the painful results of] evil deeds. It may be ill with the doer of good as long as the good ripens not. But when it does ripen, then the doer of good sees [the pleasant results of] good deeds. . . . Nowhere in the world is there a place where one may escape from the results of evil deeds. (*Dhammapada* 119–120, 127)

One must look to the ripening of evil action and of good action to see which one is truly advantageous. The ultimate consequences are the ultimate test of advantage.[361]

Similarly, Paul urges his converts to "take the long view" in regard to the gratification of the impulses of the flesh over against devoting oneself to disciplined following where the Spirit leads. Giving oneself over to the impulses of the "flesh" (as the bundle of self-centered, self-gratifying drives that are inimical to loving the neighbor as oneself) results in "corruption," by which Paul means the death and the decay of one's body, one's "flesh" as the "meat" in which we live.[362] Ultimately, the "flesh" in the first sense offers no power to escape the fate of the "flesh" in the second sense, so that self-seeking drives and impulses turn out, ironically, to be the most self-destructive drives and impulses. This is a warning comparable to Paul's warning about exclusion from the kingdom of God (5:21); it is the antithesis of "eternal life."

Conversely, the Spirit that currently works to transform us into the likeness of Jesus, such that Jesus takes on flesh anew, as it were, in our bodies, also has the power to "transform the bodies of our humiliation into the likeness of his glorified body" through resurrection from the dead (Phil 3:21). Sowing to the Spirit by giving oneself over more and

361. The *Dhammapada* opens, in fact, with a pair of sayings that foreground the consequences of sowing to lower desires versus higher motives: "If with an impure mind a person speaks or acts suffering follows that person like the wheel that follows the foot of the ox. . . . If with a pure mind a person speaks or acts happiness follows him like his or her never-departing shadow" (*Dhammapada* 1–2).

362. Fung, *Galatians*, 295; Longenecker, *Galatians*, 281.

more to the other-centered, self-giving love that characterized Jesus and that fulfills the righteous demands of the Law becomes, then, the way to secure one's own life for the long haul of eternity. Without showing thereby that he knows Jesus' sayings on this subject, Paul comes very close to expressing what Jesus meant when he asserted that "whoever wants to secure his or her own life will destroy it, and whoever throws away his or her life for my sake and the sake of the Gospel will make it secure" (Mark 8:35).

The farmer sows knowing that he or she will have to invest a lot of work and care into the crop for a lengthy period of time before enjoying the fruits thereof. The person who wants instant gratification for his or her labors cannot be a farmer. So, Paul implies, it is with the journey of the Christian. It calls for continuous investment, promising its most significant rewards at a distant, future time. Nevertheless, Paul is himself certain and communicates certainty about the "harvest time" of the last judgment. He urges Christians to keep on living, as he does, for *that* Day and the honor and joy it will bring to those who have taken the "long view" on reaping the benefits of faithful, Spirit-led action—"doing what is good" or "virtuous" (6:9)—in the here and now.

This paragraph is not about "earning" eternal life, any more than sowing "earns" a harvest, which depends on so many factors beyond human control. But sowing *is* prerequisite to enjoying a harvest, and a harvest is a natural consequence of sowing. Paul is not crossing a line into "justification on the basis of works" or "earning salvation," but he is also not shying away from warning us that our "sowing" now has eternal consequences. God has graciously given us the opportunity and the privilege even of sowing to the Spirit, giving our lives over more and more to the Spirit's promptings and guidance. Doing so, then, more and more—giving God's gift to us of the Spirit the proper attention and esteem—connects us to the promise of eternal life as surely as sowing is connected to harvest.

Now is the time, the "season," for sowing, and so Paul urges that believers make the best use of the opportunity we have during our mortal life to "work what is good" on behalf of every person, paying special attention to the "household of faith," the family of those who are related by adoption into God's household as God's sons and daughters

(4:5–7), who are children by virtue of trusting God's promise. Early Christian leaders like Paul, beginning with Jesus himself (Mark 3:31–35; 10:29–30), spoke of the early church as a kinship group. In connection with this identification, they sought also to shape the ethos of the church (a group of largely unrelated people) after the ethos of family. For example, family members (at their best) sought to cooperate with one another and avoid competition. They would seek to advance one another's honor and interests, not competing for honor at one another's expense, as was typical among non-kin. They would more readily hide one another's shame from public view rather than parade it. Because of this mutual commitment to each other's interests, kin could share a deep level of trust in one another. They would also share resources freely, seek to maintain harmony and unity, and work attentively toward forgiveness and reconciliation.[363] Many facets of this ethos are apparent behind Paul's exhortations to his "sisters and brothers" in Galatia.

Paul draws two concentric circles of care and benevolence. While Christians are to reflect God's love in this world, thus offering loving care and assistance to all people even as God gives the gifts of sun and rain to all (Matt 5:44–48), they need to especially be sure to support fellow Christians, since these would now largely lack the support of non-Christian networks.[364]

6:11–18: PAUL'S PARTING SUMMARIES AND SHOTS

[11]Look at what large letters I made as I wrote to you with my own hand! [12]As many as wish to make a good showing in the flesh, these are the people who are compelling you to get circumcised, only so that they will not be persecuted for the cross of Christ. [13]For those who are circumcised don't keep the Torah themselves, but they want you to get circumcised in order that they may make a boast in your flesh. [14]But may it never be that I boast, except in the cross of our Lord Jesus Christ, through which the cosmos was being crucified to me and I to the cosmos. [15]For neither circumcision nor uncir-

363. See, further, deSilva, *Honor, Patronage, Kinship & Purity*, 165–73, 194–239.
364. See Paul's similar exhortations in 1 Thess 3:12; 5:15b.

cumcision is anything, but a new creation—*now that's worth something.* ¹⁶And as many as fall in line with this measuring stick, peace and mercy be upon them—even upon the Israel of God. ¹⁷For the rest, let no one lay any further burdens on me, for I myself carry the brand marks of Jesus in my body. ¹⁸The generous kindness of our Lord Jesus Christ be with your spirit, brothers and sisters. Amen.

The peroration (or conclusion) of a classical speech could be expected to attend to a number of goals. It might provide a closing summary of the position advanced or course of action urged in the speech. It might seek to arouse strategic emotions among the audience, to leave them in a frame of mind especially well suited to follow the speaker's agenda for their situation. It might give some parting attention to issues of credibility, both affirming the speaker's own credibility and taking parting shots at the credibility of rival speakers or opponents, thus "disposing the hearer favourably towards oneself and unfavourably towards the adversary" (Aristotle, *Rhet.* 3.19.1).[365]

Paul's closing lines in Galatians admirably and succinctly address all of these purposes. Galatians 6:11–18 is especially reminiscent of 5:7–12 in its attention to undermining the rivals' credibility and affirming Paul's credibility (in part against the assertions that rivals have made about him), and of 5:2–6 in terms of theological and ethical content. Indeed, were it not for the need to address the pressing question concerning the sufficiency of the Spirit to empower and lead one to the "completion" of the journey begun in Christ by trust (cf. 3:3), Paul could well have ended his letter at 5:12 (though perhaps a wish for grace to be with the audience might be a bit jarring after such a wish in regard to the rival teachers). Having addressed the question of how "walking in the Spirit" would better equip the disciples for victory over the power of the flesh than the Torah ever could have done, Paul wants to leave the hearers where he had brought them in 5:1–12. To this end, Paul delivers a "knock-out punch" to the rival teachers and their position in 6:11–18.

Paul begins his peroration by drawing attention to his handwriting: "Look at what large letters I made as I wrote to you with my own hand!"

365. For an extensive discussion of the purposes typical of perorations of speeches, see Aristotle, *Rhetoric* 3.19.

(6:11). We have discussed this verse and its implications at some length in the introduction. While Paul often used a secretary or co-worker in the writing of his letters, and often takes the quill or stylus himself to add a closing greeting in his own hand, Gal 6:11 points instead to the probability that Paul wrote the entire letter personally. Here, at the letter's close (as he looks back at what he has written himself), he draws attention to the unusually large size of his handwriting. It has not been the professional, precise, economically-sized lettering of a professional scribe, but rather the oversized scrawl of a writer who was emotionally agitated and personally invested in the communication and its outcome. Paul draws attention here at the end once again to his emotional and personal investment in the Galatian believers, as it is a consequence of their close bond, Paul's personal love for and commitment to them, and the amplitude of the danger of their situation.

The source of this agitation is the topic of the following two verses: "As many as wish to make a good showing in the flesh, these are the people who are compelling you to get circumcised, only so that they will not be persecuted for the cross of Christ. For those who are circumcised don't keep the Torah themselves, but they want you to get circumcised in order that they may make a boast in your flesh" (6:12–13). Paul accuses the rival teachers of operating out of selfish and cowardly motives, not because they are well disposed toward the Galatians. They are conforming the Gospel to what will "look good" to the people whom they fear, namely non-Christian Jews. These fellow Jews would be readier to accept Christianity if they began to see it as a movement that kept Jews in line with the Torah while bringing Gentiles in line with the same, rather than a movement that encouraged Jews to be looser in their obedience to Torah for the sake of accommodating the Gentiles in their midst. "Making a good showing *in the flesh*" retains the very negative associations of "the flesh" in 5:13–26; 6:7–10, but now shifting back from an ethical sense of "flesh" to the realm of the merely physical ("to put up a good show for the sake of the non-Christian Jewish audience"). In the end, the rival teachers are motivated by their own cowardice, trying to avoid the kind of persecution that Paul formerly *inflicted* upon Christian Jews and that Paul now *suffers* as a preacher of the Torah-free Gospel. Acting from selfish motives, rather than for the good of the

Galatians, the character of the rival teachers will be diminished in the church's eyes.

Paul does not stop there, however. He also accuses the rival teachers of being themselves insincere, failing to keep the Torah themselves even as they attempt to fasten this yoke upon the Galatian converts. Exactly what Paul meant by this allegation is not clear. Was he judging them by his own exacting, pre-Christian standards of faithful Torah observance as a member of the Pharisees, the "strictest sect" of the Jewish way of life (see Acts 26:4)? Was he referring, perhaps, to their holding to Christ as the fulfillment of the cultic facets of the Torah, and thus their break with the sacrificial system of the temple (that is, their neglect of a great deal of Torah)? Was Paul's point simply that, in seeking to serve their own interests by pressuring the Galatian Gentile Christians to do what was against the Galatians' best interests in Christ, they were failing even to keep the commandment to love one's neighbor as oneself?[366] Whatever Paul might have thought in regard to these specifics, he is clear on one point: the rival teachers are promoting circumcision not because they are wholeheartedly devoted to Torah, but because this will enhance their prestige in the eyes of their significant others, the larger Jewish population. Paul puts this even more crassly: "they want to claim honor for themselves (back home, or in the eyes of other Jews) on the basis of your flesh (your circumcised penis)." They want to make personal trophies out of the Galatian converts.

While Paul may not have access to all the motives of the rival teachers, which may have *included* some good motives as well, he was in a position to see the larger picture of the dynamics within which he and the rivals were operating. He knew—and sometimes felt firsthand in the form of a lashing or stoning—the pressures that were put on the Jewish Christian community, and asserts that such pressures cannot be ignored when assessing the motives of Jewish Christian teachers who come around trying to turn Gentile Christians into Christian Jews and keep at least the appearance of loyalty to the Torah among the Christian groups spreading through the Diaspora.

Paul, however, claims to be free from such selfish motives as trying to make the Galatians into a trophy for himself, statistics of ministry

366. Nanos, *Irony of Galatians*, 227–28.

success on the basis of which he could claim honor within the Christian movement and circle of Christian missionaries and leaders. The only thing on the basis of which he is willing to claim honor (to "boast") is "the cross of our Lord Jesus Christ, through which the cosmos was being crucified to me and I to the cosmos" (6:14).[367] Paul revels in the stark juxtaposition of the concept of "claiming honor" and the image of a cross with a victim hanging upon it. We can hardly imagine the revulsion witnesses felt at the long, agonizing, messy, degrading death of a condemned criminal writhing in pain on two pieces of wood. But because God's own Son hung on such a cross to accomplish God's beneficent purposes *for us*, the cross becomes the perfect symbol for how completely upside-down the world's values and operating principles are (see, for example, 1 Cor 1:17–31). Serving one another is the path to distinction. Obedience to God, even when it leads to utter disgrace, is the path to eternal honor. Giving oneself away is the path to securing oneself for eternity. The cross that was meant to be a judgment upon Jesus becomes instead a judgment upon the world that placed him there.

Because he is united with Jesus, Jesus' death on the cross becomes Paul's crucifixion to the *kosmos* and the crucifixion of the *kosmos* to Paul. Being crucified to the *kosmos* does not mean detachment from the world of people, human needs, and beneficent relationships: the cross compels us to invest ourselves more and more fully in this "world."[368] *Kosmos* here denotes the ordering of the world under the *stoicheia* that create divisions between people—the ethnic, class/caste, and gender divisions and related valuations that have been transcended in Christ (3:28). *Kosmos* is the present, evil age and its guiding principles and powers, the distorted, fallen, old creation. This is also the death that all

---

367. The relative pronoun could grammatically refer to the cross or to Christ; more likely Paul has in mind the "cross" as instrument by which anything is "crucified." Boasting is also a topic in 2 Cor 11:21b-29 and Phil 3:4–14 (Longenecker, *Galatians*, 293–94). In both passages, as here, Paul renounces finding and promoting his own honor and worth in his Israelite pedigree and his record of Torah observance in favor of finding that claim to honor in what Jesus' death on the cross on his behalf has done to him and for him, turning the world's systems of value on their heads and revealing what really matters in God's sight. In both, as here, Paul is also contrasting his own approach to "boasting" quite explicitly with the approach of rival teachers.

368. Longenecker, *Galatians*, 295.

disciples are to share, as they crucify the "flesh with its impulses and desires" in union with Christ, and live in the freedom beyond the old codes of the present, evil age that honor the boundaries between Jew and Gentile, between person and person.

Death to this *kosmos* gives Paul the opportunity to give a summation of his position: "For neither circumcision nor uncircumcision is anything, but a new creation—*now that's worth something*. And as many as line up with this measuring stick, peace and mercy be upon them—even upon the Israel of God" (6:15–16).[369] The boundaries of Israel, the people of God, have been redrawn by the decisive act of God in Christ at the close of this present, evil age. Inclusion in the household of God, among the children of Abraham, happens not through circumcision, just as uncircumcision cannot exclude one. What matters is the emergence of the new creation in each person and in the community of faith: a dying to the world with Christ and rising to new life, the life of the Spirit reforming the person, forming Christ within the believer. This statement directly recalls Paul's earlier, similar formulation: "in Christ Jesus neither circumcision nor uncircumcision has any force, but rather faith working through love" (Gal 5:6). Paul would return to this formulation once again in his writings, when writing to the believers in Corinth: "Neither circumcision nor uncircumcision matters, but keeping God's commandments" (1 Cor 7:19). Paul foregrounds the irony of his position in this third statement. Circumcision (a "commandment of Torah") is no longer within the sphere of "the commandments of God."

Paul names that which matters—"a new creation"—in such a brief and formulaic fashion, it appears to be a "catch phrase" with which the Galatians would have had to have been familiar, perhaps from Paul's earlier instruction (see 2 Cor 5:16–17, another passage where this con-

369. Scribes show an increasing tendency to adapt the statement in 6:15 to the very similar statement earlier in Gal 5:6, "For in Christ Jesus neither circumcision nor uncircumcision avails anything." Hence the KJV of Gal 6:15, following the Majority Text, reads "For in Christ Jesus neither circumcision availeth any thing, nor uncircumcision." Such harmonization of one passage to another is a very common source of variants, but also a clear sign of scribal alteration of the text. The shorter and more fully differentiated reading, "For neither circumcision nor uncircumcision is anything" (P[46], Codex Vaticanus), is more likely to stand closer to Paul's original at this point.

cept emerges, and in somewhat more detail).[370] "New creation" is what is coming about by the Spirit's indwelling in each Christian and, thus, in Christian community. "New creation" is taking shape as Christ, the New Adam, is fully formed in the believers (2:20; 4:19), who thus come to bear the image of the New Adam rather than the Old Adam, who was crucified in them in their union with Christ.

Walking in the Spirit, or falling in step with the Spirit, is the path forward into this new creation. Paul uses once again the verb *stoicheō* (cf. 5:25), the verb related to the noun *stoicheia* that had figured so prominently in naming the systems of powers and operating principles that dominate this present, evil age, institutionalizing its unjust, violent, subjugating practices (4:1–11). Paul invokes God's blessings of peace and mercy only upon those who walk toward the realization of this new creation, and who leave behind the boundary-making codes and principles of the old creation. There is some question concerning whether or not Paul pronounces this blessing of "peace and mercy" upon two different groups (those who walk in line with the "rule" of 6:15, on the one hand, and "the Israel of God," namely ethnic Israel, on the other hand) or upon one group only (those who walk in line with the "rule" of 6:15, who constitute the "Israel of God"). Paul's qualification of "Israel" here as "*God's* Israel" would seem to distinguish this group from "Israel according to the flesh" (*kata sarka*), to use a phrase from Paul's later work (1 Cor 10:18) in a manner similar to his distinction between the "children *kata sarka*" (non-Christian Jews and Judaizers) and "children of promise" (Jewish and Gentile Christians together) in 4:21–31. It seems more likely that Paul is identifying those Christians who walk in line with the rule of 6:15, namely Jews and Gentiles bound together in Christ, as "God's Israel," the reconstituted people of God in the "new creation."[371] After taking such pains to demonstrate the equality and unity of Jews and Gentiles in Christ throughout the letter, Paul would hardly reintroduce the divisions between the church and "Israel" as an ethnic entity defined by Torah in his closing benediction.[372]

---

370. Betz, *Galatians,* 319.

371. Schlier, *Galater,* 283; Ridderbos, *Galatians,* 227; Fung, *Galatians,* 311.

372. Longenecker, *Galatians,* 298.

Paul points to his own scars as proof of his sincerity and reliability: "For the rest, let no one lay any further burdens on me, for I myself carry the brand marks (*stigmata*) of Jesus in my body" (6:17).[373] By the time Paul wrote 2 Corinthians, he had amassed quite a catalog of beatings and hardships endured because of the unpopularity of his message with both Jewish and Roman officials. Compared with other traveling Christian teachers, Paul could "boast" of being more fully Christ's servant on the basis of having endured "labors more abundantly, imprisonments more abundantly, and beatings surpassing abundantly, often in danger of death: five times I received the forty stripes minus one from the Jews, three times I was beaten [by Roman authorities] with rods, once I was stoned" (2 Cor 11:23–25).

Paul wrote this catalog sometime between 54 and 57 CE. There would have been considerably fewer items on it at the time he wrote Galatians in 49 or early 50 CE. Nevertheless, Paul's South Galatian mission gave ample opportunity for scars (Acts 13–14; 2 Tim 3:11). Far from being signs of disgrace, Paul pointed to his scars as *stigmata*, a word often used to name the brands or tattoos showing ownership of a particular slave. Paul's scars are the marks that show whose he is, in whose service he labors. They are also the marks of his sincerity in his preaching. Despite the opposition he encountered and the physical pains he endured, Paul had not altered the message that God had entrusted to him. He was not a coward, nor was he an opportunist. Unlike the rival teachers (6:12–13), he has been willing to suffer beatings and whippings for telling the truth about what God has done in Jesus, however unpopular this has made him with those same people whom the rivals fear. These same scars are also proof that Paul has not "preached circumcision" where it suited him (see Gal 5:11); he has preached the Torah-free Gospel wherever he has gone, even when it meant being whipped for it. The absence of such marks on the bodies of the rival

373. Three of the earliest manuscripts (P[46], Vaticanus, Alexandrinus) support the reading "the brand marks of Jesus," while the Majority Text expands this to "the brand marks of the Lord Jesus." Sinaiticus, surprisingly, reads "the brand marks of the Lord Jesus Christ," showing that the tendency to embellish titles of Jesus was quite early. The longer readings are clearly the result of scribes being accustomed to refer to "Jesus" as "the Lord Jesus" or "Jesus Christ." Variants of this kind are very common in the manuscript tradition.

teachers becomes, at the same time, a stroke against them. Their smooth skin proves that they are unwilling to face the hostility that the "truth of the Gospel" arouses (6:12). Paul thus asserts here at the end the physical evidence of his unassailable credibility, and on this basis he commands that "no one keep making trouble for me" by calling Paul's Gospel or apostleship into question, as the rival teachers have done.

Paul normally closes his letters with a prayer for "the favor of the Lord Jesus Christ" to be with the addressees (Rom 16:20b; 1 Cor 16:23; 2 Cor 13:14; Gal 6:18; Eph 6:24; Phil 4:23; Col 4:18b; 1 Thess 5:28; 2 Thess 3:18; Phlm 25), though this is the only letter in which Paul also addresses the hearers as "brothers and sisters" specifically in this wish for grace to be with them. Indeed, *adelphoi* ("brothers and sisters") is the last word of the letter itself, apart from the formulaic "Amen." Appropriately, grace and kinship sound the last note of the letter. Paul has argued at length that what the Galatians have received through the generous favor of Christ, who redeemed them, and of God, who poured out the Spirit upon them, is sufficient to bring them into the unending life of God's kingdom. Now at the letter's end he directs their hearts and minds to Christ's favor, in order that they may continue to rely upon it and walk in it. Paul has also argued that they have been made one family in Christ, having been joined to the family of Abraham by virtue of being united with the Seed that is Christ, and by virtue of having been adopted as God's own sons and daughters, as the Spirit testifies. He has also sought to orient them to one another as kin, so that they would banish rivalry, competition, and all that is divisive from their midst, and invest in one another's successful walk in the Spirit through the trials of the present, evil age. Now at the end, he reminds them again of their kinship with each other and with Paul, so that they will remember to nurture the ethos of kin between them.

READING GALATIANS 6 WITH SRI LANKAN CHRISTIANS

Gracious Accountability and Burden-Bearing

Early Christian leaders show an intense and consistent awareness that the steady progress of the individual disciple moving out from being driven by the flesh toward being fully Spirit-led requires the investment, input, and support of other disciples.[374] We are, as individuals, easily prone to self-deception in regard to what comes from the Spirit and what comes from the flesh; we are easily prone to our own weakness, such that we are indeed "overtaken" by some sin. There are many occasions when other Christians could help us see that we're not speaking the truth to ourselves about some direction or practice we've embraced. There are many occasions when the support and encouragement and admonition of fellow Christians could give us the resolve we require to resist the enticements of sin and to give ourselves fully to the Spirit's victory over our fleshly impulses. Simply put, we need the intervention of fellow Christians who will confront sin in our lives *and* who will do it gently, or with forbearance.

Pastors and leaders can too often rebuke harshly and in an authoritarian manner, humiliating the wayward. Shaming often leads to backlash, for example, an individual or family leaving the church, trying to harm the pastor's reputation and work, even going off and starting a new church. Conversely, Christian leaders overtaken in a trespass are often dealt with harshly rather than redemptively. Restoration is a challenge, especially for evangelicals. All of us are weak in some areas in our lives. Therefore there should be a restoration procedure for pastors, lay leaders, and all believers who fall into sin.

Insofar as Sri Lanka is a shame-oriented society, processes of confrontation and restoration that keep knowledge that might bring shame as private as possible, that thus defuse the challenge to honor inherent in confrontation, and that celebrate the honor of the restored person so that no lingering shame debilitates his or her standing and operation in the Christian community might be more effective. Care in regard to these matters may also help protect the reputation of the Christian church as a whole in a land in which it is a vulnerable minority presence. Issues of shame, and the challenges of overcoming the private/public boundaries that the Western-minded tend to draw at our domestic doorstep, are particularly acute around issues of domestic violence and sexual abuse. People in most cultures would be quite reluctant to talk about domestic abuse, sexual abuse, other sorts of issues that show the

374. See, for example, Heb 3:12–13; 10:24–25, 32–34; 12:15–17; 13:1–3.

underside of family life, but this is made even more difficult in cultures like Sri Lanka's where shame is a key issue. Churches are challenged therefore to find ways to make it safe to speak about such things, so that these situations can be better addressed and redeemed within the church's processes of confrontation and restoration.

The kind of mutual reinforcement in matters of Christian practice, and the level of trust that is required for one person poking around in another's progress on the way out from domination by fleshly drives toward wholehearted submission to the Spirit's guidance, presume a level of mutual involvement and investment that is rare in the Western world. In the West, the values (one might even say, the *stoicheia*) of individualism and of the boundary between private and public are so strong that it is highly counter-cultural for believers now to practice Paul's exhortations. To the extent that Sri Lankans have been influenced by Western individualism over the course of three centuries of colonization and the ongoing process of neocolonialism—over against the more traditional community orientation indigenous to Sri Lankan culture—the effective exercise of mutual accountability and "restoring" the sinner will be hindered. Some Sri Lankan churches have also become far more program-focused, another characteristic and emphasis imported from Western congregational practice. Such a focus puts a lot of energy into having strong and winsome activities for youth, Sunday school, children, outreach, and the like, but tends therefore to look more to the structures, schedule, and delivery of services and (in a broad sense) curriculum to the congregation (and community) as "consumers." This emphasis runs a strong risk of replacing a focus on relationships and on persons. Once again, then, as churches in Sri Lanka try to imitate or employ the programs observed in (and exported from) the West, the relational base for applying the kind of restorative discipline prescribed by Paul is eroded.

The intentional restoration of the wayward is traditionally referred to as "church discipline," or at least as coming under the umbrella of the same. Processes of discernment, confrontation, and restoration would be far more effective where the leaders of local churches cooperate with one another, reinforcing the work of restoration rather than providing a back door for escaping necessary confrontation and amendment of life. If a person or family leaves a church because of some dispute with the leadership or fellow members over some personal issue, and another church receives them with no questions asked, opportunities for that person's (or family's) transformation into Christ-likeness (and even that first church's growth in Christ as a whole) through confronting some difficult issues are bypassed because the second church is just happy to increase its numbers. The health of the whole Body of Christ is compromised when such a scenario eventuates. This is not to say that a second church should not welcome a believer leaving a first church because of some disciplinary issue. It can happen that the disciplinary issue itself reflects the lack of health in that first church! I have encountered several congregations whose over-rigorous application of disciplinary procedures (and over issues that Paul, for example, would *never* have encouraged a church to regulate or legislate) resulted in harm to the individual believer, and have myself encouraged such brothers and sisters to seek out a more healthful congregation. But it is part of our responsibility as local cells of the whole Body of Christ to examine these issues and determine whether or not we need to stand beside the first church in saying that a particular issue in that disciple's life needs to be considered and addressed for the disciple's own good, and for the health of any congregation of which he or she is a part.

The Spirit-filled community is expected to bear one another's burdens, because none of us can bear alone all the burdens of temptation, of self-delusion, and of the persistence of the *stoicheia* reasserting their power over our thinking and practices.

The community is called to come alongside the struggling members within its number; the community is also called not to shy away from evangelizing and restoring the more "obvious" sinners like prostitutes, drunkards, drug addicts, or the like. Christians often fear that bringing such people into their communities may cause damage to their church, or that their burdens are too heavy or serious to bear effectively. Therefore, they only evangelize the ordinary people, who fall within their comfort zone. Paul would challenge the church to prepare itself to bear the burdens of people from every walk of life, since Christ bore our burdens and *theirs* as well. Bearing the burdens of our sisters and brothers (those already in our churches, and those *yet* to be in our churches) who may have fallen into some sin or may be going through some difficulty in life is a primary venue for showing forth the sacrificial love of the Lord who bore all our burdens on the cross.

Mutual accountability "in a spirit of forbearance" and mutual burden-bearing are specific applications of "serving one another as slaves through love" (Gal 5:13). The model of the servant is no more appealing in Sri Lanka than it is in the rest of the world. No one aspires to be a servant, and the hierarchy between householder and servant, with the former priding themselves often at the expense of the latter, is still a powerful *stoicheion* in Sri Lanka. But Paul's call, accurately reflecting Jesus' own call to his followers (see Mark 10:41–45), is to become servants one of another in love. Conceitedness is generally tied to thinking oneself to be better than others. Sri Lankan society has several overlapping social hierarchies that feed conceit. English-speaking people may look down upon Sinhala- or Tamil-speaking people on the basis of their superior educational achievements and resulting opportunities. The Sinhalese may look down upon Tamils due to being the ethnic, empowered majority. Within Tamil society, people of one caste may look down upon people of "lower" castes. There is no room in the church for the hierarchy systems of the present, evil age nor for the conceitedness and opposition these systems foster. Christ died for all without considering the hierarchy system of Sri Lanka, and calls us to mutual burden-bearing and mutual accountability in a way that obliterates these hierarchies and lines of division.

What Kind of Harvest Are You Sowing?

Throughout this study of Galatians, we have tried to do justice to justification as "gift and task."[375] It is "gift" insofar as Christ gave himself, as an expression of God's love and generosity toward us, on our behalf, to reconcile us to God and to redeem us from this present, evil age. It is "gift" insofar as God pours his Holy Spirit out upon all who are joined to Jesus, the Seed, in trust. It is "gift" insofar as this Holy Spirit, freely

---

375. Käsemann, "The Righteousness of God in Paul," 168–82, especially p. 170. Karl Paul Donfried offers a brilliant study of the relationship of justification, sanctification, and deliverance at the last judgment in his article, "Justification and Last Judgment in Paul," 90–110.

lavished upon us, is sufficient to guide us into and empower us for living righteously before God, specifically by living fully in line with the commandment to love our neighbor with the care, investment, and commitment that the fleshly person reserves for himself or herself *above* the neighbor. It is "task," however, insofar as we must "walk by the Spirit" (5:16), "fall in line with the Spirit" (5:25), "serve one another as slaves through love" (5:13), and "stand fast," not submitting again to the powers and principles that formerly enslaved us, from which Christ freed us at such cost to himself (5:1). "As disciples continue to participate obediently in the process of sanctification granted them by God, this process will lead to the final fulfillment of that which began in justification, namely, the gift of salvation to be consummated at the last day."[376] Paul closes his exhortations in Galatians by reminding them—and us—of our ultimate responsibility before God to use God's gifts well, to submit our lives fully to the Spirit that came upon us only because Jesus bore the cost of submitting his life fully to God's good will for us. He concludes with the solemn warning that we can't fool God. No theology of justification or eternal security or other conceptual construct that we espouse and hold up will pull the wool over God's eyes as he peers into our hearts and minds to learn: Did we spend our lives sowing to the flesh, or sowing to the Spirit? Did we dedicate ourselves to making the best use of the gifts God gave us to bring us fully in line with his righteousness, to bring Christ to life within us and, through us, ongoingly to life to work throughout the world? Does God recognize his Son in the people we came to be? Was it God's Spirit or our own fleshly impulses at work in our lives, evidenced by the traces of the flesh's works or Spirit's fruit that we left behind in our wake?

Here is a strong point of commonality between Paul's Gospel and the major religions of Sri Lanka: our actions and the attitudes of our hearts have consequences, as sure and certain as the wheel that follows the ox's foot. But precisely here is also the "good news" of the Gospel most evident: there is a God, and he lavishly supplies all that is needed for us to walk in righteousness and enjoy the consequences of living righteous lives. What is required of us is, essentially, to cultivate aware-

---

376. Donfried, "Justification and Last Judgment," 99 (modified slightly for the sake of inclusive language).

ness (including honesty with ourselves before God) and steady commitment. Cultivation of awareness could be achieved by the regular practice of asking ourselves: Where is this impulse or this reaction coming from? Is it coming from something fleshly, self-protective, self-promoting, or self-gratifying within us? Or is it coming from something within us that protects or promotes God's goals, the well-being of the other, the health and vitality of Christian witness? "Commitment" comes in to play insofar as we consistently turn away from following the direction of the former set of impulses and consistently invest ourselves in the latter. This is what it means to remain "in grace," living by the direction and in the power of God's gift, the Spirit, which allows us, in turn, to produce what is pleasing to God.

Sowing, for Paul, involves first and foremost "doing good" to other human beings, fulfilling the command to "love one's neighbor as oneself" in concrete, practical, beneficent, helpful, needful ways. Christian practice is to differ from the typical practice of other religious groups in this regard. While we are especially entrusted with looking after the needs of other believers, we are not to care *only* for "our own." Doing good is a life practice, to be pursued "whenever we have opportunity," and not a practice limited to particular religious days or seasons. Our commitment to "sow" by investing ourselves in doing good for others creates a twofold witness: our care for other believers shows the quality of fellowship we have with each other in Christ; our care for nonbelievers witnesses to the love, care, and mercy of the God who looks after everyone in this earth (Matt 5:45). Christians are empowered by the Holy Spirit to realize the ideal of *metta* in action, and to go beyond this through personal involvement in and attachment to those whom we encounter and help.

Sowing here includes financial spending. Buddhists and Hindus are accustomed to providing for the material needs of priests and other facilitators of religious ceremonies. While giving to the Christian church is not something to be regulated (e.g., through prescribing the "tithe"), the church cannot carry on its mission without financial support. Christians therefore need to think about their spending as "sowing" as well. We are expected to spend the money we receive from our employment on what is truly needful for life. Beyond the necessities, however, it is a *spiritual* practice to ask ourselves how much we are spending on our desires and pleasures, and how much we are spending on advancing God's interests in this world through God's churches and other channels. Spending can never "buy" salvation, as if we can ever indebt God to us (see Rom 11:35!), but our spending does show where the interests of our hearts lie—in providing for our own pleasures, or providing for others' necessities and encounter with the Gospel.

As a sidebar on sowing and reaping, we need to hear Paul's instruction concerning those who devote themselves to the study and teaching of the word, as well as to the formation of Christian disciples, to the extent that they take necessary time away from engaging in other kinds of work by means of which a person typically supports himself or herself. Those who are blessed by the ministry of such people, exercised at the cost of looking after their own material needs first, should share their material gifts with their instructors (6:6). In Sri Lanka, many pastors and other leaders who have dedicated themselves to full-time ministry are not paid well as they are expected by the church and its leadership to depend on God's provision alone and live by faith. They are paid a small allowance to look after their family. Because of this, many pastors and leaders have left their ministries in order to go abroad for study and settled there without returning, or have moved into secular work to sustain their families.

As Paul would later write to the Christians in Rome using the imagery of sowing and reaping, "If the Gentiles received a share of their [the Judean Christians'] spiritual blessings, they ought also to be of service to them in regard to material blessings" (Rom 15:27). What was said in regard to the partnership of Judean Christians and (largely) Gentile Christians in Macedonia and Greece expressed by Paul in his collection project could be said as well of the partnership between a church community and those who devote themselves to its growth and nurture. Pastors ought also not to be neglected in their old age or retirement. This partnership continues long after the pastor ceases to be able to perform as once he or she did—at least as a function of bearing one another's burdens.

Integrity as Christian Leaders and as Christian Disciples

Paul's parting words in Galatians raise several important issues regarding our integrity as ministers or missionaries of the Gospel, which spill over into the area of our integrity as Christ-followers (and, so, can apply to lay and clergy alike). What disqualifies the rival teachers? What gives Paul credibility as a leader? Paul raises three considerations for examining integrity: (1) Are we adapting the message to what will make us personally more popular or our message more palatable? (2) Are we guided in our ministries or missions by a desire to "make a good showing in the flesh" or to build up our own reputation? (3) Are we taking our ministry and mission in certain directions, and avoiding other directions, out of a desire to avoid persecution? These become essential points for self-examination for Christian leaders and disciples alike.

Paul has from the beginning affirmed that he is not a "people-pleaser" and that, indeed, the drive to please people tends to undermine one's ability to be a servant of Christ (1:10–11). The rival teachers appear to have asserted that Paul has been guilty of adapting his message to suit his audience, promoting circumcision where it would win the support of Jewish converts and downplaying the requirement of keeping Torah where it would win the support of Gentile converts. Paul, however, vehemently denies adapting the essence of the message to that which will make him more popular or his message more palatable (5:11).

Two areas in which this presents a challenge in the contemporary Sri Lankan Christian environment are "seeker-sensitivity" and syncretism. The church is indeed called to be sensitive to developing worship experiences that will reach out to and welcome non-Christian "seekers" who are invited into the church or who come out of a desire to explore the Christian way. At the same time, however, the church is challenged to present the full Gospel to such seekers and to worship in the presence of such seekers in an authentically Christian manner. That is to say, considerations of relevance or accessibility or winsomeness—all of which are important, to be sure—cannot trump authenticity and faithfulness to the Gospel itself. Sri Lankan Christians need to test models of seeker-sensitive worship imported from the Western world, being wary of buying into the "market mentality" that infuses much Western material on evangelism and church growth.

The second area calls us to examine the degree to which we make room for practices native to Hindu and Buddhist religious practice within the context of church life and individual practice. The rival teachers sought to import significant features of Judaism into Christian practice for the sake of easing the social tension between themselves and other Jews who had not moved with them into faith in Christ, and perhaps even for the sake of recognition in the eyes of non-Christian Jews (6:12–13). Paul resists this, accepting the consequences of the tension (6:17). In Sri Lanka, the majority surrounding the church practice Buddhism and Hinduism; the majority of people within the church ultimately come from a Buddhist or Hindu background. We are challenged to discern, in conversation with our fellow believers, what facets of Buddhist or Hindu practice may continue to be permitted on the basis of Christian freedom, and what ought to be resisted for the sake of preserving the integrity of the Gospel and its witness to the One God, and as part of our essential allegiance to One Lord and one faith. Paul suggests that, whatever the answers might be, they not be driven by people-pleasing or by cowardice (that is, the unwillingness to pay the cost of letting the stumbling block of the cross remain evident and poignant), so as to preserve both the integrity of the Gospel and our witness to the Gospel, visible in our practices and behaviors.

Integrity in ministry and discipleship is hindered by people-pleasing; it is also hindered by using ministry and mission as an opportunity for pleasing ourselves. Paul suggests that the rival teachers were pursuing their work, in part at least, out of a desire to make a name for themselves among the Jerusalem leadership and even among non-Christian Jews. Their negative example cautions us against engaging in outreach or building up a church for the sake of our own ego and reputation among other Christian leaders. Serving other people and serving God's purposes means eliminating competition and fostering cooperation among Christian leaders and churches. When pastors baptize people without any confirmation that their faith is genuine (as opposed to seeking better schooling for their children or securing a place for a wedding), focusing merely on increasing their church membership as this would bring outward credit for these pastors with their church or denomination, their ministry, the "converts," and the health of the whole Body all suffer as a result. Paul emphasizes here that wrong motives and purposes will lead us to wrong actions.

Competition between churches and other organizations of Christians is a product, in many instances, of our commitment not to the work of God, but to our establishing our own reputation and making a good showing in our own ministries. In some cases, churches will seek to outdo one another by augmenting their facilities and programs on the strength of foreign aid. It is a matter of integrity as well to seek to support our own loads in terms of resources and facilities. This does not mean that the Sri Lankan Christian community should not raise funds from foreign countries, but if foreign Christians encounter Sri Lankan Christians chiefly as people seeking to raise funds from them, this may hinder the formation of genuine—and equal—relationships. It also hurts the witness of the church to be overly dependent on foreign funds, appearing as though the church is not truly an indigenous phenomenon, but rather a means of Westernization (where conversion, moreover, is potentially purchased).

The third point of integrity involves our being willing to accept the opposition, hostility, even attacks that the "stumbling block of the cross" and the "truth of the Gospel" provoke. In recent years, the possibility of passing an "unethical conversion bill" raised questions about whether or not Christians would be able to engage in sharing the Gospel or seeking to evangelize the people that they helped, mixing mission and relief work. As the bill itself represents the crystallization of a fair sector of public opinion, Christians might be tempted to focus their efforts more on "relief" without evangelizing in order to become more acceptable and provoke less hostility from the more powerful majority that feels threatened when individuals turn from the ancestral religions to the Christian faith. God, however, calls us to both (though, indeed, without imposing any conditions such that receiving aid is in any way dependent upon conversion, or even upon listening to the Gospel). Ministering with integrity means ministering in line with Paul's rule that, through the cross, "the cosmos was being crucified to me and I to the cosmos" (6:16). The minister and the disciple have been crucified to the world's lines of divisions between ethnic groups, castes, socio-economic strata, and the like. As Christians bear witness to this in their own relationships and practice, their neighbors, for whom these lines are still often vitally important to their own identity and sense of order, may react with scorn or worse. It is a matter of integrity, however, not to accommodate one's practice to the demands of worldly thinkers, but always to the demands of the Spirit and the rule of the "new creation."

For Paul, suffering for Christ was proof of his genuineness (6:17). The marks on his body were a testimony to his faithfulness to his commission and his Commissioner, communicating that he was obedient first to the latter and that he was faithful to preach and practice the truth of the Gospel, when it would have been far easier and more comfortable to alter it here and there so as to avoid opposition and hostility. These scars were signs that he was Christ's follower and he belonged to Christ. The "marks of Christ" or "marks of a Christian" are not the wearing of a cross on a chain or donning of a "WWJD" ("What would Jesus do?") bracelet or carrying the Bible everywhere. The "marks" involve developing Christ-like character and cultivating the fruit of the Spirit (Gal 5:22–23), showing Jesus himself branded in our lives so that, in any situation, we can be only what Jesus would have us be. It leaves marks in other ways as well. It leaves marks on how we spend our time and energies, investing perhaps in a homeless person to teach him new skills or help reconnect him with family. It leaves marks on how we use our homes, as when perhaps a family takes in a young girl from the street to give her an option other than a life of prostitution. It still may leave marks on our feelings and bodies, as others express their rage and prejudice against Christianity through violence.

Paul challenges us to embrace the freedom and the challenge of living by the Spirit, trusting this gift of God to bring us fully in line with the character and standards of God, to transform us into the likeness of Jesus, the image of the Father. He challenges us to use this freedom responsibly, as spiritual adults. Christian freedom is never an occasion for self-serving, but always an occasion to serve and to love beyond the limits set on us by our upbringing, our socialization, our customs. The righteousness that God seeks to impart will be manifested in the character of our Christian community. Are we other-centered, or self-centered? Are we marked by cooperation, or competition? Do we live out the vision where, indeed, ethnic, social, and gender distinctions—and the hierarchical evaluations, limitations, abuses, or avoidances that are fostered by such distinctions—are transcended in the one family of God's children and heirs? Only by following the Spirit will we, as a Christian community, arrive at the full freedom and glorious inheritance of the sons and daughters of God.

Bibliography

Alexander, Loveday. "Chronology of Paul." Pages 115–23 in *Dictionary of Paul and his Letters.* Edited by Gerald F. Hawthorne, Ralph P. Martin, and Daniel G. Reid. Downers Grove, IL: InterVarsity, 1995.

Aus, R. D. "Three Pillars and Three Patriarchs: A Proposal Concerning Gal 2:9." *Zeitschrift für die neutestamentliche Wissenschaft* 70 (1979) 252–61.

Barclay, J. M. G. *Obeying the Truth.* Minneapolis: Fortress, 1991.

———. "Mirror-Reading a Polemical Letter: Galatians as a Test Case." *Journal for the Study of the New Testament* 31 (1987) 73–93.

Barclay, William. *Flesh and Spirit: An Examination of Gal 5:19–23.* London: SCM, 1962.

Barrett, C. K. "The Allegory of Abraham, Sarah, and Hagar in the Argument of Galatians." Pages 1–16 in *Rechtfertigung. FS für Ernst Käsemann zum 70. Geburtstag.* Edited by J. Friedrich, et al. Tübingen: Mohr Siebeck, 1976.

———. *Essays on Paul.* Philadelphia: Westminster, 1982.

———. *Freedom and Obligation.* London: SPCK, 1985.

Barth, Markus. "Jew and Gentile: The Social Character of Justification in Paul." *Journal of Ecumenical Studies* 5 (1968) 241–67.

Bauckham, Richard. "Barnabas in Galatians." *Journal for the Study of the New Testament* 2 (1979) 61–71.

Bauernfeind, O. "*Aselgeia,*" *TDNT* 1:490.

Becker, Jürgen. *Paul: Apostle to the Gentiles.* Louisville: Westminster John Knox, 1993.

Beker, Johan C. *Paul the Apostle: The Triumph of God in Life and Thought.* Philadelphia: Fortress, 1980.

Belleville, Linda L. "'Under Law': Structural Analysis and the Pauline Concept of Law in Galatians 3.21–4.11." *Journal for the Study of the New Testament* 26 (1986) 53–78.

Berger, Peter L. *The Sacred Canopy: Elements of a Sociological Theory of Religion.* New York: Doubleday, 1967.

————. *Invitation to Sociology: A Humanistic Perspective*. New York: Anchor, 1963.

Betz, Hans D. *Galatians*. Hermeneia. Philadelphia: Fortress, 1979.

————. "The Literary Composition and Function of Paul's Letter to the Galatians." *New Testament Studies* 21 (1974–75) 353–79.

Blinzler, Josef. "Lexicalisches zu dem Terminus *ta stoicheia tou kosmou*." Pages 427–43 in *Studiorum Paulinorum Congressus Internationalis Catholicus II*. Rome: Pontifical Biblical Institute, 1963.

Boers, Hendrikus. *The Justification of the Gentiles: Paul's Letters to the Romans and the Galatians*. Peabody, MA: Hendrickson, 1994.

————. "We Who Are by Inheritance Jews, Not from the Gentiles, Sinners." *Journal of Biblical Literature* 111 (1992) 273–81.

Borgen, Peder. "Paul Preaches Circumcision and Pleases Men." Pages 37–46 in *Paul and Paulinism. Essays in Honor of C. K. Barrett*. Edited by M. D. Hooker and S. G. Wilson. London: SPCK, 1982.

Bornkamm, Gunther. "The Revelation of Christ to Paul on the Damascus Road and Paul's Doctrine of Justification and Reconciliation." Pages 90–103 in *Reconciliation and Hope*. Edited by R. Banks. Exeter: Paternoster, 1974.

————. *Paul*. New York: Harper & Row, 1971.

Boyarin, Daniel. *A Radical Jew: Paul and the Politics of Identity*. Berkeley: University of California Press, 1994.

Brehm, H. A. "Paul's Relationship with the Jerusalem Apostles in Galatians 1 and 2." *Southwestern Journal of Theology* 37 (1994) 11–16

Bruce, F. F. *The Epistle to the Galatians*. New International Greek Testament Commentary. Grand Rapids: Eerdmans, 1982.

————. "The Curse of the Law." Pages 27–36 in *Paul and Paulinism. Essays in Honor of C. K. Barrett*. Edited by M. D. Hooker and S. G. Wilson. London: SPCK, 1982.

————. *Paul: Apostle of the Heart Set Free*. Grand Rapids: Eerdmans, 1977.

————. "Galatian Problems. 2: North or South Galatia?" *Bulletin of the John Rylands Library* 52 (1970) 243–66.

Buck, C. H. "The Date of Galatians." *Journal of Biblical Literature* 70 (1951) 113–22.

Bultmann, Rudolf. "Das Problem der Ethik bei Paulus." *Zeitschrift für die neutestamentliche Wissenschaft* 23 (1924) 123–140.

Burkitt, F. C. *Christian Beginnings*. London: University of London, 1924.

Burton, Ernest de Witt. *A Critical and Exegetical Commentary on the Epistle to the Galatians*. International Critical Commentary. New York: Scribners, 1920.

Caird, G. B. *Principalities and Powers*. Oxford: Oxford University Press, 1956.

Callan, Terence "Pauline Midrash: The Exegetical Background of Gal 3:19b." *Journal of Biblical Literature* 99 (1980) 549–67.

———. "The Background of the Apostolic Decree (Acts 15:20, 29; 21:25)." *Catholic Biblical Quarterly* 55 (1993) 284–97.

Callaway, M. C. "The Mistress and the Maid: Midrashic Traditions Behind Galatians 4:21–31." *Radical Religion* 2 (1975) 94–101.

Campbell, Doulgas. *The Rhetoric of Righteousness in Romans 3.21–26.* Journal for the Study of the New Testament, Supplement Series 65. Sheffield: JSOT Press, 1992.

Carson, D. A., P. T. O'Brien, and M. A. Seifrid, eds. *Justification and Variegated Nomism.* Vol. 1, *The Complexities of Second Temple Judaism.* Grand Rapids: Baker Academic, 2001.

———. *Justification and Variegated Nomism.* Vol. 2, *The Paradoxes of Paul.* Grand Rapids: Baker Academic, 2004.

Catchpole, David R. "Paul, James, and the Apostolic Decree." *New Testament Studies* 23 (1977) 428–44.

Cook, David. "The Prescript as Programme in Galatians." *Journal of Theological Studies* 42 (1992) 511–19.

Corley, Bruce. "Reasoning 'by Faith': Whys and Wherefores of the Law in Galatians." *Southwestern Journal of Theology* 37 (1991) 17–22.

Cosgrove, C. H. "Arguing like a Mere Human Being: Galatians 3:15–18 in Rhetorical Perspective." *New Testament Studies* 34 (1988) 536–49.

———. "The Mosaic Law Teaches Faith: A Study in Galatians 3." *Westminster Theological Journal* 41 (1978) 146–64.

Cranfield, C. E. B. "St. Paul and the Law." *Scottish Journal of Theology* 17 (1964) 43–68.

Cranford, M. "The Possibility of Perfect Obedience: Paul and an Implied Promise in Galatians 3:10 and 5:3." *Novum Testamentum* 36 (1994) 242–58.

Daube, David. "Rabbinic Methods of Interpretation and Hellenistic Rhetoric." *Hebrew Union College Annual* 22 (1949) 239–64.

Davies, W. D. "Paul and the Dead Sea Scrolls: Flesh and Spirit." Pages 157–82 in *The Scrolls and the New Testament.* Edited by Krister Stendahl. New York: Harper, 1957.

———. *The Setting of the Sermon on the Mount.* Cambridge: Cambridge University Press, 1963.

Deissmann, Adolf. *Light from the Ancient East: The New Testament Illustrated by Recently Discovered Texts of the Greco-Roman World.* Translated by L. R. M. Strachan. London: Hodder & Stoughton, 1909.

———. *Paul: A Study of Social and Religious History.* New York: Harper & Brothers, 1957.

Dennison, W. D. "Indicative and Imperative: The Basic Structure of Pauline Ethics." *Calvin Theological Journal* 14 (1979) 55–78.

deSilva, D. A. *4 Maccabees: Introduction and Commentary on the Greek Text of Codex Sinaiticus*. Leiden: Brill, 2006.

———. *4 Maccabees*. Guides to the Apocrypha and Pseudepigrapha; Sheffield: Sheffield Academic, 1998.

———. *Honor, Patronage, Kinship & Purity: Unlocking New Testament Culture*. Downers Grove, IL: InterVarsity, 2000.

———. *Introducing the Apocrypha: Message, Context, and Significance*. Grand Rapids: Baker Academic, 2002.

———. *An Introduction to the New Testament: Contexts, Methods & Ministry Formation*. Downers Grove, IL: InterVarsity, 2004.

———. *Seeing Things John's Way: The Rhetoric of the Book of Revelation*. Louisville: Westminster John Knox, 2009.

Dibelius, Martin. *From Tradition to Gospel*. London: Nicholson and Watson, 1934.

Dodd, C. H. "*Ennomos Christou*." Pages 134–48 in *More New Testament Studies*. Manchester: Manchester University Press, 1968.

Donaldson, T. L. "The 'Curse of the Law' and the Inclusion of the Gentiles: Galatians 3.13–14." *New Testament Studies* 32 (1986) 94–112.

———. "Zealot and Convert: The Origin of Paul's Christ-Torah Antithesis." *Catholic Biblical Quarterly* 51 (1989) 655–82.

Donfried, Karl P. "Justification and the Last Judgment in Paul." *Zeitschrift für die neutestamentliche Wissenschaft* 67 (1976) 90–110.

Drane, John. *Paul, Libertine or Legalist?* London: SPCK, 1975.

Dunn, J. D. G. "4QMMT and Galatians." *New Testament Studies* 43 (1997) 147–53.

———. *Christology in the Making: A New Testament Inquiry into the Origins of the Doctrine of the Incarnation*. 2nd ed. Grand Rapids: Eerdmans, 1996.

———. "Echoes of Intra-Jewish Polemic in Paul's Letter to the Galatians." *Journal of Biblical Literature* 113 (1993) 459–77.

———. *The Epistle to the Galatians*. Peabody, MA: Hendrickson, 1993.

———. "The Incident at Antioch (Gal 2:11–18)." *Journal for the Study of the New Testament* 18 (1983) 3–57.

———. "The Justice of God." *Journal of Theological Studies* NS 43 (1992) 1–22.

———. "'A Light to the Gentiles', or 'The End of the Law'? The Significance of the Damascus Road Christophany for Paul." Pages 89–107 in *Jesus, Paul, and the Law*. Louisville: Westminster John Knox, 1990.

———. "The New Perspective on Paul." Pages 183–214 in *Jesus, Paul, and the Law*. Louisville: Westminster John Knox, 1990.

———. "The Relationship Between Paul and Jerusalem according to Galatians 1 and 2." *New Testament Studies* 28 (1982) 461–78.

———. *Romans 1–8* and *Romans 9–16*. Word Biblical Commentary 38. Dallas: Word, 1988.

———. *The Theology of Paul the Apostle*. Grand Rapids: Eerdmans, 1998.

———. *The Theology of Paul's Letter to the Galatians*. Cambridge: Cambridge University Press, 1993.

———. "Works of the Law and the Curse of the Law (Gal 3.10–14)." *New Testament Studies* 31 (1985) 523–42.

Ebeling, Gerhard. *The Truth of the Gospel*. Philadelphia: Fortress, 1985.

Ellis, E. Earle. "The Circumcision Party and the Early Christian Mission." *Texte und Untersuchungen* 102 (1968) 390–99.

Engberg-Pedersen, Troels, editor. *Paul in His Hellenistic Context*. Minneapolis: Fortress, 1995.

Fairweather, Janet. "The Epistle to the Galatians and Classical Rhetoric: Parts 1 and 2." *Tyndale Bulletin* 45 (1994) 1–38.

———. "The Epistle to the Galatians and Classical Rhetoric: Part 3." *Tyndale Bulletin* 45 (1994) 213–43.

Fee, Gordon D. *Galatians*. Pentecostal Commentary Series. Blanford Forum, UK: Deo, 2007.

———. *God's Empowering Presence: The Holy Spirit in the Letters of Paul*. Peabody, MA: Hendrickson, 1994.

Fitzmyer, Joseph A. *To Advance the Gospel*. New York: Crossroad, 1981.

———. "Crucifixion in Ancient Palestine, Qumran Literature, and the New Testament." *Catholic Biblical Quarterly* 40 (1978) 493–513.

Fredericksen, Paula. "Judaism, the Circumcision of the Gentiles, and Apocalyptic Hope: Another Look at Galatians 1 and 2." *Journal of Theological Studies* (n.s.) 42 (1991) 532–64.

Fuller, D. P. "Paul and 'the Works of the Law.'" *Westminster Theological Journal* 38 (1975–76) 28–42.

Fung, Ronald Y. K. *The Epistle to the Galatians*. New International Commentary on the New Testament. Grand Rapids: Eerdmans, 1988.

Gaston, Lloyd. *Paul and the Torah*. Vancouver: University of British Columbia Press, 1987.

Gaventa, Beverly R. "Our Mother St. Paul: Toward the Recovery of a Neglected Theme." *Princeton Seminary Bulletin* 17 (1996) 29–44.

———. "The Maternity of Paul: An Exegetical Study of Gal 4:19." Pages 189–201 in *The Conversation Continues: Studies in Paul and John in Honor of J. Louis Martyn*. Edited by R. T. Fortna and B. R. Gaventa. Nashville: Abgindon, 1990.

———. "Galatians 1 and 2: Autobiography as Paradigm." *Novum Testamentum* 28 (1986) 309–26.

Goldin, J. "Not by Means of an Angel and Not by Means of a Messenger." Pages 412–24 in *Religions in Antiquity*. Edited by Jacob Neusner. *Numen* Supplements 14. Leiden: Brill, 1968.

Goodenough, E. R., and A. T. Kraabel. "Paul and the Hellenization of Christianity." Pages 23–68 in *Religions in Antiquity*. Edited by J. Neusner. Leiden: Brill, 1968.

Goodman, M. "Jewish Proselytizing in the First Century." Pages 53–78 in *The Jews Among Pagans and Christians in the Roman Empire*. Edited by Judith Lieu, J. North, and Tessa Rajak. London: Routledge, 1992.

Grant, Robert M. "Jewish Christianity in Antioch in the Second Century." *Religious Studies Review* 60 (1972) 97–108.

Gundry, Robert H. "Grace, Works, and Staying Saved in Paul." *Biblica* 66 (1985) 1–38.

Haenchen, Ernst. *Acts of the Apostles*. Translated by R. McL. Wilson. Philadelphia: Westminster, 1971.

———. "The Book of Acts as Source Material for the History of Early Christianity." Pages 258–78 in *Studies in Luke-Acts*. Edited by Leander E. Keck and J. Louis Martyn. Nashville: Abingdon, 1966.

Hall, Robert G. "Arguing like an Apocalypse: Galatians and an Ancient Topos outside the Greco-Roman Rhetorical Tradition." *New Testament Studies* 42 (1996) 434–53.

———. "The Rhetorical Outline for Galatians: A Reconsideration." *Journal of Biblical Literature* 106 (1987) 277–287.

Hansen, G. W. *Abraham in Galatians: Epistolary and Rhetorical Contexts*. Sheffield: Sheffield Academic, 1989.

Hanson, R. P. C. *Allegory and Event*. London: SCM, 1959.

Harrisville, R. A. "ΠΙΣΤΙΣ ΧΡΙΣΤΟΥ: Witness of the Fathers." *Novum Testamentum* 36 (1994) 233–41.

Hawthorne, G. F., R. P. Martin, and D. G. Reid, editors. *Dictionary of Paul and His Letters*. Downers Grove, IL: InterVarsity, 1993.

Hays, Richard B. "Christology and Ethics in Galatians: The Law of Christ." *Catholic Biblical Quarterly* 49 (1987) 268–90.

———. *Echoes of Scripture in the Letters of Paul*. New Haven, CT: Yale University Press, 1989.

———. *The Faith of Jesus Christ: An Investigation of the Narrative Substructure of Galatians 3:1—4:11*. Society of Biblical Literature Dissertation Series 56. Chico, CA: Scholars, 1983.

————. "ΠΙΣΤΙΣ and Pauline Christology: What Is at Stake?" Pages 35–60 in *Pauline Theology IV: Looking Back, Pressing On*, edited by David Hay and Elizabeth Johnson. Atlanta: Scholars, 1997.

Hemer, Colin J., and Conrad H. Gempf. *The Book of Acts in the Setting of Hellenistic History*. Wissenschaftliche Untersuchungen zum Neuen Testament, II 49. Tübingen: Mohr Siebeck, 1989.

Hemer, Colin J. "Acts and Galatians Reconsidered." *Themelios* 2 (1977) 81–88.

————. "Observations on Pauline Chronology." Pages 3–18 in *Pauline Studies: Essays Presented to F. F. Bruce*. Edited by Donald A. Hagner and Murray J. Harris. Exeter: Paternoster, 1980.

Hengel, Martin. *The Pre-Christian Paul*. Valley Forge, PA: Trinity, 1991.

————. *The Hellenization of Judaea in the First Century after Christ*. London: SCM, 1989.

————. *Jews, Greeks, Barbarians*. Philadelphia: Fortress, 1980.

————. *Acts and the History of Earliest Christianity*. Translated by John Bowden. London: SCM, 1979.

————. *Judaism and Hellenism*. 2 vols. Philadelphia: Fortress, 1974.

Hengel, Martin, and Anna Maria Schwemer. *Paul between Damascus and Antioch: The Unknown Years*. Louisville: Westminster John Knox, 1997.

Hester, J. D. "The Rhetorical Structure of Galatians 1:11–2:14." *Journal of Biblical Literature* 103 (1984) 223–44.

Hoenig, S. B. "Circumcision: The Covenant of Abraham." *Jewish Quarterly Review* (n.s.) 53 (1962–63) 322–34.

Hofius, Otfried. "Das Gesetz Mose und das Gesetz Christi." *Zeitschrift für Theologie und Kirche* 80 (1983) 262–86.

Hooker, Morna D. "ΠΙΣΤΙΣ ΧΡΙΣΤΟΥ." *New Testament Studies* 35 (1989) 321–42.

Howard, George. *Paul: Crisis in Galatia*. Cambridge: Cambridge University Press, 1979.

Hübner, Hans. "Der Galaterbrief und das Verhältnis von der antiker Rhetorik und Epistolographie." *Theologische Literaturzeitung* 109 (1984) 241–50.

Hultgren, A. J. "Paul's Pre-Christian Persecutions of the Church: Their Purpose, Locale, and Nature." *Journal of Biblical Literature* 95 (1976) 97–111.

————. "The *Pistis Christou* Formulations in Paul." *Novum Testamentum* 22 (1980) 248–63.

Hurtado, L. W. "The Jerusalem Collection and the Book of Galatians." *Journal for the Study of the New Testament* 5 (1979) 46–62.

Jeremias, Joachim. *The Prayers of Jesus*. London: SCM, 1967.

Jewett, Robert. "The Agitators and the Galatian Congregations." *New Testament Studies* 17 (1971) 198–212.

———. *A Chronology of Paul's Life.* Philadelphia: Fortress, 1979.

Johnson, J. F. "Paul's Argument from Experience: A Closer Look at Galatians 3:1–5." *Concordia Journal* 19 (1993) 234–37.

Käsemann, Ernst. "The Righteousness of God in Paul." In *New Testament Questions of Today*, 168–82. Philadelphia: Fortress, 1969.

Kennedy, George. *New Testament Interpretation through Rhetorical Criticism.* Chapel Hill: University of North Carolina Press, 1984.

Kim, Seyoon. *Paul and the New Perspective.* Grand Rapids: Eerdmans, 2001.

Knox, John. *Chapters in a Life of Paul.* Rev. ed. Macon, GA: Mercer University Press, 1987.

Kruger, M. A. "Law and Promise in Galatians." *Neotestamentica* 26 (1992) 311–27.

Kuck, D. W. "Each Will Bear His Own Burden: Paul's Creative Use of an Apocalyptic Motif." *New Testament Studies* 40 (1994) 289–97.

Lake, Kirsopp. *The Beginnings of Christianity.* Part I: *The Acts of the Apostles.* 5 vols. London: MacMillan, 1922.

Lambrecht, Jan. "The Line of Thought in Gal. 2.14b–21." *New Testament Studies* 24 (1977–78) 484–95.

———. "Transgressor by Nullifying God's Grace. A Study of Gal 2,18–21." *Biblica* 72 (1991) 217–36.

Lategan, B. "The Argumentative Situation of Galatians." *Neotestamentica* 26 (1992) 257–77.

———. "Is Paul Defending His Apostleship in Galatians? The Function of Galatians 1:11–12 and 2:19–20 in the Development of Paul's Argument." *New Testament Studies* 34 (1988) 411–30.

Lemmer, H. R. "Mnemonic Reference to the Spirit as a Persuasive Tool (Gal. 3:1–6 within the argument 3:1—4:11)." *Neotestamentica* 26 (1992) 359–88.

Liddell, Henry G. Robert Scott, and Henry S. Jones, editors. *A Greek-English Lexicon, Ninth Edition with a Revised Supplement.* New York: Oxford University Press, 1996.

Lietzmann, H. *An die Galater. Handbuch zum Neuen Testament* 10, 4th ed. Tübingen: Mohr Siebeck, 1971.

Lightfoot, J. B. *St. Paul's Epistle to the Galatians.* 10th ed. London: Macmillan, 1890.

Longenecker, Richard N. *Galatians.* Word Biblical Commentary. Dallas: Word, 1990.

———. "The Pedagogical Nature of the Law in Galatians 3:19–4:7." *Journal of the Evangelical Theological Society* 25 (1982) 53–61.

Loubser, J. A. "The Contrast Slavery/Freedom as Persuasive Device in Galatians." *Neotestamentica* 28 (1994) 163–76.

Lüdemann, Gerd. *Paul: Apostle to the Gentiles. Studies in Chronology.* Philadelphia: Fortress, 1984.

Lührmann, Dieter. *Galatians.* Minneapolis: Fortress, 1992.

———. "*Pistis* im Judentum." *Zeitschrift für die neutestamentliche Wissenschaft* 64 (1973) 19–38.

Lull, D. J. "'The Law Was Our Pedagogue': A Study in Galatians 3:19–25." *Journal of Biblical Literature* 105 (1986) 481–98.

Lütgert, Wilhelm. *Gesetz und Geist: Eine Untersuchung zur Vorgeschichte des Galaterbriefes.* Gütersloh: Gerd Mohn, 1919.

Luther, Martin. *A Commentary on St. Paul's Epistle to the Galatians.* Translated by P. S. Watson. London: James Clarke, 1953.

Lyall, F. "Roman Law in the Writings of Paul—Adoption." *Journal of Biblical Literature* 88 (1969) 458–66.

Lyons, George. *Pauline Autobiography: Toward a New Understanding.* Atlanta: Scholars, 1985.

Marcus, Joel. "The Evil Inclination in the Letters of Paul." *Irish Biblical Studies* 8 (1986) 8–21.

Martyn, J. Louis. *Galatians.* Anchor Bible 33A. Garden City, NY: Doubleday, 1997.

———. "A Law-Observant Mission to the Gentiles: The Background of Galatians." *Southwest Journal of Theology* 38 (1985) 307–24.

———. *Theological Issues in the Letters of Paul.* Edinburgh: T. & T. Clark; Nashville: Abingdon, 1997.

Matera, Frank J. "The Culmination of Paul's Argument to the Galatians." *Journal for the Study of the New Testament* 32 (1988) 79–91.

———. *Galatians.* Sacra Pagina. Collegeville, MN: Liturgical, 1992.

Matlock, Barry. "Detheologizing the ΠΙΣΤΙΣ ΧΡΙΣΤΟΥ Debate: Cautionary Remarks from a Lexical Semantic Perspective." *Novum Testamentum* 42 (2000) 1–23.

———. "'Even the Demons Believe': Paul and πίστις Χριστοῦ." *Catholic Biblical Quarterly* 64 (2002) 300–318.

McGrath, Alister E., editor. *The Christian Theology Reader.* Oxford: Blackwell, 1995.

McNamara, M. "'To de (Hagar) Sina oros estin en tē Arabia' (Gal. 4:25a): Paul and Petra." *Milltown Studies* 2 (1978) 24–41.

Meeks, Wayne A. *The First Urban Christians: The Social World of the Apostle Paul.* New Haven, CT: Yale University Press, 1983.

———. "Understanding Early Christian Ethics." *Journal of Biblical Literature* 105 (1986) 3–11.

Metzger, Bruce M. *A Textual Commentary on the New Testament.* Rev. ed. New York: United Bible Societies, 1994.

Meyer, P. W. "The Holy Spirit in the Pauline Letters." *Interpretation* 33 (1979) 3–18.

Mihindukulasuriya, Prabo. "Without Christ I Could Not Be a Buddhist: An Evangelical Response to Christian Self-Understanding in a Buddhist Context." *Journal of the Colombo Theological Seminary* 6 (2010) 83–110.

Moffatt, J. An *Introduction to the Literature of the New Testament.* 3rd ed. Edinburgh: T. & T. Clark, 1918.

Moo, Douglas J. "Law, 'Works of the Law', and Legalism in Paul." *Westminster Theological Journal* 45 (1983) 73–100.

Moore-Crispin, D. R. "Galatians 4:1–9: The Use and Abuse of Parallels." *Evangelical Quarterly* 60 (1989) 203–23.

Moule, C. F. D. "The Biblical Conception of 'Faith.'" *Expository Times* 68 (1957) 157, 221–22.

———. "Obligation in the Ethic of Paul." Pages 389–406 in *Christian History and Interpretation.* Edited by W. R. Farmer, et al. Cambridge: Cambridge University, 1967.

Moulton, J. H., and G. Milligan. *The Vocabulary of the Greek New Testament.* Grand Rapids: Eerdmans, 1930.

Mullins, T. Y. "Formulas in New Testament Epistles." *Journal of Biblical Literature* 91 (1972) 380–90.

Munck, Johannes. *Paul and the Salvation of Mankind.* London: SCM, 1959.

Murphy-O'Connor, Jerome. *Paul: A Critical Life.* Oxford: Clarendon, 1996.

———. "Pauline Missions before the Jerusalem Conference." *Revue Biblique* 89 (1982) 71–91.

Nanos, Mark. *The Irony of Galatians: Paul's Letter in First-Century Context.* Minneapolis: Fortress, 2002.

Neyrey, J. H. "Bewitched in Galatia: Paul and Cultural Anthropology." *Catholic Biblical Quarterly* 50 (1988) 73–100.

Nock, A. D. *St. Paul.* London: Butterworth, 1938.

O'Neill, J. C. *The Recovery of Paul's Letter to the Galatians.* London: SPCK, 1972.

Patte, Daniel, editor. *The Global Bible Commentary.* Nashville: Abingdon, 2004.

Perriman, A. C. "The Rhetorical Strategy of Galatians 4:21—5:1." *Evangelical Quarterly* 65 (1993) 27–42.

Räisänen, Heiki. "Galatians 2.16 and Paul's Break With Judaism." *New Testament Studies* 31 (1985) 543–53.

———. *Paul and the Law.* Tübingen: Mohr Siebeck, 1983.

Ramachandra, Vinoth. "Authentic Partnerships." Online: http://vinothra machandra.wordpress.com/2010/10/01/authentic-partnerships.

———. *Subverting Global Myths: Theology and the Public Issues Shaping Our World.* Downers Grove, IL: InterVarsity, 2008.

Ramsay, William. *A Historical Commentary on St. Paul's Epistle to the Galatians.* 2nd ed. London: Hodder & Stoughton, 1900.

———. *The Teaching of Paul in Terms of the Present Day.* London: Hodder & Stoughton, 1913.

Reicke, Bo. "The Law and This World According to Paul. Some Thoughts Concerning Gal 4.1–11." *Journal of Biblical Literature* 70 (1951) 259–76.

Richardson, P. "Pauline Inconsistency: 1 Cor 9:19–23 and Gal 2:11–14." *New Testament Studies* 26 (1980) 347–61.

Ridderbos, H. N. *The Epistle of Paul to the Churches of Galatia.* Translated by H. Zylstra. New International Commentary on the New Testament. Grand Rapids: Eerdmans, 1953.

———. *Paul: An Outline of His Theology.* Grand Rapids: Eerdmans, 1975.

Robinson, J. A. T. *Redating the New Testament.* London: SCM Press, 1976.

Roetzel, Calvin. *The Letters of Paul: Conversations in Context.* 2nd ed. Atlanta: John Knox, 1985.

Ropes, James H. *The Singular Problem of the Epistle to the Galatians.* Harvard Theological Studies 14. Cambridge, MA: Harvard University Press, 1929.

Royalty, Robert. "The Rhetoric of Revelation." Pages 596–617 in *Society of Biblical Literature Seminar Papers, 1997.* Atlanta: Scholars, 1997.

Rusam, D. "Neue Belege zu dem *stoicheia tou kosmou* (Gal 4,3.9; Kol 2,8.20)." *Zeitschrift für die neutestamentliche Wissenschaft* 83 (1992) 119–25.

Russell, W. B. "Rhetorical Analysis of the Book of Galatians, Part 1." *Bibliotheca Sacra* 150 (1993) 341–58.

———. "Rhetorical Analysis of the Book of Galatians, Part 2." *Bibliotheca Sacra* 150 (1993) 416–39.

Sampley, Paul. "'Before God, I do not lie' [Gal. i. 20]: Paul's Self-Defense in the Light of Roman Legal Praxis." *New Testament Studies* 23 (1976–77) 477–82.

Sanders, E. P. *Paul.* New York: Oxford, 1991.

———. *Paul, the Law, and the Jewish People.* Philadelphia: Fortress, 1983.

———. *Paul and Palestinian Judaism.* Philadelphia: Fortress, 1977.

Schlier, H. *Der Brief an die Galater. Kritisch-exegetischer Kommentar über das Neue Testament 7.* 10th ed. Göttingen: Vandenhoeck & Ruprecht, 1949.

Schmithals, Walter. *Paul and the Gnostics.* Nashville: Abingdon, 1971.

———. "Die Häretiker in Galatien." *Zeitschrift für die neutestamentliche Wissenschaft* 47 (1956) 25–67.

Schrenk, Gottlob. "*dikaioō*." *Theological Dictionary of the New Testament* 2:211–219.

———. "Was bedeutet 'Israel Gottes'?" *Judaica* 5 (1949) 81–94.

Schüssler-Fiorenza, E. "Neither Male Nor Female: Gal 3:28 – Alternative Vision and Pauline Modification." Pages 205–241 in *In Memory of Her.* New York: Crossroad, 1984.

Schweizer, Eduard. "Slaves of the Elements and Worshipers of Angels: Gal 4:3, 9 and Col 2:8, 18, 20." *Journal of Biblical Literature* 107 (1988) 455–68.

Scott, J. M. *Adoption as Sons of God: An Exegetical Investigation into the Background of huiothesia in the Pauline Corpus.* Tübingen: Mohr Siebeck, 1992.

———. "Paul's Use of Deuteronomistic Tradition." *Journal of Biblical Literature* 112 (1993) 645–65.

Segal, Alan. *Paul the Convert: The Apostolate and Apostasy of Saul the Pharisee.* New Haven, CT: Yale University Press, 1990.

Silva, Moises. *Explorations in Exegetical Method: Galatians as a Test Case.* Grand Rapids: Baker, 1996.

Slingerland, Dixon. "Acts 18:1–8, the Gallio Inscription, and Absolute Pauline Chronology." *Journal of Biblical Literature* 110 (1991) 439–49.

Smit, Joop. "The Letter of Paul to the Galatians: A Deliberative Speech." *New Testament Studies* 35 (1989) 1–26.

Snodgrass, Klyne. "Spheres of Influence: A Possible Solution to the Problem of Paul and the Law." *Journal for the Study of the New Testament* 32 (1988) 93–113.

Snyman, A. H. "Modes of Persuasion in Galatians 6:7–10." *Neotestamentica* 26 (1992) 475–84.

Stanley, C. D. "'Under a Curse': A Fresh Reading of Galatians 3.10–14." *New Testament Studies* 36 (1990) 481–511.

Stanton, Graham. "The Law of Moses and the Law of Christ: Galatians 3.1–6.2." Pages 99–116 in *Paul and the Mosaic Law.* Edited by J. D. G. Dunn. Tübingen: Mohr Siebeck, 1996.

Stein, Robert H. "The Relationship of Galatians 2:1–10 and Acts 15:1–35: Two Neglected Arguments." *Journal of the Evangelical Theological Society* 17 (1974) 239–42.

Stowers, Stanley. *A Rereading of Romans: Justice, Jews, and Gentiles.* New Haven, CT: Yale University Press, 1994.

Stuhlmacher, Peter. *Revisiting Paul's Doctrine of Justification: A Challenge to the New Perspective.* With an essay by Donald A. Hagner. Downers Grove, IL: InterVarsity, 2001.

Talbert, Charles. "Again: Paul's Visits to Jerusalem." *Novum Testamentum* 9 (1967) 26–40.

Taubenschlag, R. *The Law of Greco-Roman Egypt in Light of the Papyri*. New York: Herald Square, 1948.

Thielman, Frank. *From Plight to Solution: A Jewish Framework for Understanding Paul's View of the Law in Galatians and Romans*. Leiden: Brill, 1989.

Tyson, J. B. "'Works of the Law' in Galatians." *Journal of Biblical Literature* 92 (1973) 423–31.

Van Daalen, D. H. "'Faith' according to Paul." *Expository Times* (1975) 83–85.

Vermes, Geza. *The Complete Dead Sea Scrolls in English*. New York: Penguin, 1998.

Verseput, D. J. "Paul's Gentile Mission and the Jewish Christian Community." *New Testament Studies* 39 (1993) 36–58.

Vielhauer, Philip. "Gesetzesdienst und Stoicheiadienst im Galaterbrief." Pages 543–555 in *Rechtfertigung. FS für Ernst Kasemann zum 70. Geburtstag*. Edited by J. Friedrich, et al. Tübingen: Mohr Siebeck, 1976.

Vos, J. S. "Paul's Argumentation in Galatians 1–2." *Harvard Theological Review* 87 (1994) 1–16.

Wallace, D. B. "Galatians 3.19–20: A *Crux Interpretum* for Paul's View of the Law." *Westminster Theological Journal* 52 (1990) 225–45.

Wan, Sze-Kar. "Abraham and the Promise of Spirit: Points of Convergence between Philo and Paul." Pages 209–220 in *Things Revealed: Studies in Early Jewish and Christian Literature in Honor of Michael E. Stone*. Edited by E. G. Chazon, D. Satran, and R.A. Clements. Leiden: Brill, 2004.

Watson, Francis. "By Faith (of Christ): An Exegetical Dilemma and Its Scriptural Solution." In *The Faith of Jesus Christ: Exegetical, Biblical, and Theological Studies*, edited by Michael Bird and Preston Sprinkle, 147–63. Peabody, MA: Hendrickson, 2009.

Watson, N. M. "Justified by Faith, Judged by Works – an Antinomy?" *New Testament Studies* 29 (1983) 209–21.

Weima, J. A. D. "Gal. 6:11–18: A Hermeneutical Key to the Galatian Letter." *Calvin Theological Journal* 28 (1993) 90–107.

Wessels, G. F. "The Call to Responsible Freedom in Paul's Persuasive Strategy. Gal 5:13–6:10." *Neotestamentica* 26 (1992) 475–84.

Westerholm, Stephen. *Israel's Law and the Church's Faith: Paul and His Recent Interpreters*. Grand Rapids: Eerdmans, 1988.

———. "Letter and Spirit: The Foundation of Pauline Ethics." *New Testament Studies* 30 (1984) 229–48.

———. "On Fulfilling the Whole Law (Gal 5.14)." *Svensk exegetisk årsbok* 51–52 (1986–87) 229–37.

————. *Preface to the Study of Paul.* Grand Rapids: Eerdmans, 1997.

White, C. Dale. *Making a Just Peace: Human Rights and Domination Systems.* Nashville: Abingdon, 1998.

Wilcox, Max. "The Promise of the 'Seed' in the New Testament and Targumim." *Journal for the Study of the New Testament* 5 (1979) 2–20.

Williams, S. K. "Again Pistis Christou." *Catholic Biblical Quarterly* 49 (1987) 431–47.

————. "The Hearing of Faith: ΑΚΩΗ ΠΙΣΤΕΩΣ in Galatians 3." *New Testament Studies* 35 (1989) 82–93.

————. "Justification and the Spirit in Galatians." *Journal for the Study of the New Testament* 29 (1987) 91–100.

————. "Promise in Galatians: A Reading of Paul's Reading of Scripture." *Journal of Biblical Literature* 107 (1988) 709–20.

Wink, Walter. *Engaging the Powers: Discernment and Resistance in a World of Domination.* Minneapolis: Fortress, 1992.

————. *Naming the Powers: The Language of Power in the New Testament.* Minneapolis: Fortress, 1984.

————. *Unmasking the Powers: The Invisible Forces That Determine Human Existence.* Minneapolis: Fortress, 1986.

Witherington III, Ben. *Grace in Galatia: A Commentary on Paul's Letter to the Galatians.* Grand Rapids: Eerdmans, 1998.

————. *New Testament History: A Narrative Account.* Grand Rapids: Baker, 2001.

————. *The Paul Quest: The Renewed Search for the Jew of Tarsus.* Downers Grove, IL: InterVarsity, 1998.

————. *Paul's Narrative Thought World.* Louisville: Westminster John Knox, 1994.

————. "Rite and Rights for Women—Galatians 3:28." *New Testament Studies* 27 (1980) 593–604.

Wright, N. T. *The Climax of the Covenant: Christ and the Law in Pauline Theology.* Edinburgh: T. & T. Clark, 1991.

————. *What Saint Paul Really Said.* Grand Rapids: Eerdmans, 1997.

Young, N. H. "*Paidagogos*: The Social Setting of a Pauline Metaphor." *Novum Testamentum* 29 (1987) 150–76.

Ziesler, J. A. *The Meaning of Righteousness in Paul: A Linguistic and Theological Inquiry.* Cambridge: Cambridge University Press, 1972.

Index of Subjects

329

Index of Modern Authors